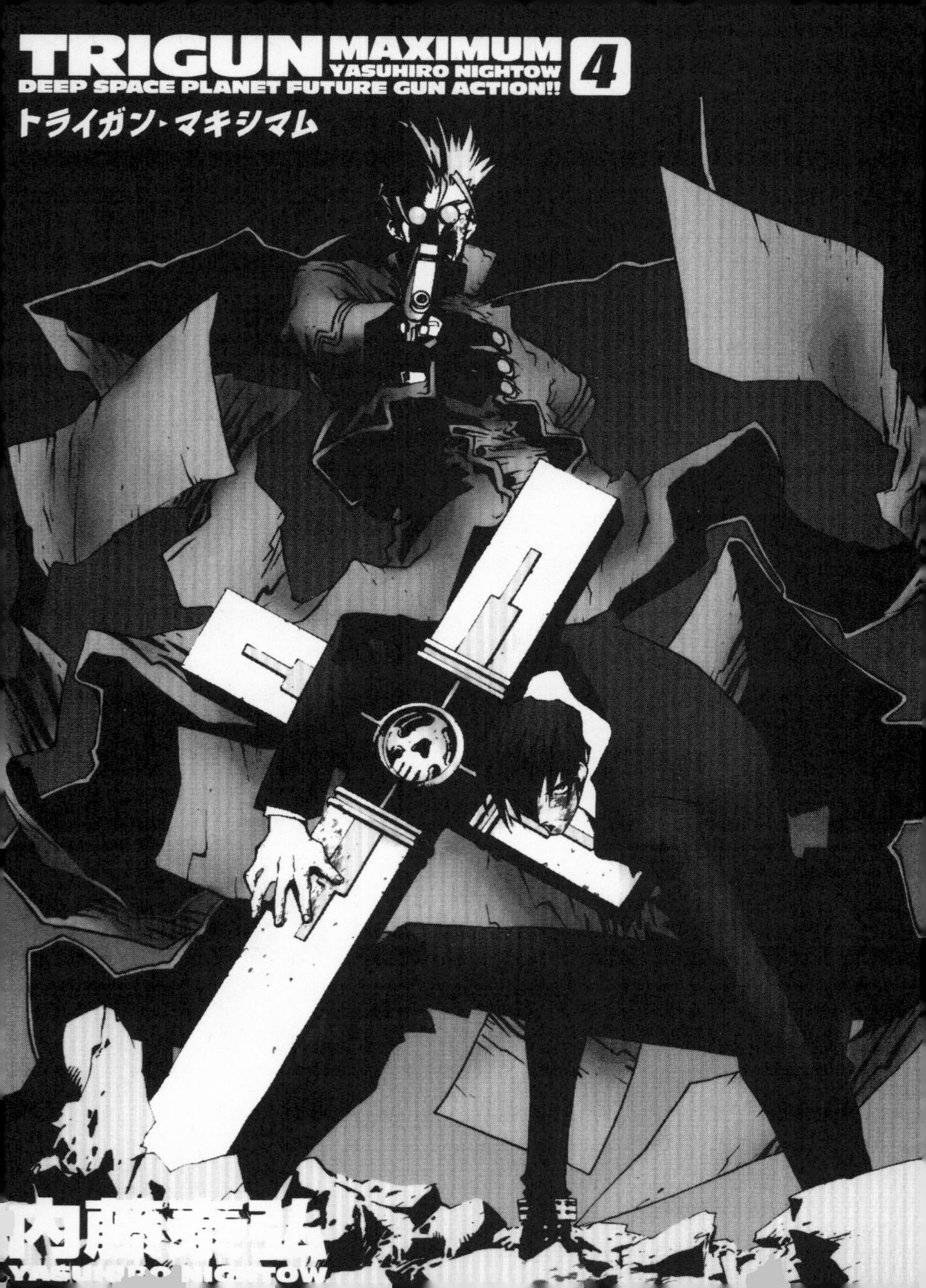
TRIGUN MAXIMUM 4
YASUHIRO NIGHTOW
DEEP SPACE PLANET FUTURE GUN ACTION!!
トライガン・マキシマム

TRIGUN MAXIMUM
YASUHIRO NIGHTOW
DEEP SPACE PLANET FUTURE GUN ACTION!!
CONTENTS

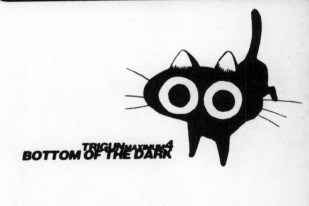

TRIGUN MAXIMUM 4
BOTTOM OF THE DARK

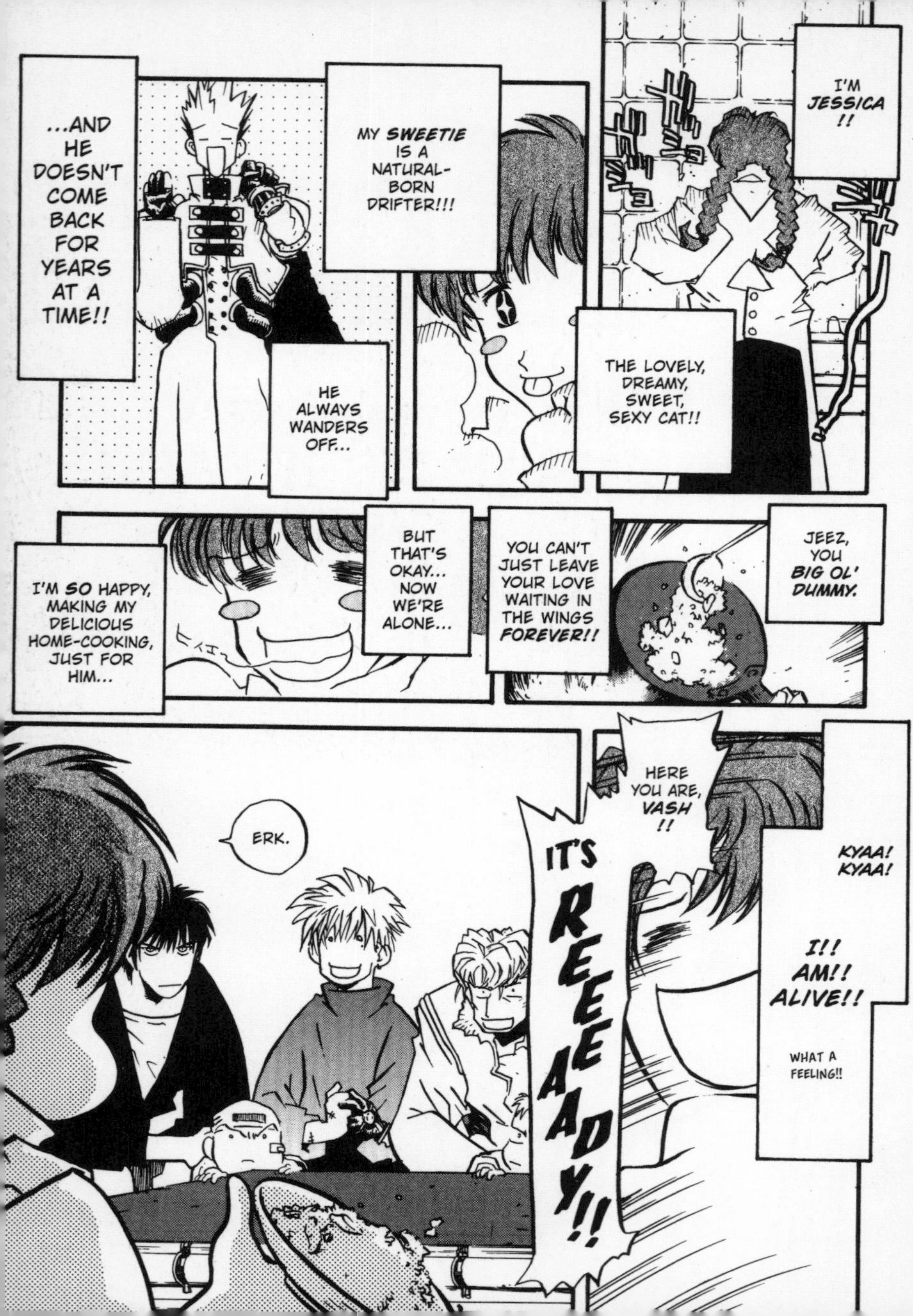
I'M JESSICA!!
THE LOVELY, DREAMY, SWEET, SEXY CAT!!
MY SWEETIE IS A NATURAL-BORN DRIFTER!!!
...AND HE DOESN'T COME BACK FOR YEARS AT A TIME!!
HE ALWAYS WANDERS OFF...
JEEZ, YOU BIG OL' DUMMY.
YOU CAN'T JUST LEAVE YOUR LOVE WAITING IN THE WINGS FOREVER!!
BUT THAT'S OKAY... NOW WE'RE ALONE...
I'M SO HAPPY, MAKING MY DELICIOUS HOME-COOKING, JUST FOR HIM...
KYAA! KYAA!
I!! AM!! ALIVE!!
WHAT A FEELING!!
HERE YOU ARE, VASH!!
IT'S REEEAADY!!
ERK.

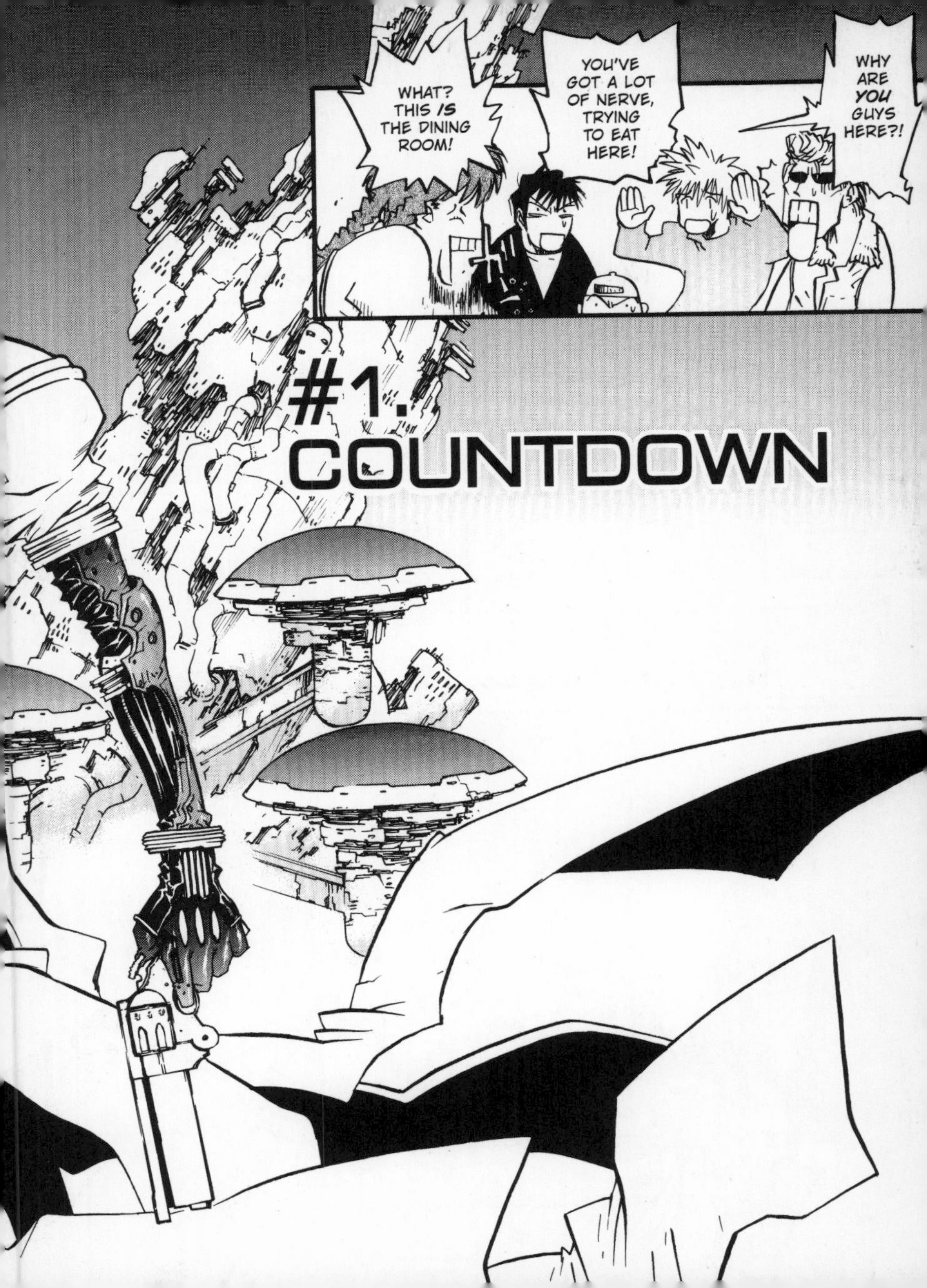
WHY ARE YOU GUYS HERE?!
YOU'VE GOT A LOT OF NERVE, TRYING TO EAT HERE!
WHAT? THIS IS THE DINING ROOM!
#1. COUNTDOWN

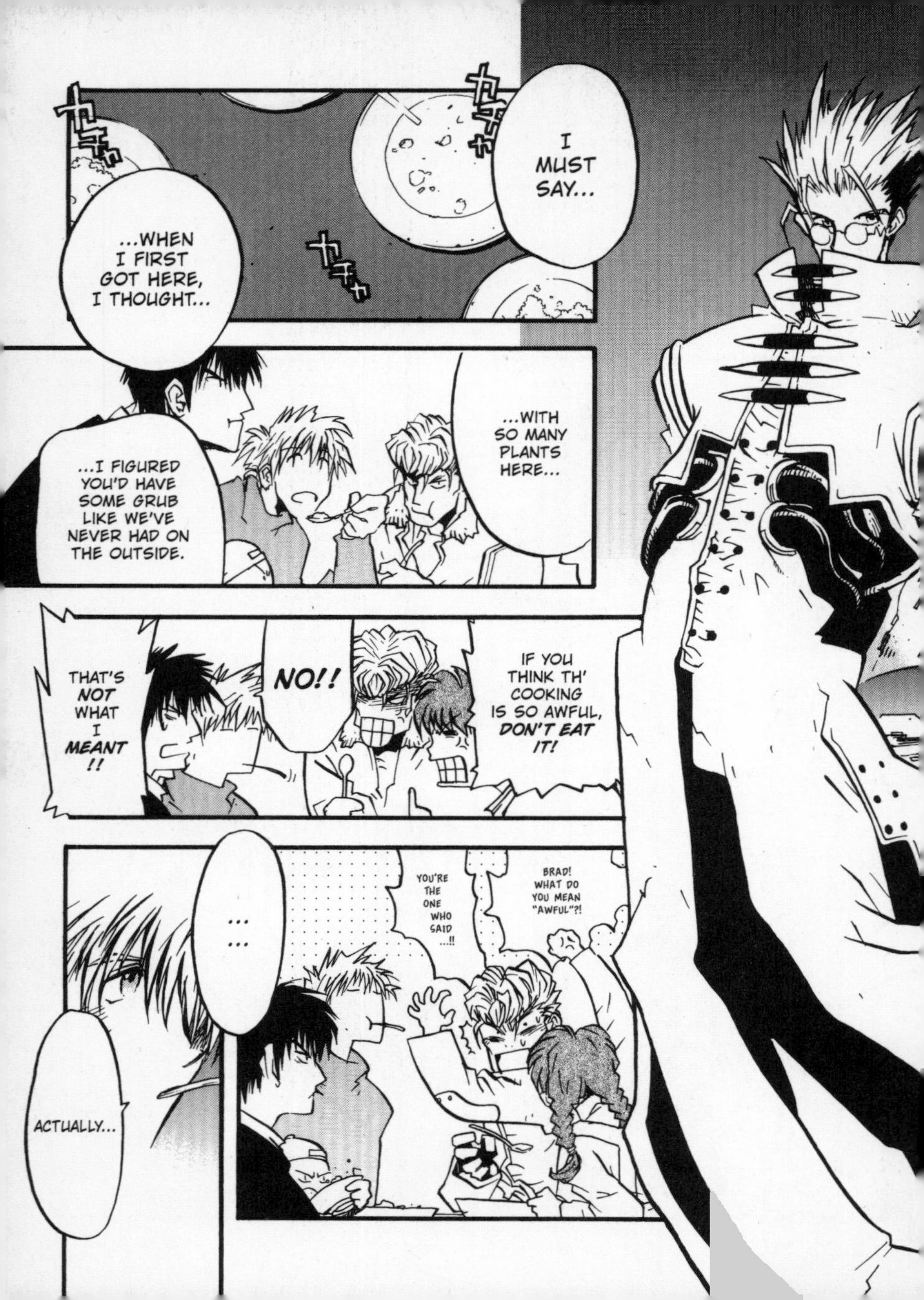
I MUST SAY...
...WHEN I FIRST GOT HERE, I THOUGHT...
...WITH SO MANY PLANTS HERE...
...I FIGURED YOU'D HAVE SOME GRUB LIKE WE'VE NEVER HAD ON THE OUTSIDE.
IF YOU THINK TH' COOKING IS SO AWFUL, DON'T EAT IT!
NO!!
THAT'S NOT WHAT I MEANT!!
BRAD! WHAT DO YOU MEAN "AWFUL"?!
YOU'RE THE ONE WHO SAID ...!!
... ...
ACTUALLY...

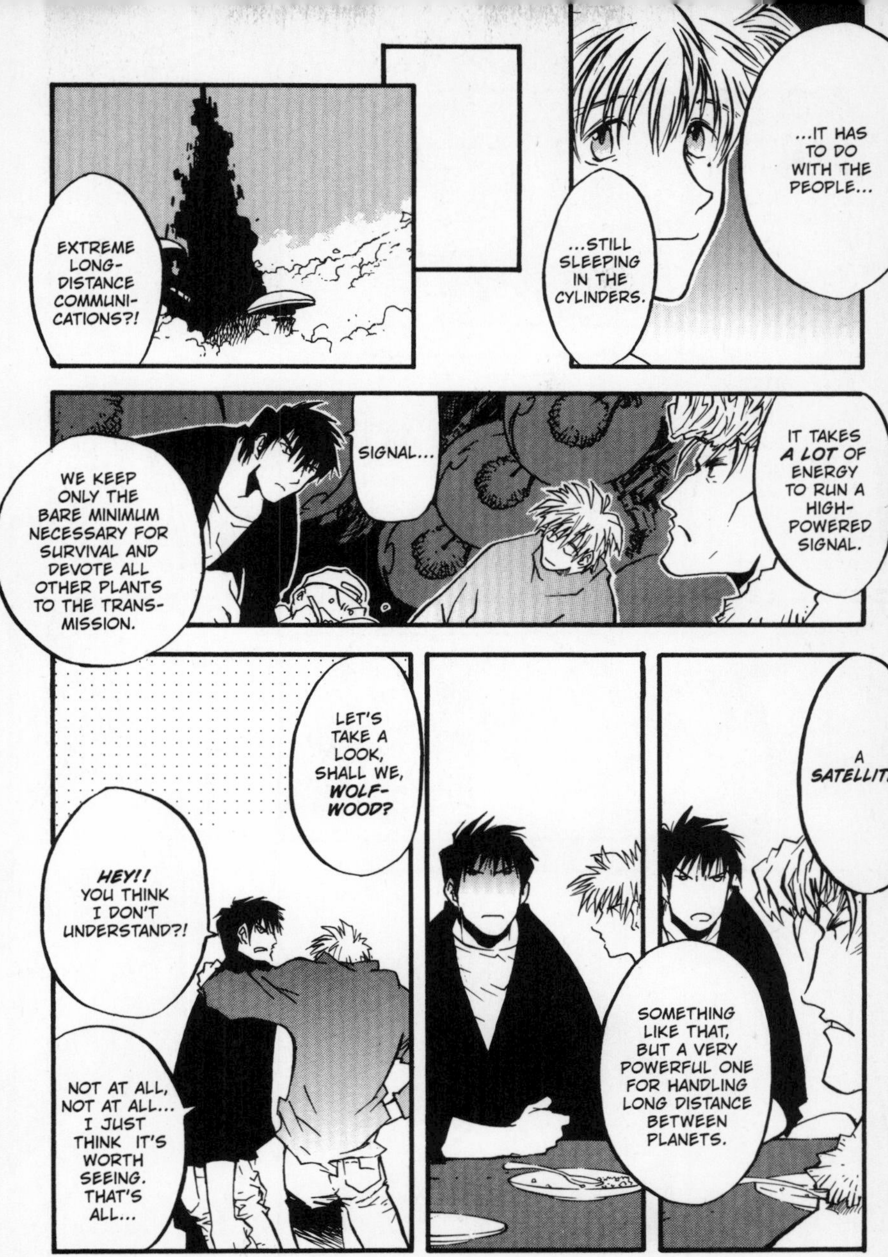
...IT HAS TO DO WITH THE PEOPLE...
...STILL SLEEPING IN THE CYLINDERS.
EXTREME LONG-DISTANCE COMMUNICATIONS?!
IT TAKES **A LOT** OF ENERGY TO RUN A HIGH-POWERED SIGNAL.
SIGNAL...
WE KEEP ONLY THE BARE MINIMUM NECESSARY FOR SURVIVAL AND DEVOTE ALL OTHER PLANTS TO THE TRANSMISSION.
A ***SATELLITE?***
SOMETHING LIKE THAT, BUT A VERY POWERFUL ONE FOR HANDLING LONG DISTANCE BETWEEN PLANETS.
LET'S TAKE A LOOK, SHALL WE, ***WOLF-WOOD?***
HEY!! YOU THINK I DON'T UNDERSTAND?!
NOT AT ALL, NOT AT ALL... I JUST THINK IT'S WORTH SEEING. THAT'S ALL...

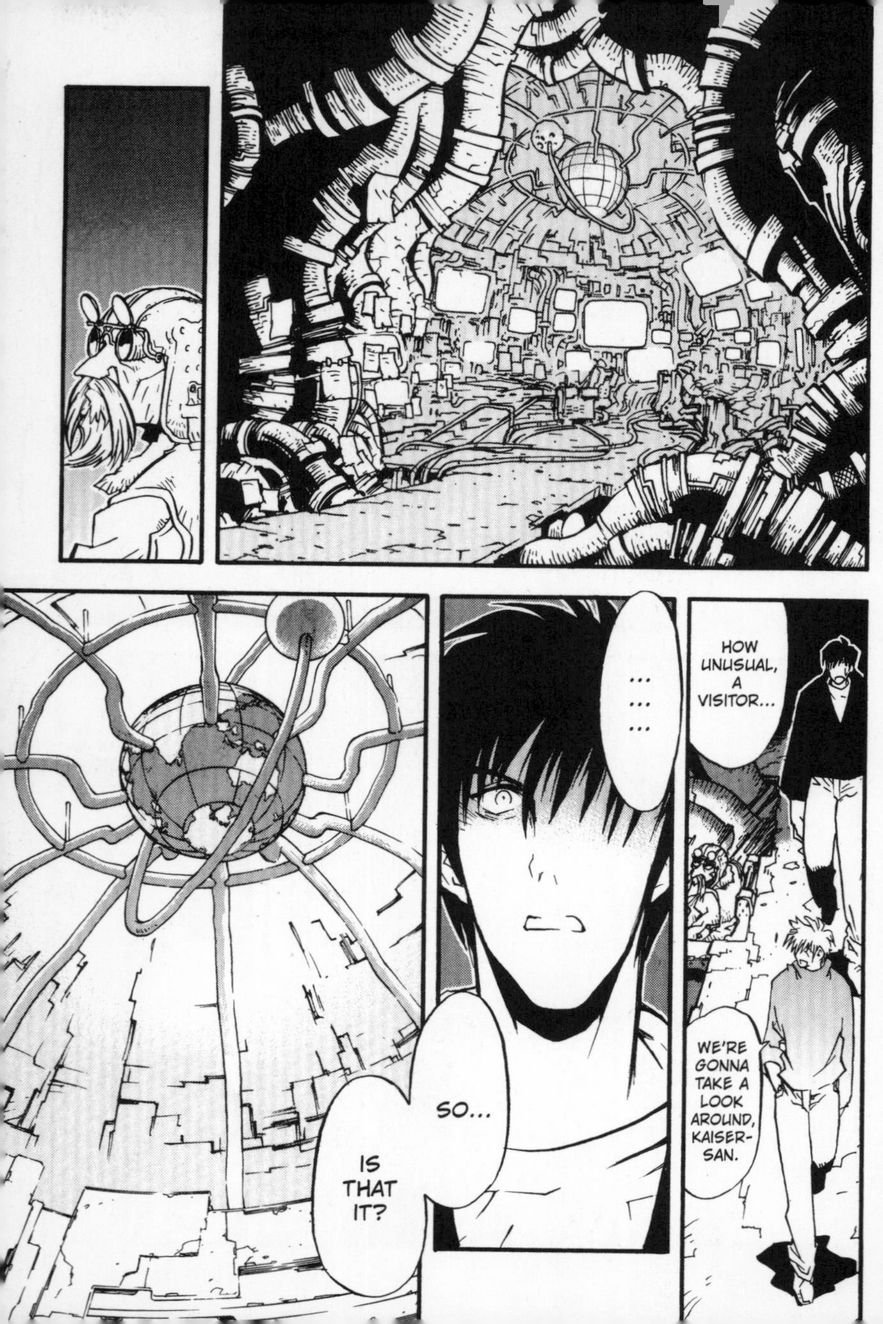

HOW UNUSUAL, A VISITOR...
WE'RE GONNA TAKE A LOOK AROUND, KAISER-SAN.
... ...
SO...
IS THAT IT?

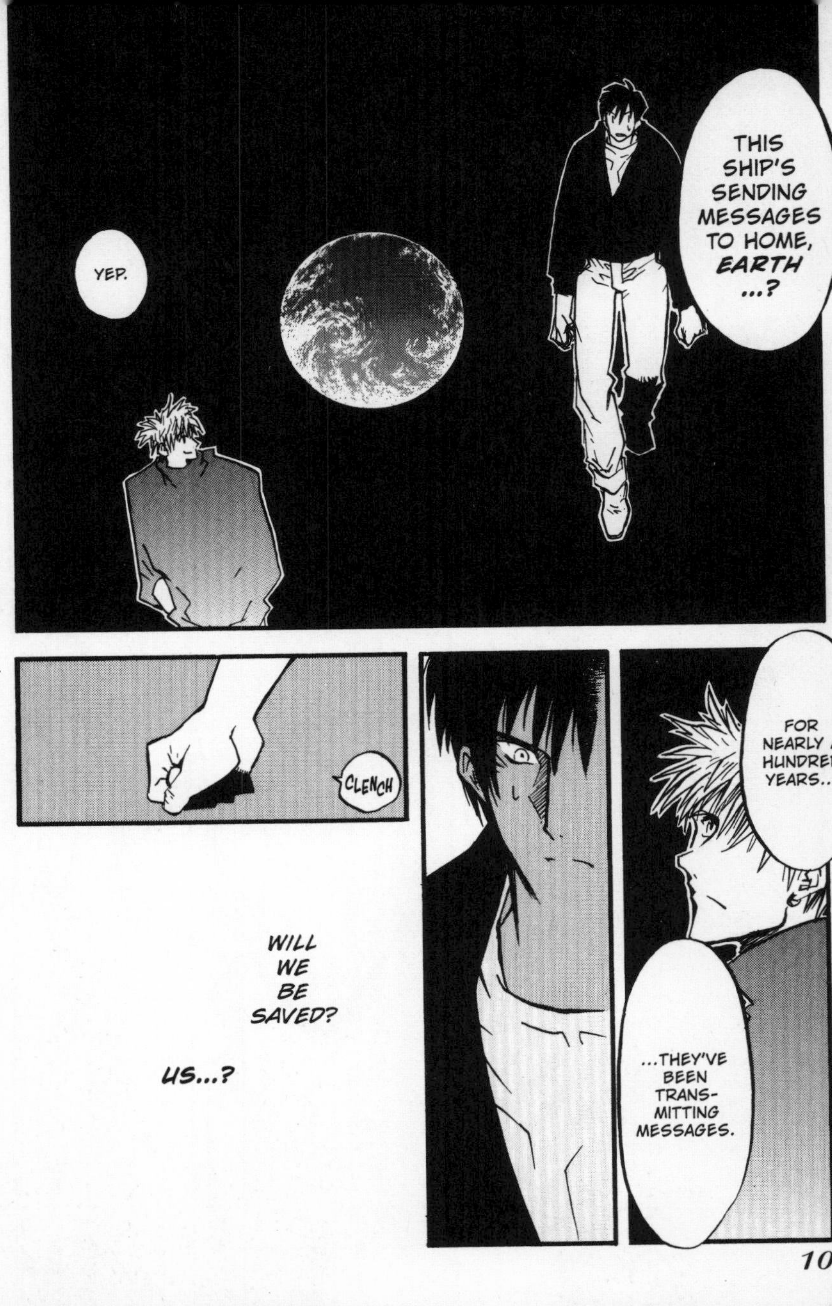
THIS SHIP'S SENDING MESSAGES TO HOME, EARTH ...?
YEP.
FOR NEARLY A HUNDRED YEARS...
...THEY'VE BEEN TRANS-MITTING MESSAGES.
CLENCH
WILL WE BE SAVED?
US...?

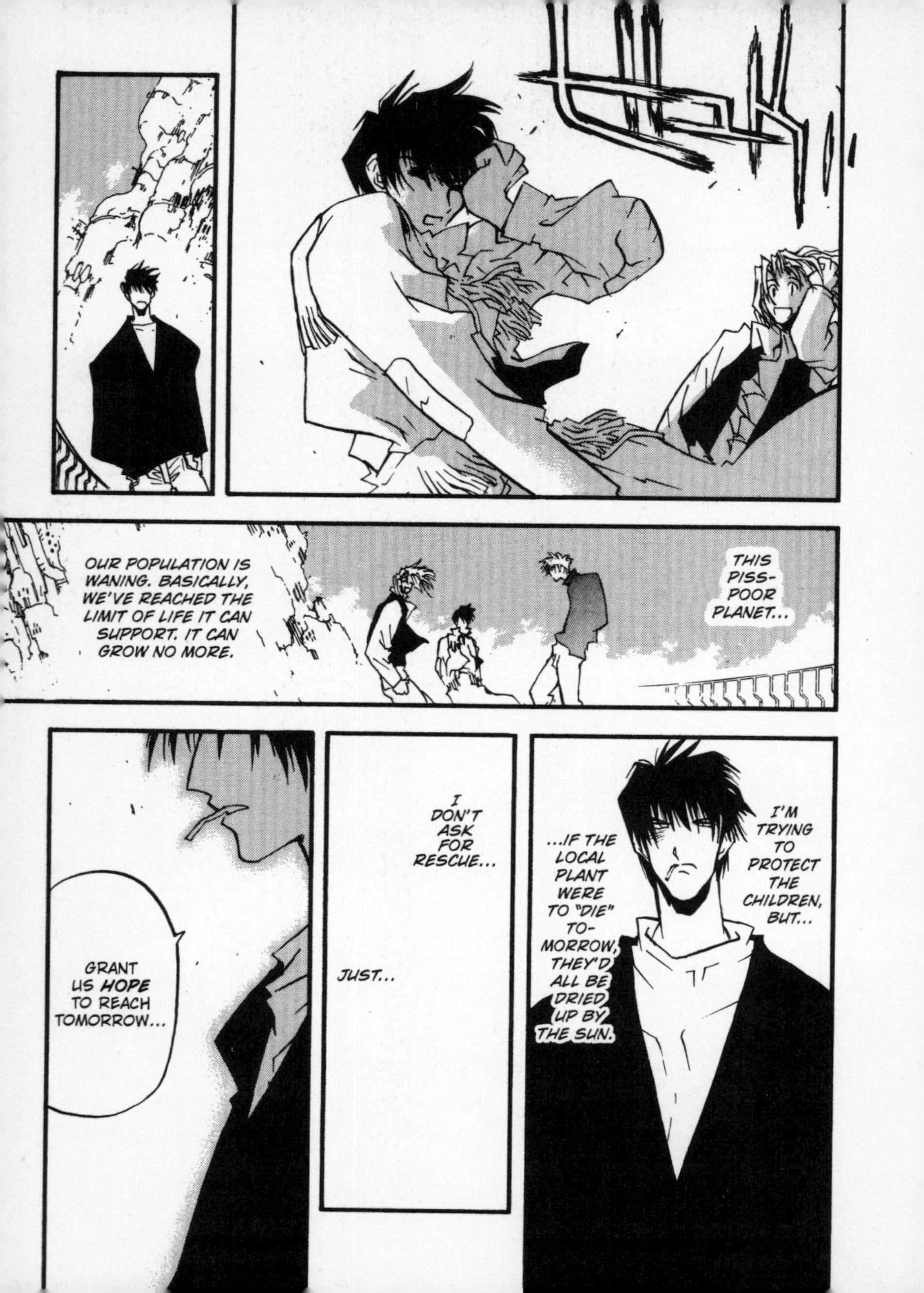
THIS PISS-POOR PLANET...
OUR POPULATION IS WANING. BASICALLY, WE'VE REACHED THE LIMIT OF LIFE IT CAN SUPPORT. IT CAN GROW NO MORE.
I'M TRYING TO PROTECT THE CHILDREN, BUT...
...IF THE LOCAL PLANT WERE TO "DIE" TO-MORROW, THEY'D ALL BE DRIED UP BY THE SUN.
I DON'T ASK FOR RESCUE...
JUST...
GRANT US *HOPE* TO REACH TOMORROW...

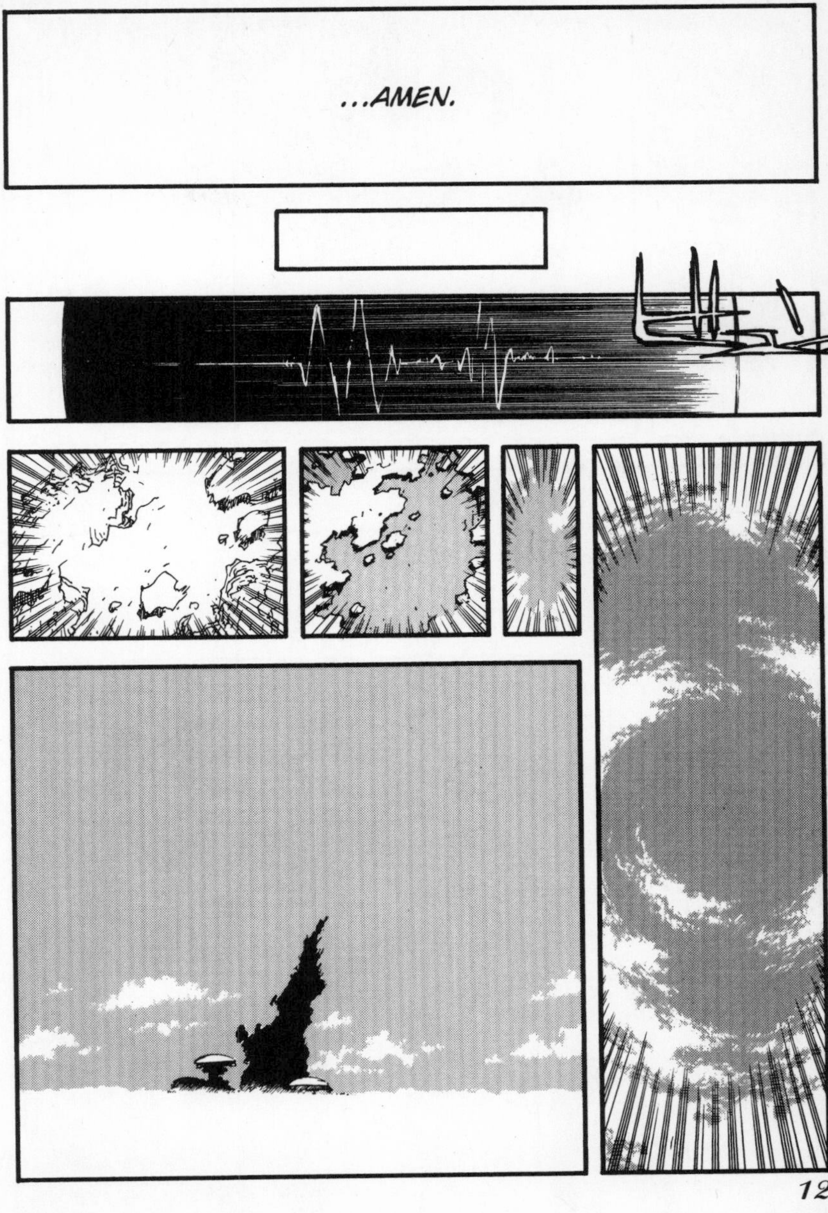
...AMEN.

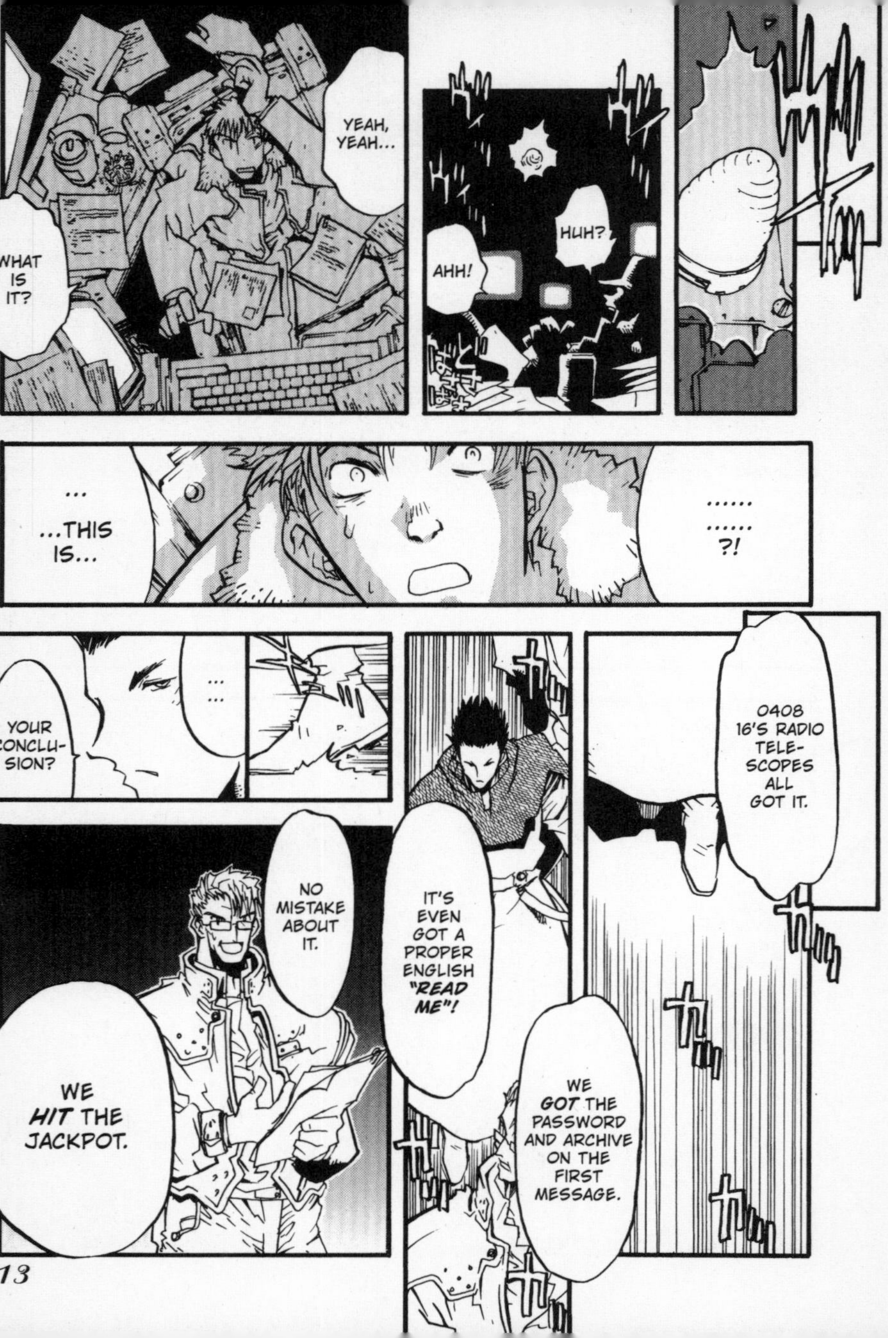
HUH?
AHH!
YEAH, YEAH...
WHAT IS IT?
......
......
?!
...
...THIS IS...
0408 16'S RADIO TELE-SCOPES ALL GOT IT.
WE GOT THE PASSWORD AND ARCHIVE ON THE FIRST MESSAGE.
IT'S EVEN GOT A PROPER ENGLISH "READ ME"!
...
...
YOUR CONCLU-SION?
NO MISTAKE ABOUT IT.
WE HIT THE JACKPOT.

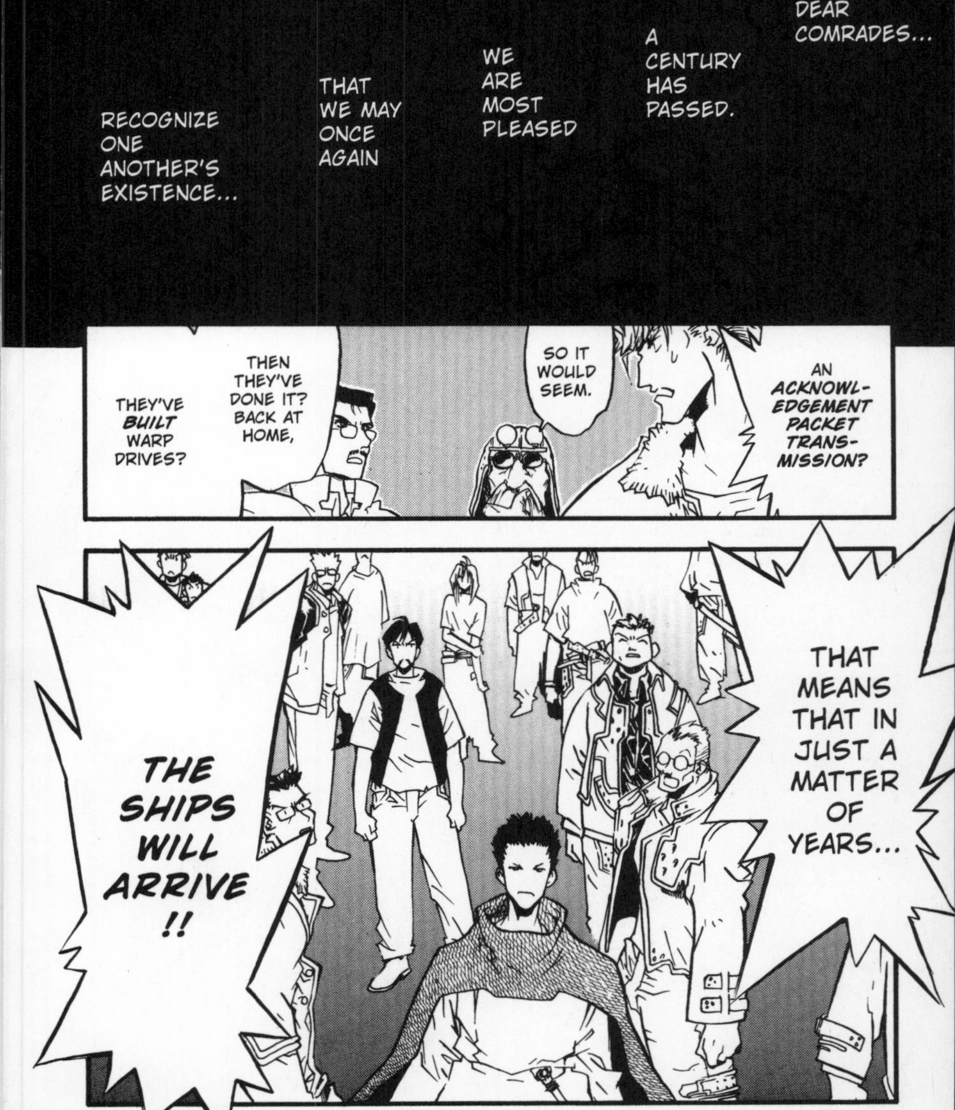
DEAR COMRADES...
A CENTURY HAS PASSED.
WE ARE MOST PLEASED
THAT WE MAY ONCE AGAIN
RECOGNIZE ONE ANOTHER'S EXISTENCE...
AN ACKNOWL-EDGEMENT PACKET TRANS-MISSION?
SO IT WOULD SEEM.
THEN THEY'VE DONE IT? BACK AT HOME,
THEY'VE *BUILT* WARP DRIVES?
THAT MEANS THAT IN JUST A MATTER OF YEARS...
THE SHIPS WILL ARRIVE!!

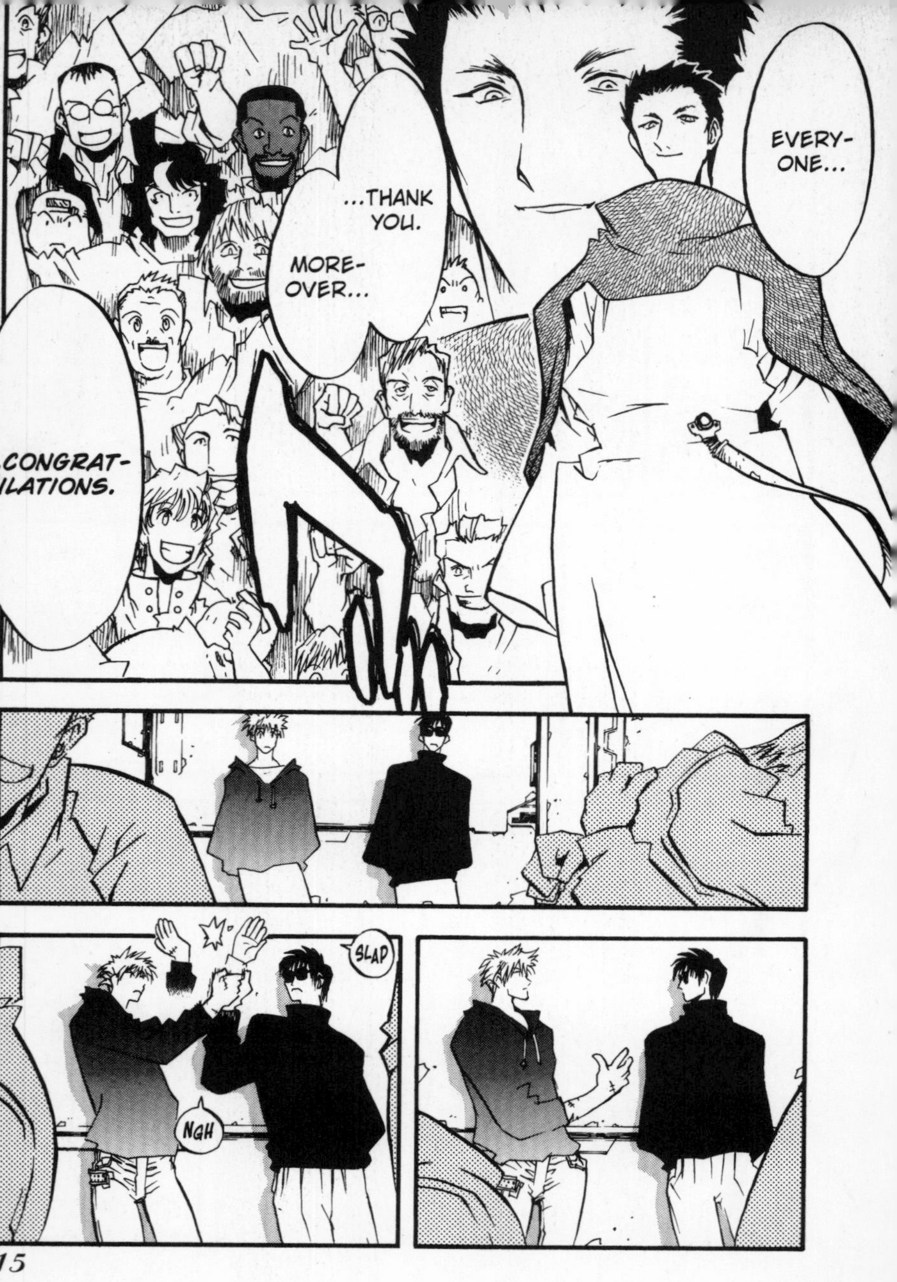
EVERY-ONE...
...THANK YOU.
MORE-OVER...
...CONGRAT-ULATIONS.
SLAP
NGH

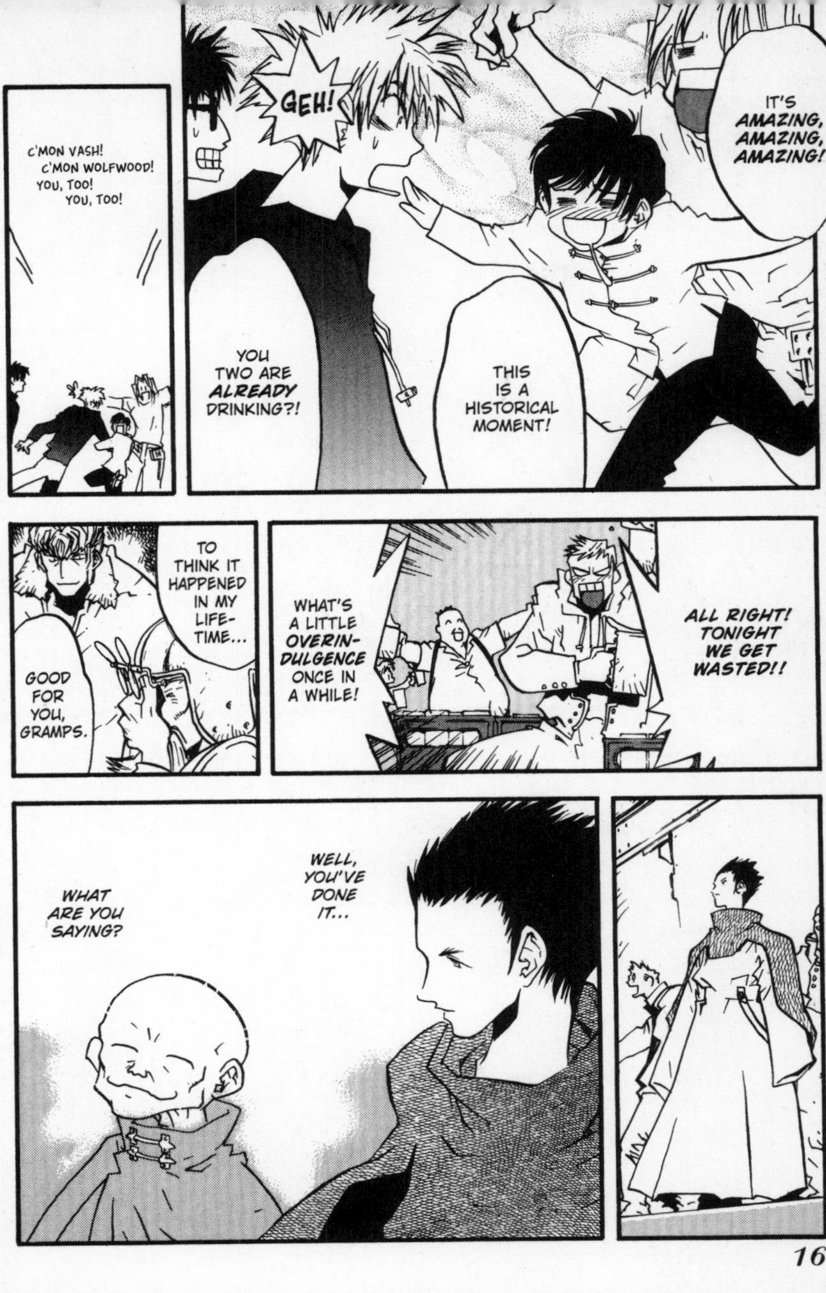
IT'S AMAZING, AMAZING, AMAZING!
GEH!
THIS IS A HISTORICAL MOMENT!
YOU TWO ARE ALREADY DRINKING?!
C'MON VASH! C'MON WOLFWOOD! YOU, TOO! YOU, TOO!
ALL RIGHT! TONIGHT WE GET WASTED!!
WHAT'S A LITTLE OVERINDULGENCE ONCE IN A WHILE!
TO THINK IT HAPPENED IN MY LIFETIME...
GOOD FOR YOU, GRAMPS.
WELL, YOU'VE DONE IT...
WHAT ARE YOU SAYING?

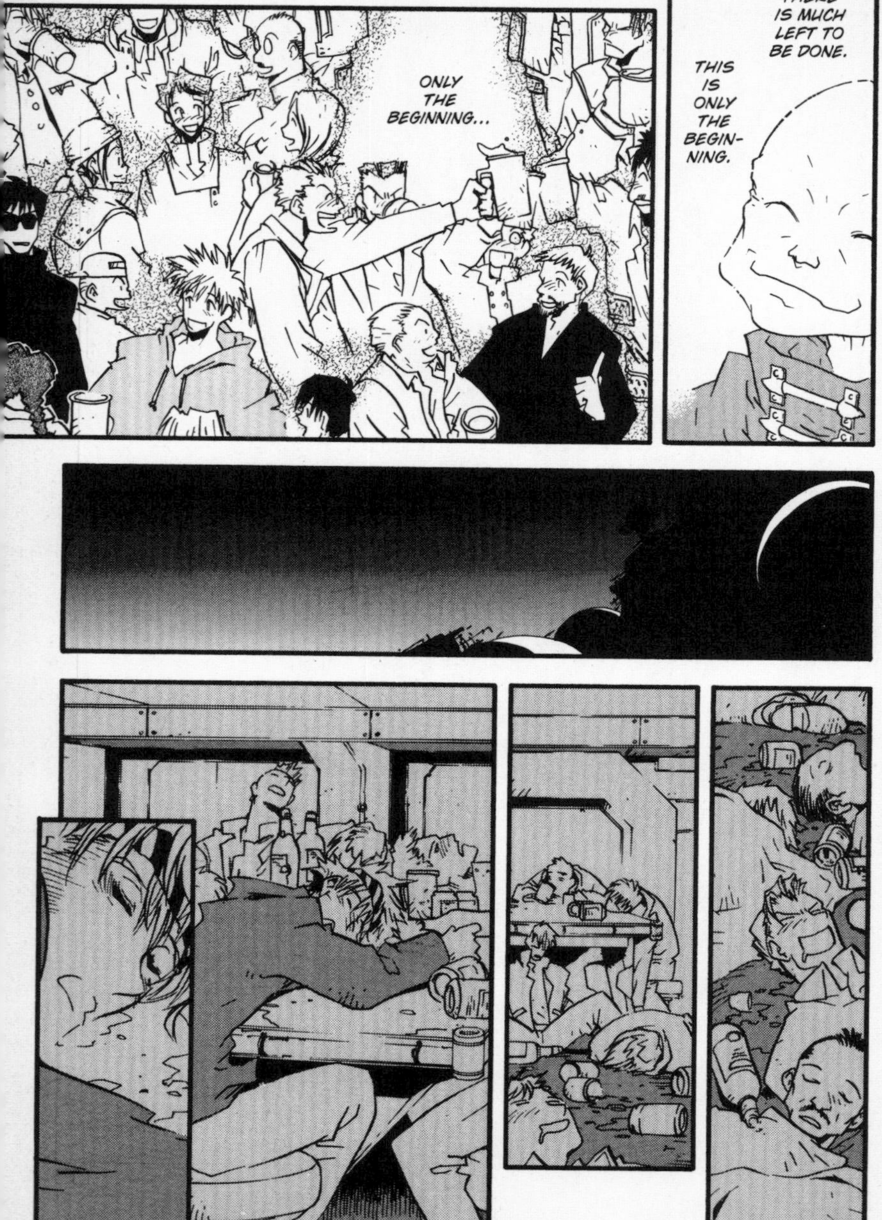
THERE IS MUCH LEFT TO BE DONE.
THIS IS ONLY THE BEGINNING.
ONLY THE BEGINNING...

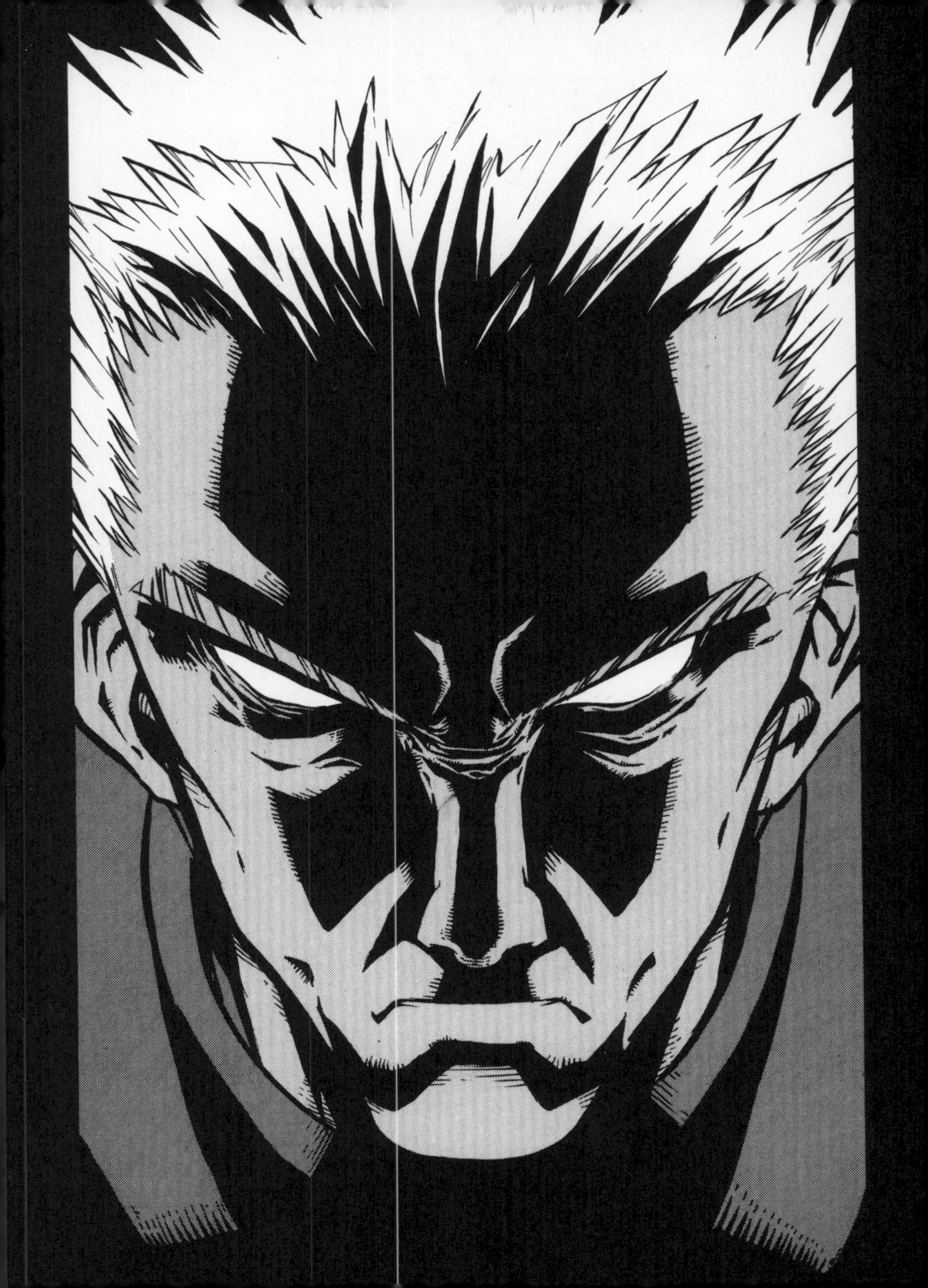

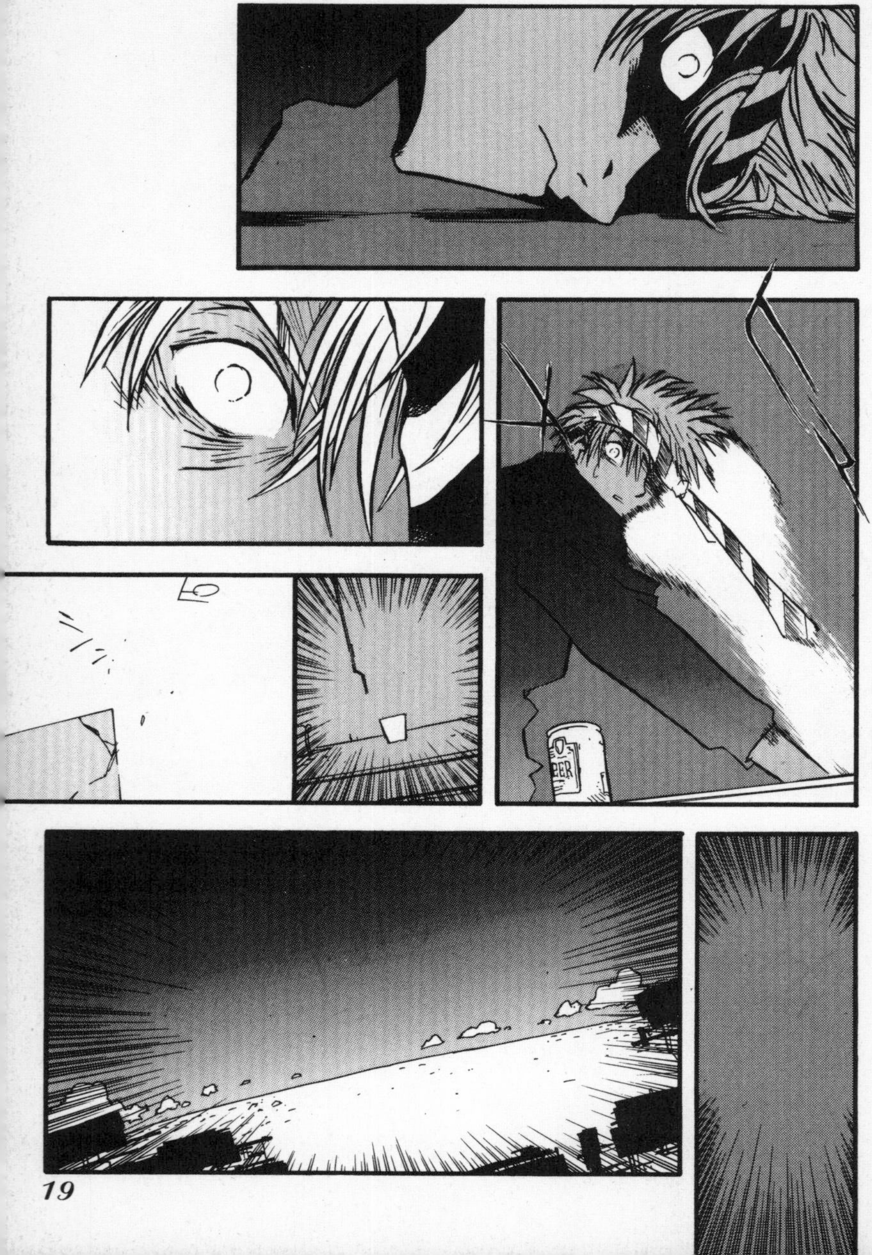

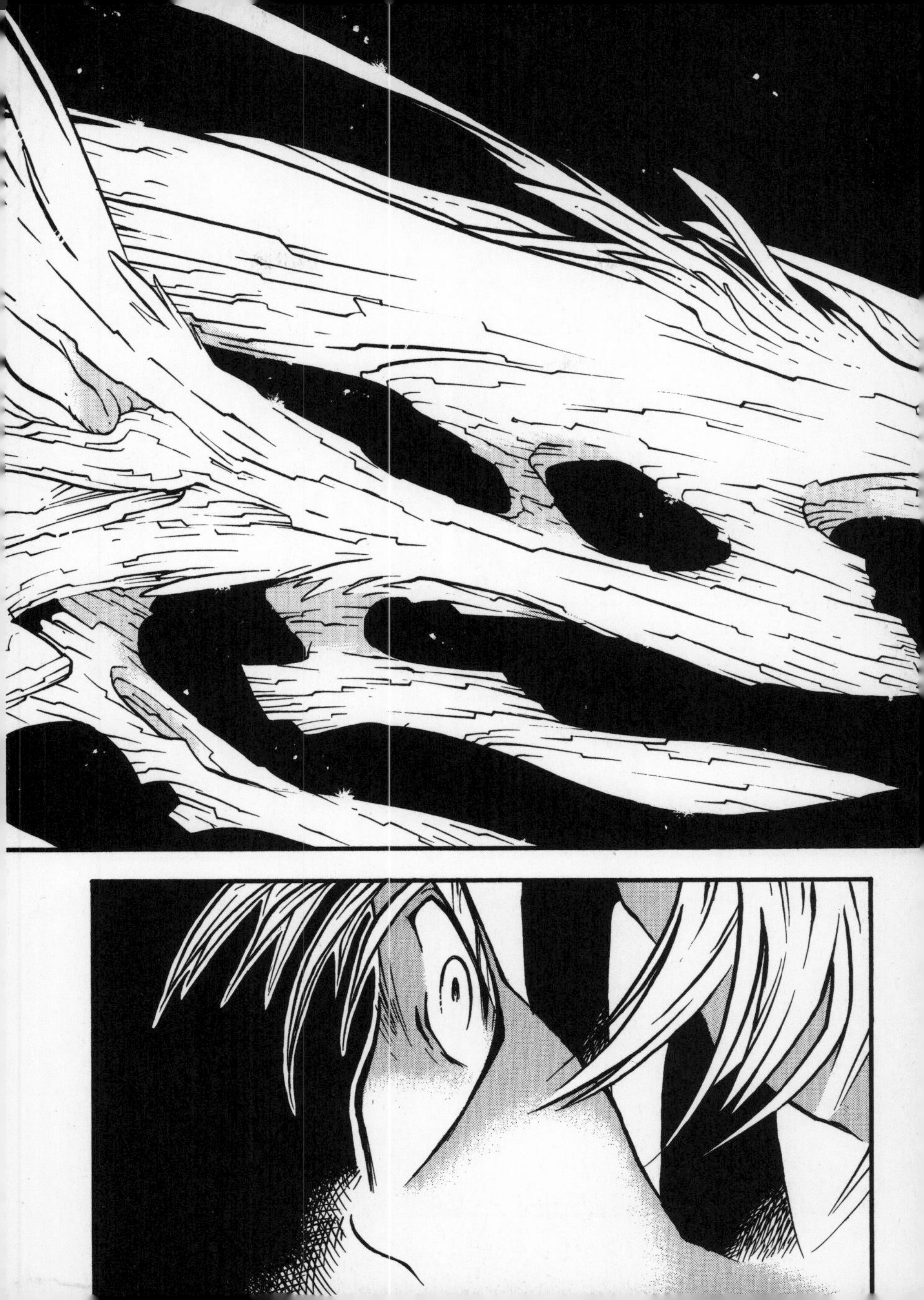

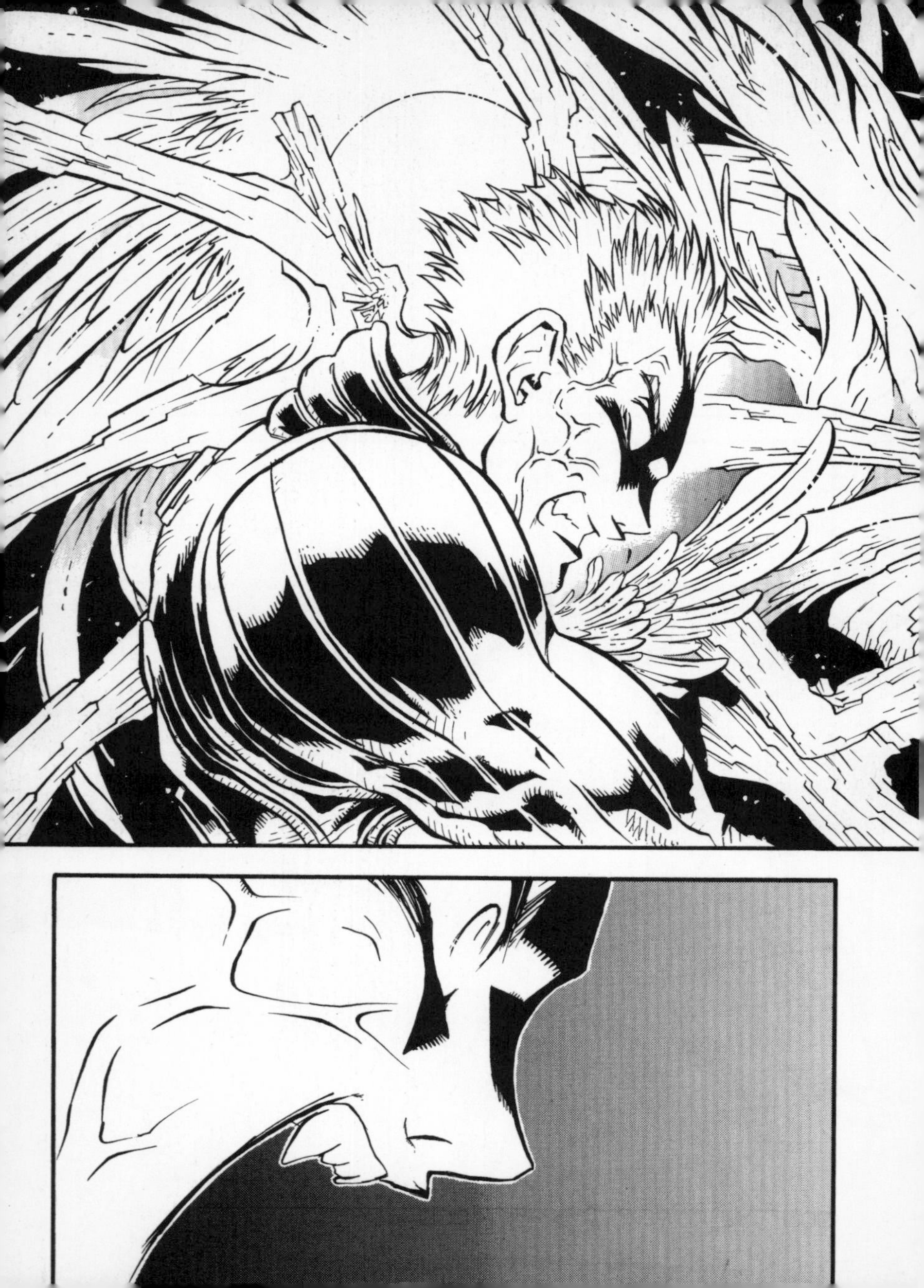

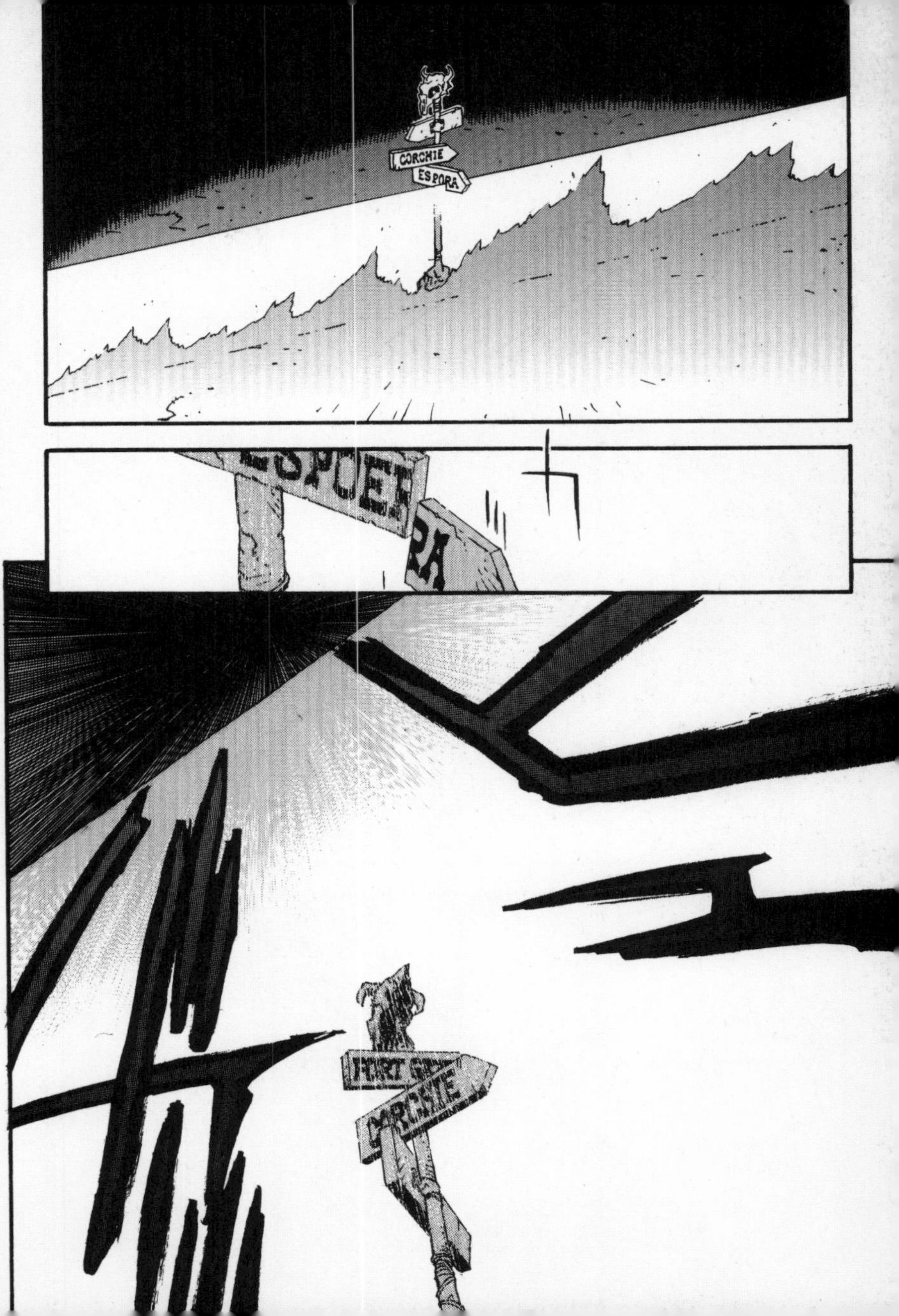
CORCHIE
ESPORA

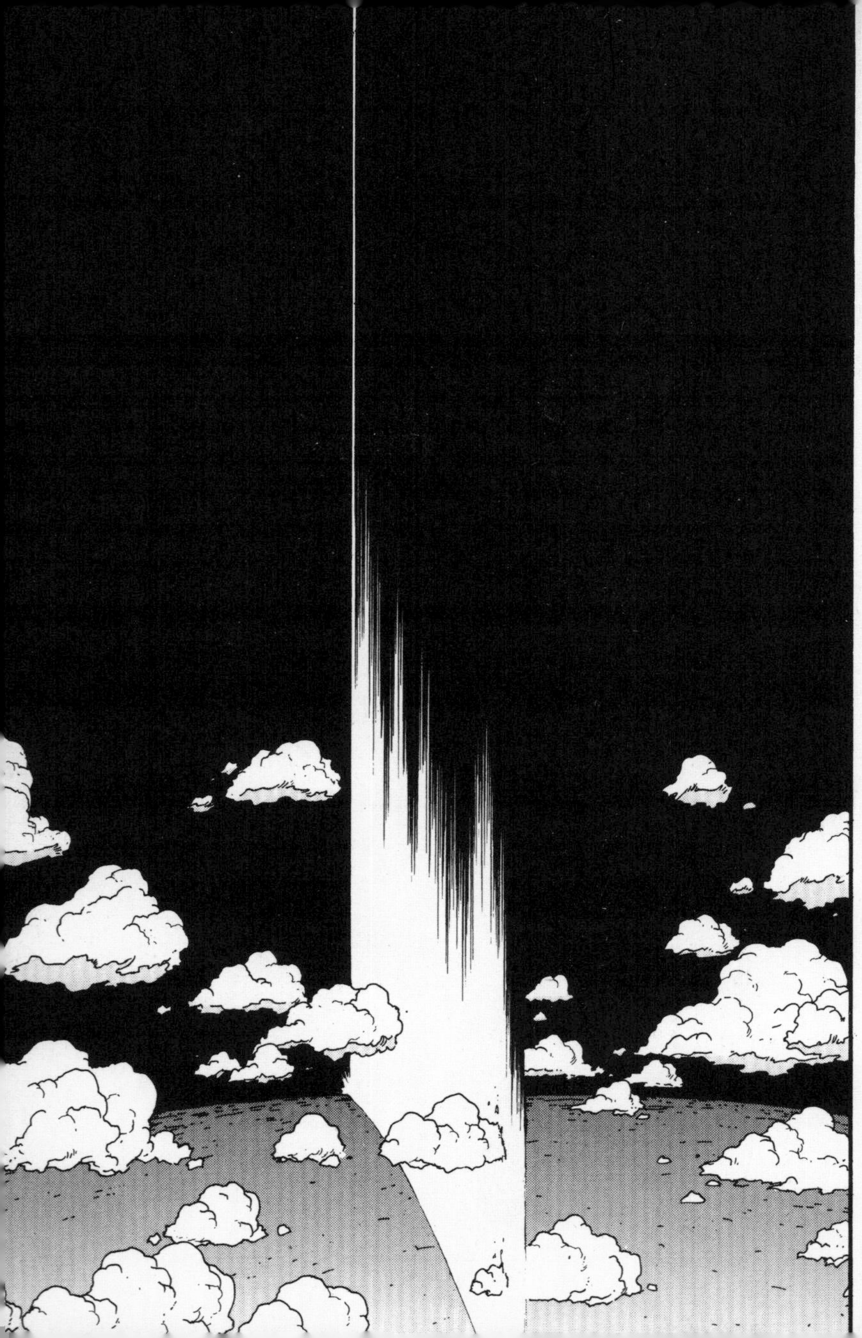

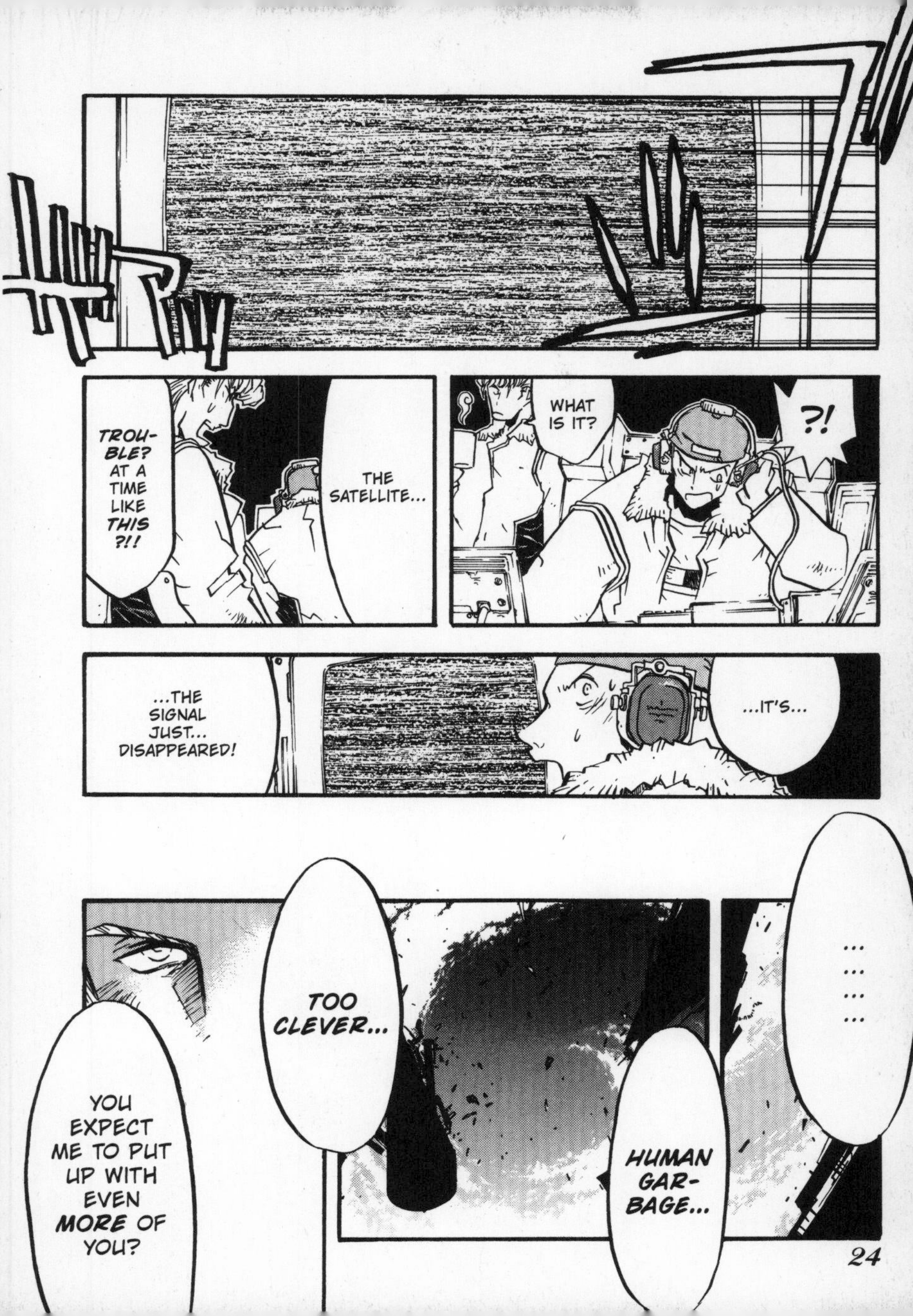
?!
WHAT IS IT?
THE SATELLITE...
TROUBLE? AT A TIME LIKE THIS?!!
...IT'S...
...THE SIGNAL JUST... DISAPPEARED!
... ...
HUMAN GARBAGE...
TOO CLEVER...
YOU EXPECT ME TO PUT UP WITH EVEN MORE OF YOU?

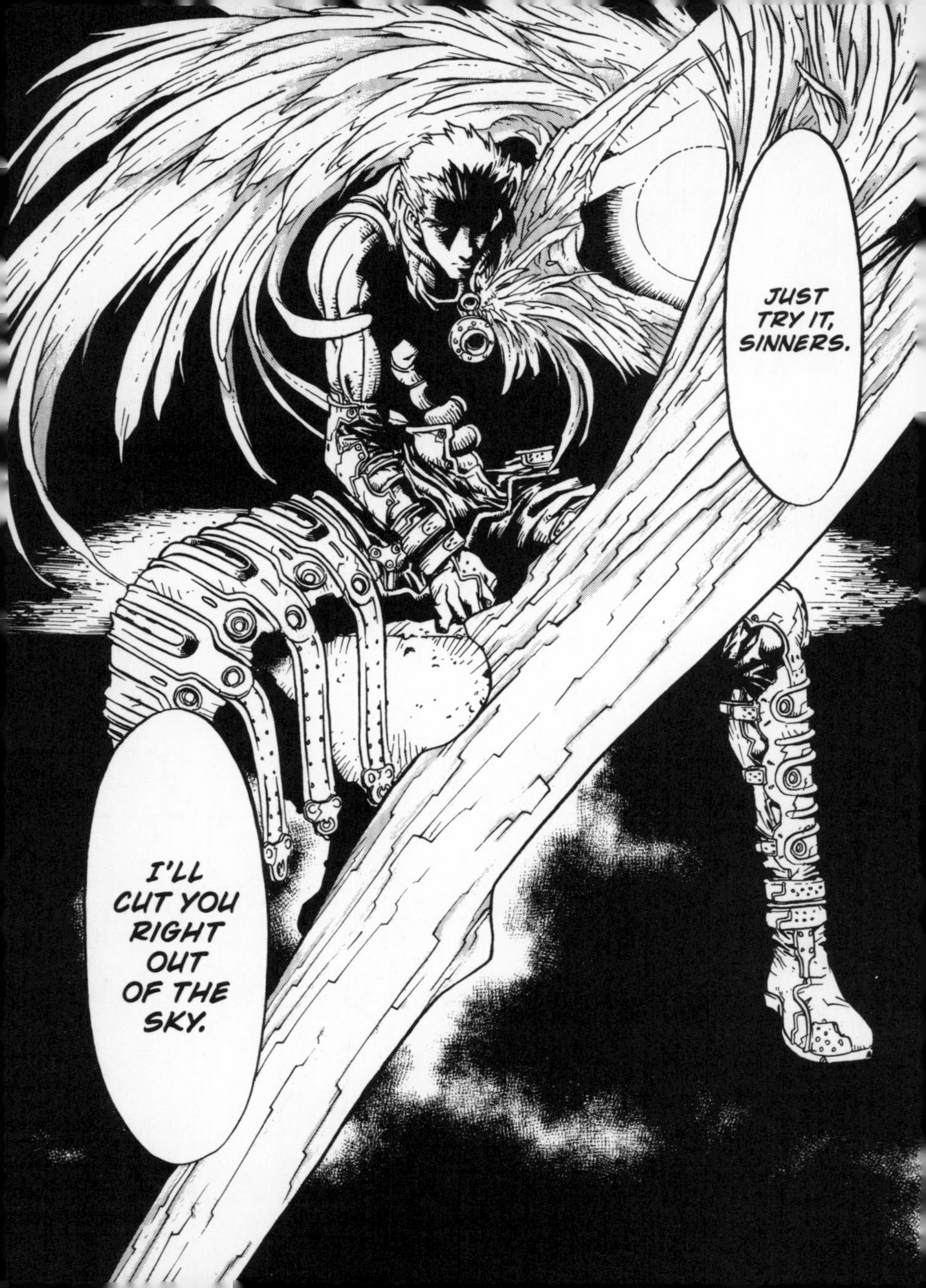
JUST TRY IT, SINNERS.
I'LL CUT YOU RIGHT OUT OF THE SKY.

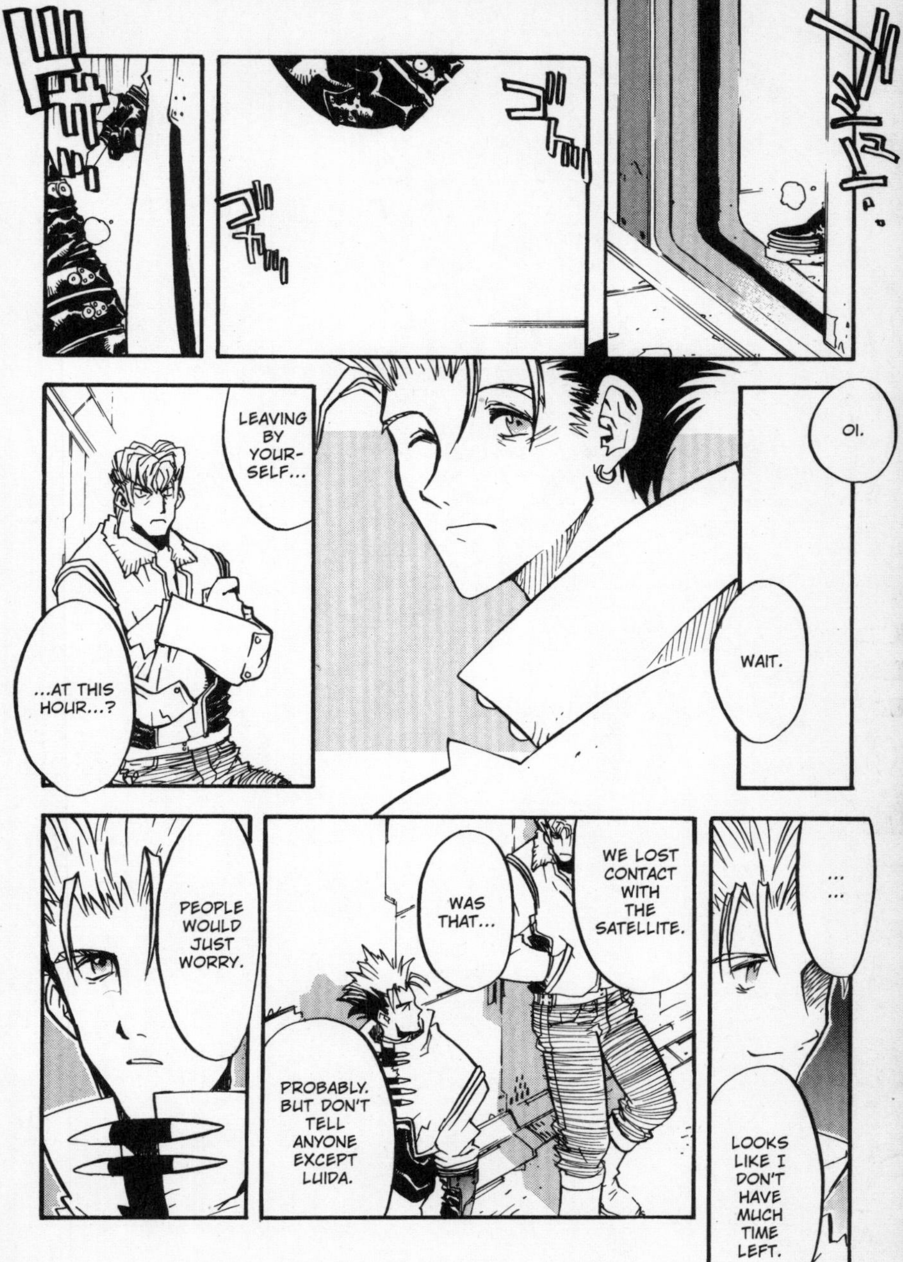
OI.
WAIT.
LEAVING BY YOURSELF...
...AT THIS HOUR...?
... ...
LOOKS LIKE I DON'T HAVE MUCH TIME LEFT.
WE LOST CONTACT WITH THE SATELLITE.
WAS THAT...
PROBABLY. BUT DON'T TELL ANYONE EXCEPT LUIDA.
PEOPLE WOULD JUST WORRY.

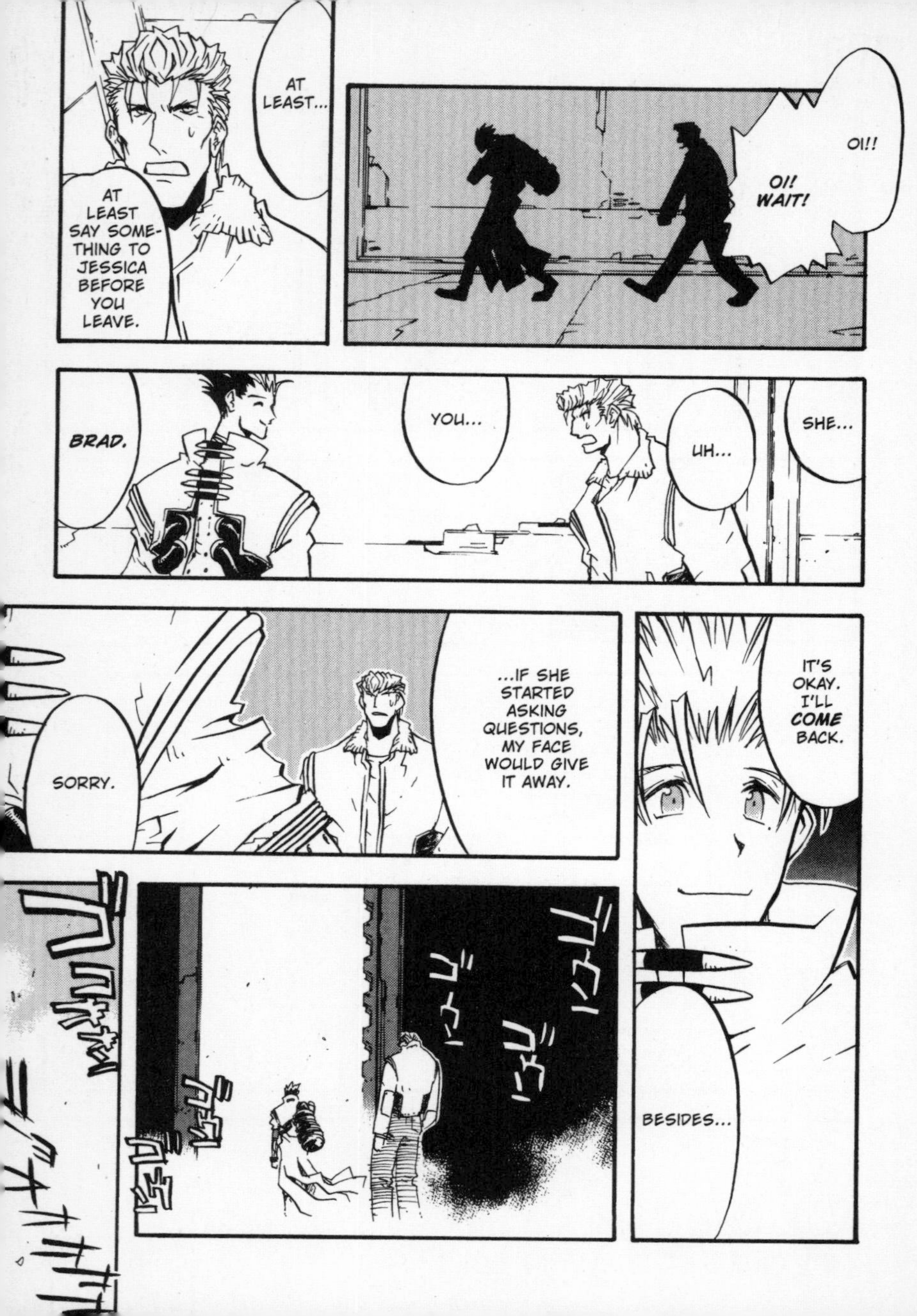
OI!!
OI! WAIT!
AT LEAST...
AT LEAST SAY SOMETHING TO JESSICA BEFORE YOU LEAVE.
SHE...
UH...
YOU...
BRAD.
IT'S OKAY. I'LL COME BACK.
BESIDES...
...IF SHE STARTED ASKING QUESTIONS, MY FACE WOULD GIVE IT AWAY.
SORRY.

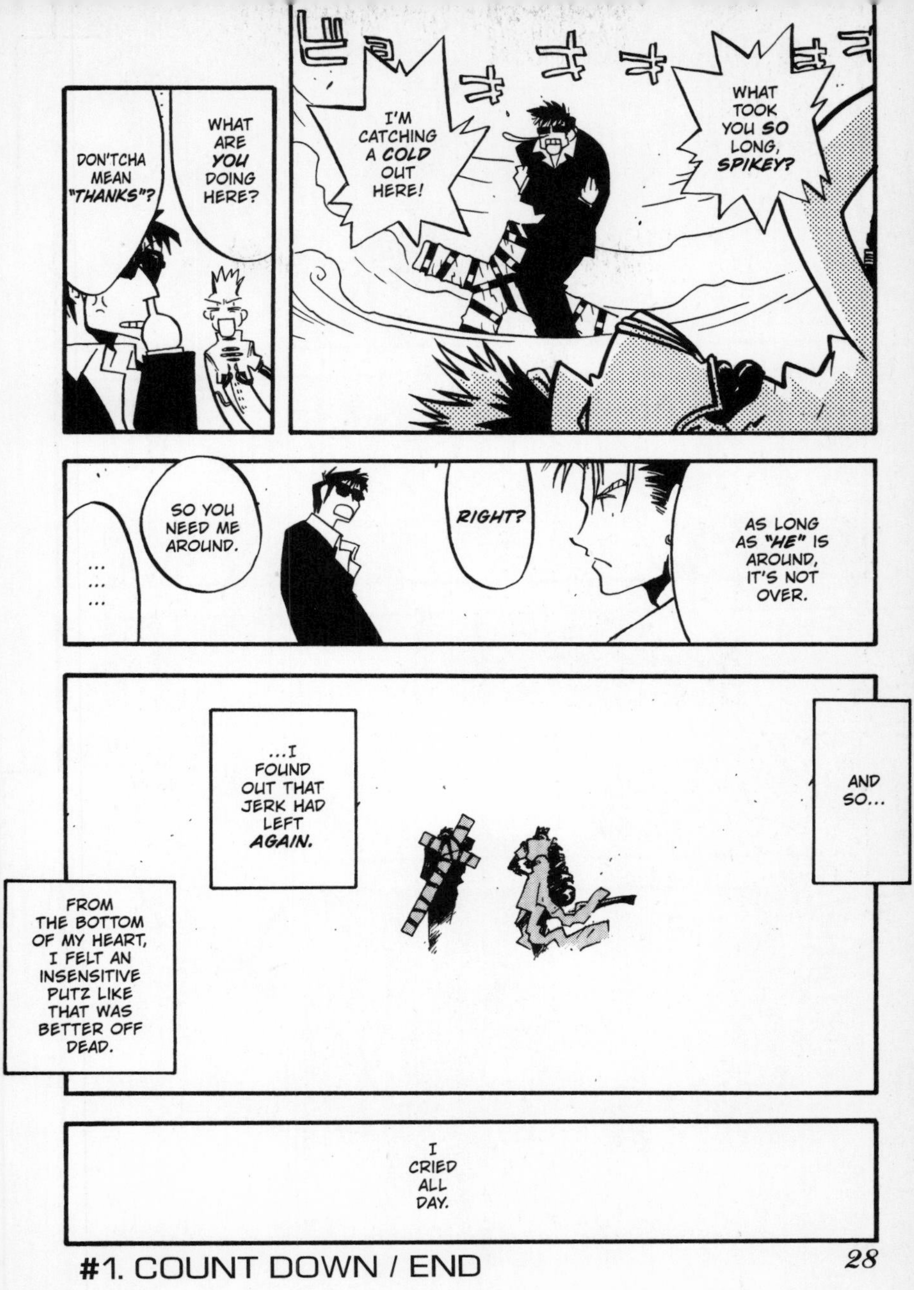
WHAT TOOK YOU SO LONG, SPIKEY?
I'M CATCHING A COLD OUT HERE!
WHAT ARE YOU DOING HERE?
DON'TCHA MEAN "THANKS"?
AS LONG AS "HE" IS AROUND, IT'S NOT OVER.
RIGHT?
SO YOU NEED ME AROUND.
... ...
AND SO...
...I FOUND OUT THAT JERK HAD LEFT AGAIN.
FROM THE BOTTOM OF MY HEART, I FELT AN INSENSITIVE PUTZ LIKE THAT WAS BETTER OFF DEAD.
I CRIED ALL DAY.

#1. COUNT DOWN / END

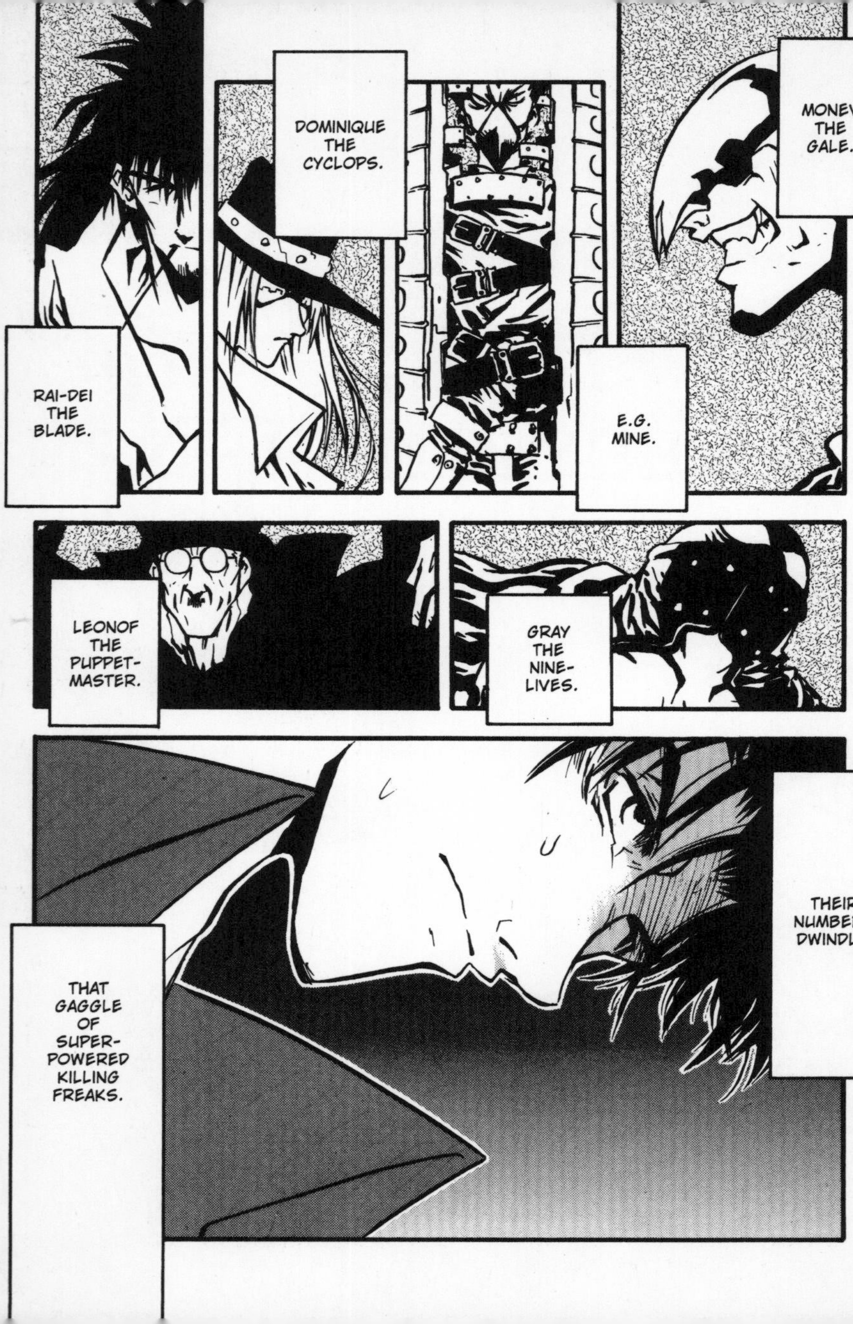
MONEV THE GALE.
E.G. MINE.
DOMINIQUE THE CYCLOPS.
RAI-DEI THE BLADE.
GRAY THE NINE-LIVES.
LEONOF THE PUPPET-MASTER.
THEIR NUMBERS DWINDLE...
THAT GAGGLE OF SUPER-POWERED KILLING FREAKS.

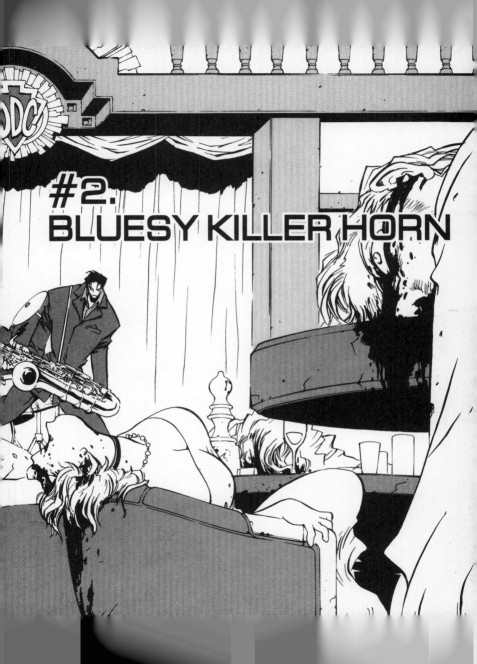

#2.
BLUESY KILLER HORN

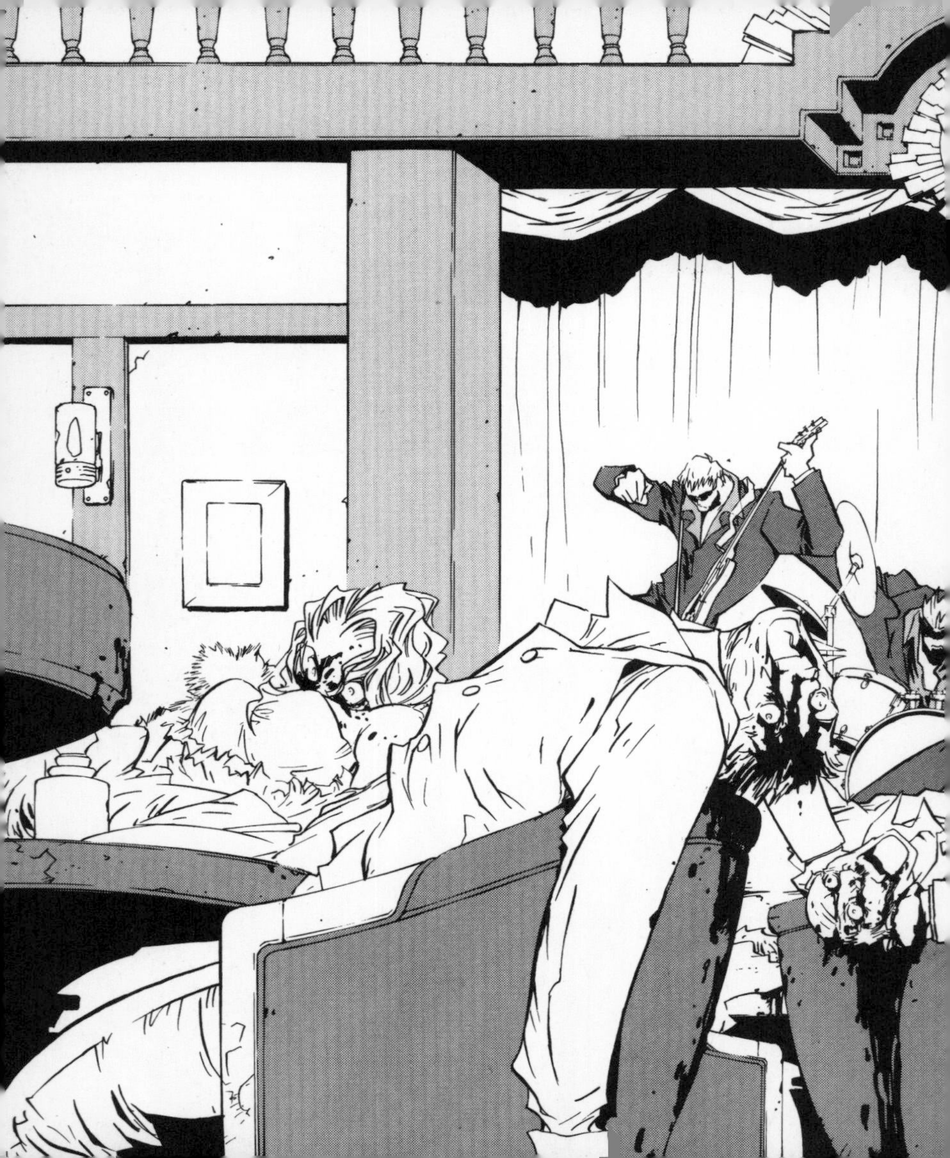

SINCE I WAS LITTLE, I'VE ALWAYS LOVED "SOUND" ALONE...

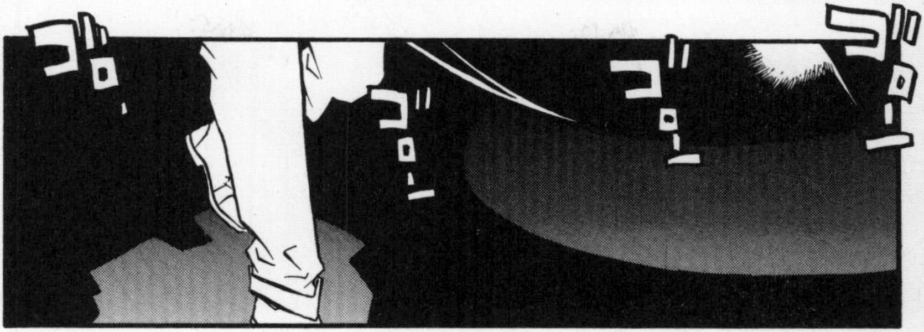

THAT'S IT...

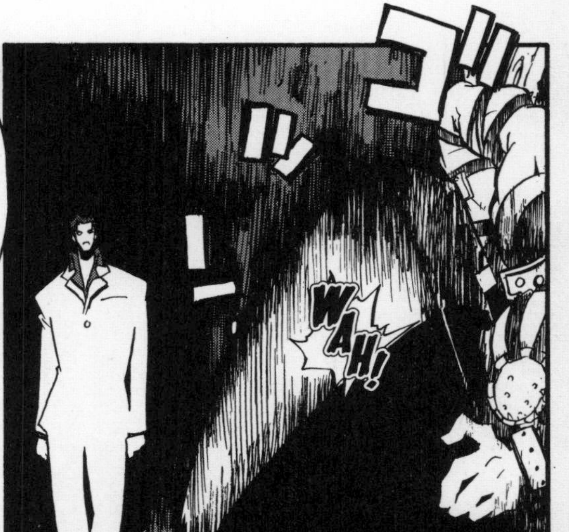
WAH!

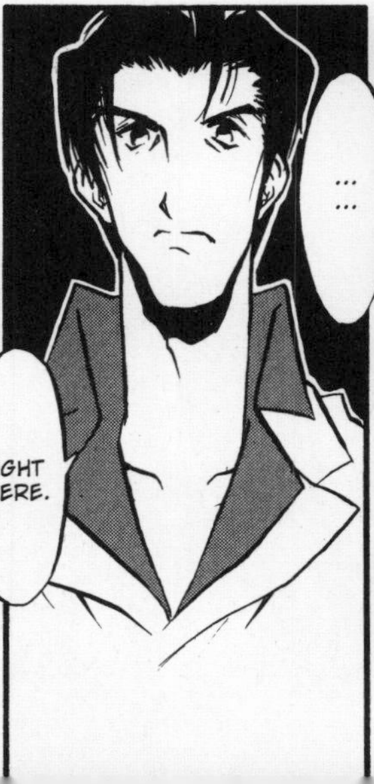
......
RIGHT THERE.

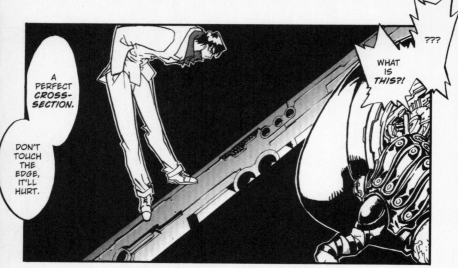

???
WHAT IS THIS?!
A PERFECT CROSS-SECTION.
DON'T TOUCH THE EDGE, IT'LL HURT.
……
THE "BLADE" WAS JUST A FEW TENTHS OF A MICRON THICK.
IT'S SLICED UP THIS WHOLE BLOCK.
… …?
HOW… DO YOU KNOW?

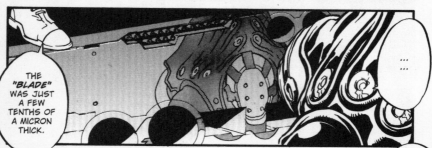

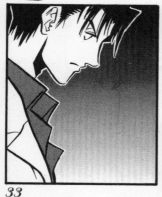

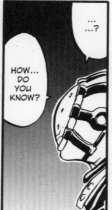

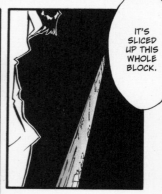

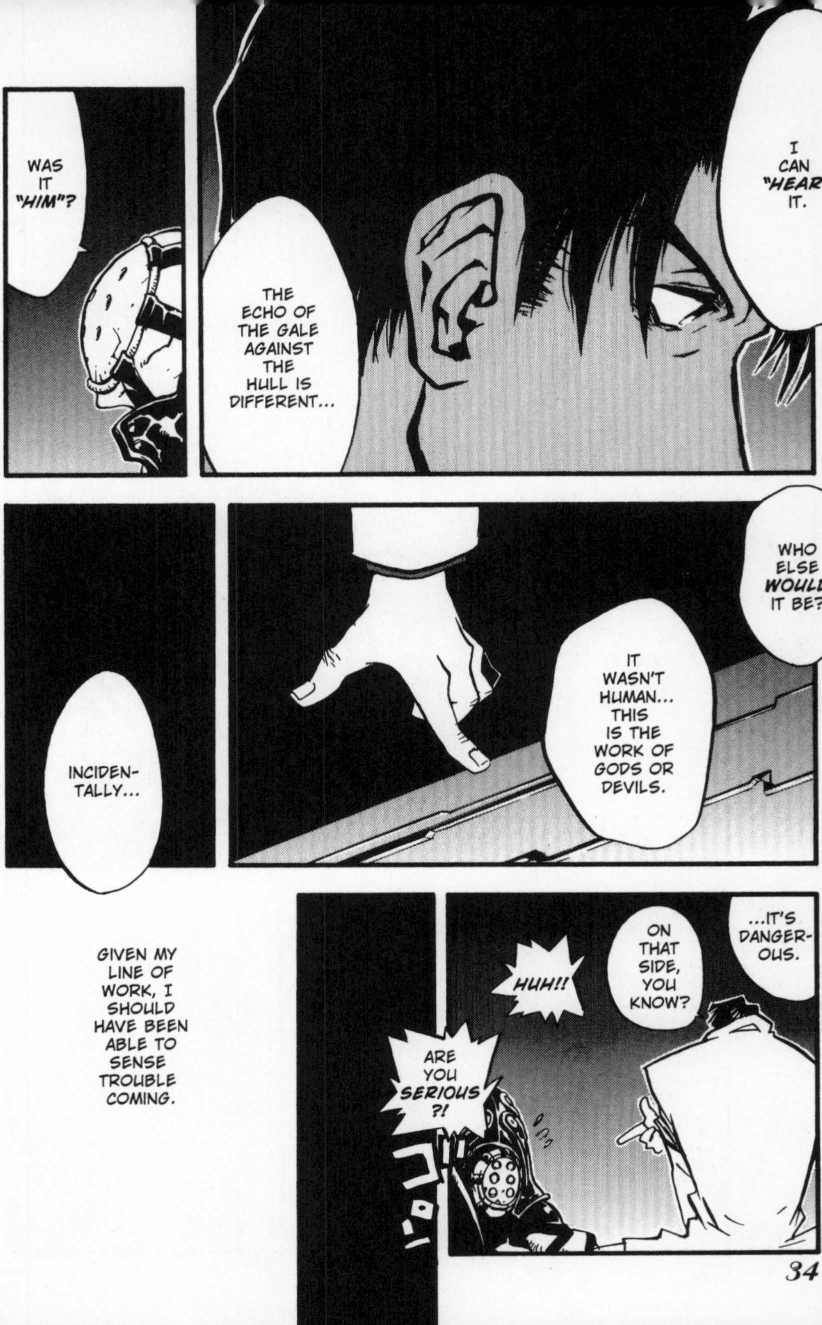
I CAN "HEAR" IT.
THE ECHO OF THE GALE AGAINST THE HULL IS DIFFERENT...
WAS IT "HIM"?
WHO ELSE WOULD IT BE?
IT WASN'T HUMAN... THIS IS THE WORK OF GODS OR DEVILS.
INCIDENTALLY...
...IT'S DANGEROUS.
ON THAT SIDE, YOU KNOW?
HUH!!
ARE YOU SERIOUS ?!
GIVEN MY LINE OF WORK, I SHOULD HAVE BEEN ABLE TO SENSE TROUBLE COMING.

BUT THAT
DOESN'T
WORK ON
PURE,
*UNMITIGATED
EVIL.*

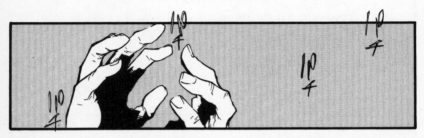

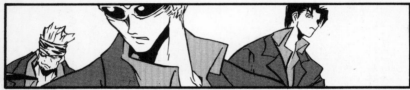

A POWER
THAT
IMMENSE
SEIZES YOUR
DESTINY
WITHOUT
WARNING.

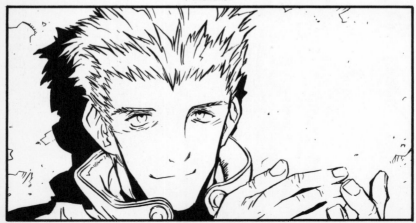

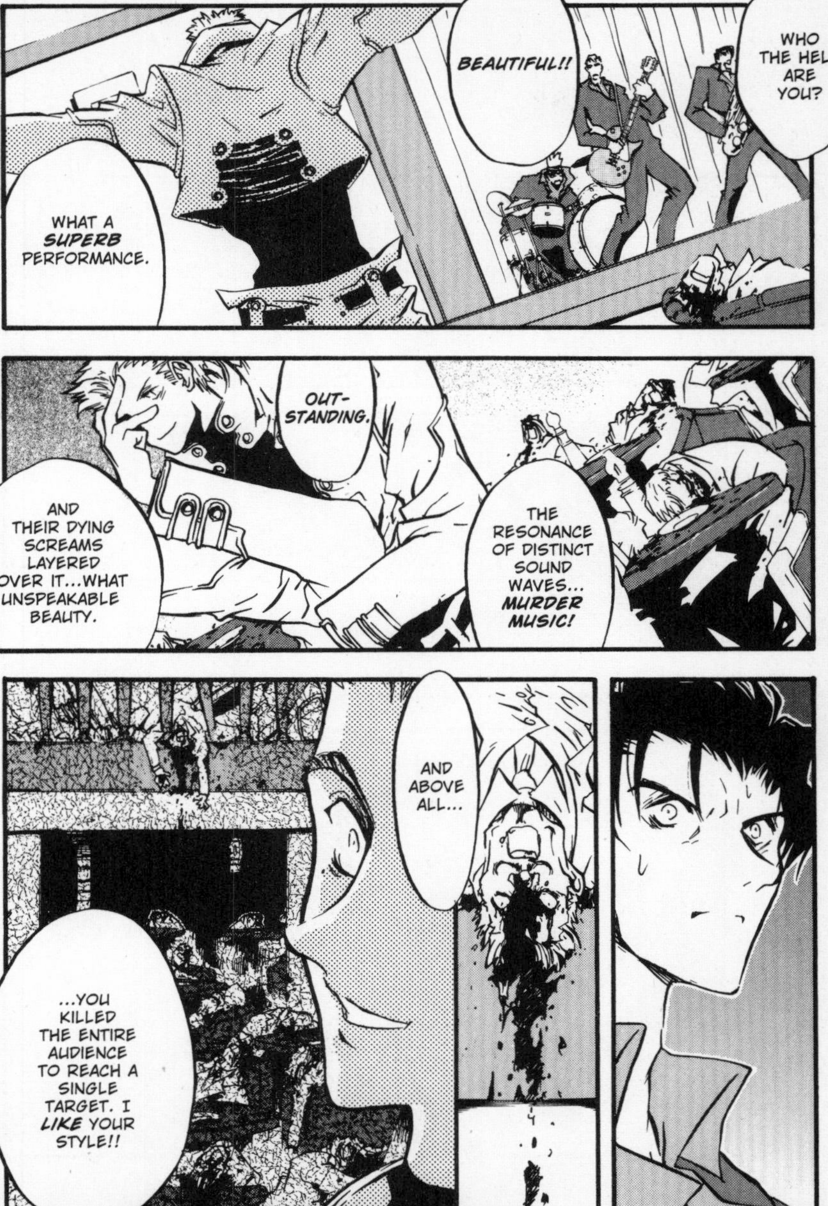
WHO THE HELL ARE YOU?
BEAUTIFUL!!
WHAT A SUPERB PERFORMANCE.
OUT-STANDING.
THE RESONANCE OF DISTINCT SOUND WAVES... MURDER MUSIC!
AND THEIR DYING SCREAMS LAYERED OVER IT...WHAT UNSPEAKABLE BEAUTY.
AND ABOVE ALL...
...YOU KILLED THE ENTIRE AUDIENCE TO REACH A SINGLE TARGET. I LIKE YOUR STYLE!!

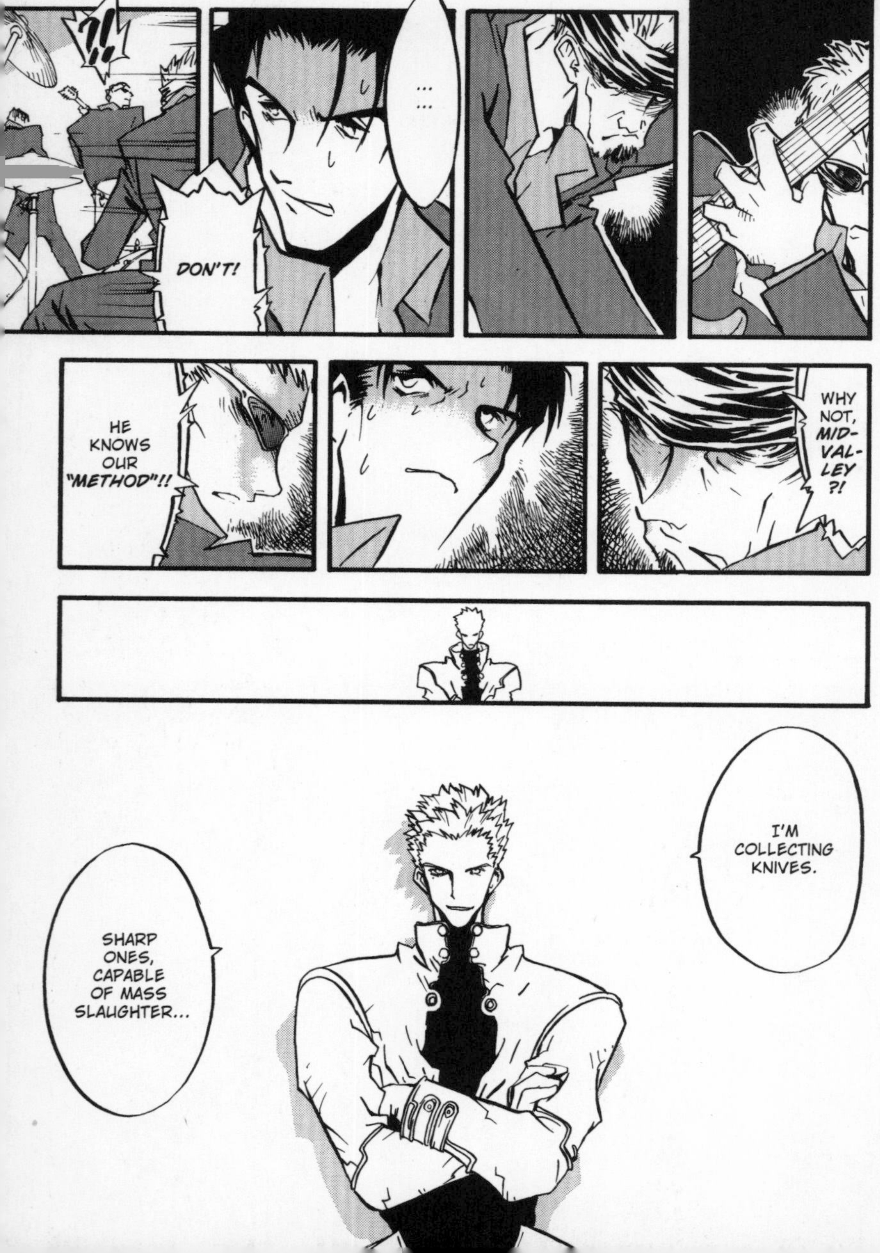
… …
?!!
DON'T!
WHY NOT, MID-VAL-LEY?!
HE KNOWS OUR "METHOD"!!
I'M COLLECTING KNIVES.
SHARP ONES, CAPABLE OF MASS SLAUGHTER…

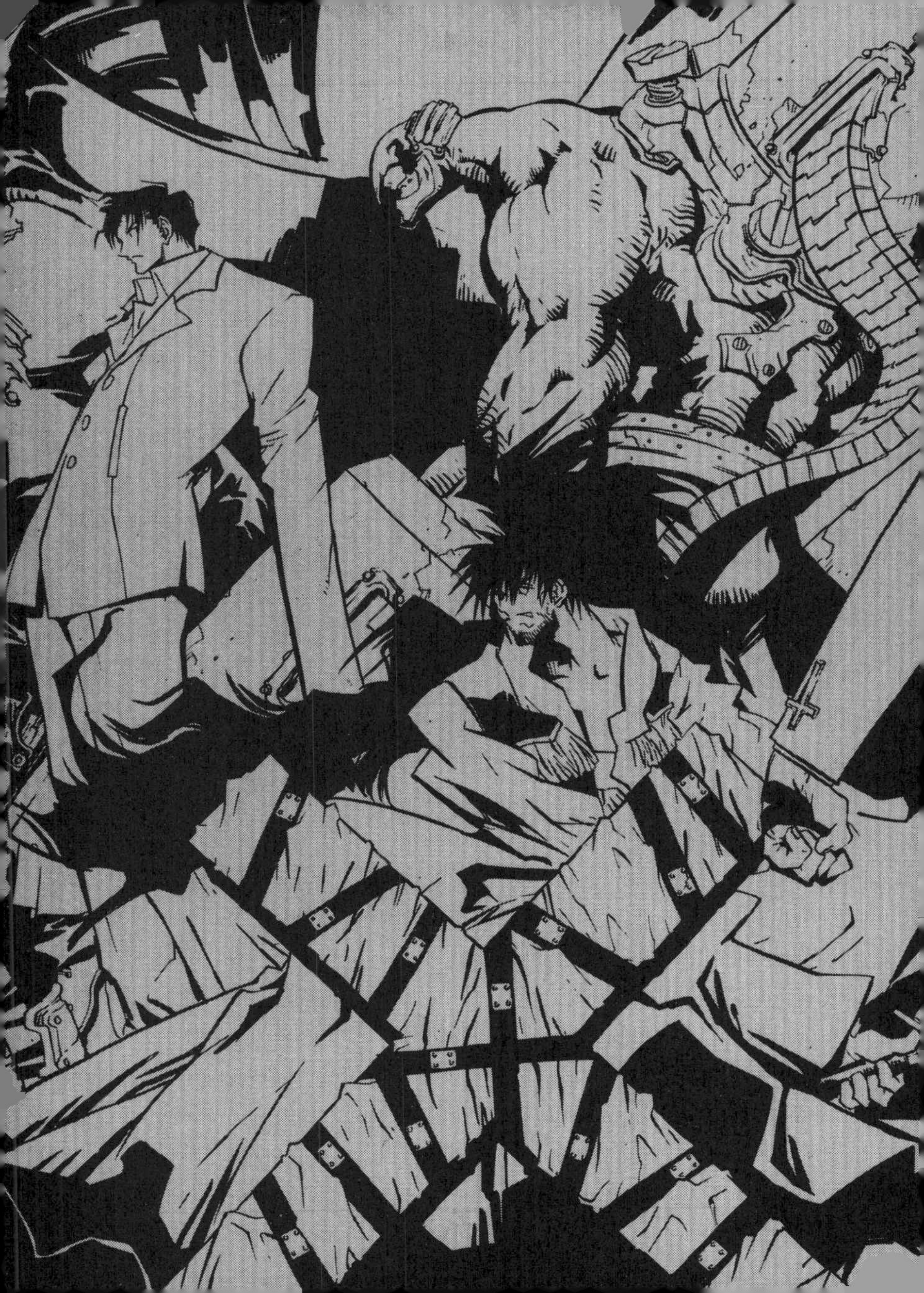

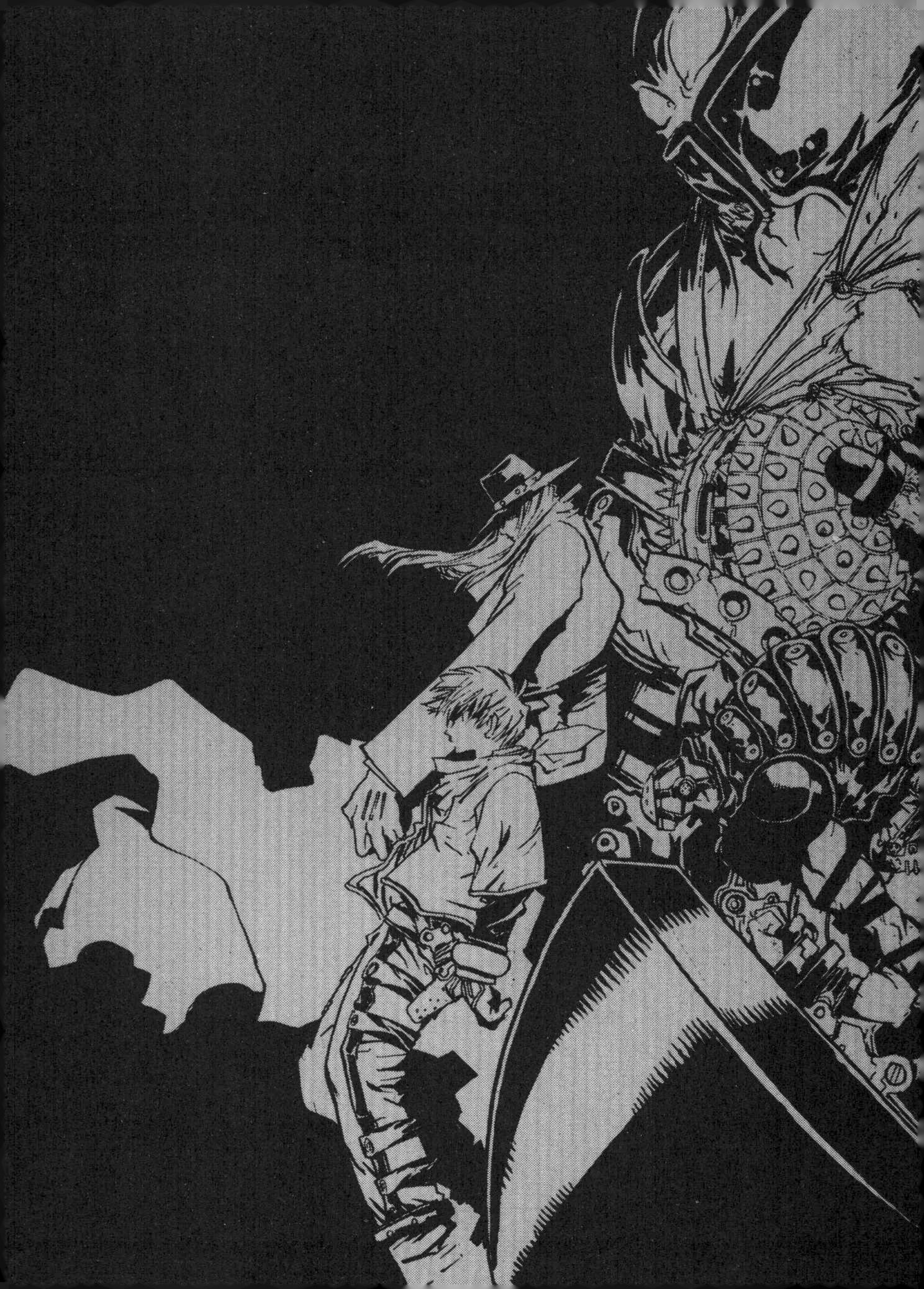

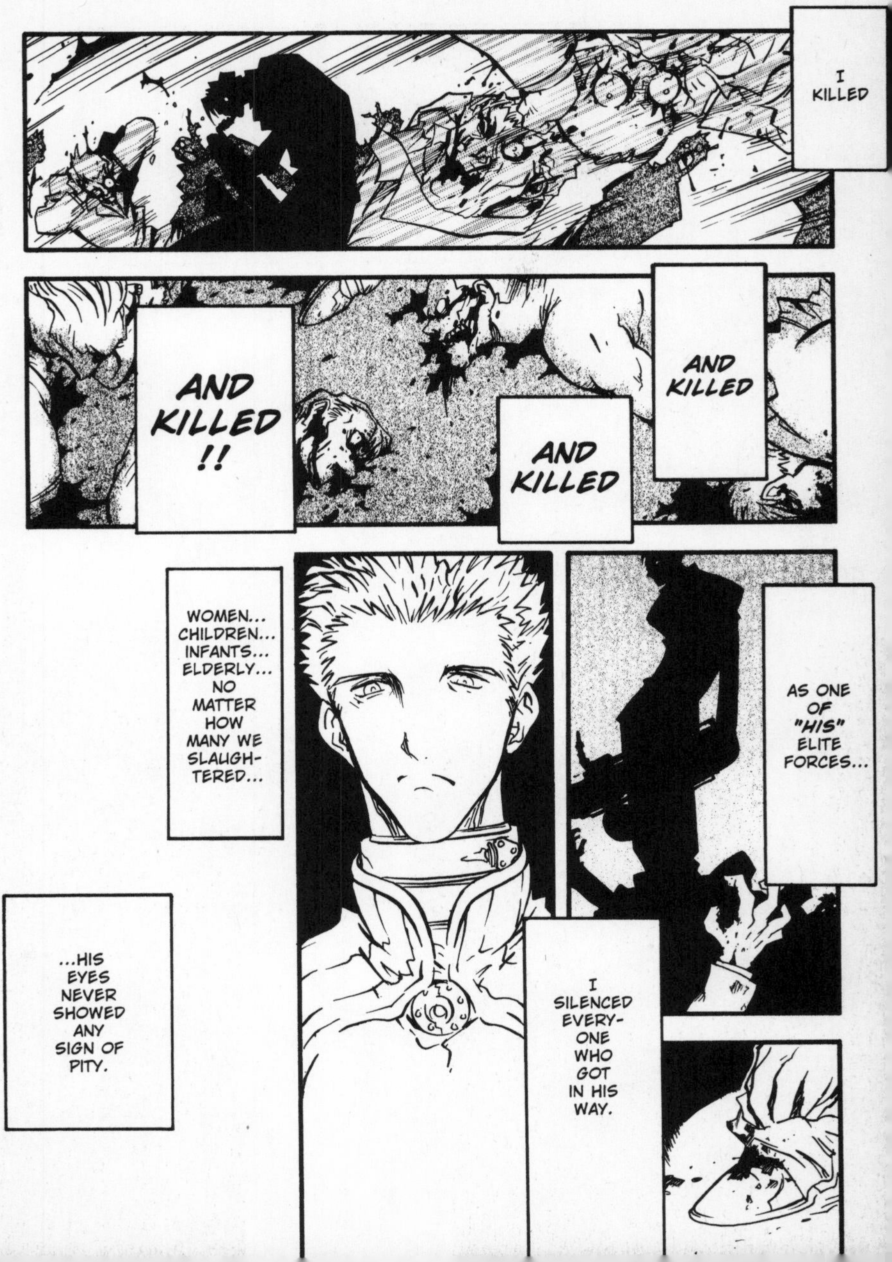
I KILLED
AND KILLED
AND KILLED
AND KILLED !!
AS ONE OF "HIS" ELITE FORCES...
I SILENCED EVERY-ONE WHO GOT IN HIS WAY.
WOMEN... CHILDREN... INFANTS... ELDERLY... NO MATTER HOW MANY WE SLAUGH-TERED...
...HIS EYES NEVER SHOWED ANY SIGN OF PITY.

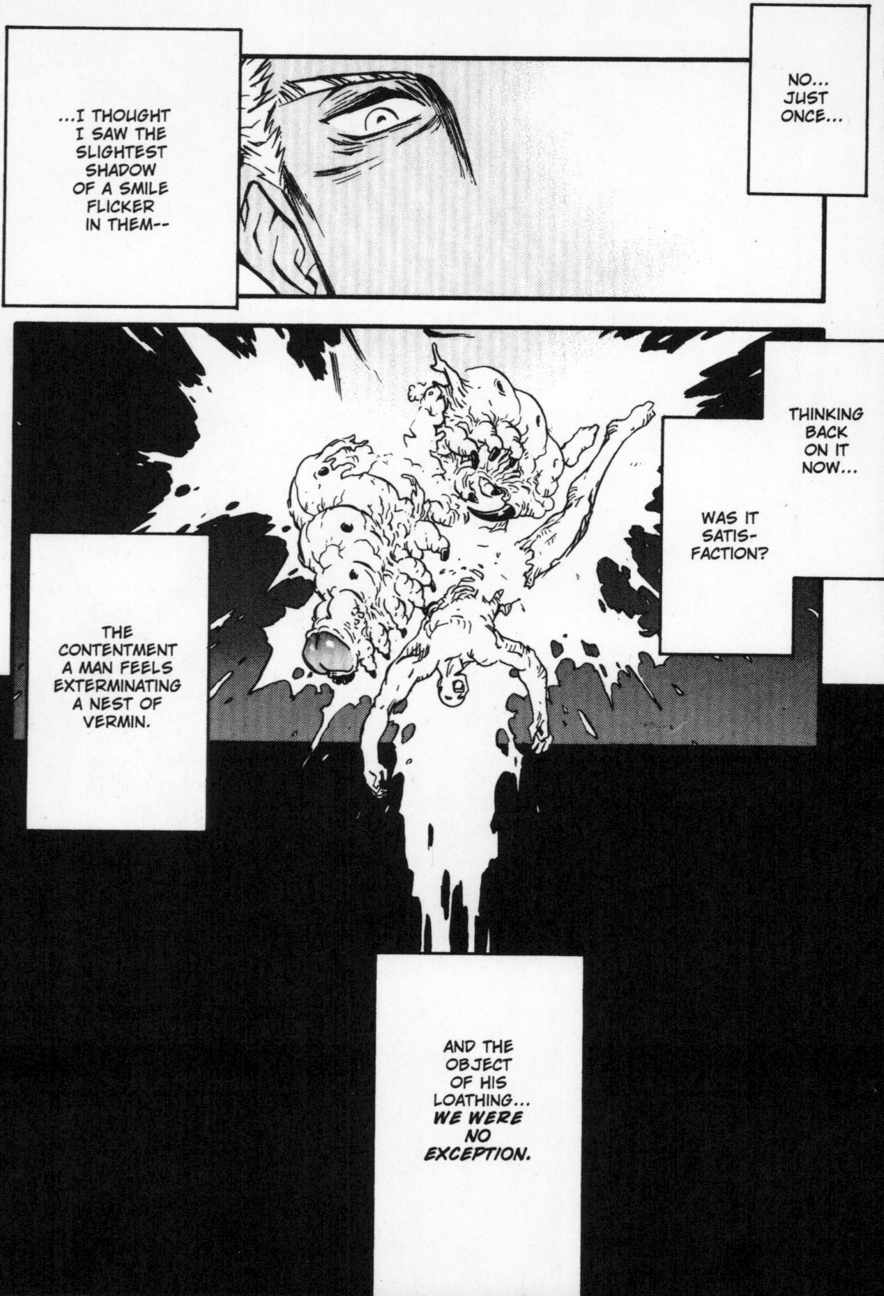
NO... JUST ONCE...
...I THOUGHT I SAW THE SLIGHTEST SHADOW OF A SMILE FLICKER IN THEM--
THINKING BACK ON IT NOW...
WAS IT SATIS-FACTION?
THE CONTENTMENT A MAN FEELS EXTERMINATING A NEST OF VERMIN.
AND THE OBJECT OF HIS LOATHING... ***WE WERE NO EXCEPTION.***

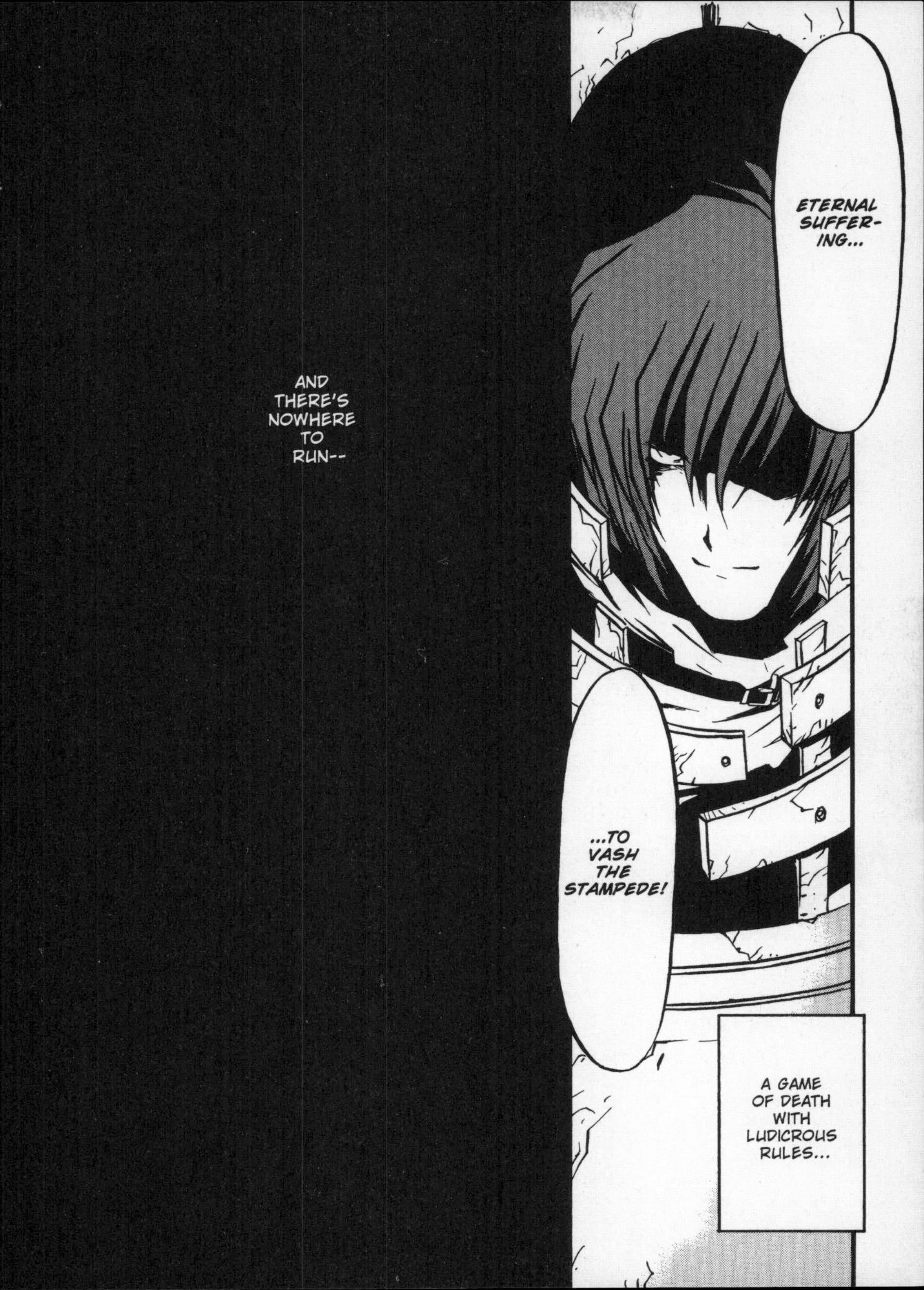
ETERNAL SUFFER- ING...
...TO VASH THE STAMPEDE!
A GAME OF DEATH WITH LUDICROUS RULES...
AND THERE'S NOWHERE TO RUN--

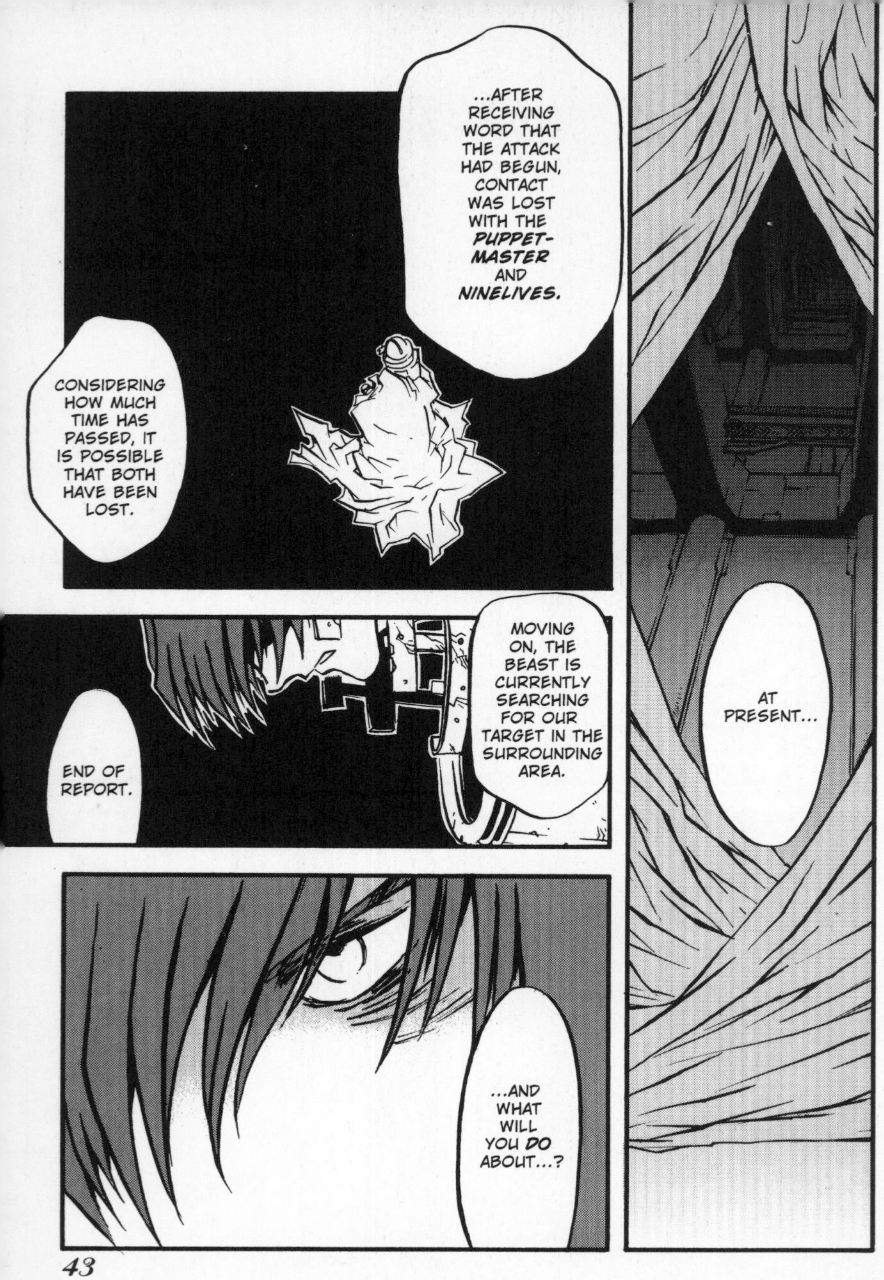
AT PRESENT...
...AFTER RECEIVING WORD THAT THE ATTACK HAD BEGUN, CONTACT WAS LOST WITH THE PUPPET-MASTER AND NINELIVES.
CONSIDERING HOW MUCH TIME HAS PASSED, IT IS POSSIBLE THAT BOTH HAVE BEEN LOST.
MOVING ON, THE BEAST IS CURRENTLY SEARCHING FOR OUR TARGET IN THE SURROUNDING AREA.
END OF REPORT.
...AND WHAT WILL YOU DO ABOUT...?

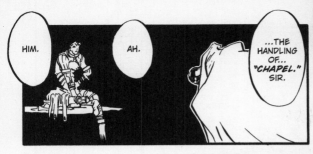

HIM.

AH.

...THE HANDLING OF... *"CHAPEL."* SIR.

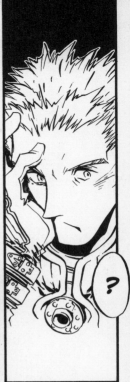

?

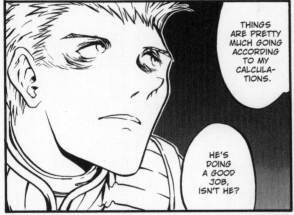

THINGS ARE PRETTY MUCH GOING ACCORDING TO MY CALCULATIONS.

HE'S DOING A GOOD JOB, ISN'T HE?

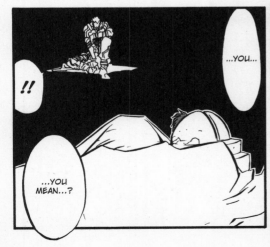

...YOU...

!!

...YOU MEAN...?

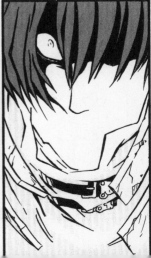

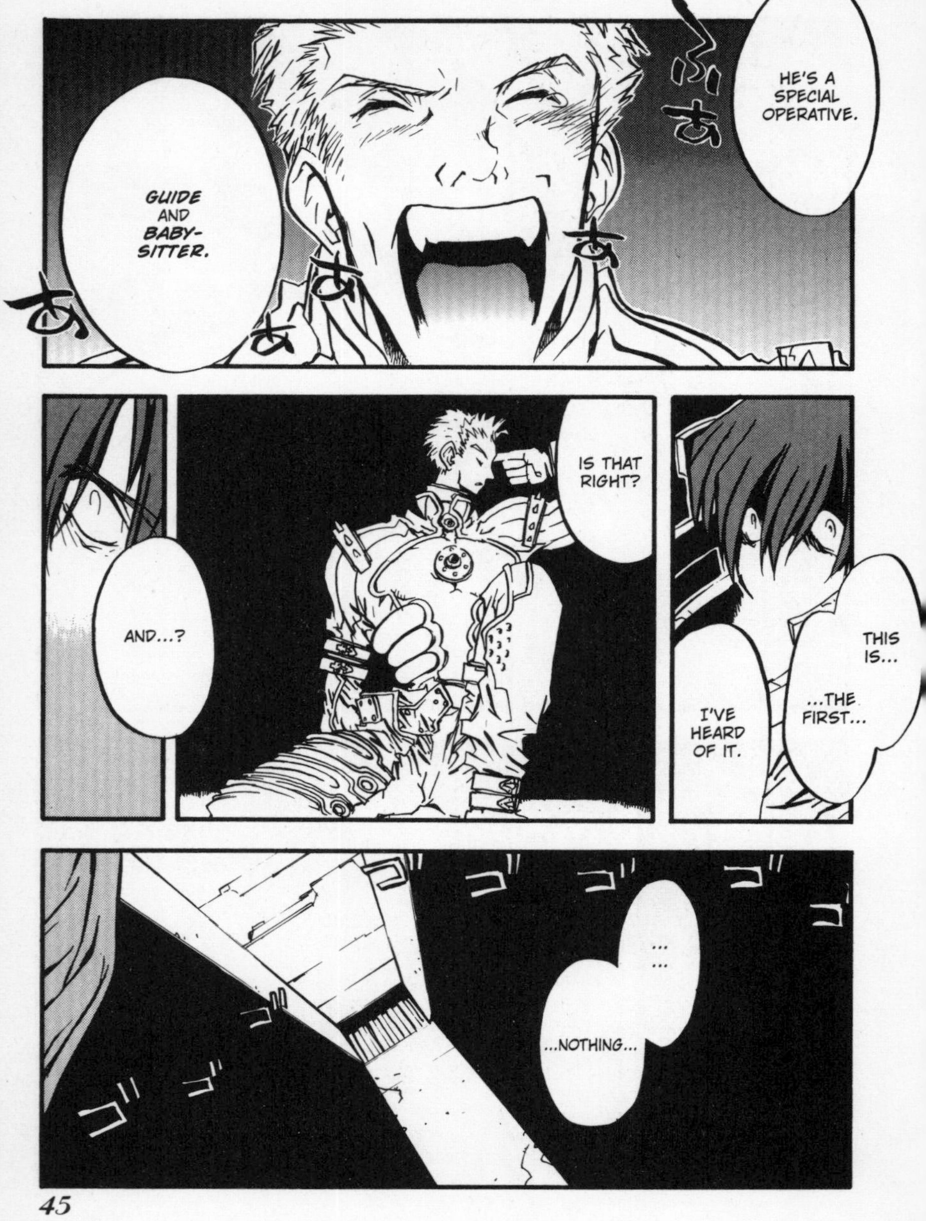
ふあ
HE'S A SPECIAL OPERATIVE.
あああ
GUIDE AND BABY-SITTER.
THIS IS...
...THE FIRST...
I'VE HEARD OF IT.
IS THAT RIGHT?
AND...?
ゴゴゴゴ
......
...NOTHING...
ゴゴゴ

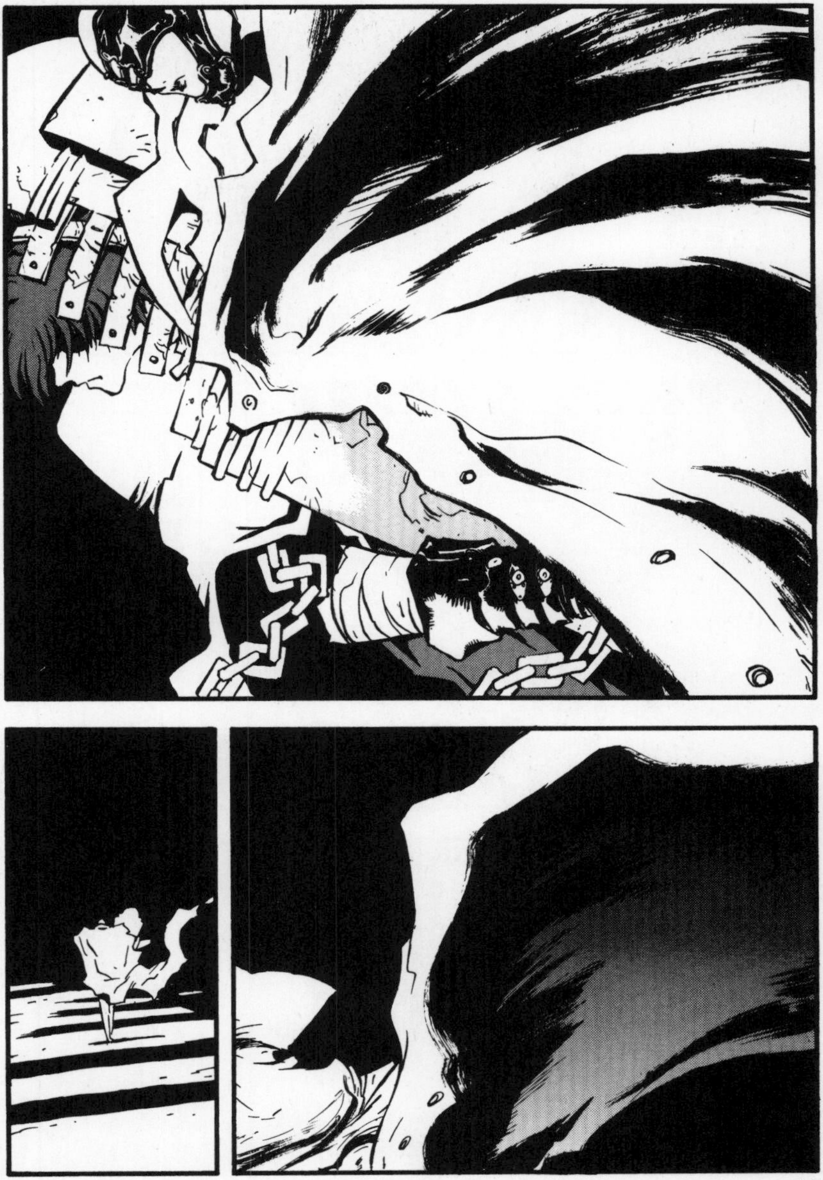

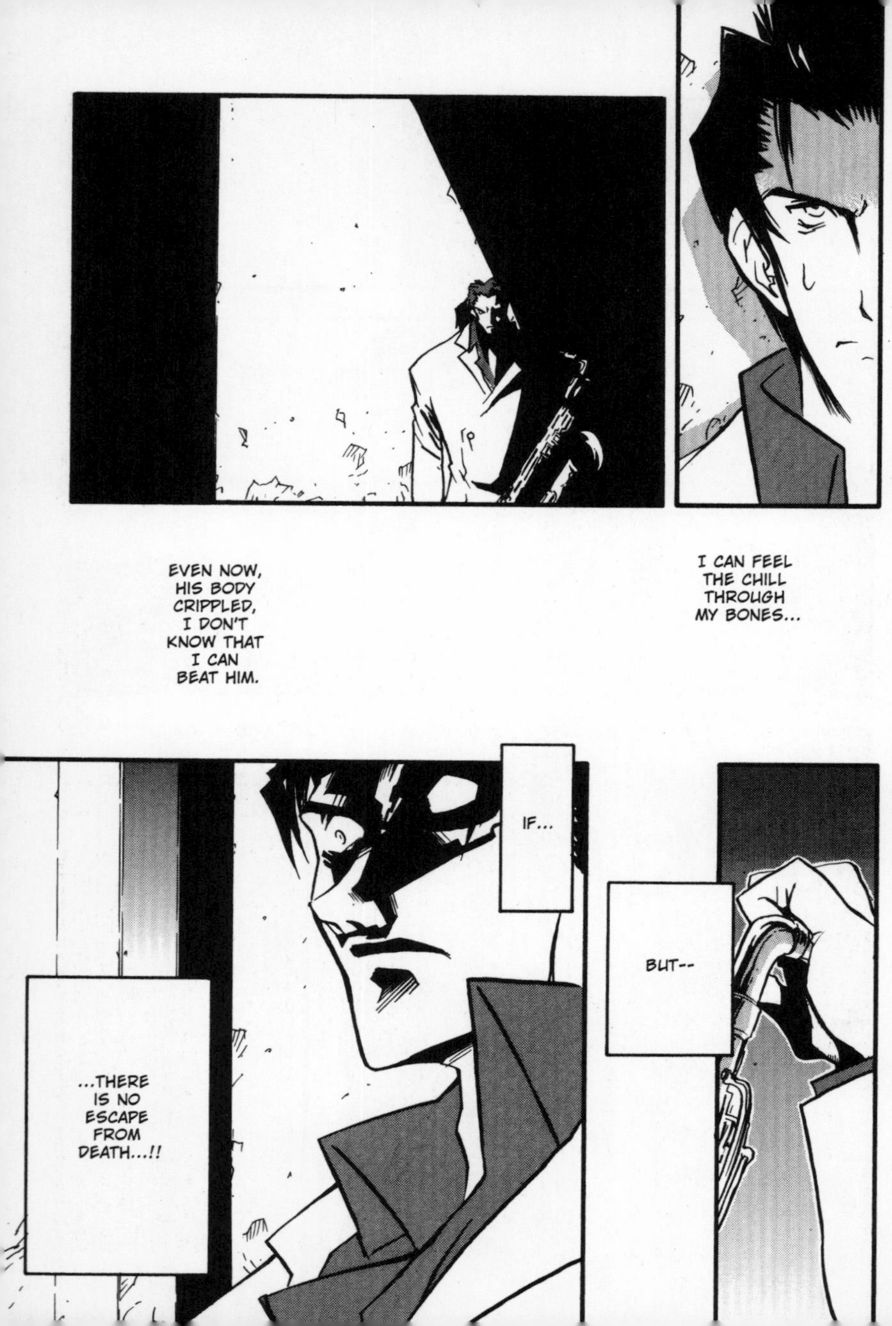
I CAN FEEL THE CHILL THROUGH MY BONES...
EVEN NOW, HIS BODY CRIPPLED, I DON'T KNOW THAT I CAN BEAT HIM.
BUT--
IF...
...THERE IS NO ESCAPE FROM DEATH...!!

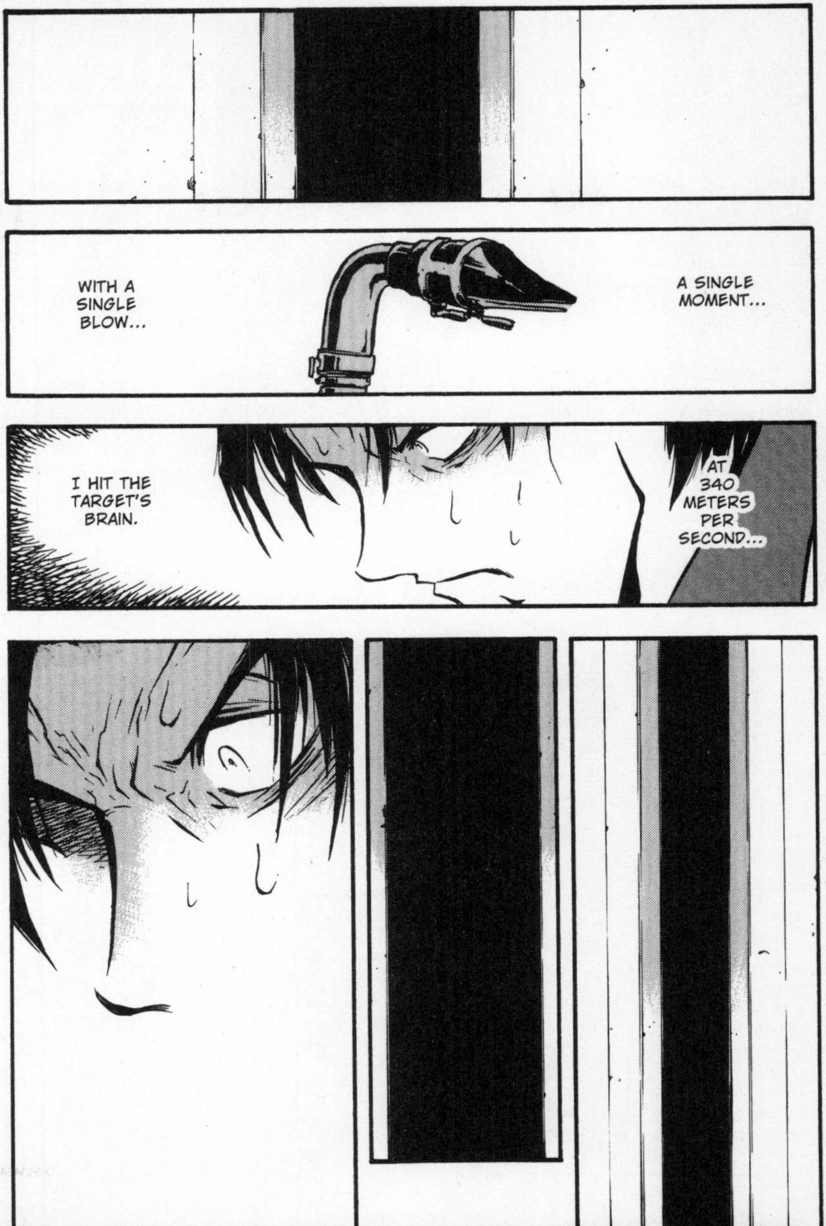
A SINGLE MOMENT...
WITH A SINGLE BLOW...
AT 340 METERS PER SECOND...
I HIT THE TARGET'S BRAIN.

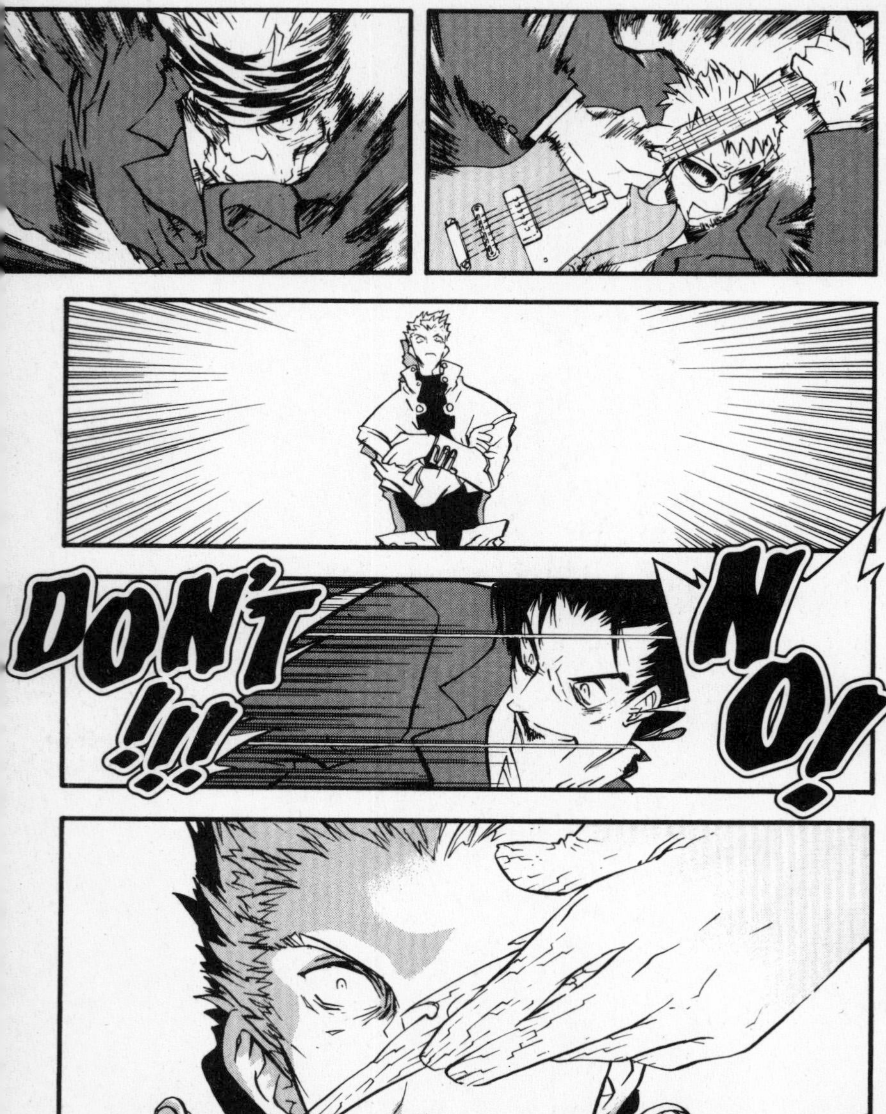
NO!
DON'T!!!

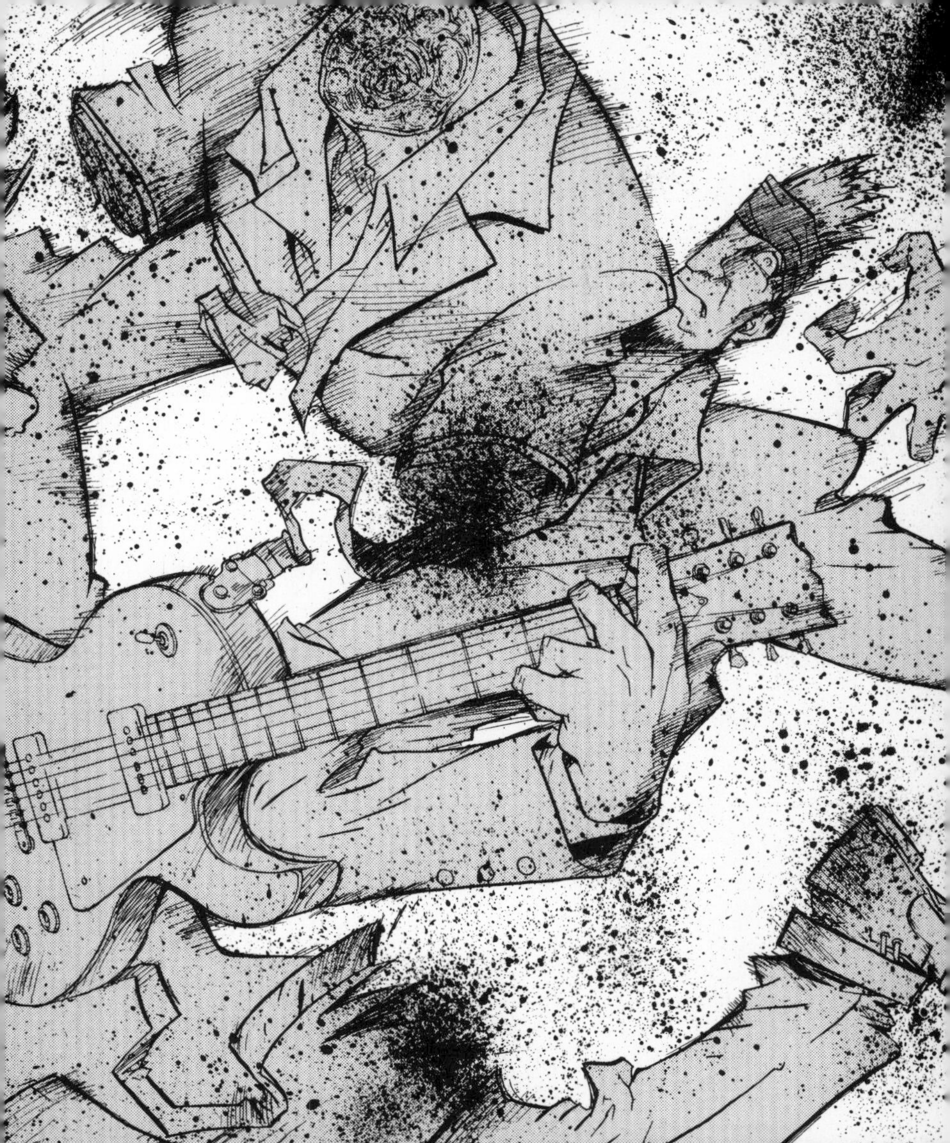

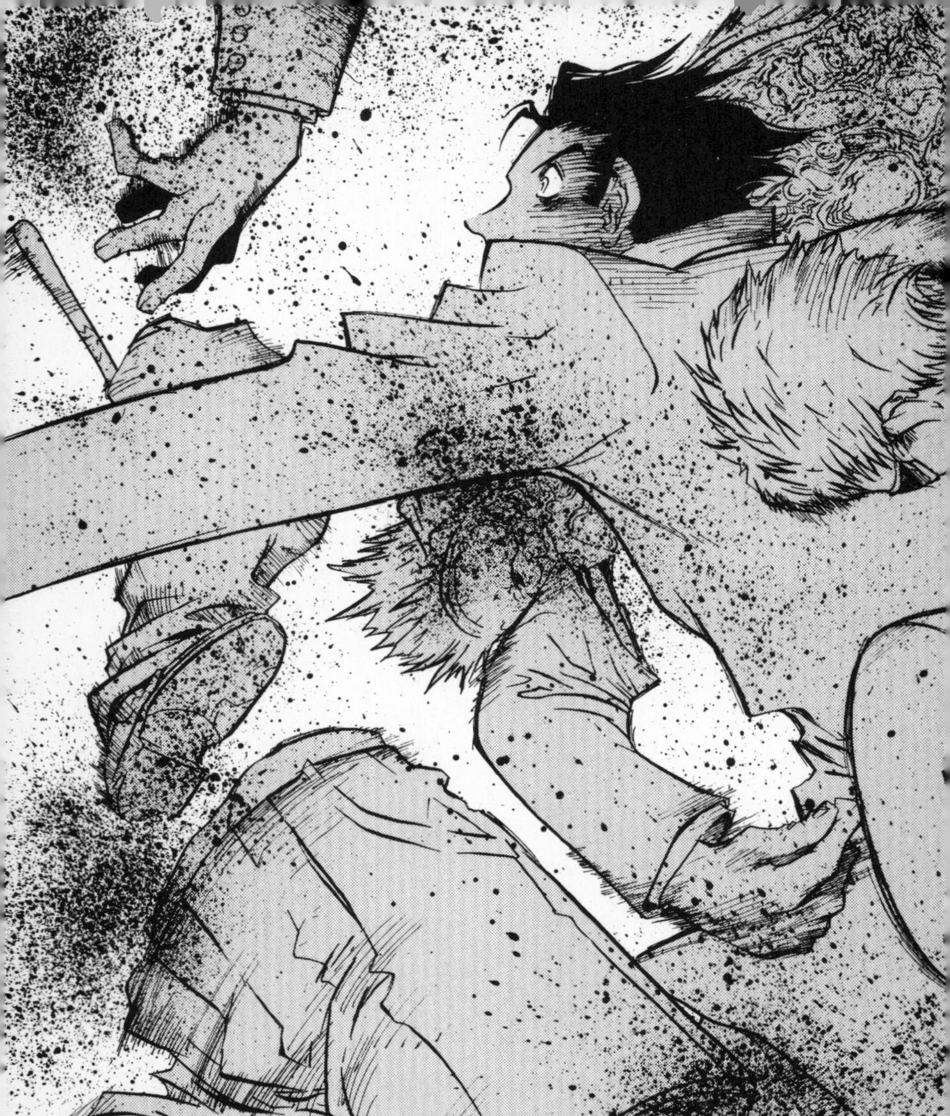

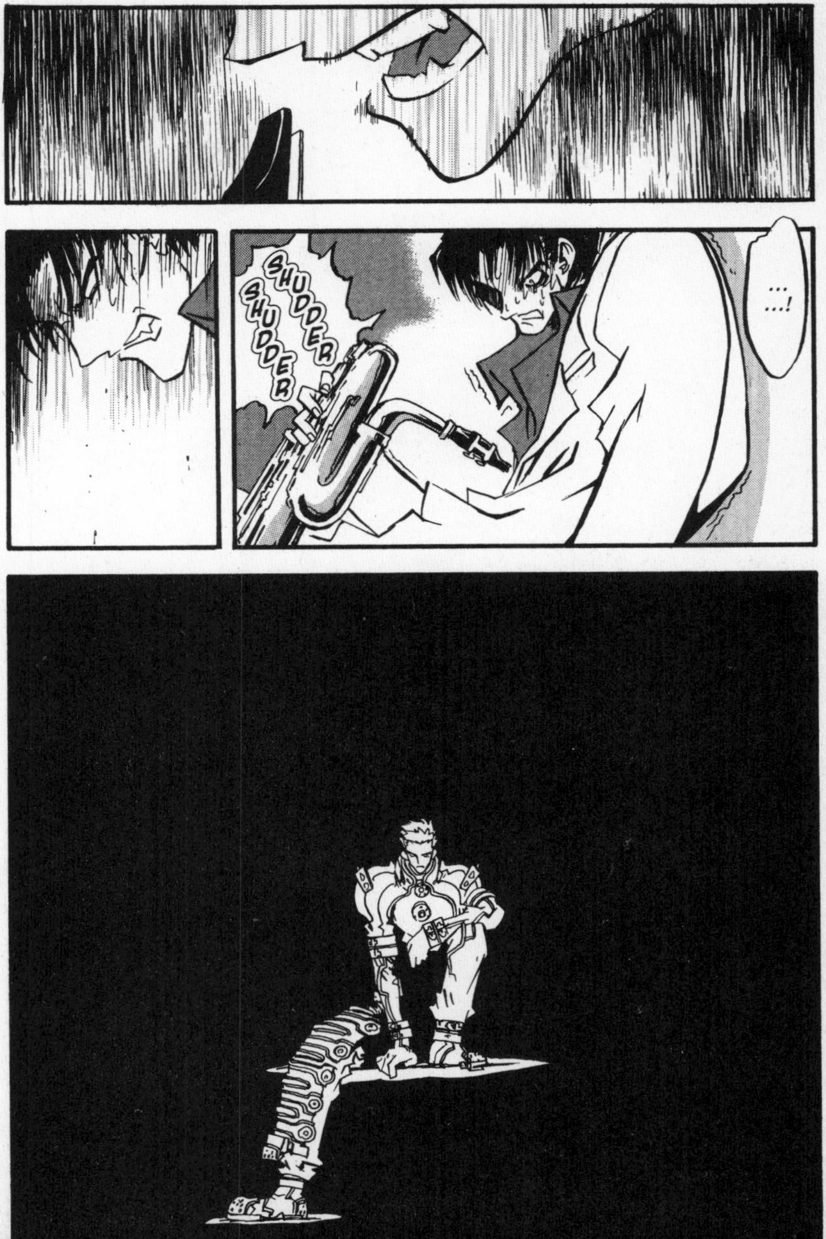
... ...!
SHUDDER SHUDDER

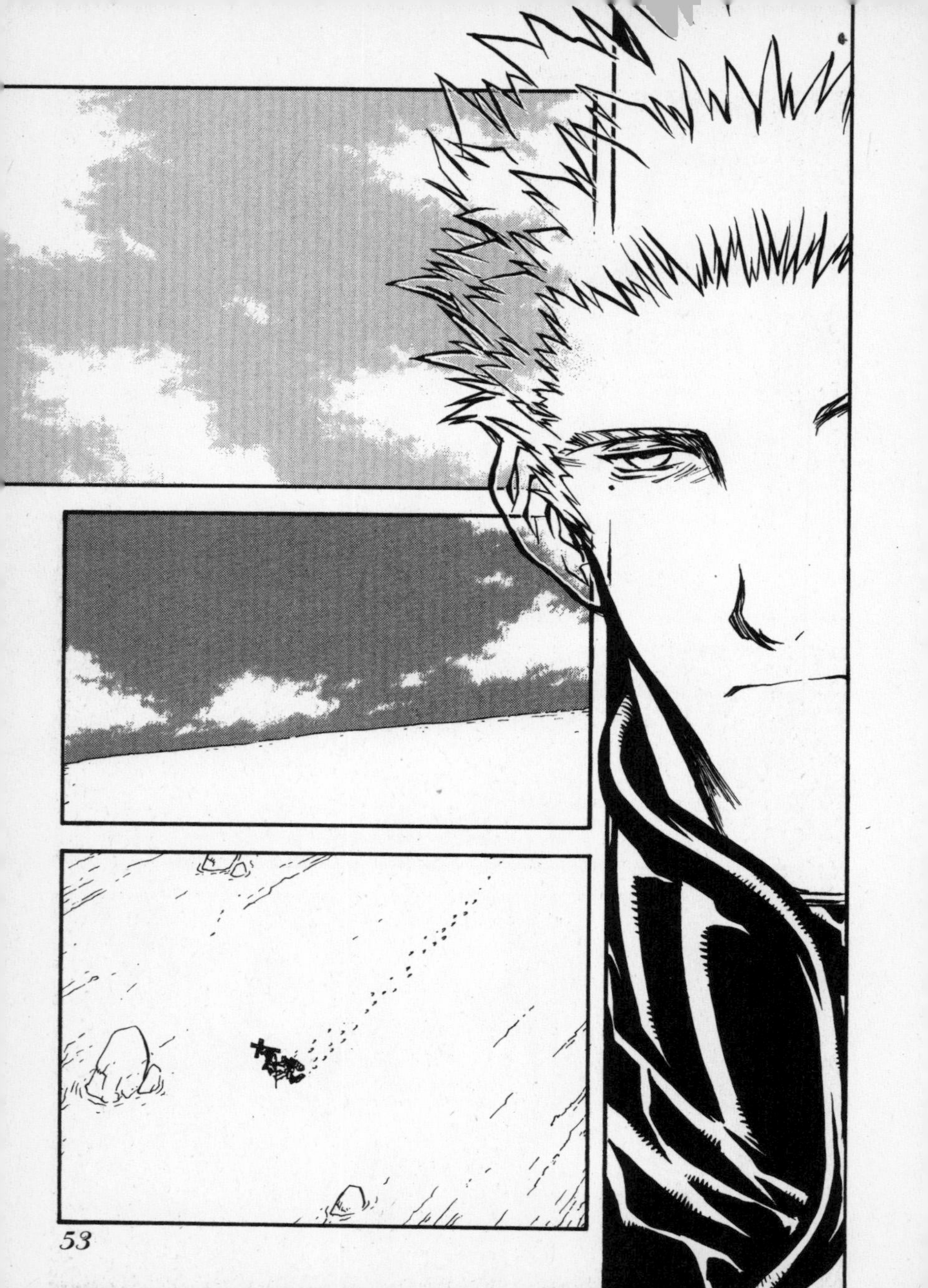

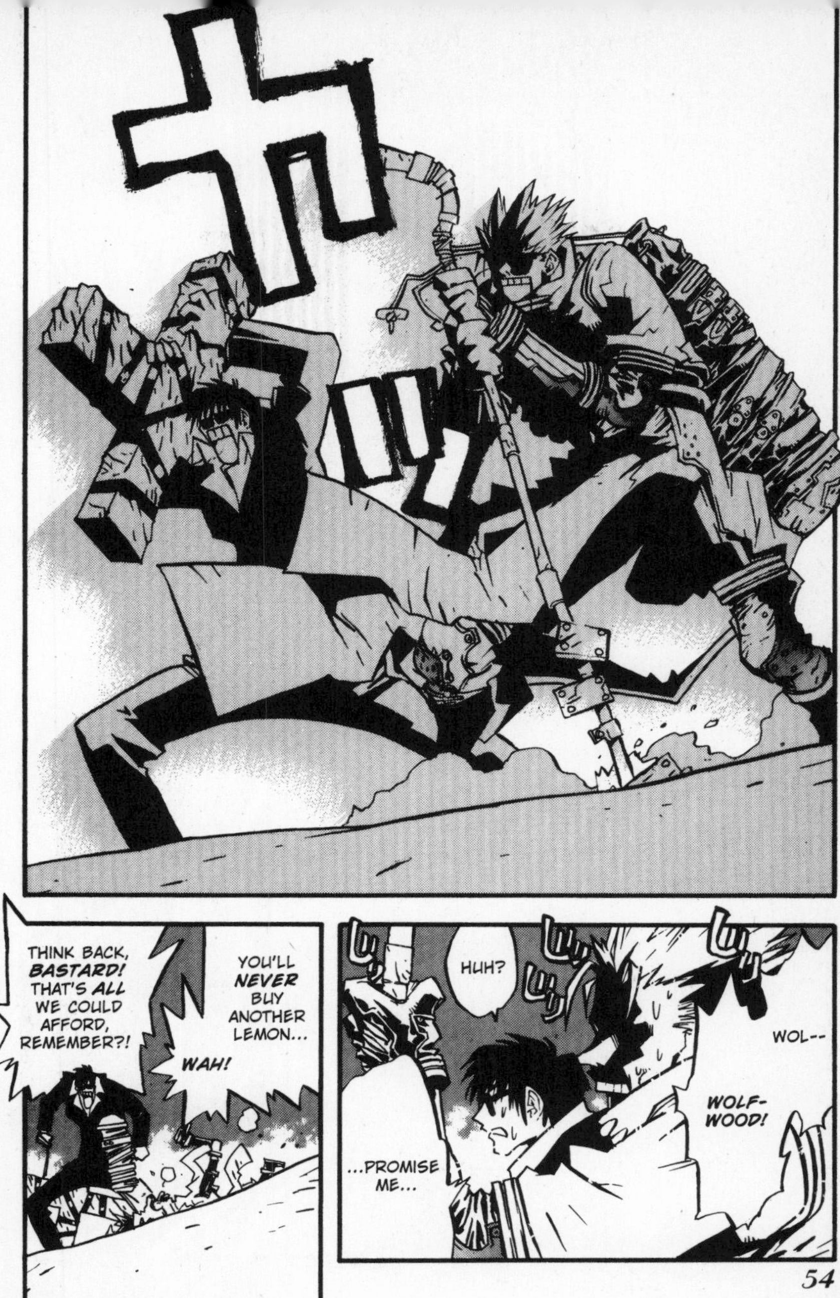
HUH?
WOL--
WOLF-WOOD!
...PROMISE ME...
YOU'LL NEVER BUY ANOTHER LEMON...
THINK BACK, BASTARD! THAT'S ALL WE COULD AFFORD, REMEMBER?!
WAH!

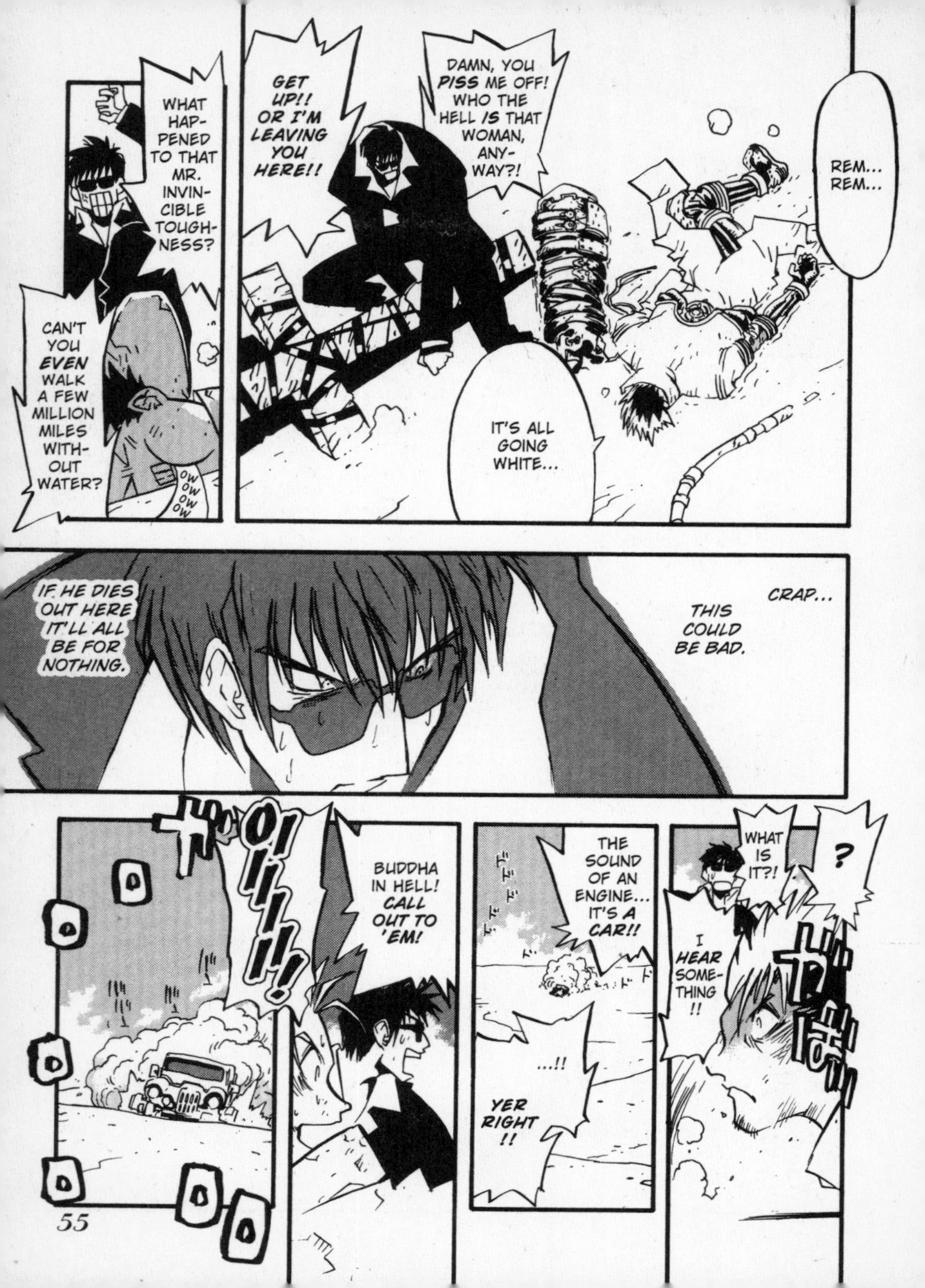

REM... REM...
IT'S ALL GOING WHITE...
DAMN, YOU *PISS* ME OFF! WHO THE HELL *IS* THAT WOMAN, ANYWAY?!
GET UP!! OR I'M LEAVING YOU HERE!!
WHAT HAPPENED TO THAT MR. INVINCIBLE TOUGHNESS?
CAN'T YOU *EVEN* WALK A FEW MILLION MILES WITHOUT WATER?
OW OW OW OW
CRAP... THIS COULD BE BAD.
IF HE DIES OUT HERE IT'LL ALL BE FOR NOTHING.
?
WHAT IS IT?!
I *HEAR* SOMETHING!!
THE SOUND OF AN ENGINE... IT'S *A CAR!!*
...!!
YER RIGHT!!
BUDDHA IN HELL! *CALL OUT TO 'EM!*

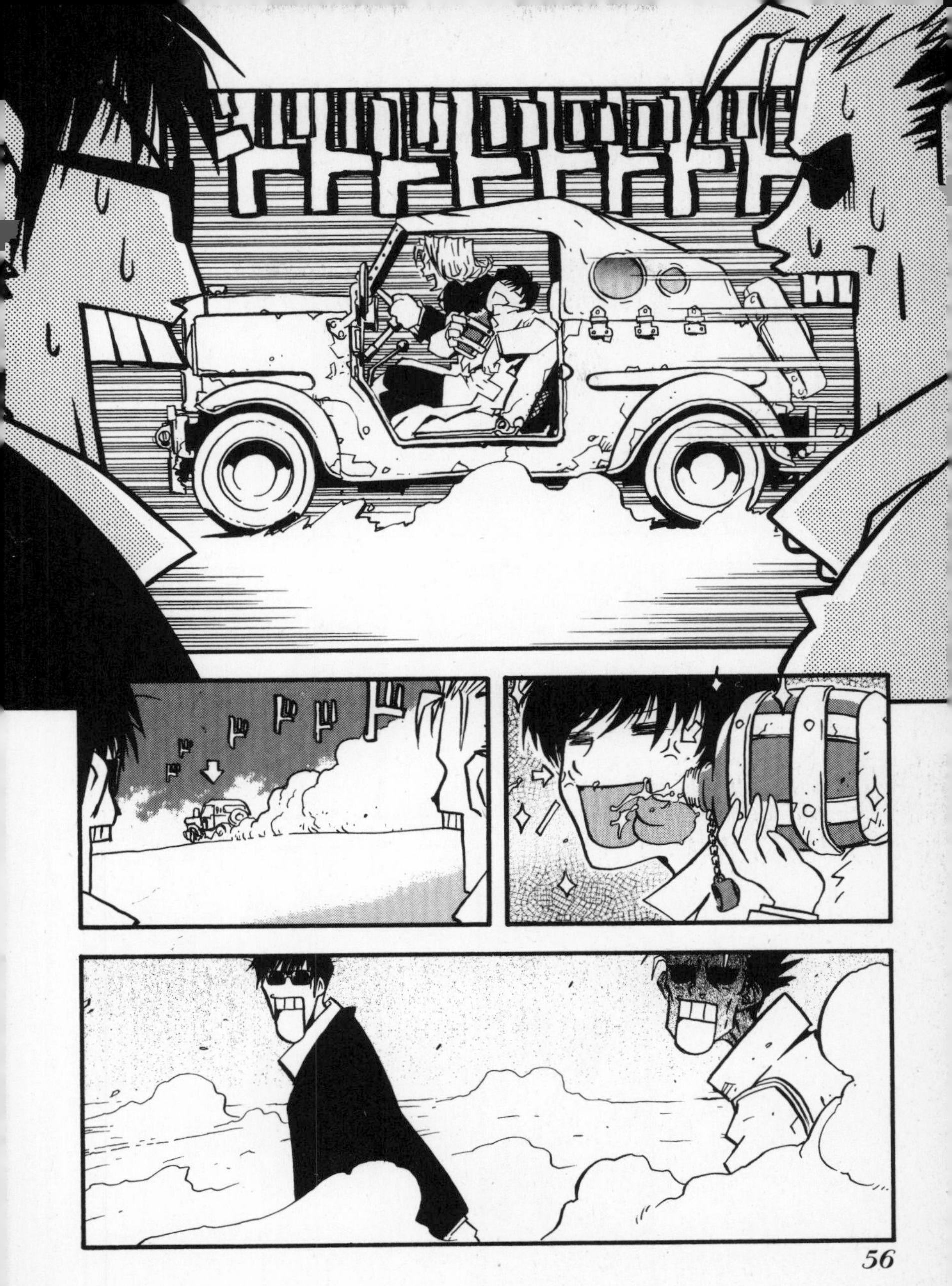

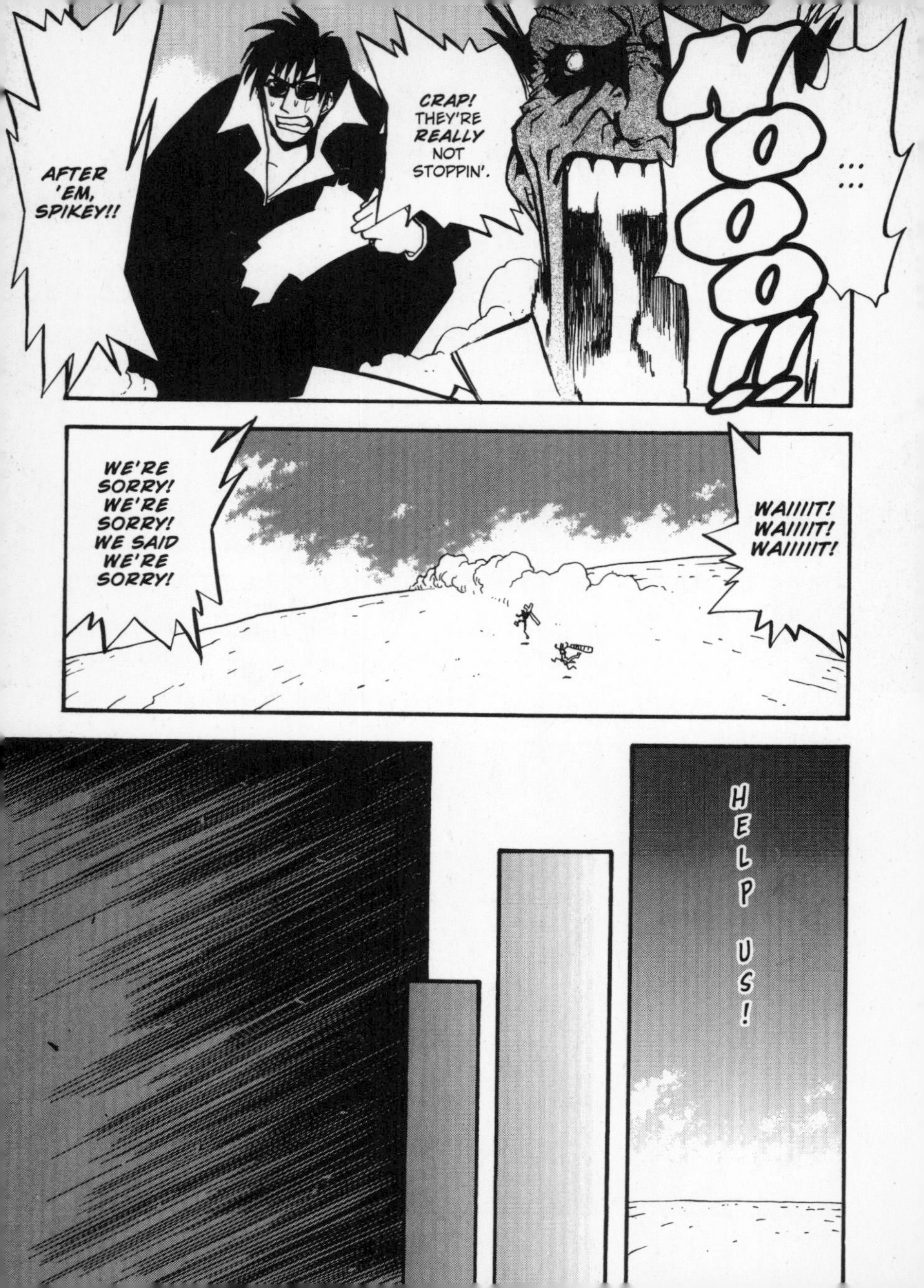
NOOOO!!
......
CRAP! THEY'RE REALLY NOT STOPPIN'.
AFTER 'EM, SPIKEY!!
WAIIIIT! WAIIIIT! WAIIIIIT!
WE'RE SORRY! WE'RE SORRY! WE SAID WE'RE SORRY!
HELP US!

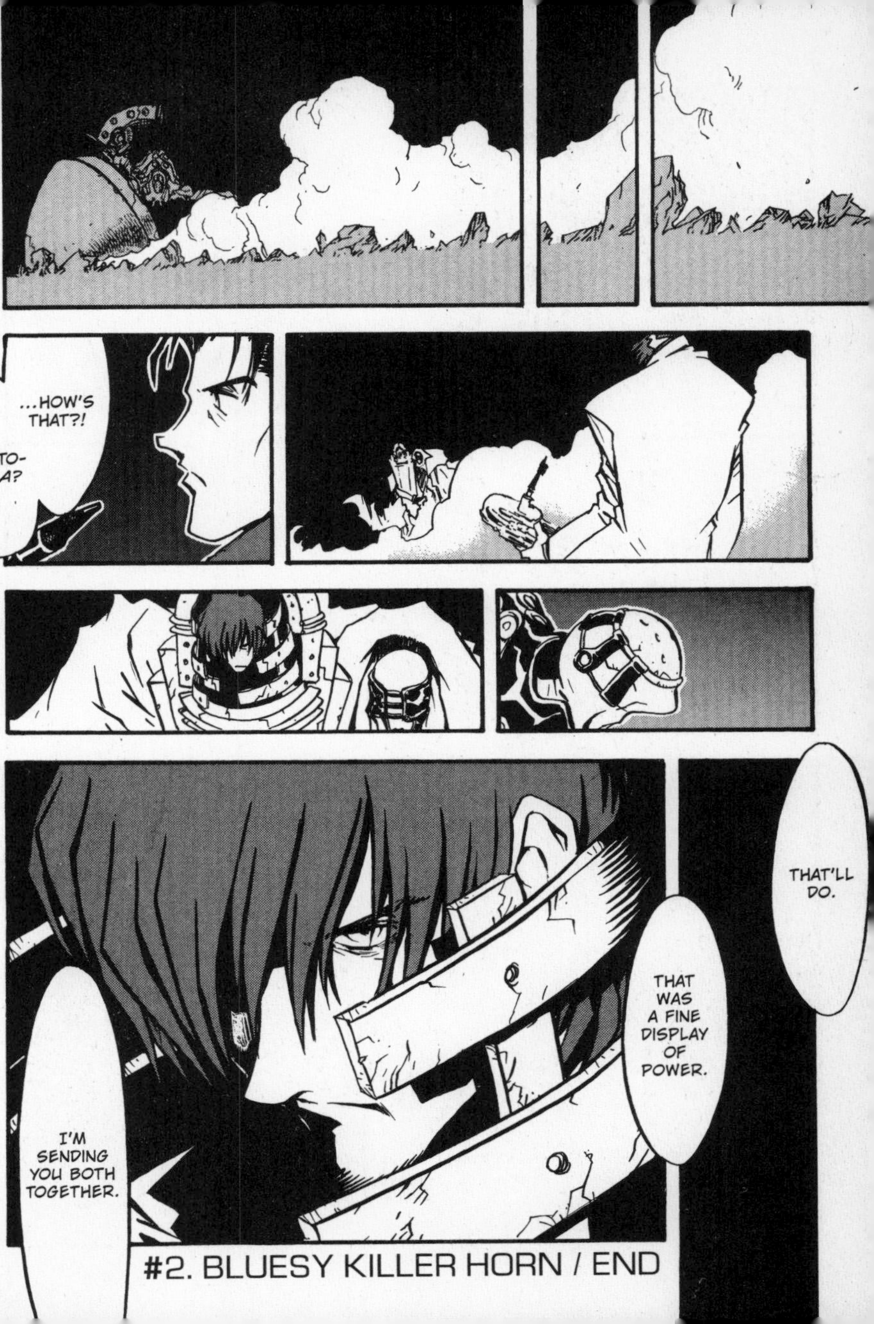
...HOW'S THAT?!
LEGATO-SAMA?
THAT'LL DO.
THAT WAS A FINE DISPLAY OF POWER.
I'M SENDING YOU BOTH TOGETHER.

#2. BLUESY KILLER HORN / END

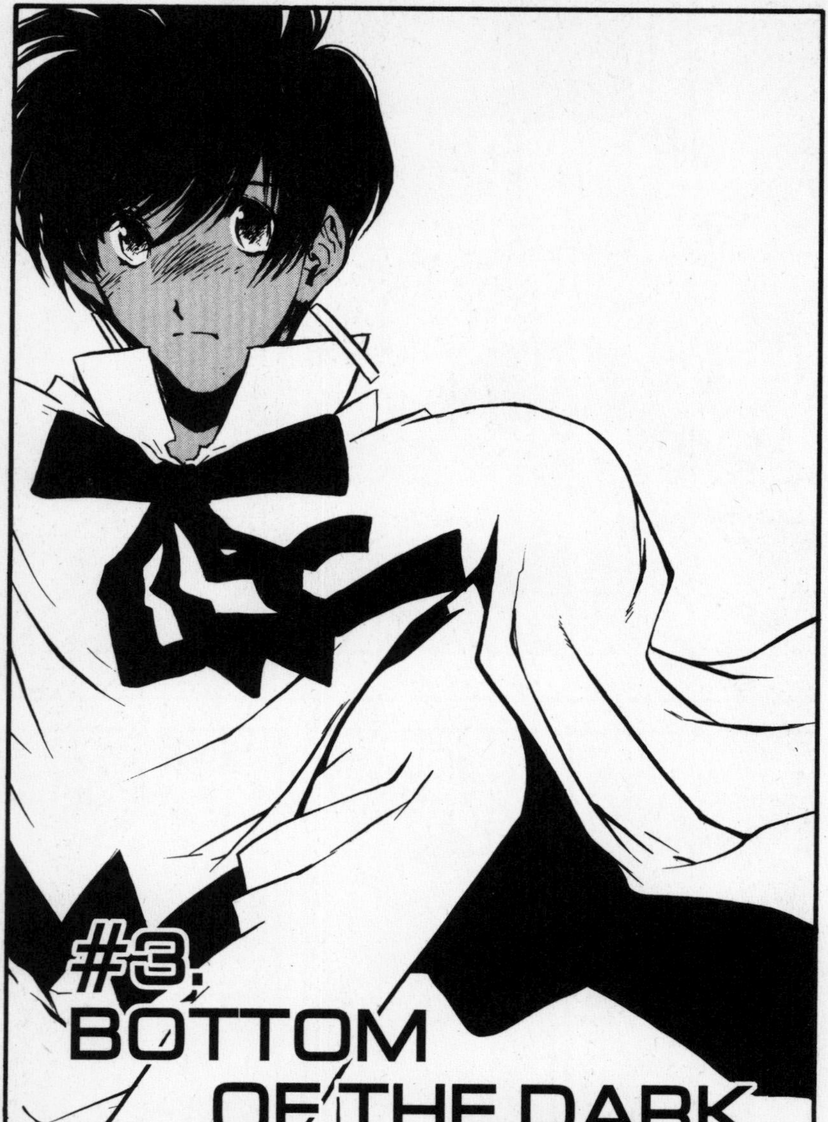
#3.
BOTTOM
OF THE DARK

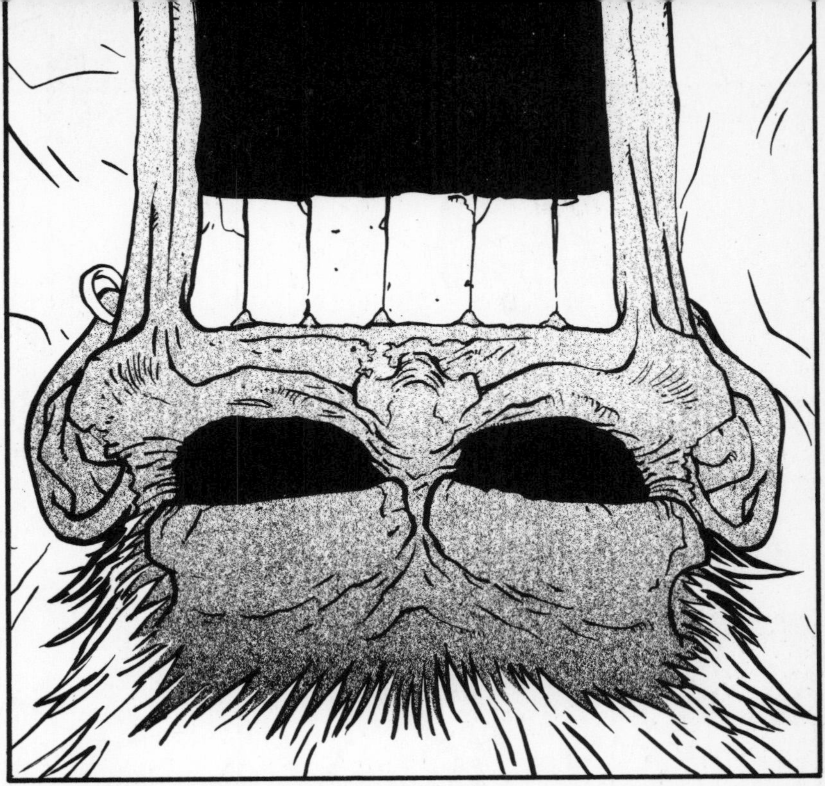

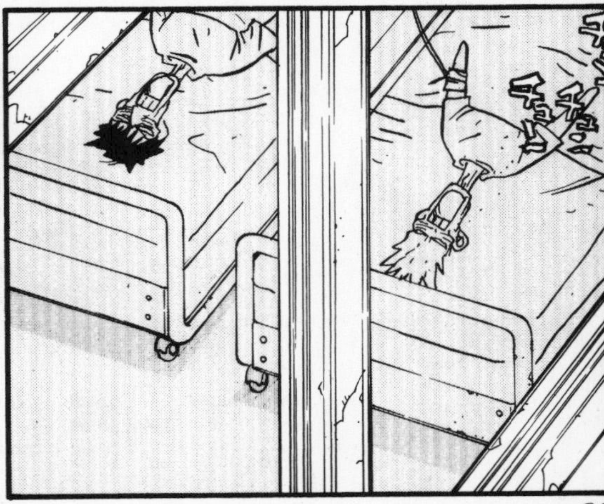

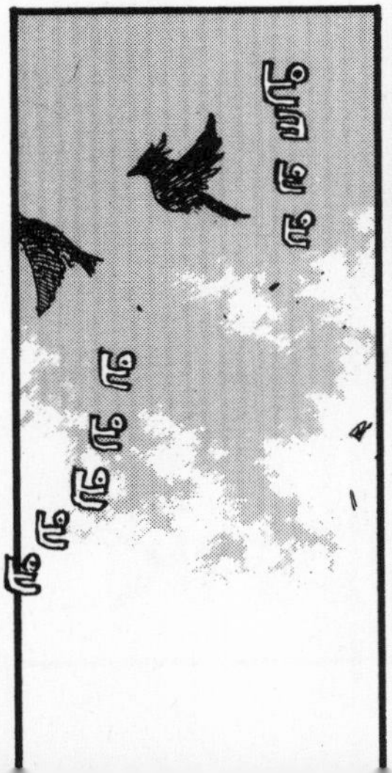

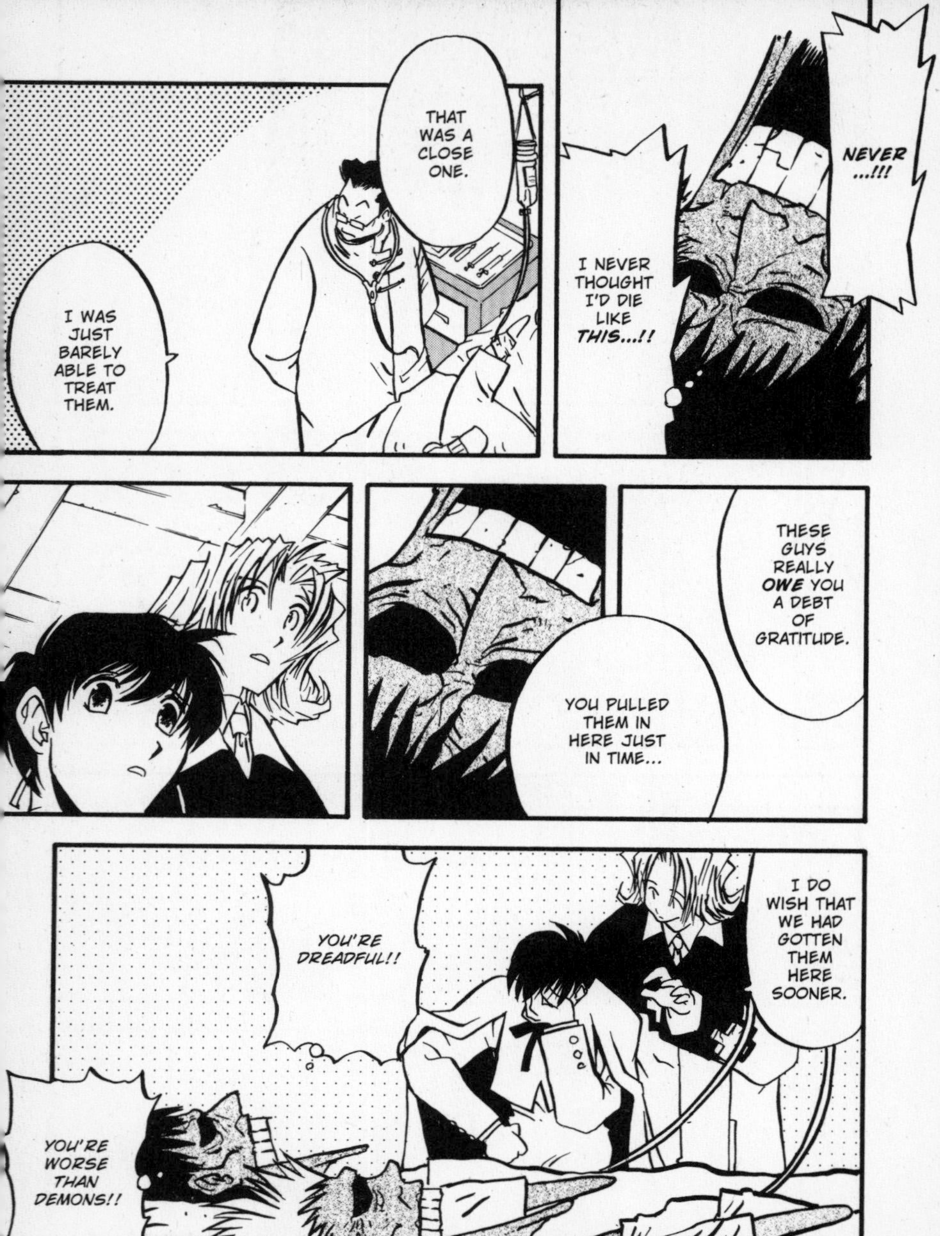
NEVER ...!!!
I NEVER THOUGHT I'D DIE LIKE THIS...!!
THAT WAS A CLOSE ONE.
I WAS JUST BARELY ABLE TO TREAT THEM.
THESE GUYS REALLY OWE YOU A DEBT OF GRATITUDE.
YOU PULLED THEM IN HERE JUST IN TIME...
I DO WISH THAT WE HAD GOTTEN THEM HERE SOONER.
YOU'RE DREADFUL!!
YOU'RE WORSE THAN DEMONS!!

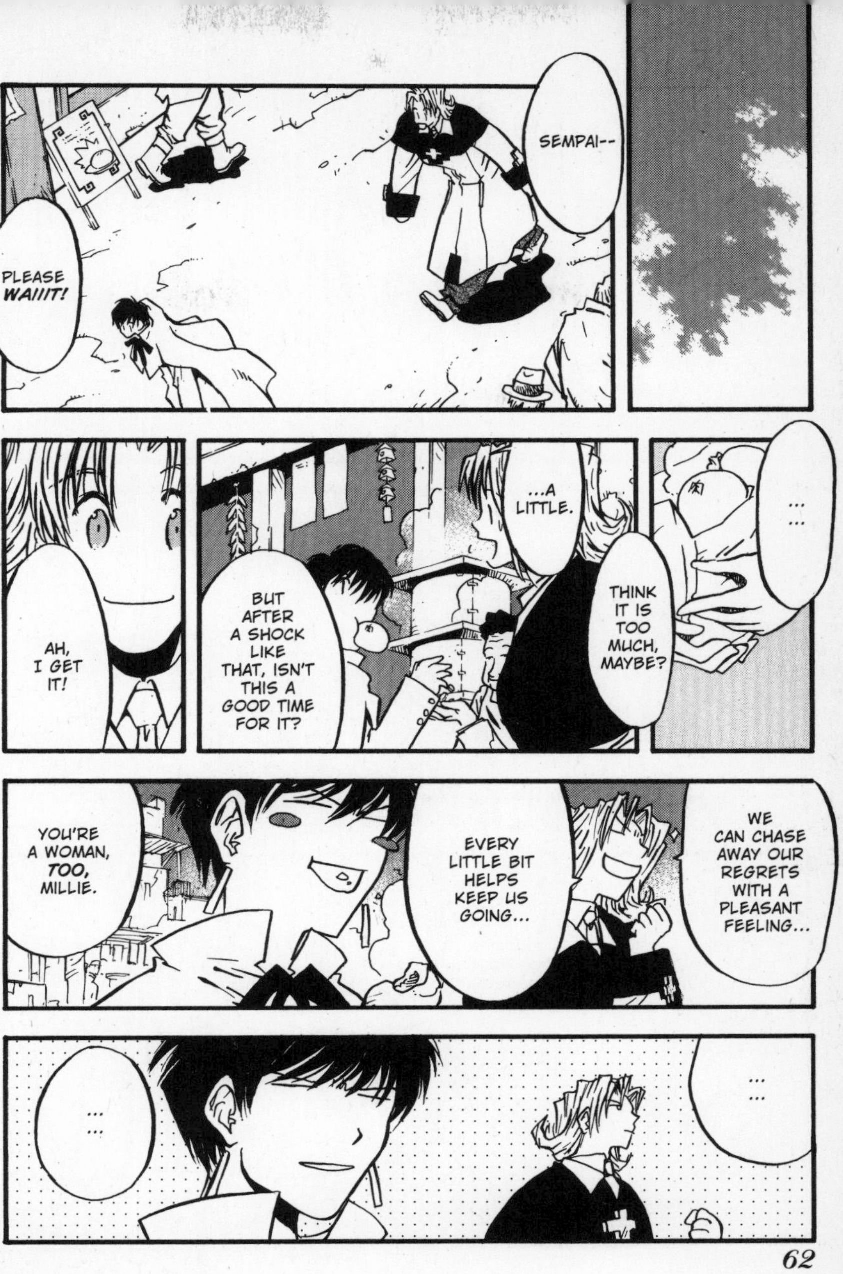
SEMPAI--
PLEASE **WAIIIT!**
... ...
THINK IT IS TOO MUCH, MAYBE?
...A LITTLE.
BUT AFTER A SHOCK LIKE THAT, ISN'T THIS A GOOD TIME FOR IT?
AH, I GET IT!
WE CAN CHASE AWAY OUR REGRETS WITH A PLEASANT FEELING...
EVERY LITTLE BIT HELPS KEEP US GOING...
YOU'RE A WOMAN, **TOO,** MILLIE.
... ...
... ...

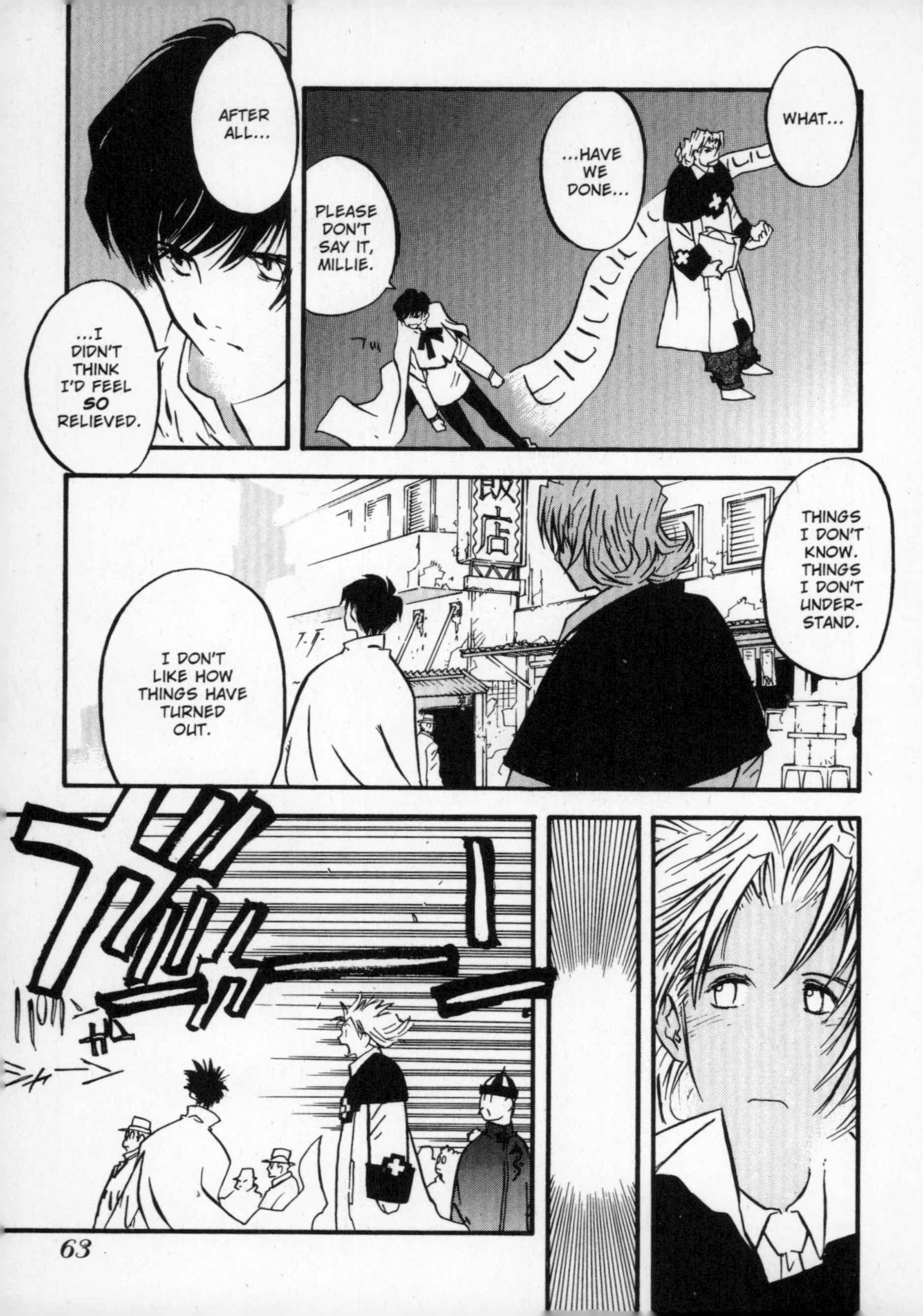
WHAT...
...HAVE WE DONE...
PLEASE DON'T SAY IT, MILLIE.
AFTER ALL...
...I DIDN'T THINK I'D FEEL SO RELIEVED.
THINGS I DON'T KNOW. THINGS I DON'T UNDERSTAND.
I DON'T LIKE HOW THINGS HAVE TURNED OUT.

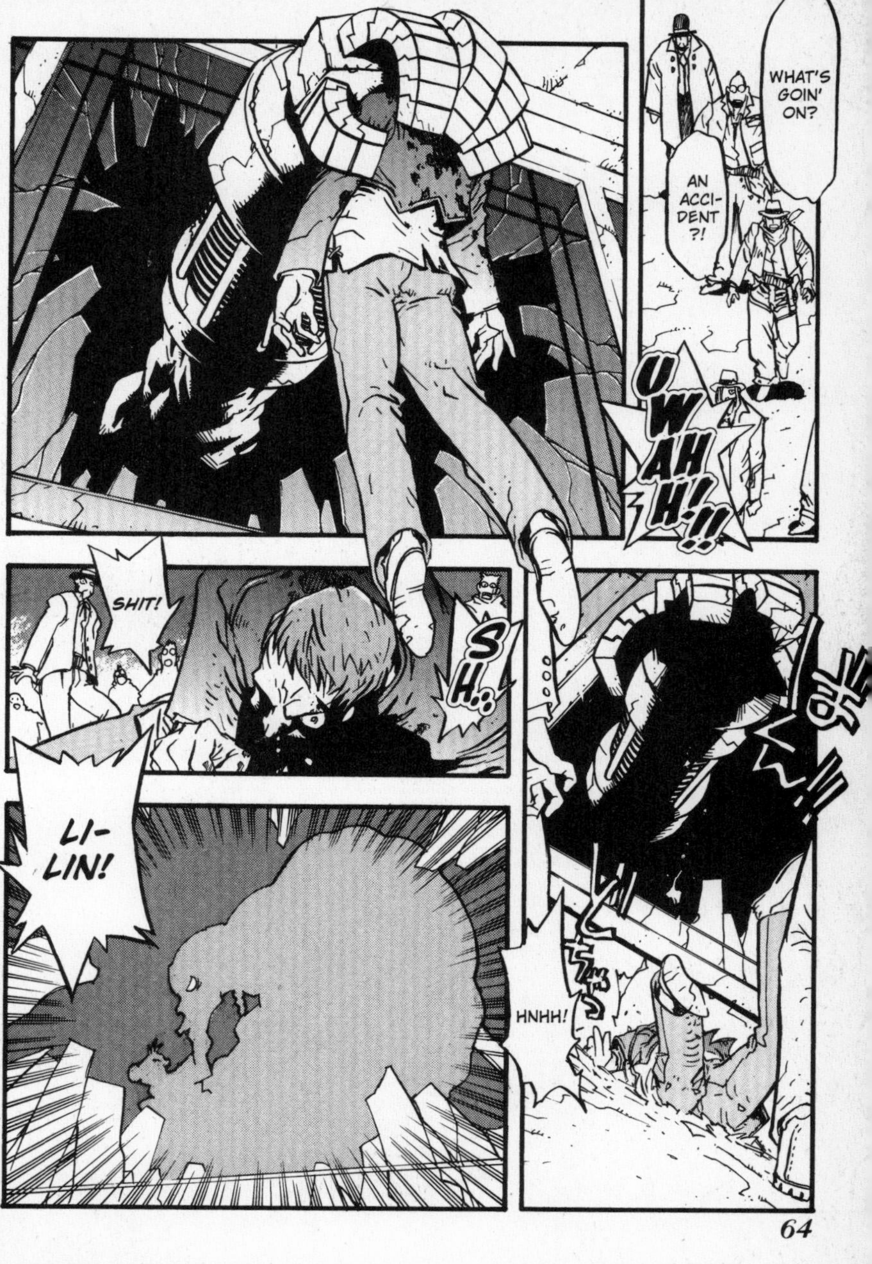
WHAT'S GOIN' ON?
AN ACCIDENT?!
UWAHH-!!
HNHH!
SHIT!
SH..:
LI-LIN!

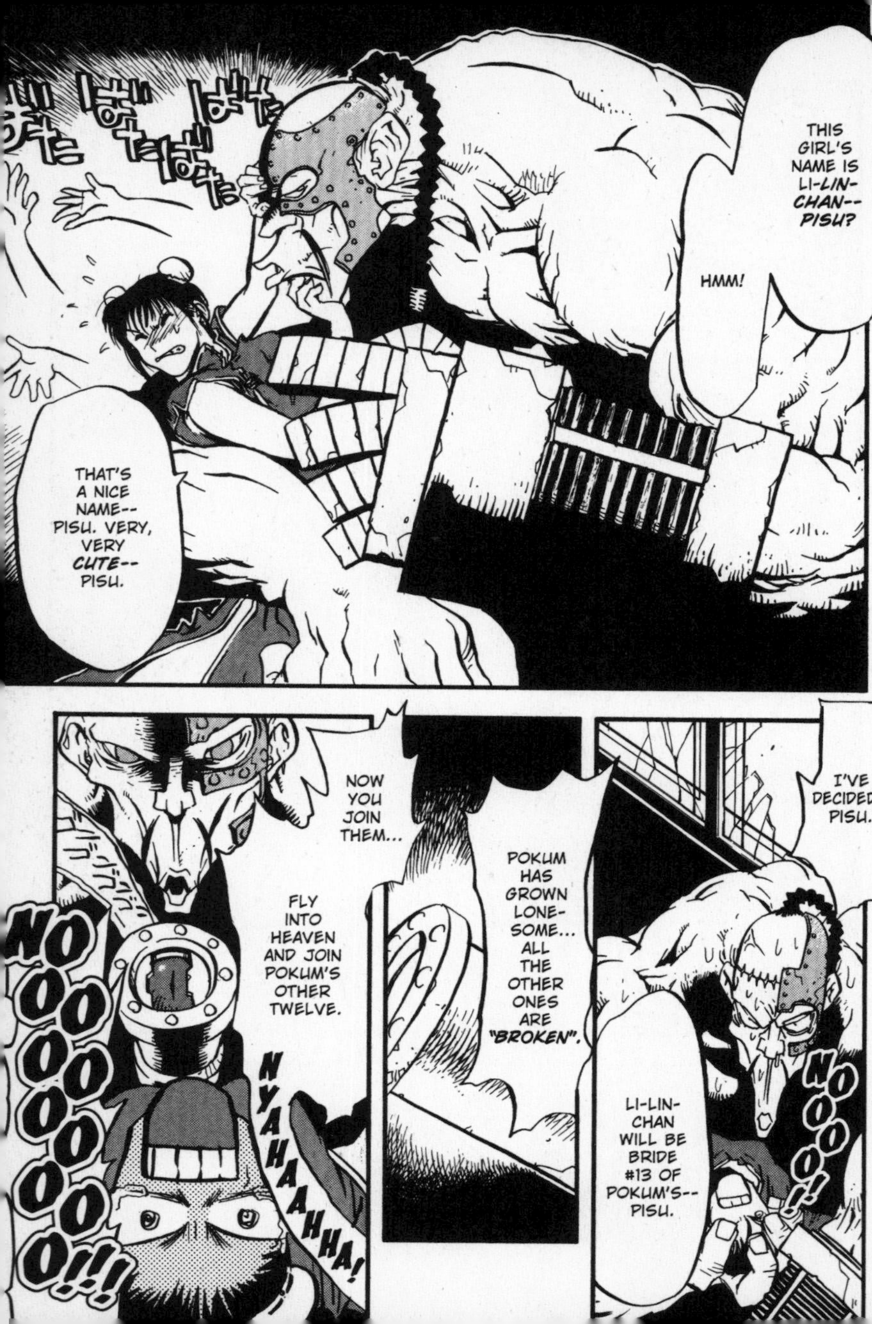
THIS GIRL'S NAME IS LI-*LIN*-*CHAN*--*PISU*?
HMM!
THAT'S A NICE NAME--PISU. VERY, VERY *CUTE*--PISU.
I'VE DECIDED--PISU.
NOOOO!
LI-LIN-CHAN WILL BE BRIDE #13 OF POKUM'S--PISU.
POKUM HAS GROWN LONESOME... ALL THE OTHER ONES ARE *"BROKEN"*.
NOW YOU JOIN THEM...
FLY INTO HEAVEN AND JOIN POKUM'S OTHER TWELVE.
NYAHAHAHHA!
NOOOOOOOOOOO!!!

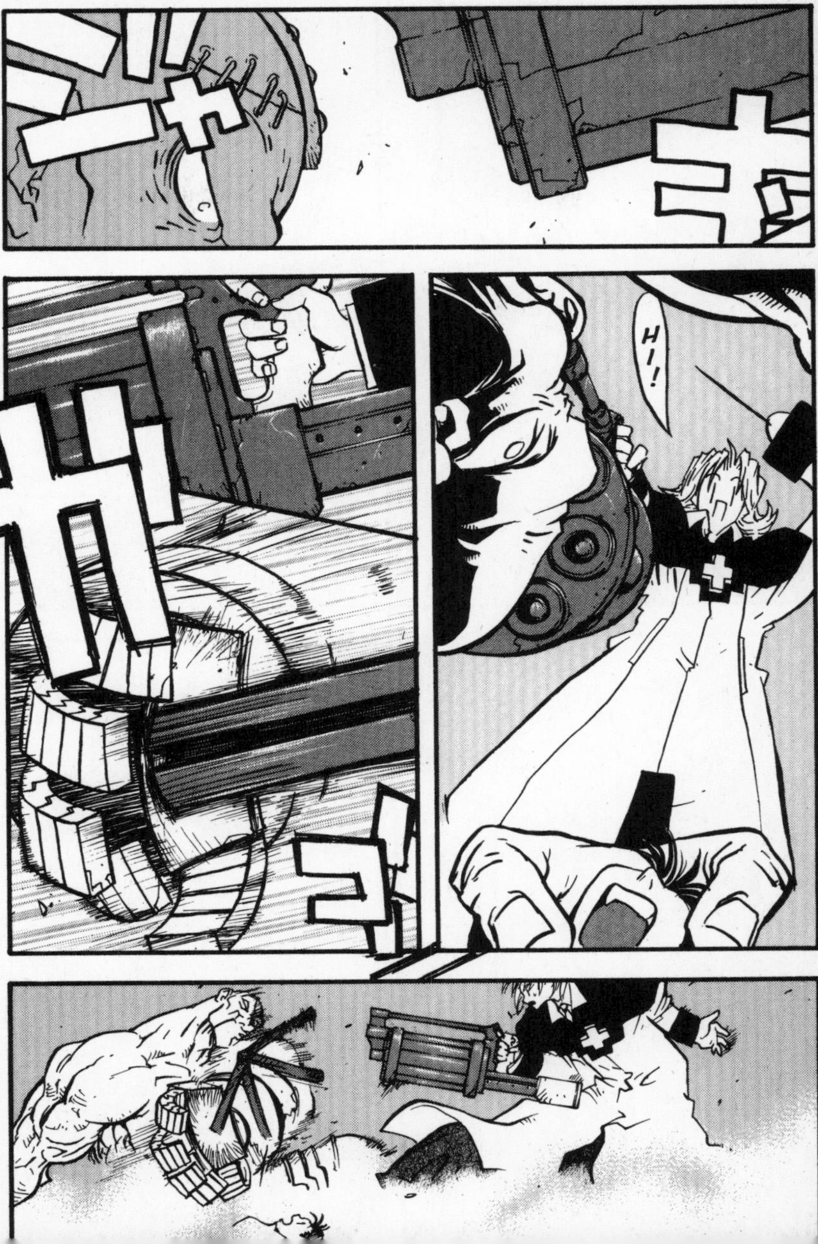
HI!

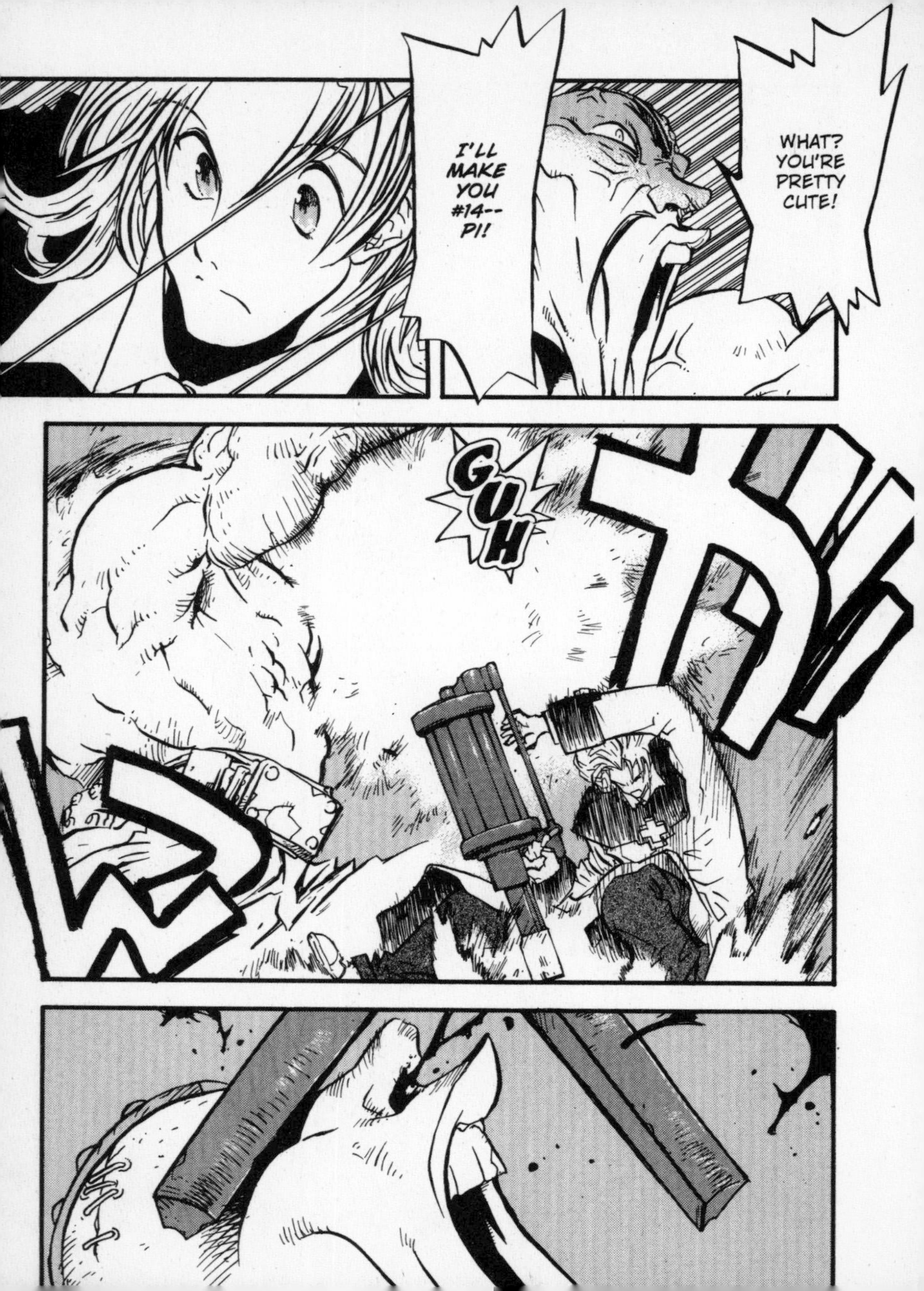
WHAT? YOU'RE PRETTY CUTE!
I'LL MAKE YOU #14-- PI!
GUH

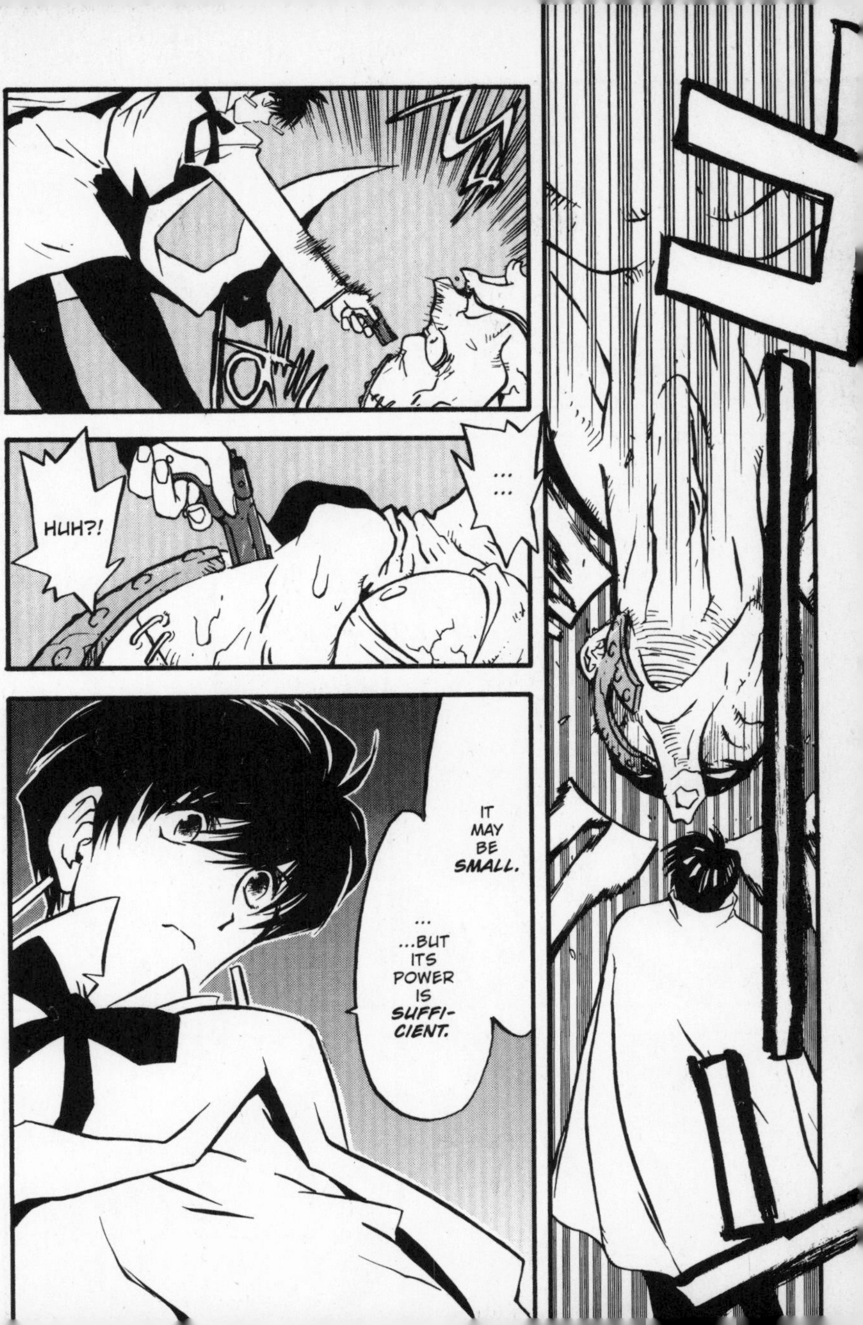
......
HUH?!
IT MAY BE SMALL.
... ...BUT ITS POWER IS SUFFICIENT.

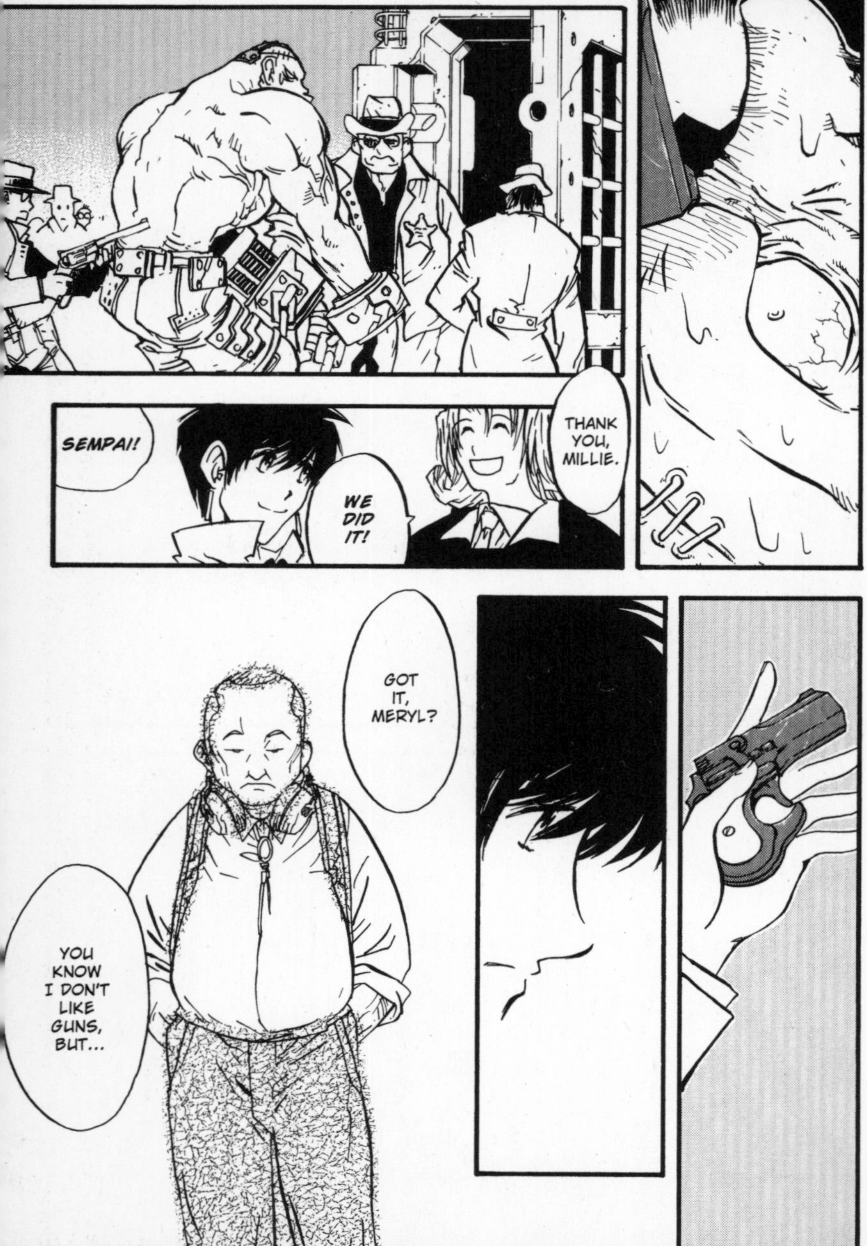
THANK YOU, MILLIE.
WE DID IT!
SEMPAI!
GOT IT, MERYL?
YOU KNOW I DON'T LIKE GUNS, BUT...

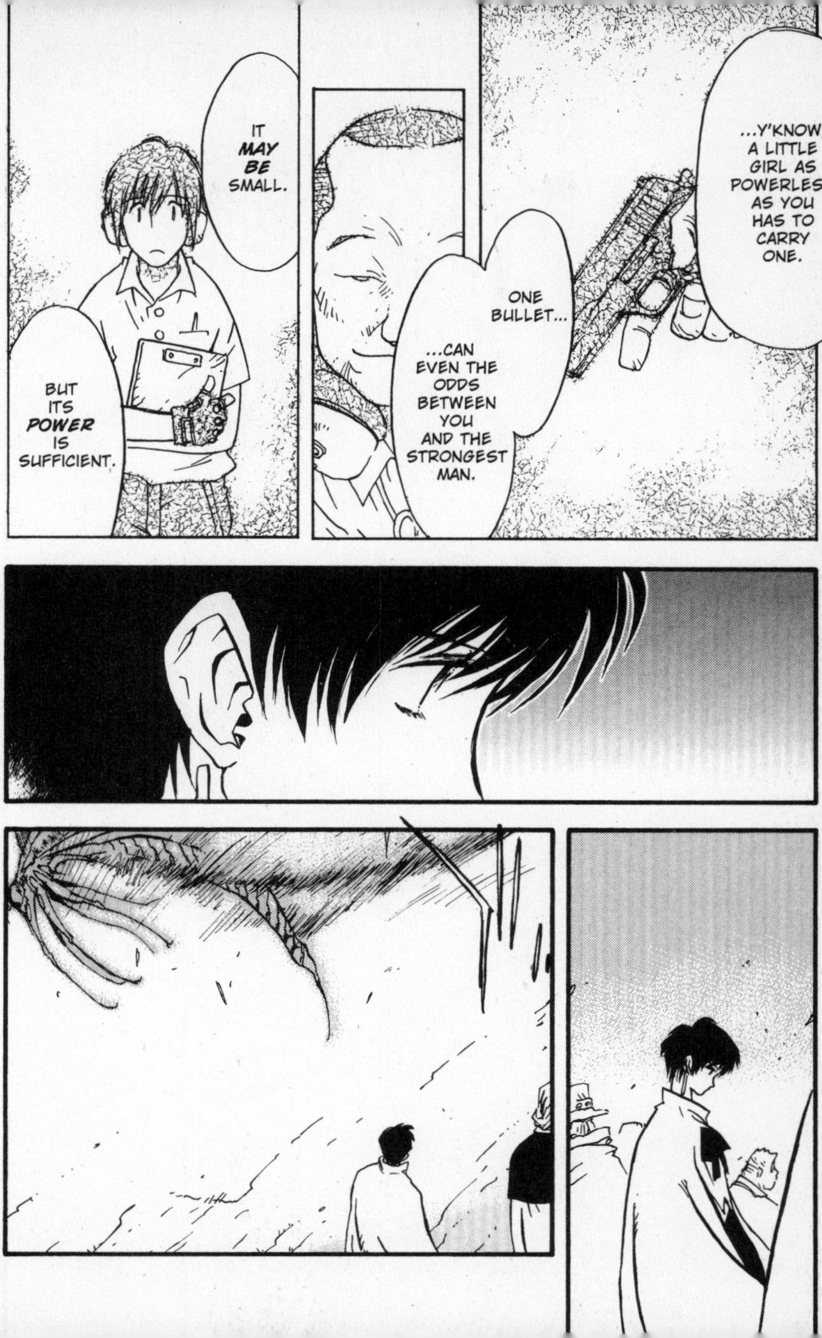
...Y'KNOW, A LITTLE GIRL AS POWERLESS AS YOU HAS TO CARRY ONE.
ONE BULLET...
...CAN EVEN THE ODDS BETWEEN YOU AND THE STRONGEST MAN.
IT *MAY BE* SMALL.
BUT ITS *POWER* IS SUFFICIENT.

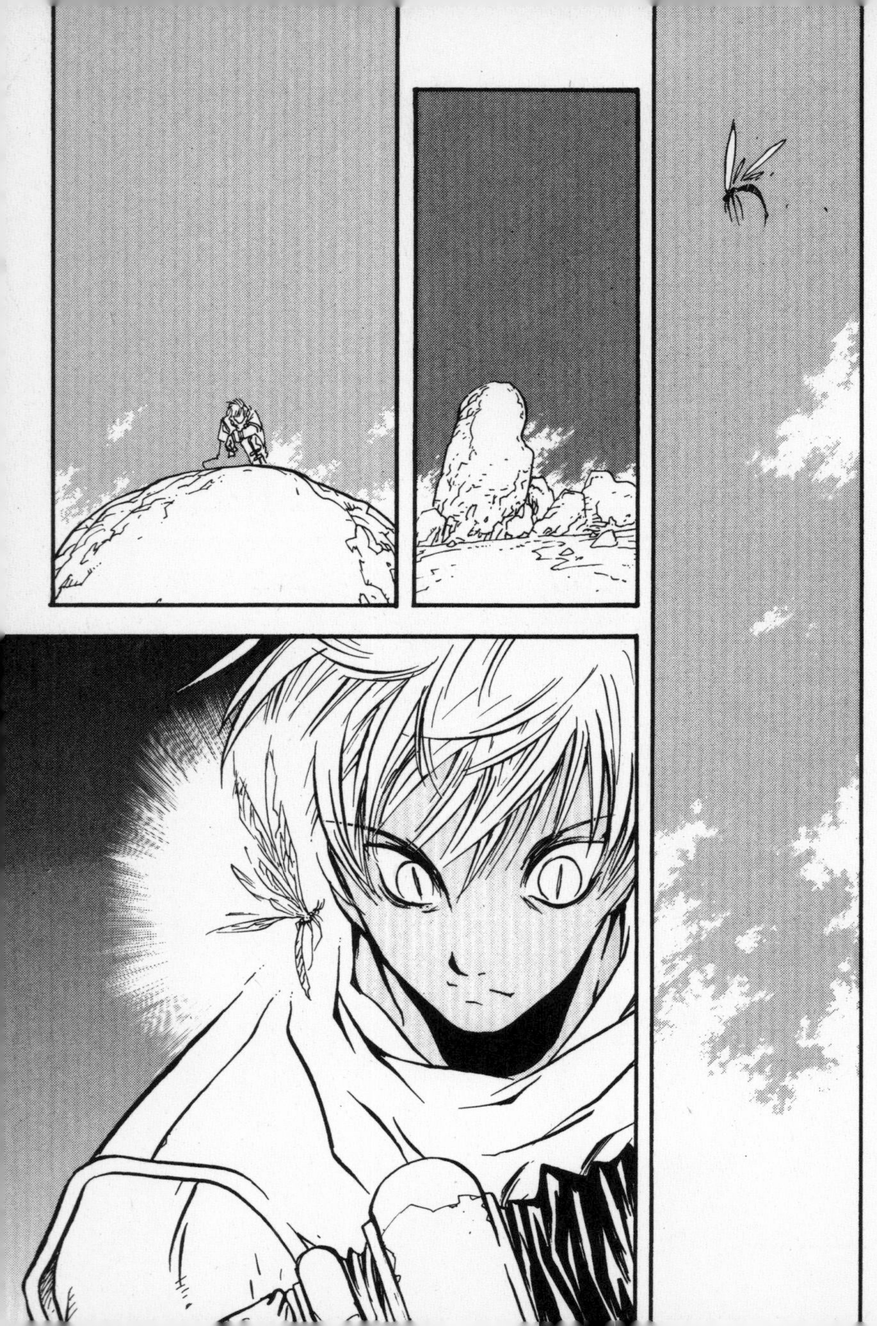

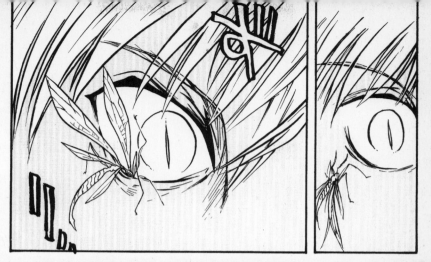

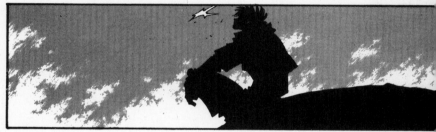

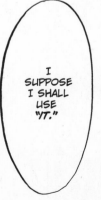

I SUPPOSE
I SHALL
USE
"YT."

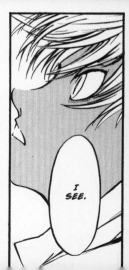

I
SEE.

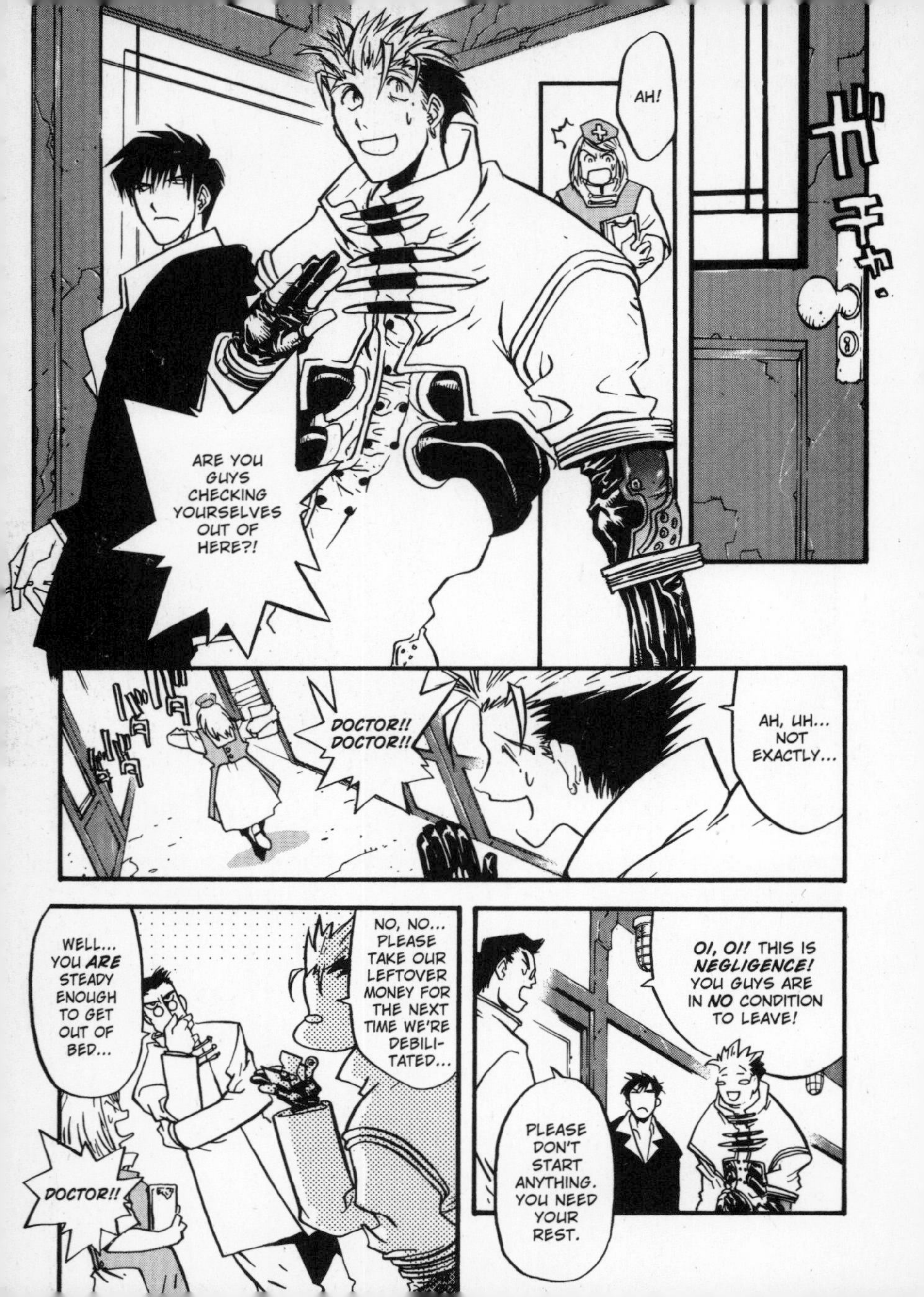
ガチャ。
AH!
ARE YOU GUYS CHECKING YOURSELVES OUT OF HERE?!
AH, UH... NOT EXACTLY...
DOCTOR!! DOCTOR!!
OI, OI! THIS IS NEGLIGENCE! YOU GUYS ARE IN NO CONDITION TO LEAVE!
PLEASE DON'T START ANYTHING. YOU NEED YOUR REST.
NO, NO... PLEASE TAKE OUR LEFTOVER MONEY FOR THE NEXT TIME WE'RE DEBILITATED...
WELL... YOU ARE STEADY ENOUGH TO GET OUT OF BED...
DOCTOR!!

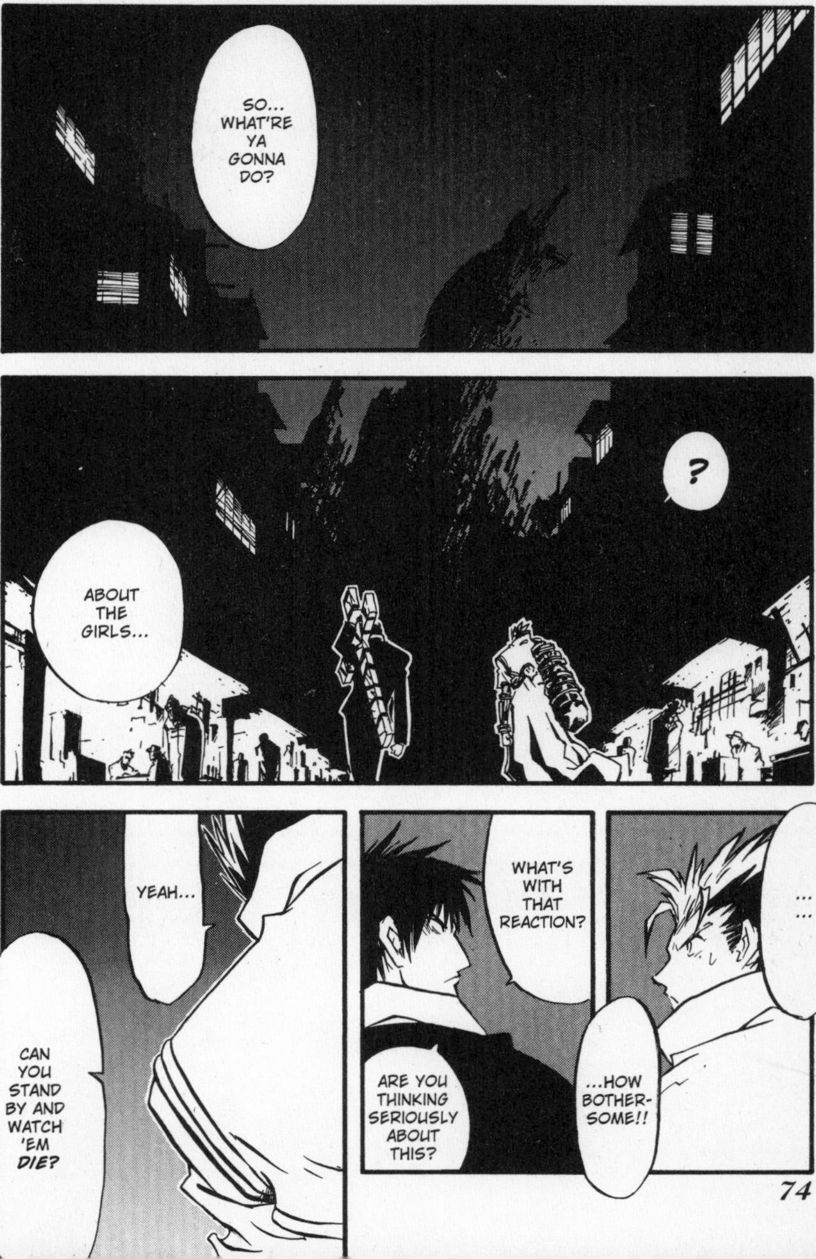
SO... WHAT'RE YA GONNA DO?
?
ABOUT THE GIRLS...
... ...
...HOW BOTHER-SOME!!
WHAT'S WITH THAT REACTION?
ARE YOU THINKING SERIOUSLY ABOUT THIS?
YEAH...
CAN YOU STAND BY AND WATCH 'EM ***DIE?***

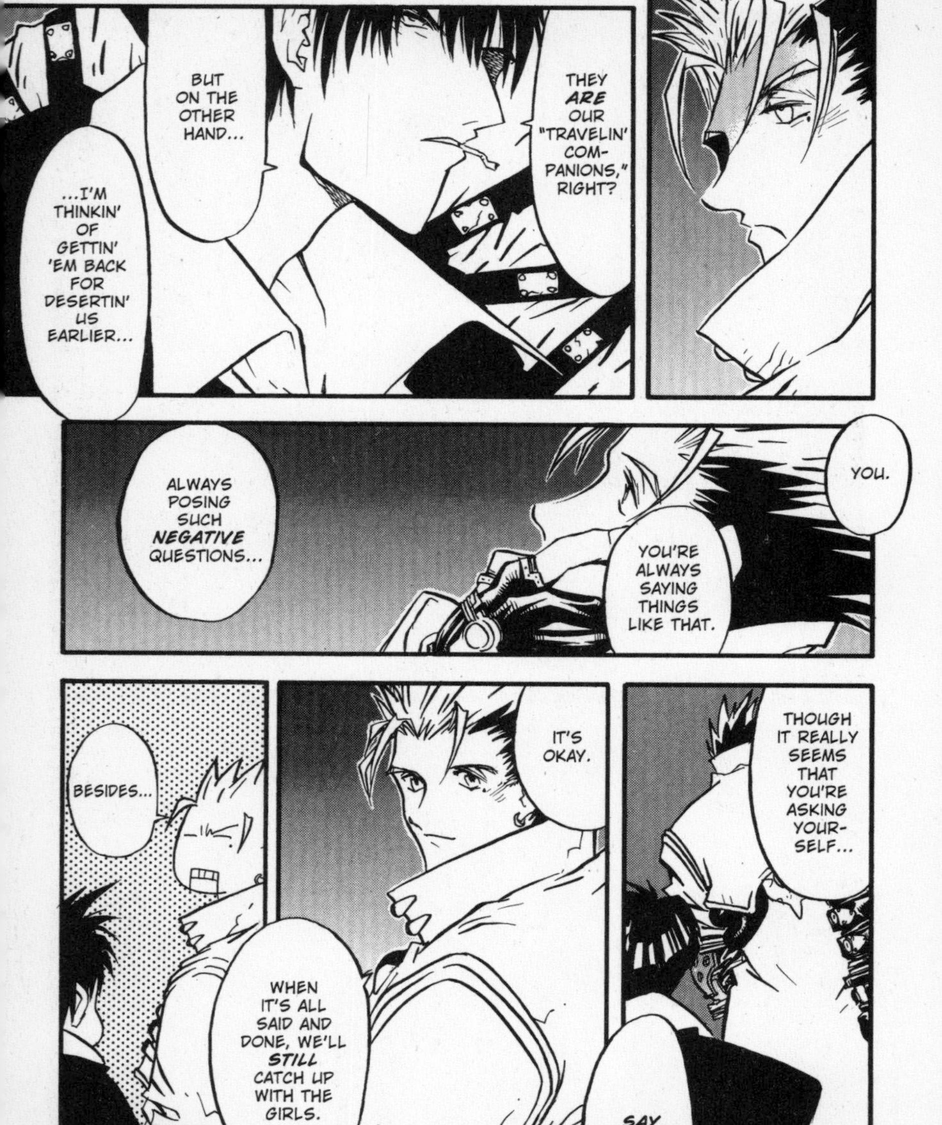
THEY *ARE* OUR "TRAVELIN' COMPANIONS," RIGHT?
BUT ON THE OTHER HAND...
...I'M THINKIN' OF GETTIN' 'EM BACK FOR DESERTIN' US EARLIER...
YOU.
YOU'RE ALWAYS SAYING THINGS LIKE THAT.
ALWAYS POSING SUCH *NEGATIVE* QUESTIONS...
THOUGH IT REALLY SEEMS THAT YOU'RE ASKING YOURSELF...
SAY WHAT?
IT'S OKAY.
WHEN IT'S ALL SAID AND DONE, WE'LL *STILL* CATCH UP WITH THE GIRLS.
BESIDES...

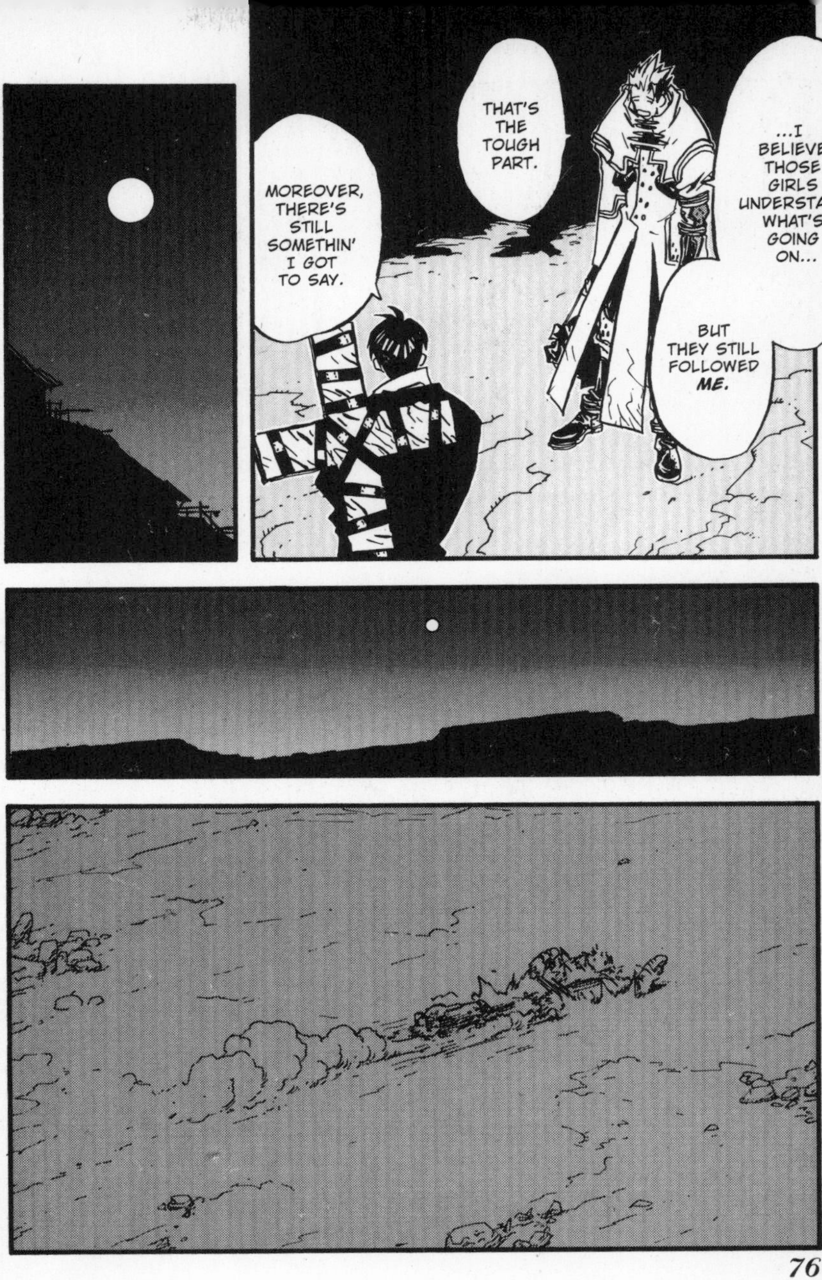
...I BELIEVE THOSE GIRLS UNDERSTAND WHAT'S GOING ON...
BUT THEY STILL FOLLOWED *ME.*
THAT'S THE TOUGH PART.
MOREOVER, THERE'S STILL SOMETHIN' I GOT TO SAY.

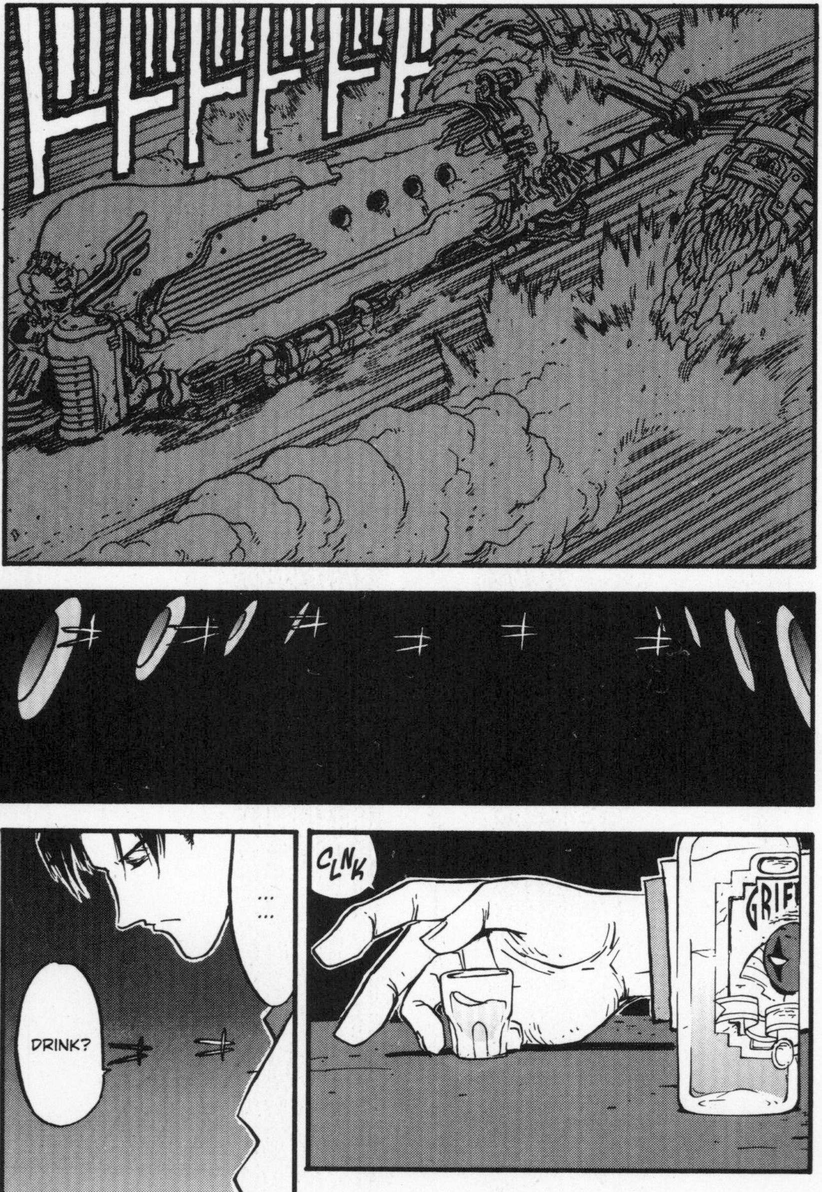
CLNK
...
...
DRINK?

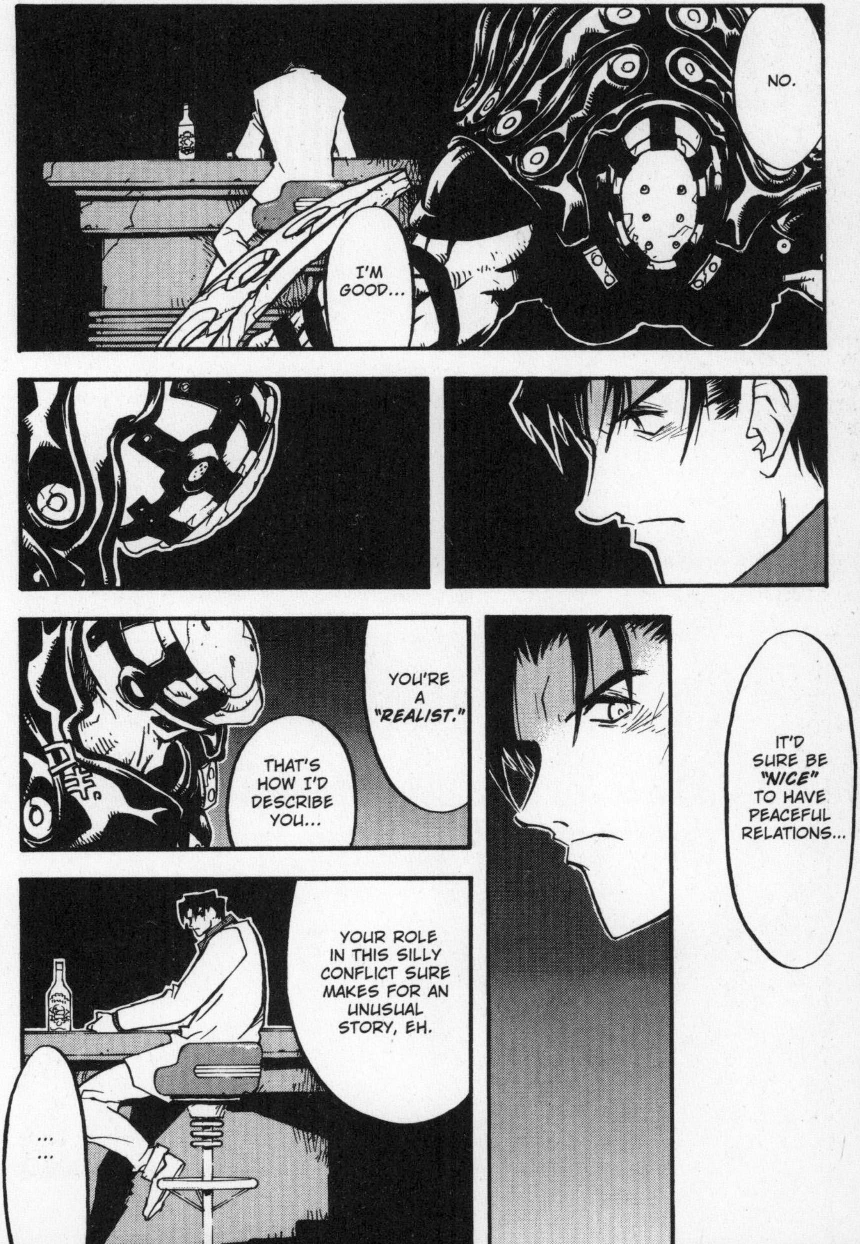
NO.
I'M GOOD...
IT'D SURE BE "NICE" TO HAVE PEACEFUL RELATIONS...
YOU'RE A "REALIST."
THAT'S HOW I'D DESCRIBE YOU...
YOUR ROLE IN THIS SILLY CONFLICT SURE MAKES FOR AN UNUSUAL STORY, EH.
... ...

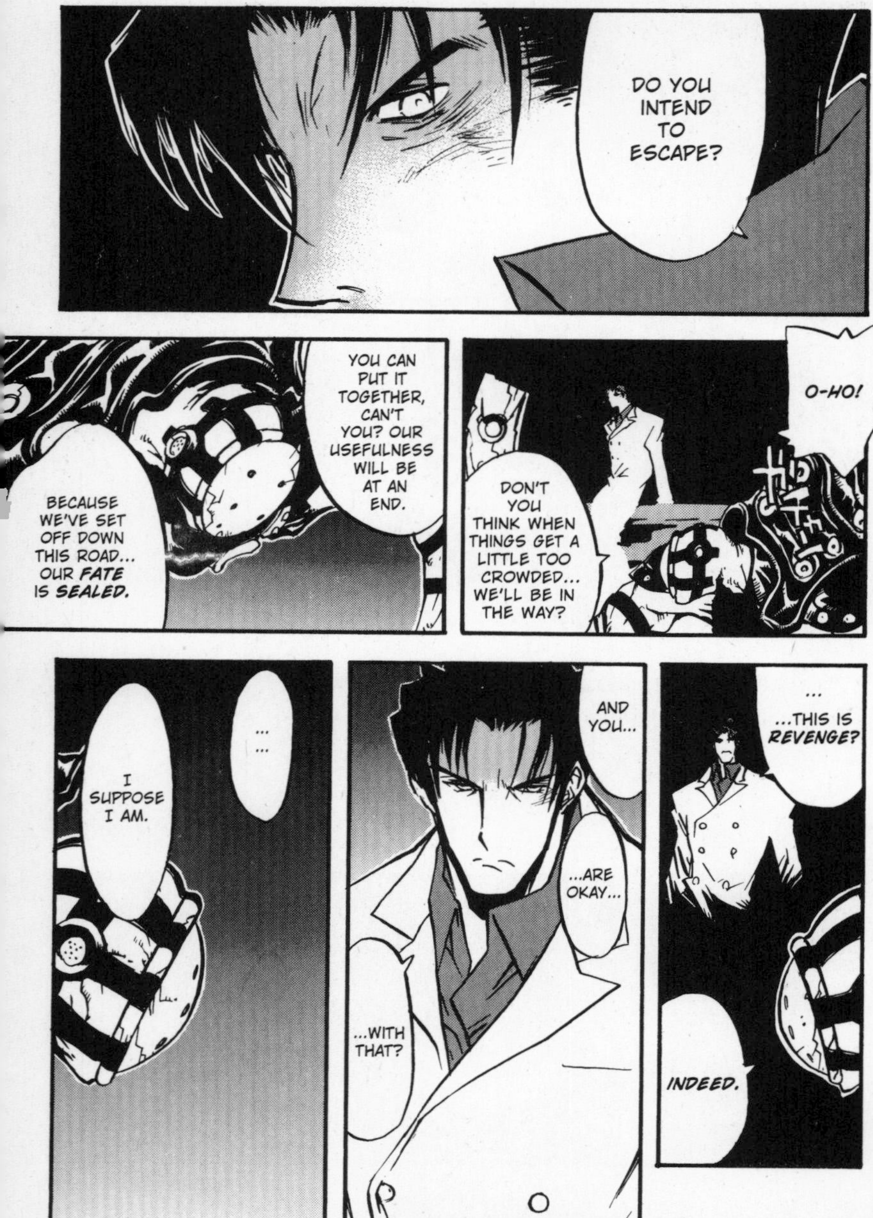
DO YOU INTEND TO ESCAPE?
O-HO!
DON'T YOU THINK WHEN THINGS GET A LITTLE TOO CROWDED... WE'LL BE IN THE WAY?
YOU CAN PUT IT TOGETHER, CAN'T YOU? OUR USEFULNESS WILL BE AT AN END.
BECAUSE WE'VE SET OFF DOWN THIS ROAD... OUR *FATE* IS *SEALED.*
... ...THIS IS *REVENGE?*
INDEED.
AND YOU...
...ARE OKAY...
...WITH THAT?
... ...
I SUPPOSE I AM.

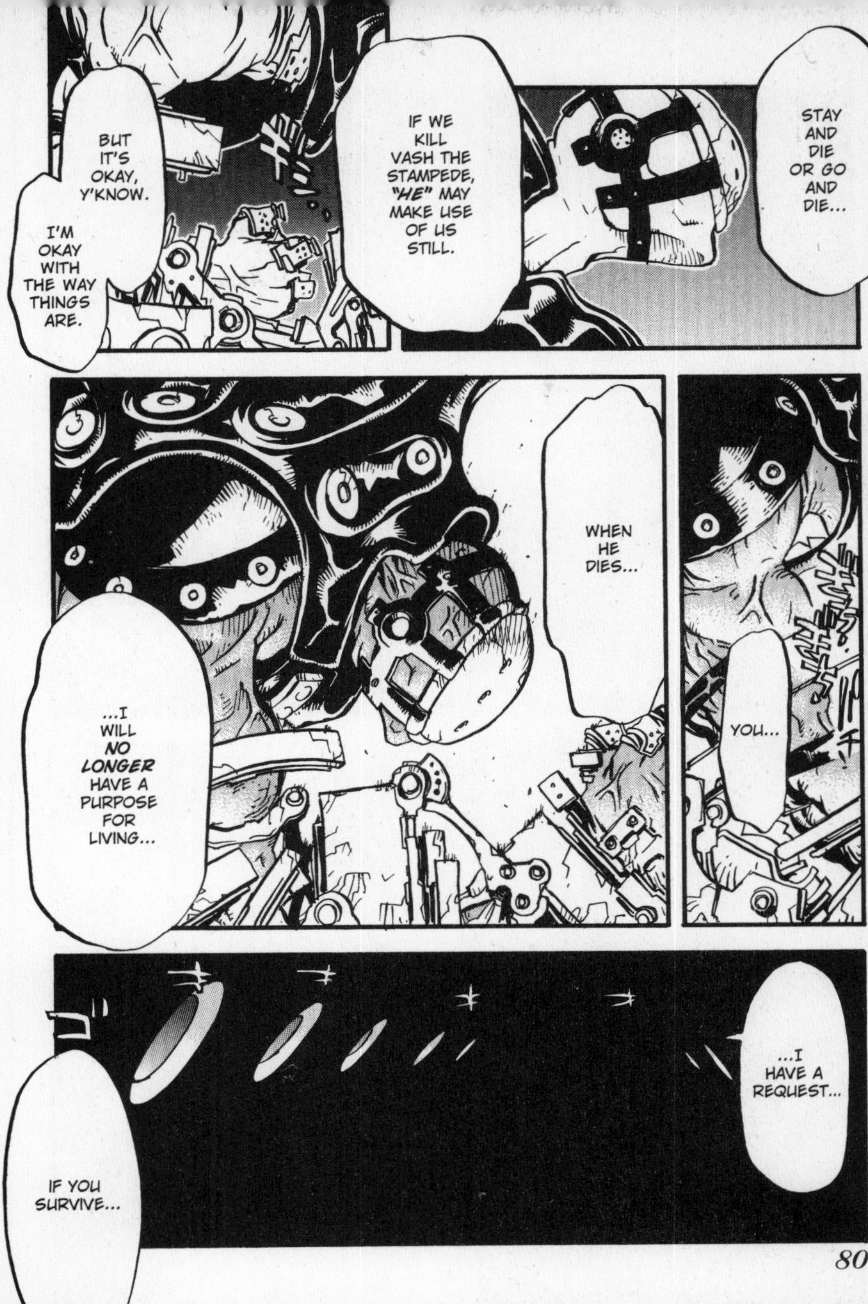
STAY AND DIE OR GO AND DIE...
IF WE KILL VASH THE STAMPEDE, "HE" MAY MAKE USE OF US STILL.
BUT IT'S OKAY, Y'KNOW.
I'M OKAY WITH THE WAY THINGS ARE.
YOU...
WHEN HE DIES...
...I WILL NO LONGER HAVE A PURPOSE FOR LIVING...
...I HAVE A REQUEST...
IF YOU SURVIVE...

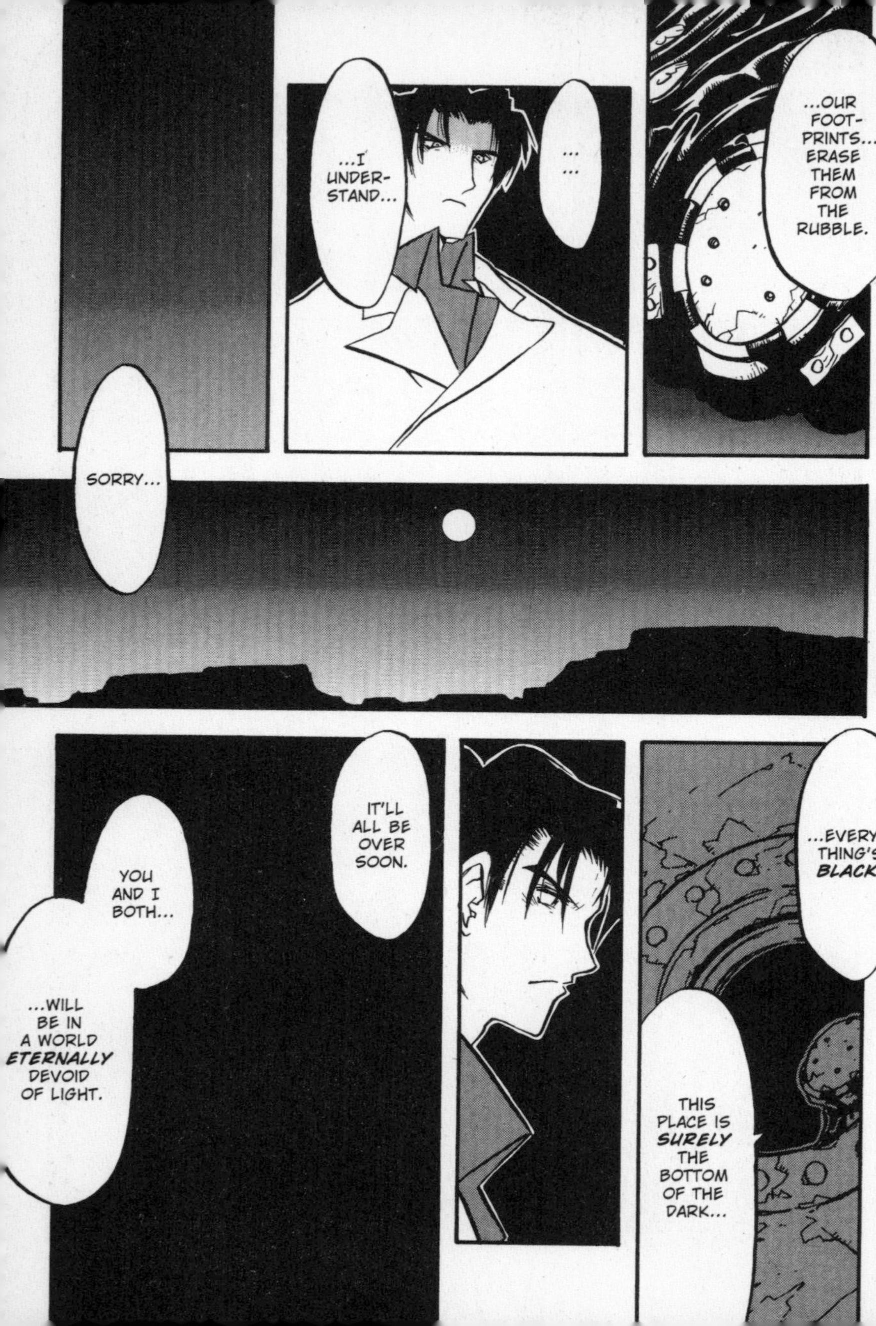
...OUR FOOT-PRINTS... ERASE THEM FROM THE RUBBLE.
... ...
...I UNDER-STAND...
SORRY...
...EVERY-THING'S **BLACK.**
THIS PLACE IS **SURELY** THE BOTTOM OF THE DARK...
IT'LL ALL BE OVER SOON.
YOU AND I BOTH...
...WILL BE IN A WORLD **ETERNALLY** DEVOID OF LIGHT.

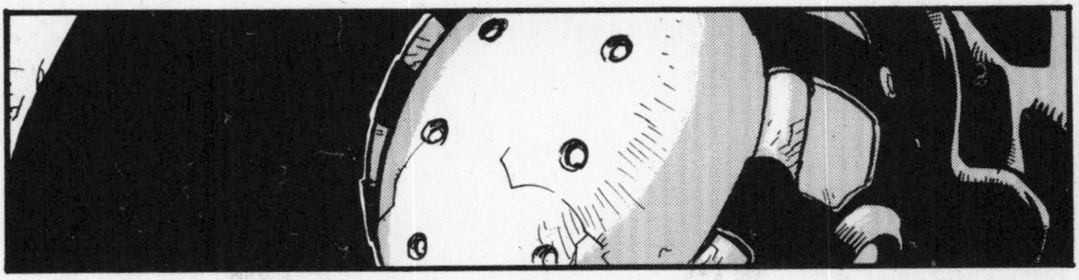
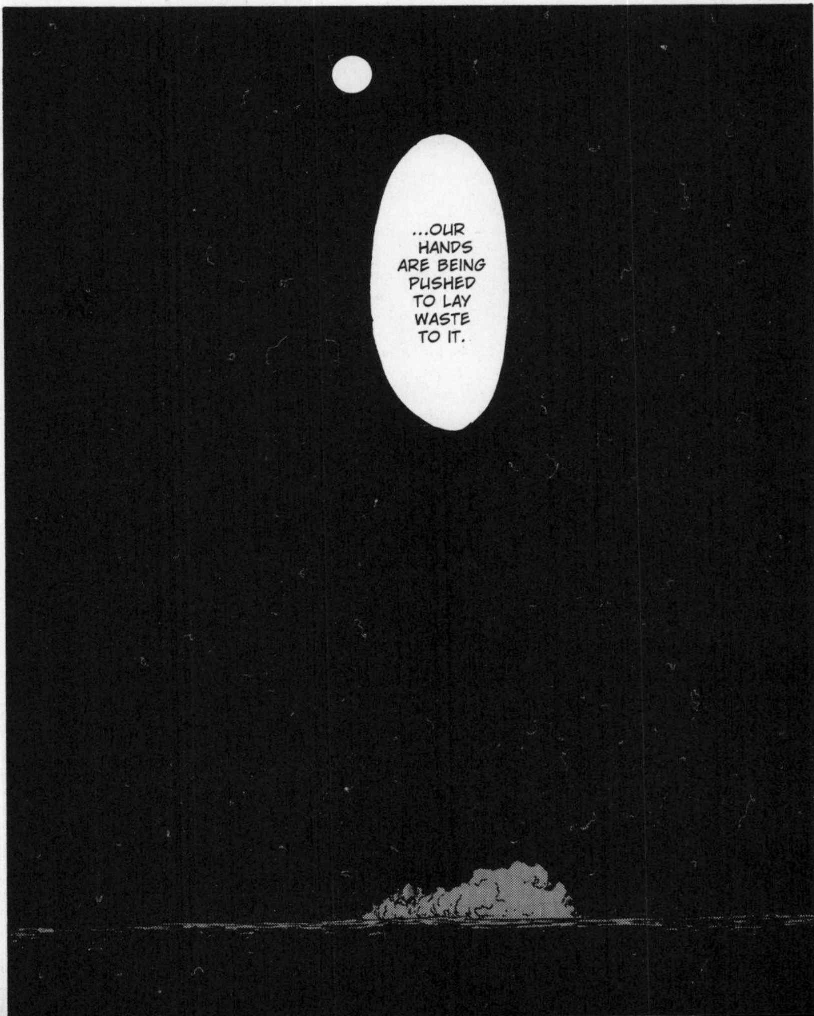
...OUR HANDS ARE BEING PUSHED TO LAY WASTE TO IT.

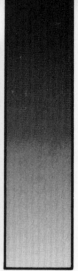

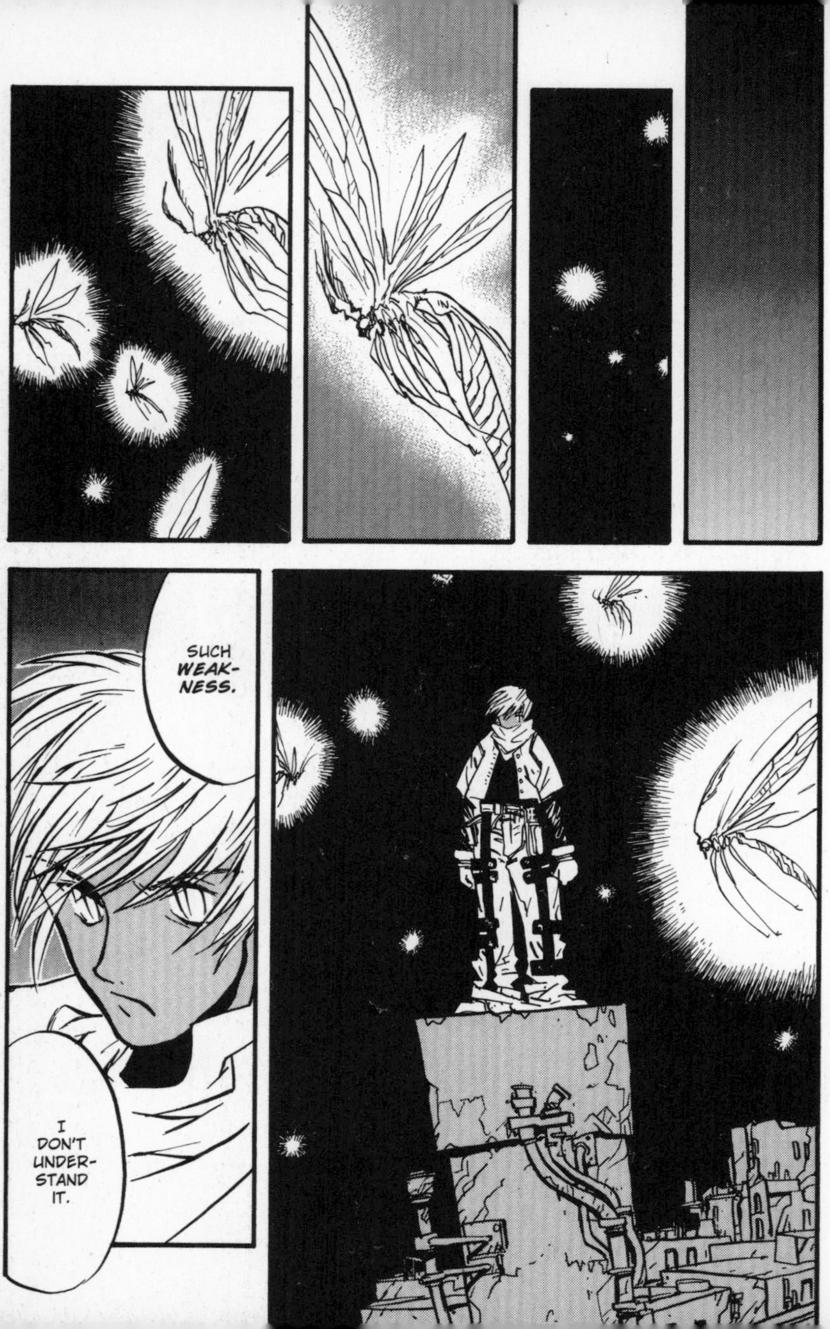
SUCH WEAK-NESS.
I DON'T UNDER-STAND IT.

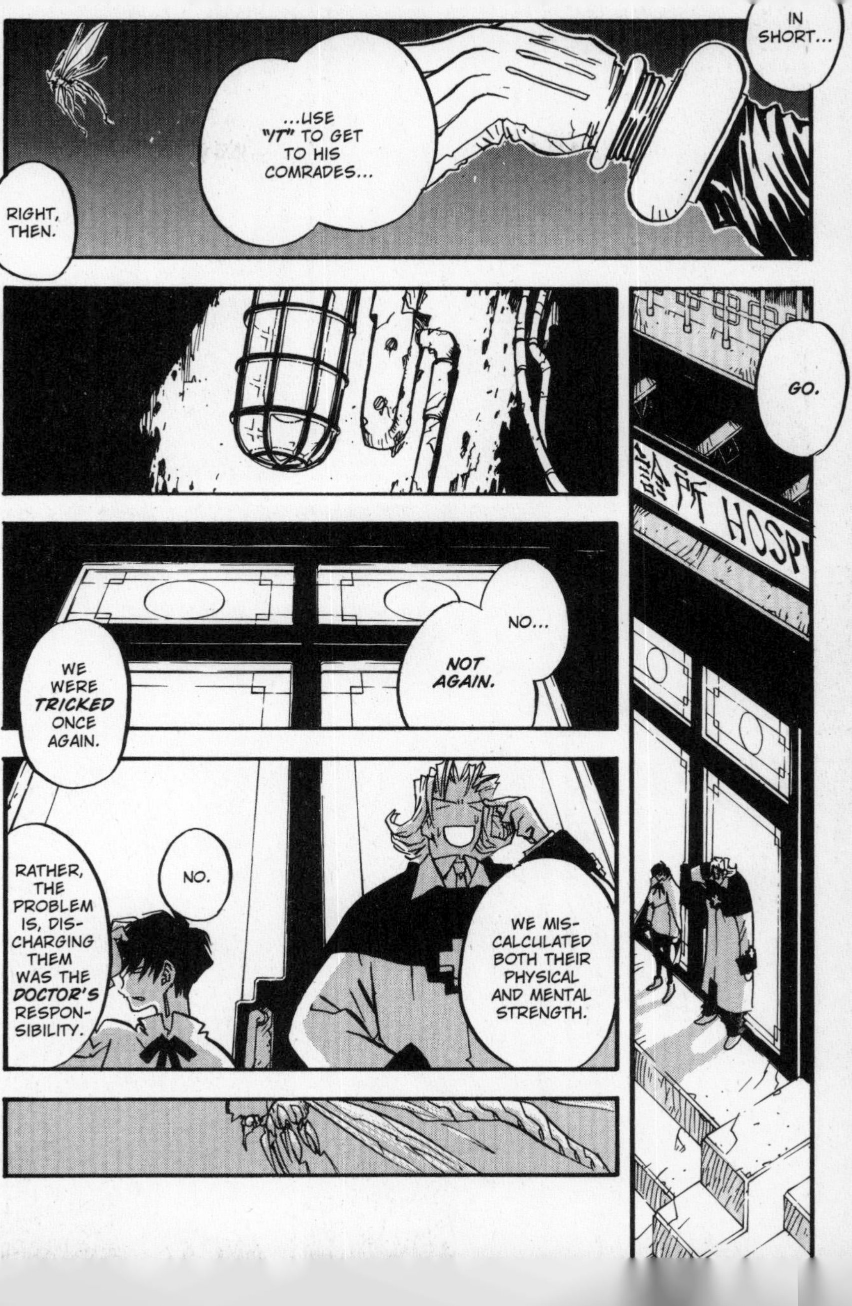
IN SHORT...
...USE "IT" TO GET TO HIS COMRADES...
RIGHT, THEN.
GO.
NO... NOT AGAIN.
WE WERE TRICKED ONCE AGAIN.
WE MIS-CALCULATED BOTH THEIR PHYSICAL AND MENTAL STRENGTH.
NO.
RATHER, THE PROBLEM IS, DIS-CHARGING THEM WAS THE DOCTOR'S RESPON-SIBILITY.

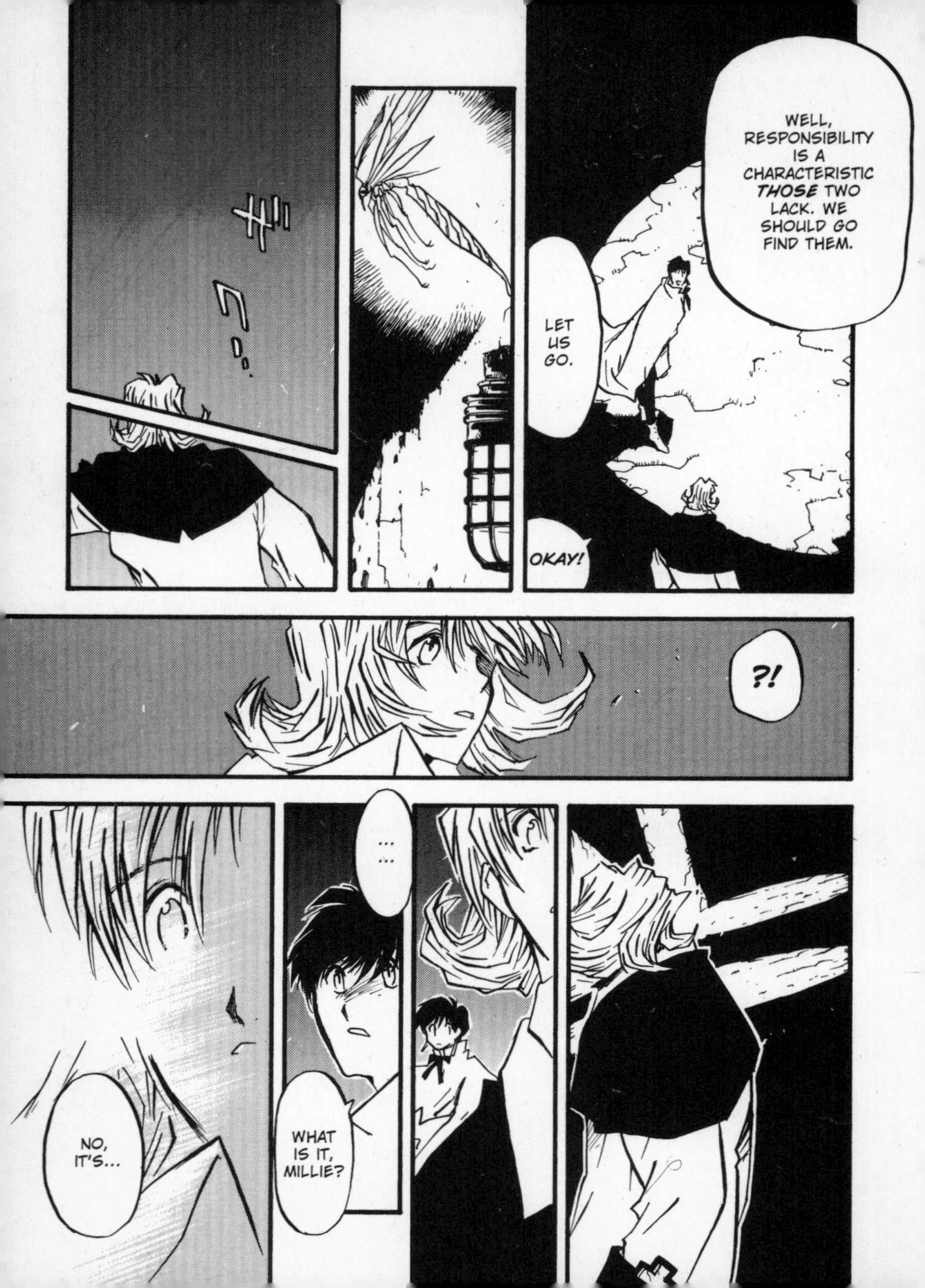
WELL, RESPONSIBILITY IS A CHARACTERISTIC *THOSE* TWO LACK. WE SHOULD GO FIND THEM.
LET US GO.
OKAY!
?!
......
WHAT IS IT, MILLIE?
NO, IT'S...

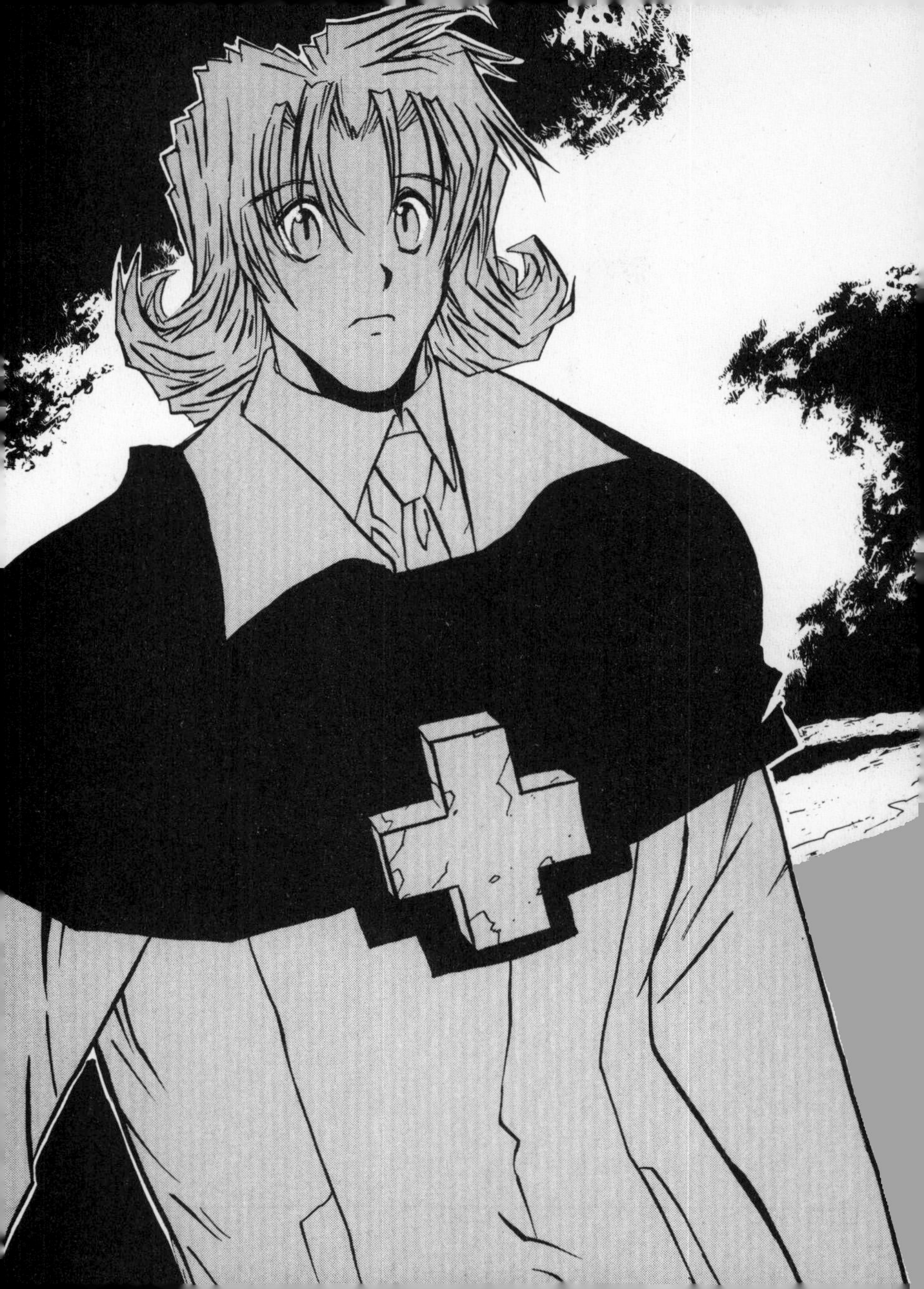

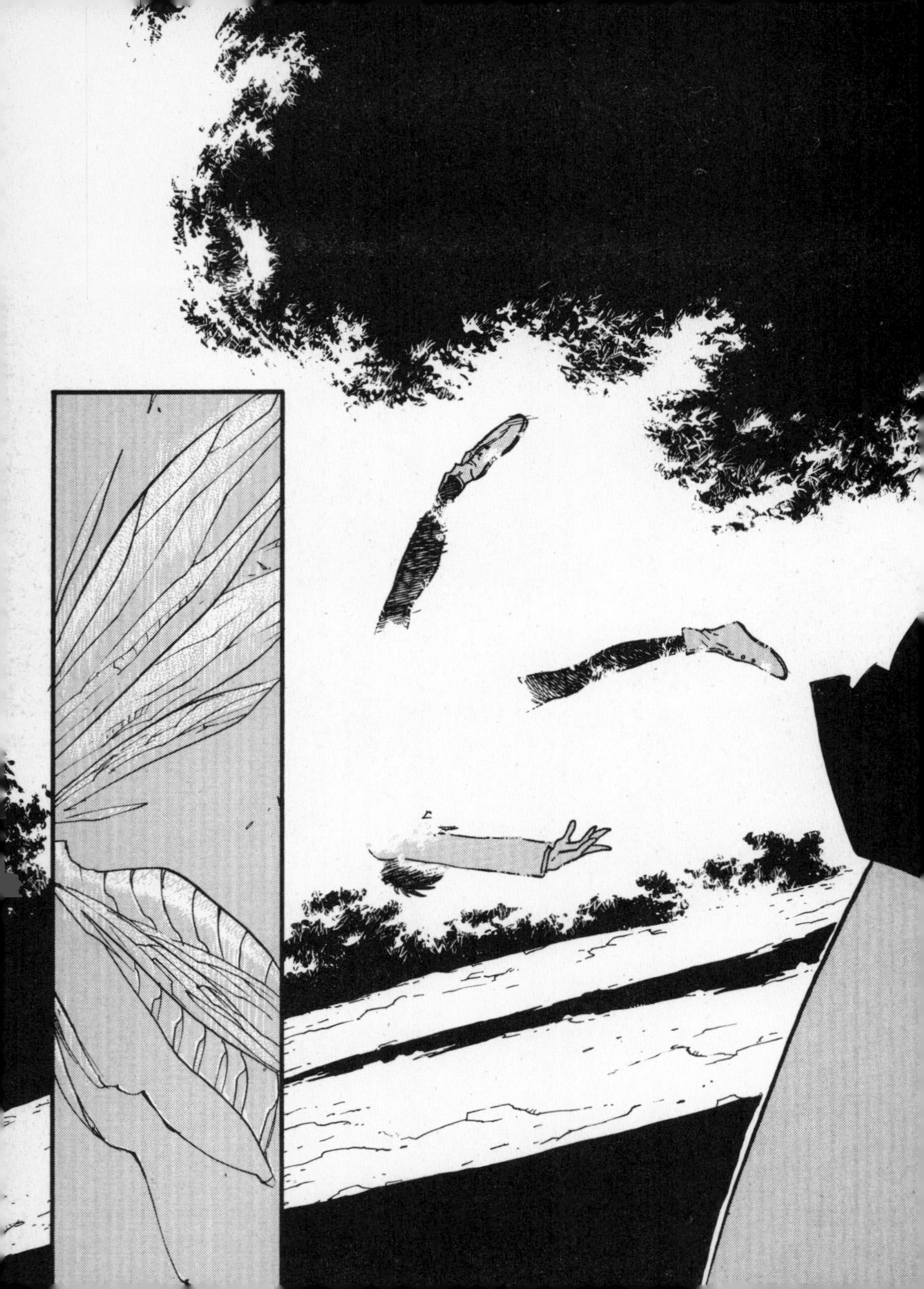

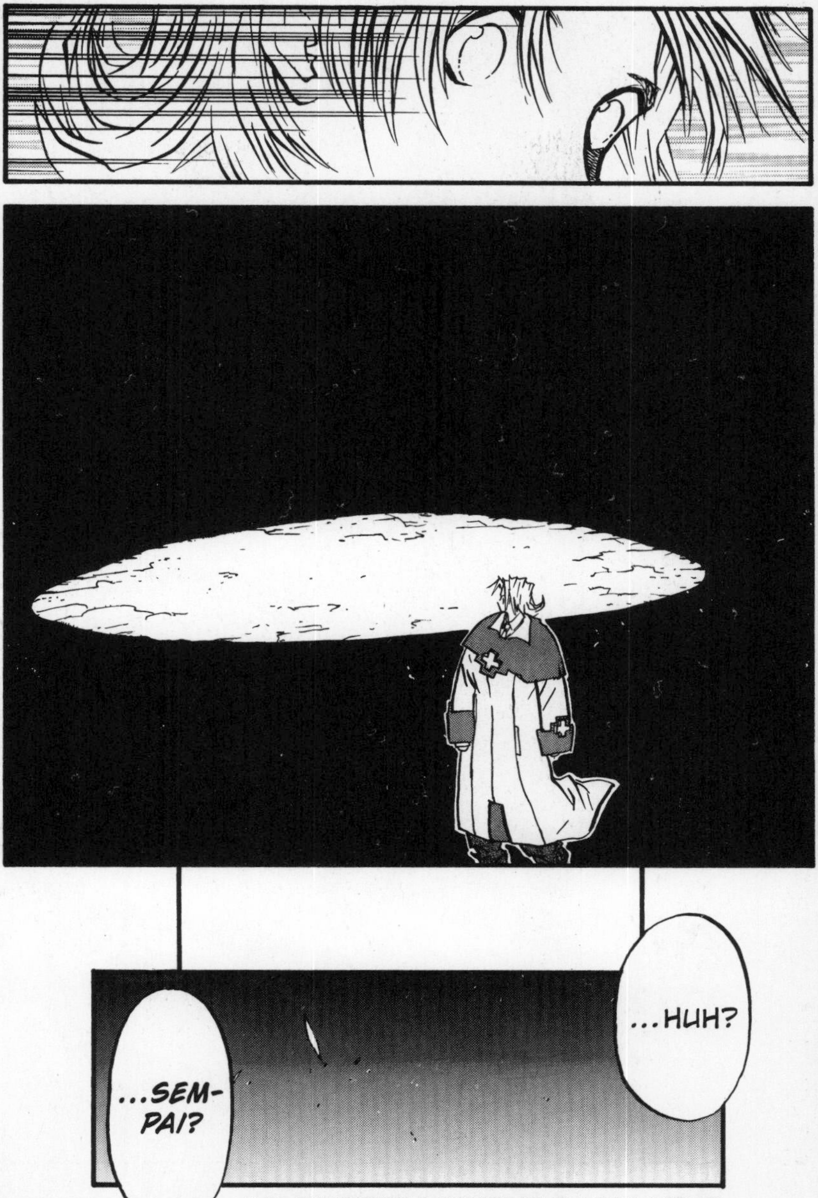
...HUH?
...SEM-PAI?

#3. BOTTOM OF THE DARK / END

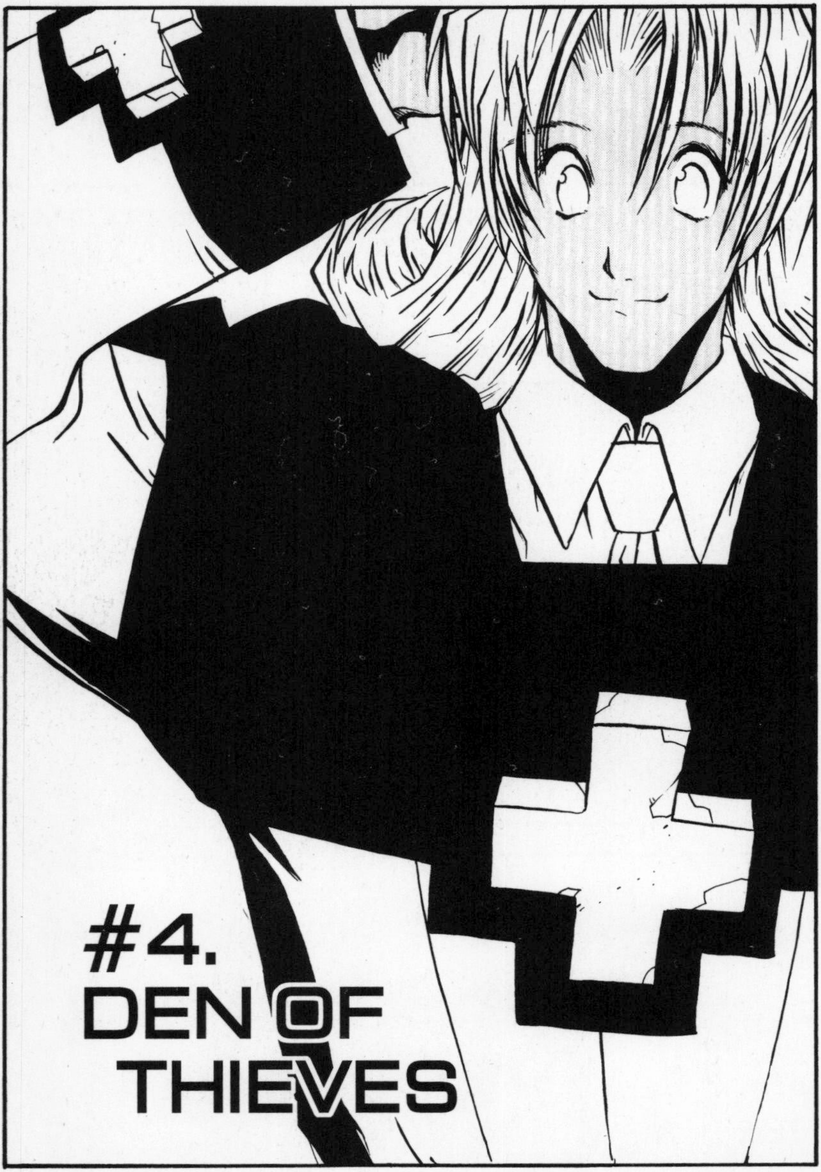
#4.
DEN OF
THIEVES

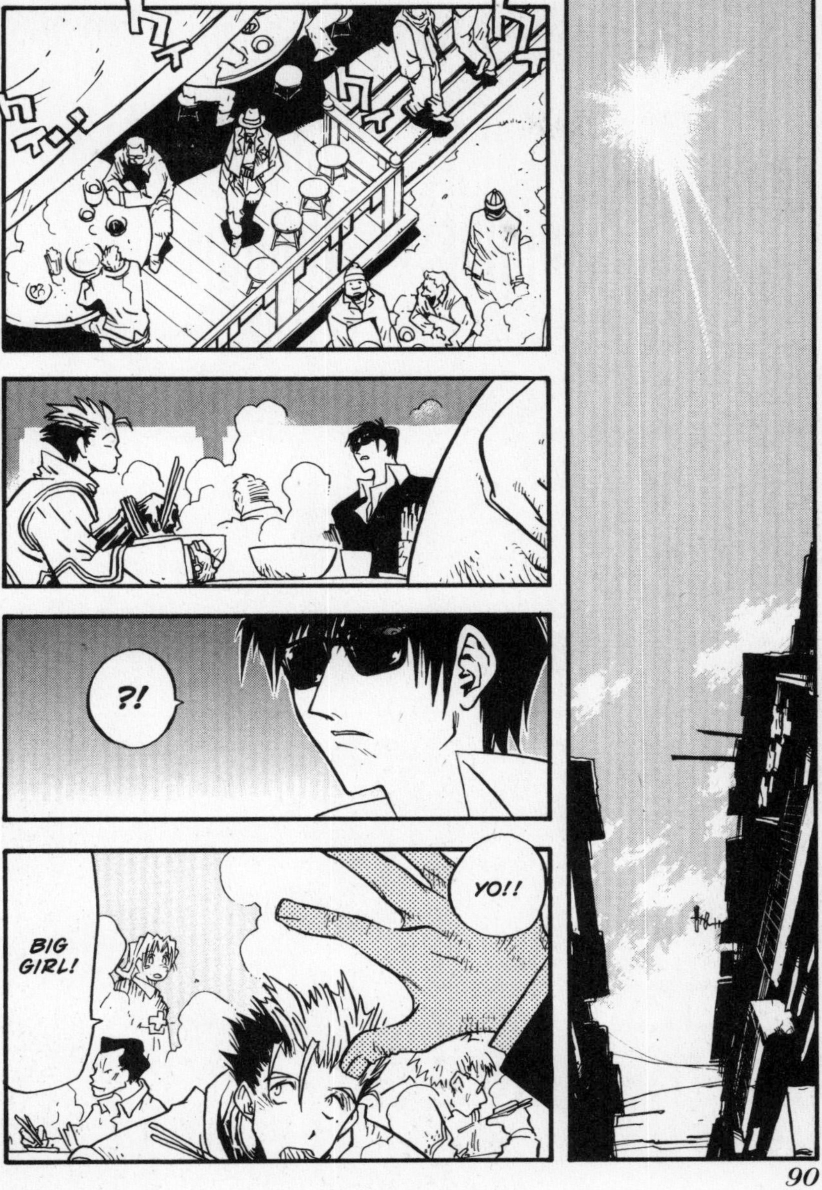
?!
YO!!
BIG GIRL!

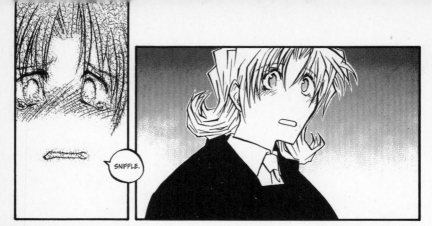

SNIFFLE.

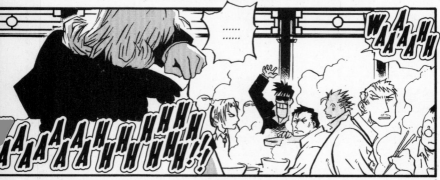

......
......

WAAAAHH

AAAAAAHHHHHH
AAAAAAHHHHHH!!

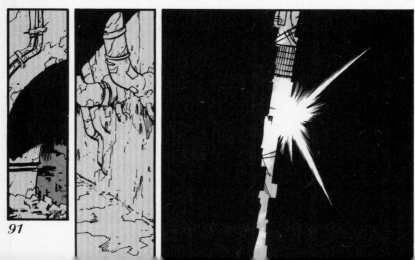

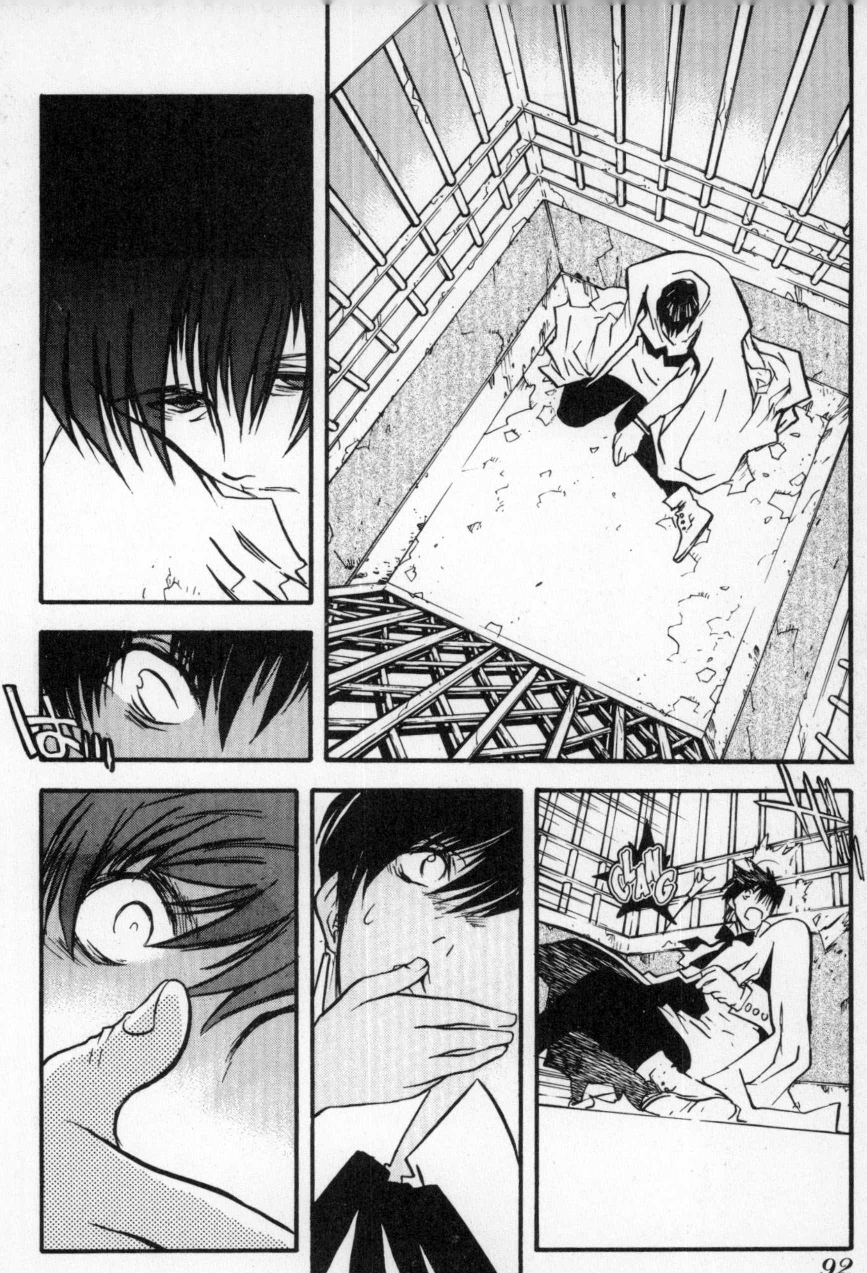
はっ
CLANG

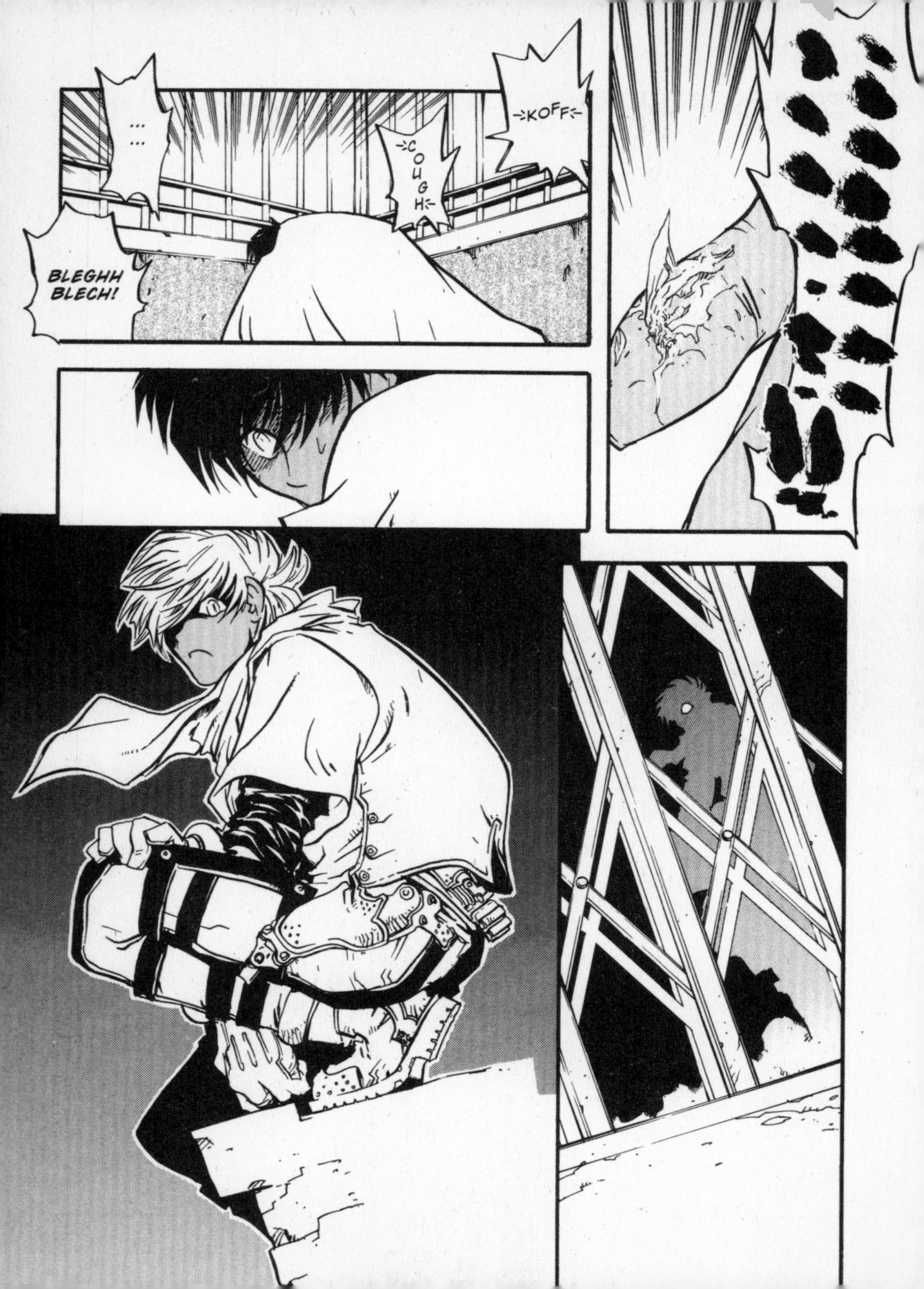
KOFF
COUGH
... ...
BLEGHH BLECH!

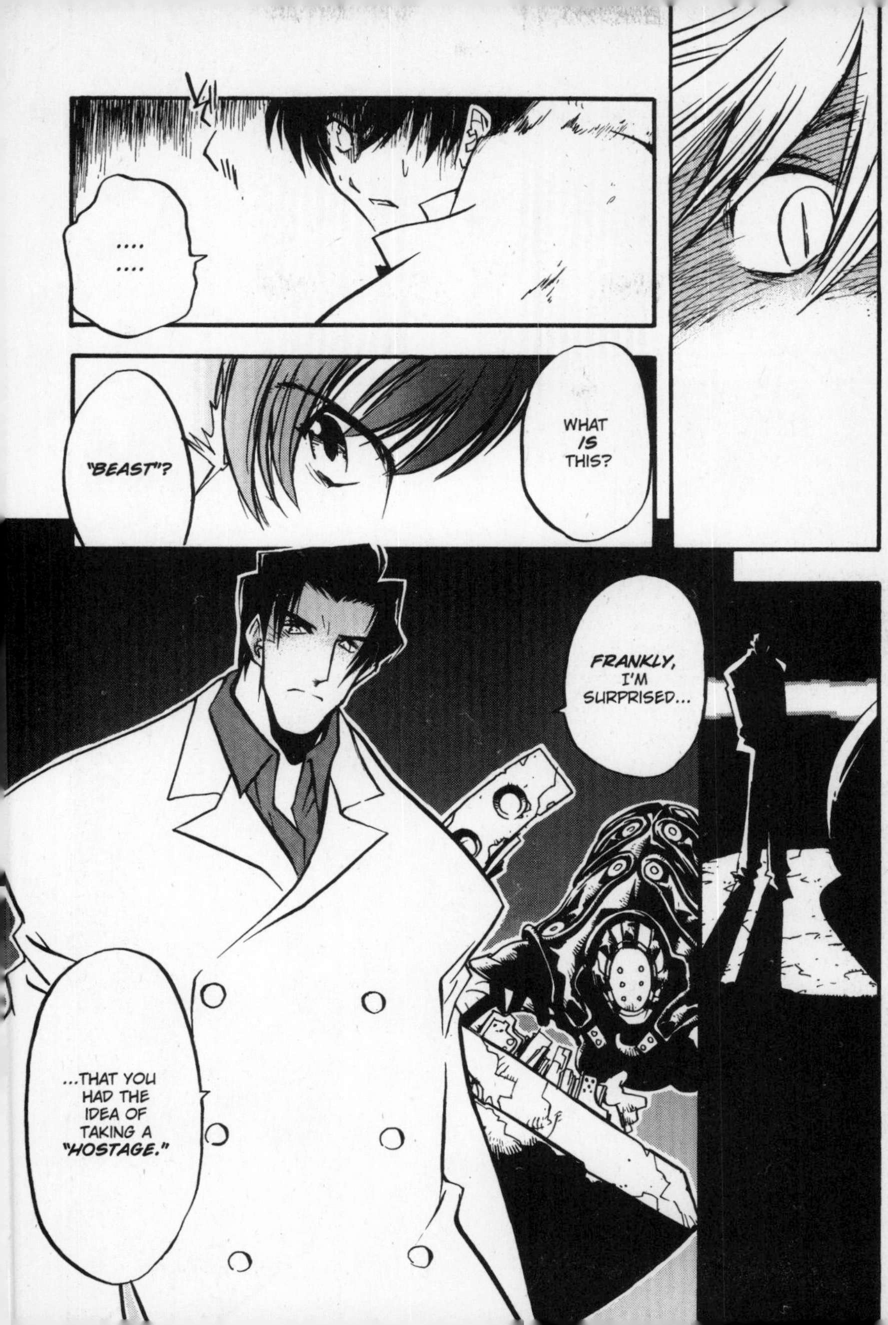
....
....
WHAT *IS* THIS?
"*BEAST*"?
FRANKLY, I'M SURPRISED...
...THAT YOU HAD THE IDEA OF TAKING A "*HOSTAGE.*"

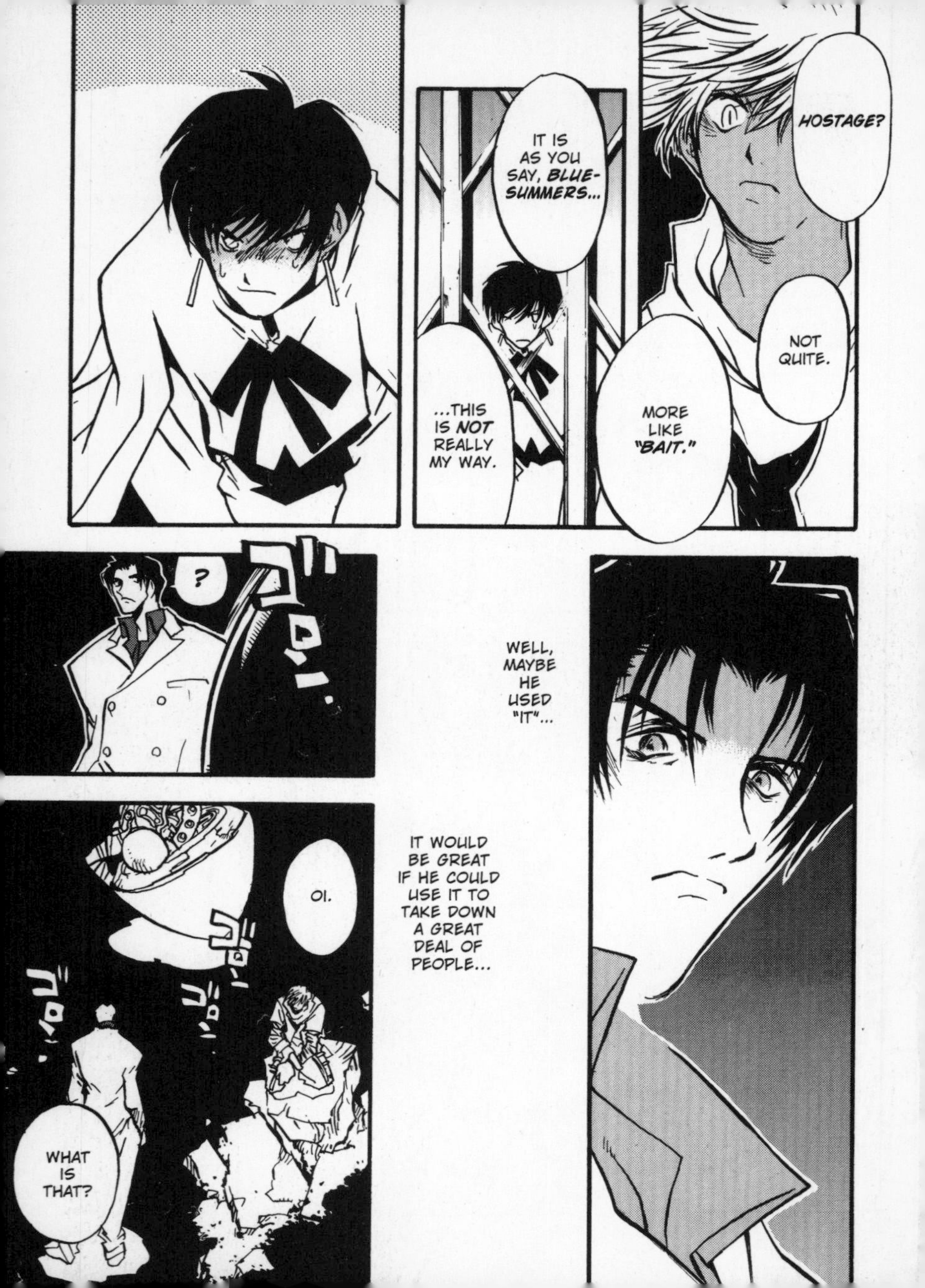
HOSTAGE?
NOT QUITE.
MORE LIKE "BAIT."
IT IS AS YOU SAY, BLUE-SUMMERS...
...THIS IS NOT REALLY MY WAY.
WELL, MAYBE HE USED "IT"...
IT WOULD BE GREAT IF HE COULD USE IT TO TAKE DOWN A GREAT DEAL OF PEOPLE...
?
OI.
WHAT IS THAT?

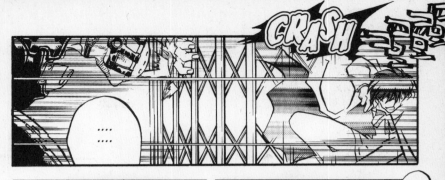

CRASH

....
....

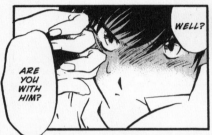

WELL?

ARE YOU WITH HIM?

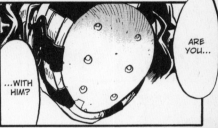

...WITH HIM?

ARE YOU...

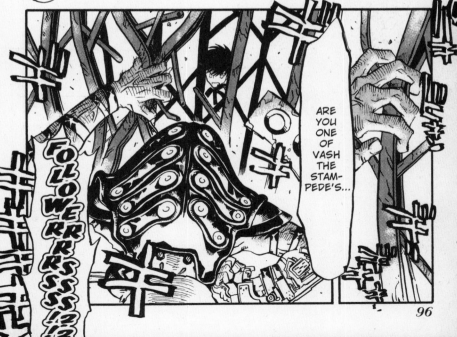

ARE YOU ONE OF VASH THE STAMPEDE'S...

FOLOWERRRSSSS!?!?

96

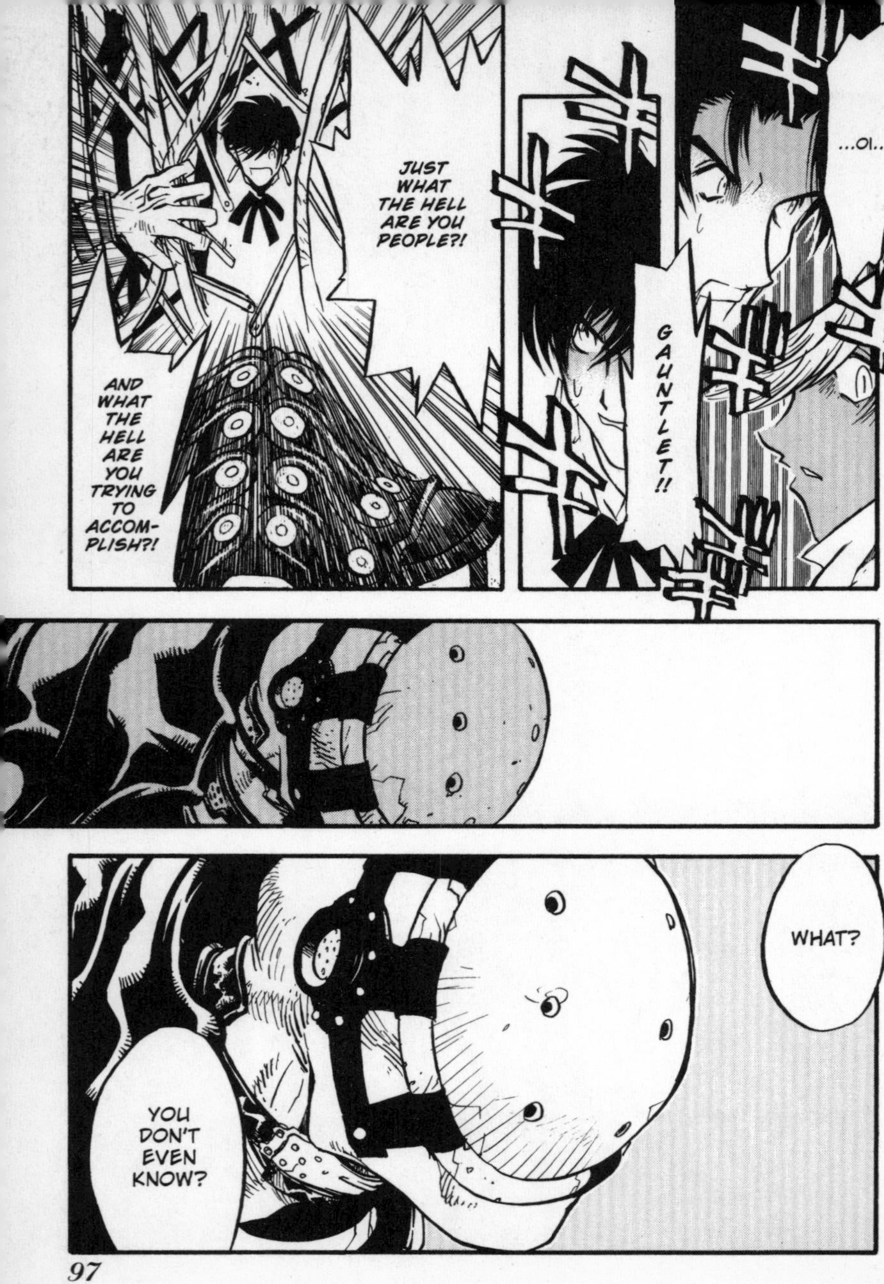
...OI...
GAUNTLET!!
JUST WHAT THE HELL ARE YOU PEOPLE?!
AND WHAT THE HELL ARE YOU TRYING TO ACCOMPLISH?!
WHAT?
YOU DON'T EVEN KNOW?

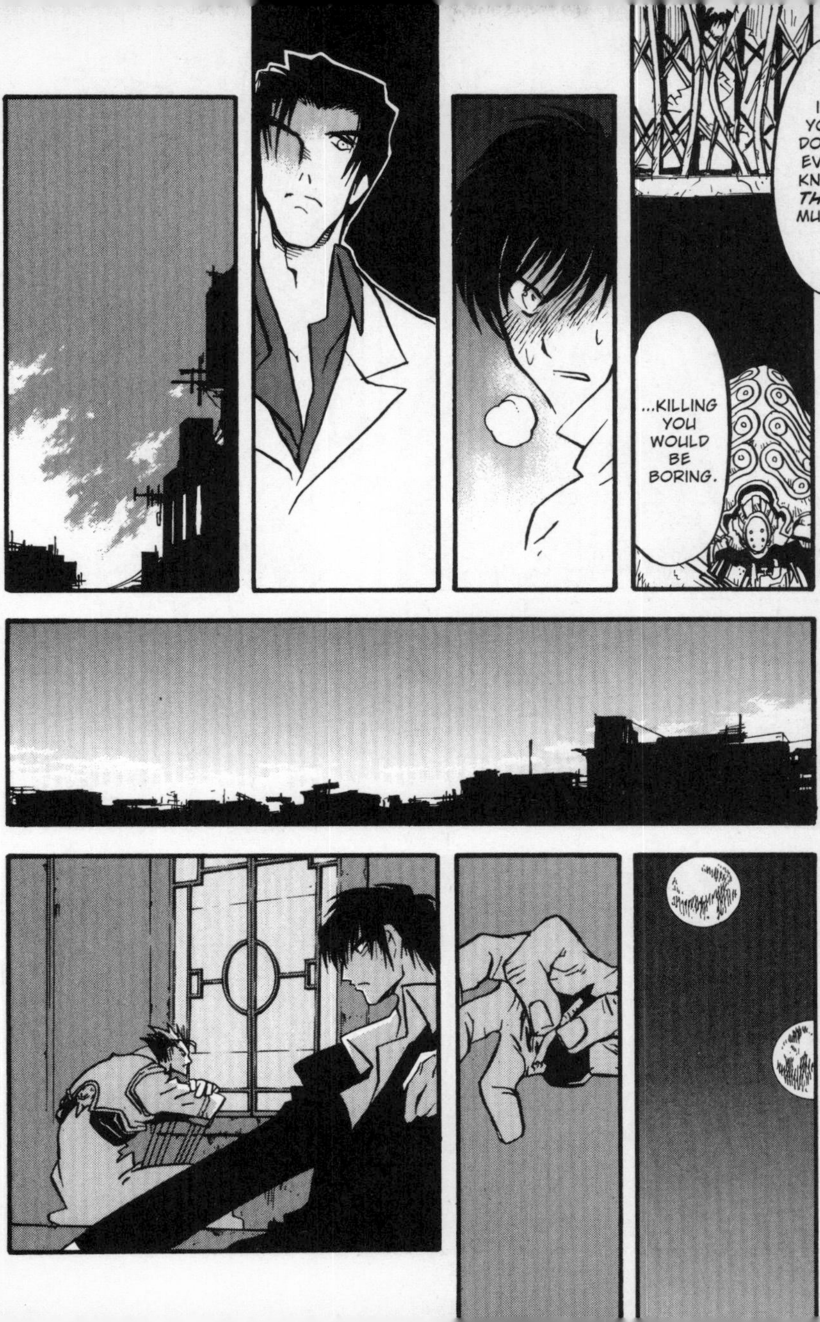
IF YOU DON'T EVEN KNOW *THAT* MUCH...
...KILLING YOU WOULD BE BORING.

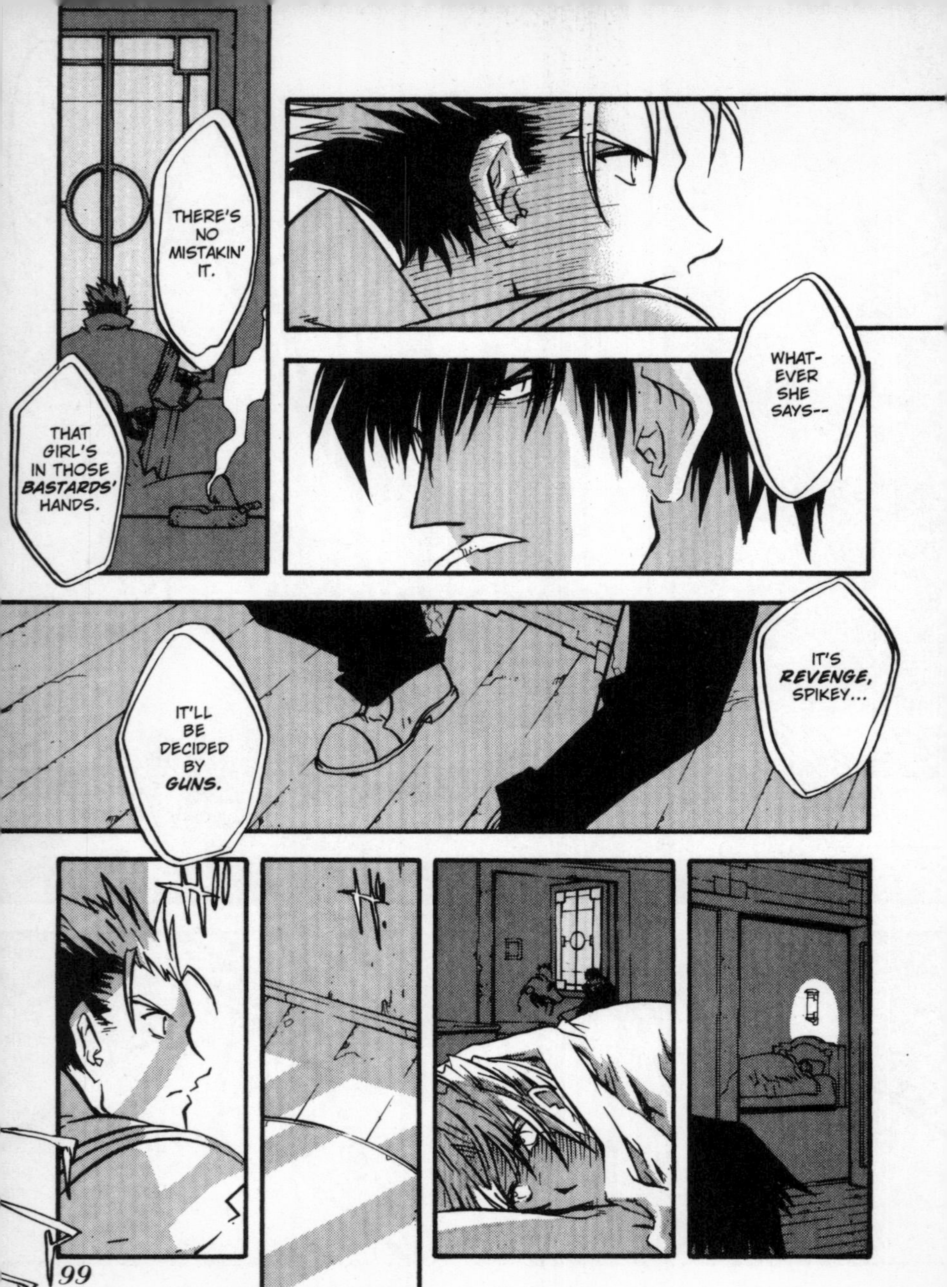
WHAT-EVER SHE SAYS--
THERE'S NO MISTAKIN' IT.
THAT GIRL'S IN THOSE *BASTARDS'* HANDS.
IT'S *REVENGE*, SPIKEY...
IT'LL BE DECIDED BY *GUNS.*

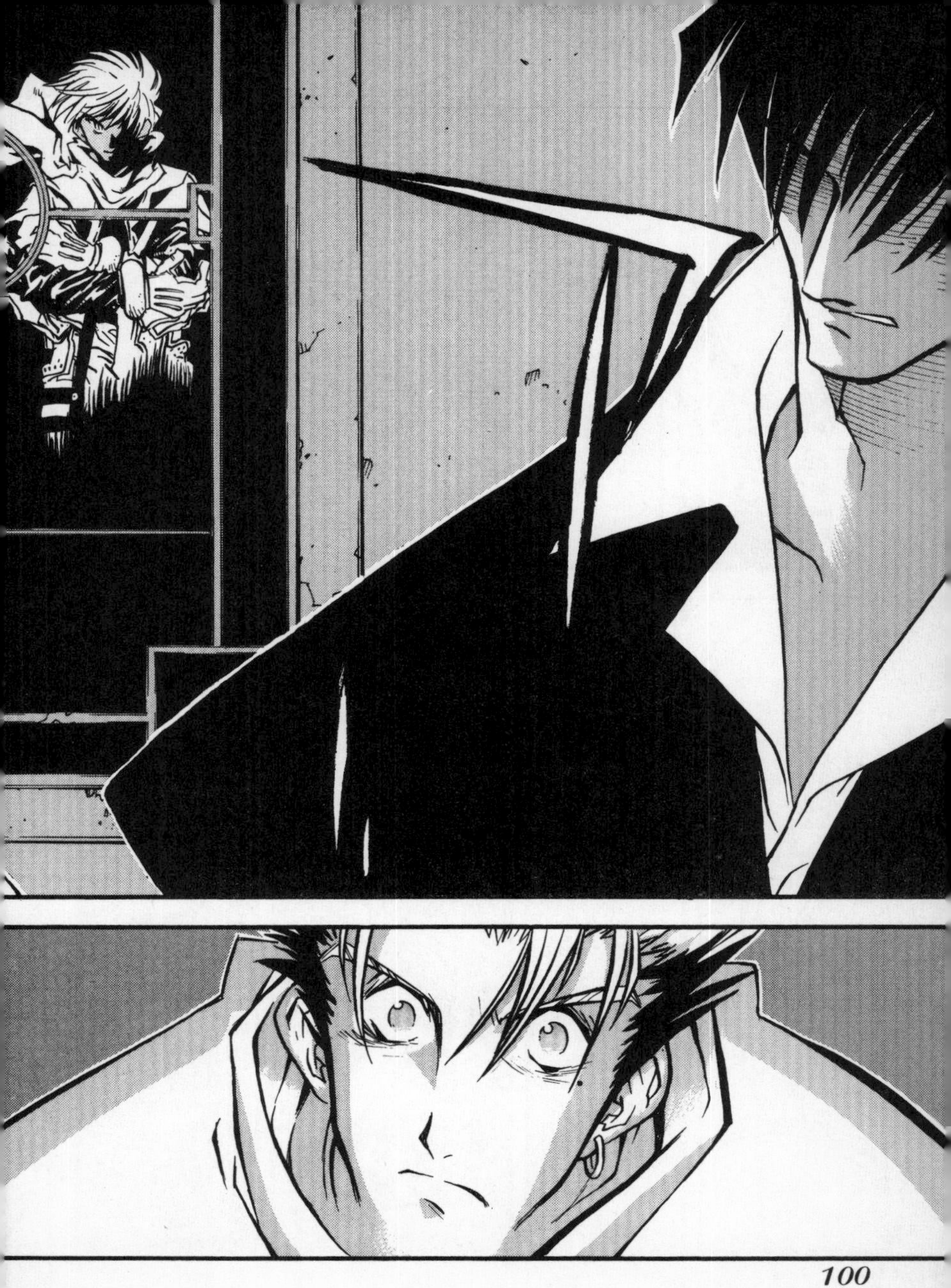

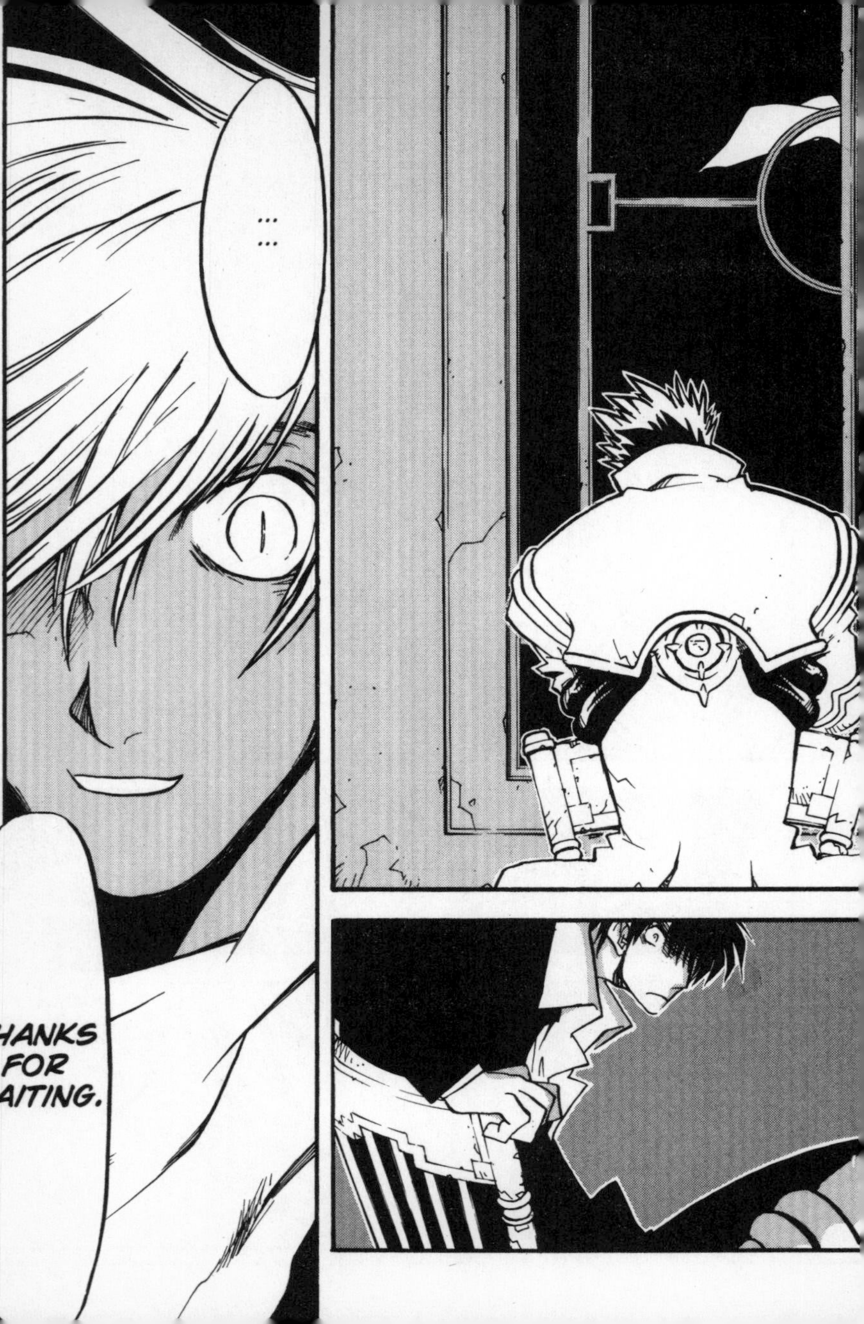
……
THANKS FOR WAITING.

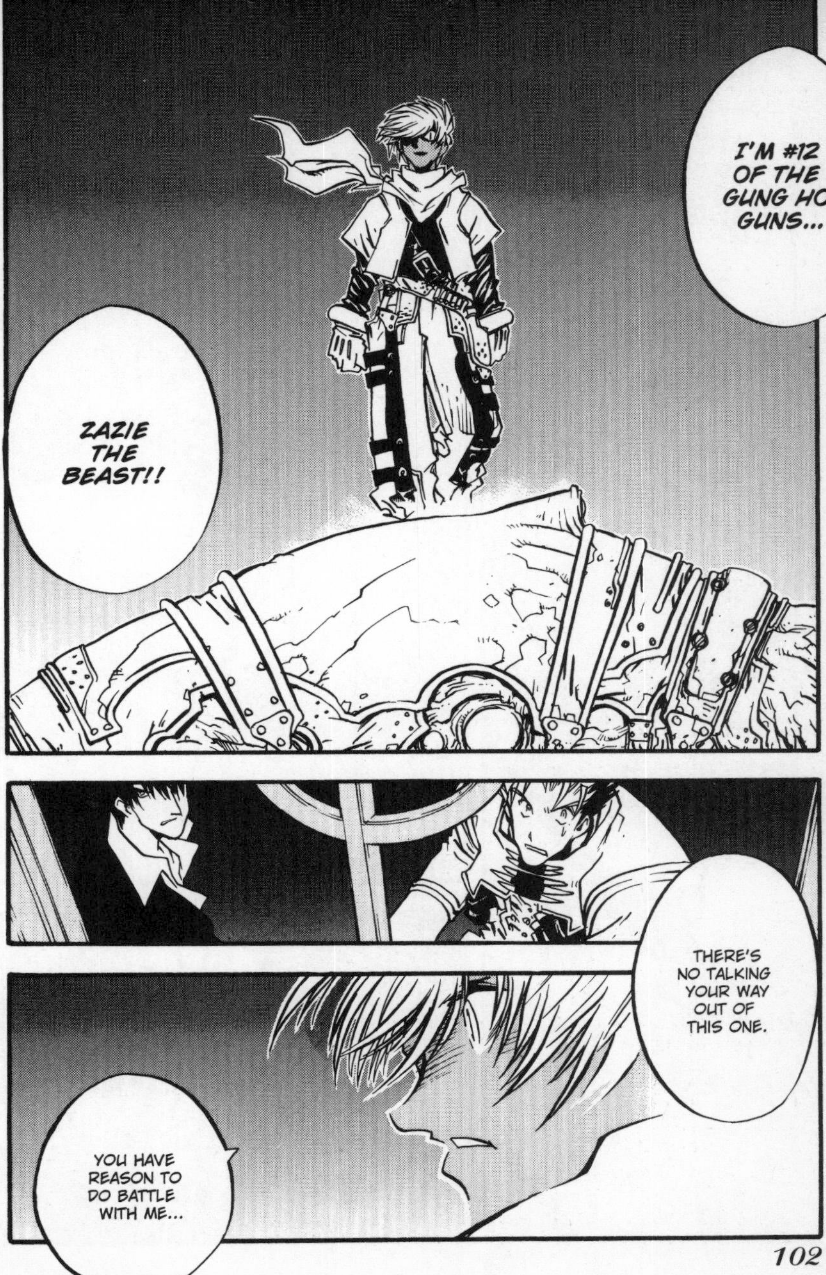
I'M #12 OF THE GUNG HO GUNS...
ZAZIE THE BEAST!!
THERE'S NO TALKING YOUR WAY OUT OF THIS ONE.
YOU HAVE REASON TO DO BATTLE WITH ME...

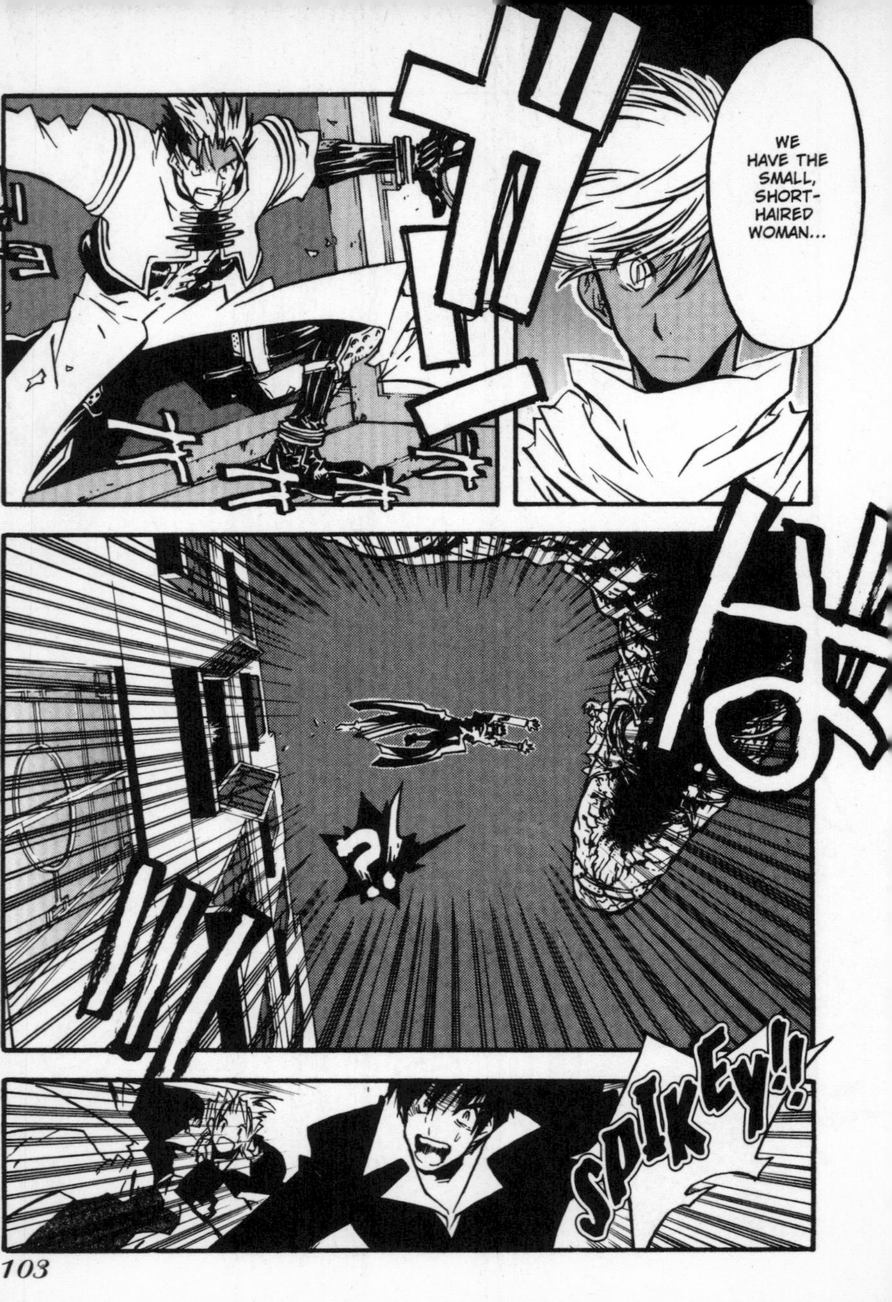
WE HAVE THE SMALL, SHORT-HAIRED WOMAN...
?!
SPIKEY!!

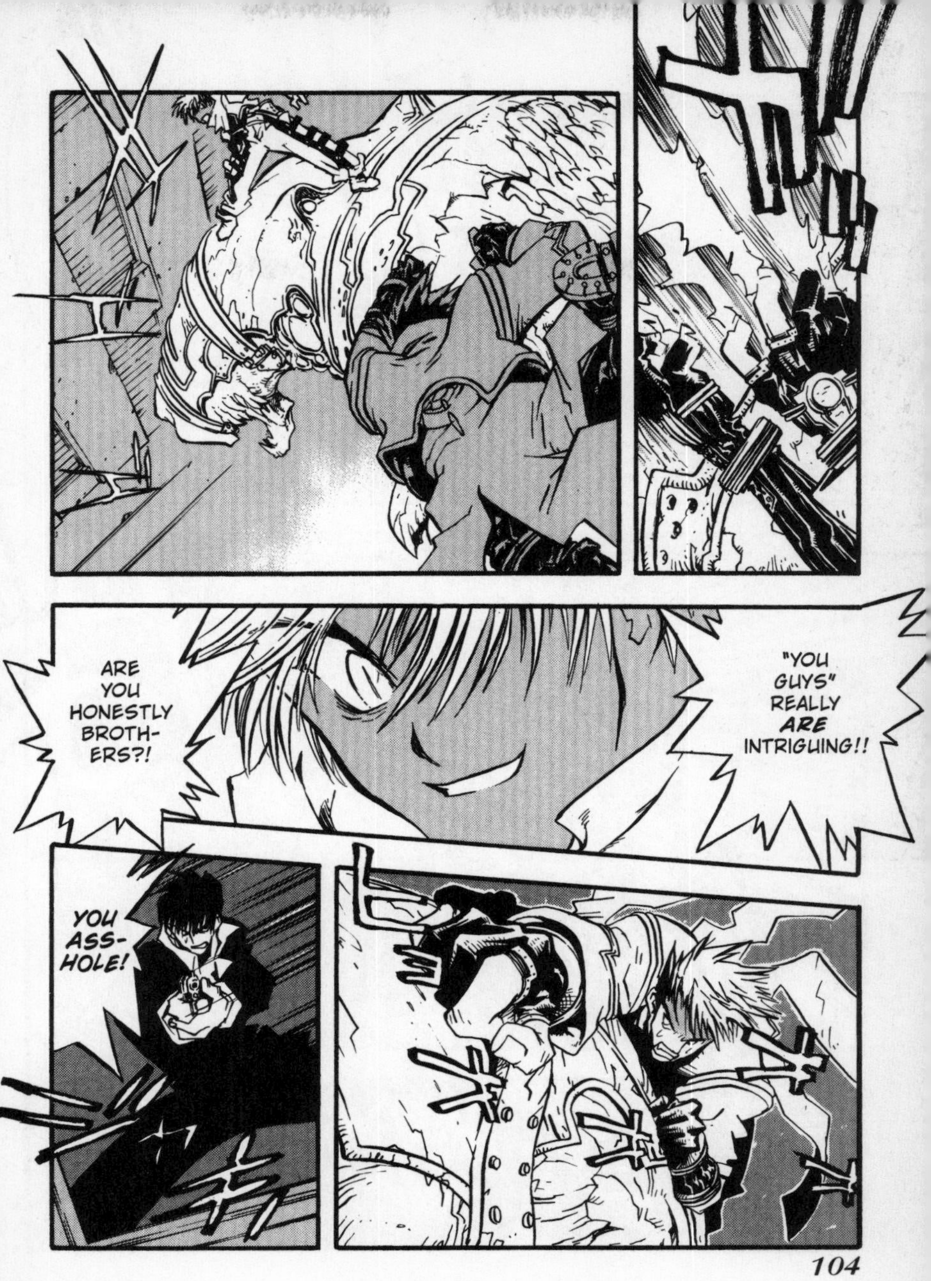
"YOU GUYS" REALLY ARE INTRIGUING!!
ARE YOU HONESTLY BROTHERS?!
YOU ASSHOLE!

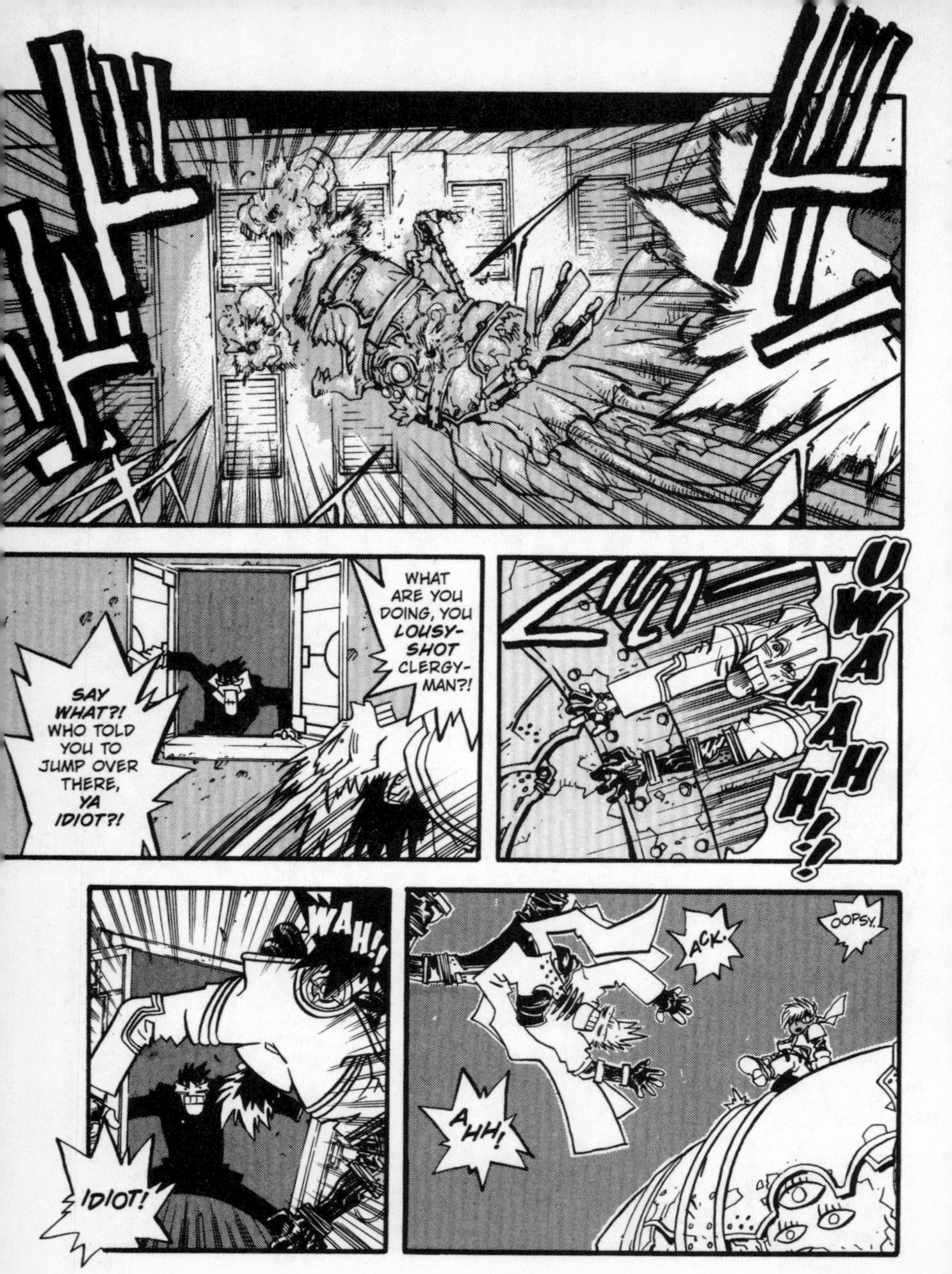
UWAAAHH!!
WHAT ARE YOU DOING, YOU *LOUSY-SHOT* CLERGYMAN?!
SAY WHAT?! WHO TOLD YOU TO JUMP OVER THERE, *YA IDIOT?!*
OOPSY.
ACK.
AHH!
WAH!!
IDIOT!

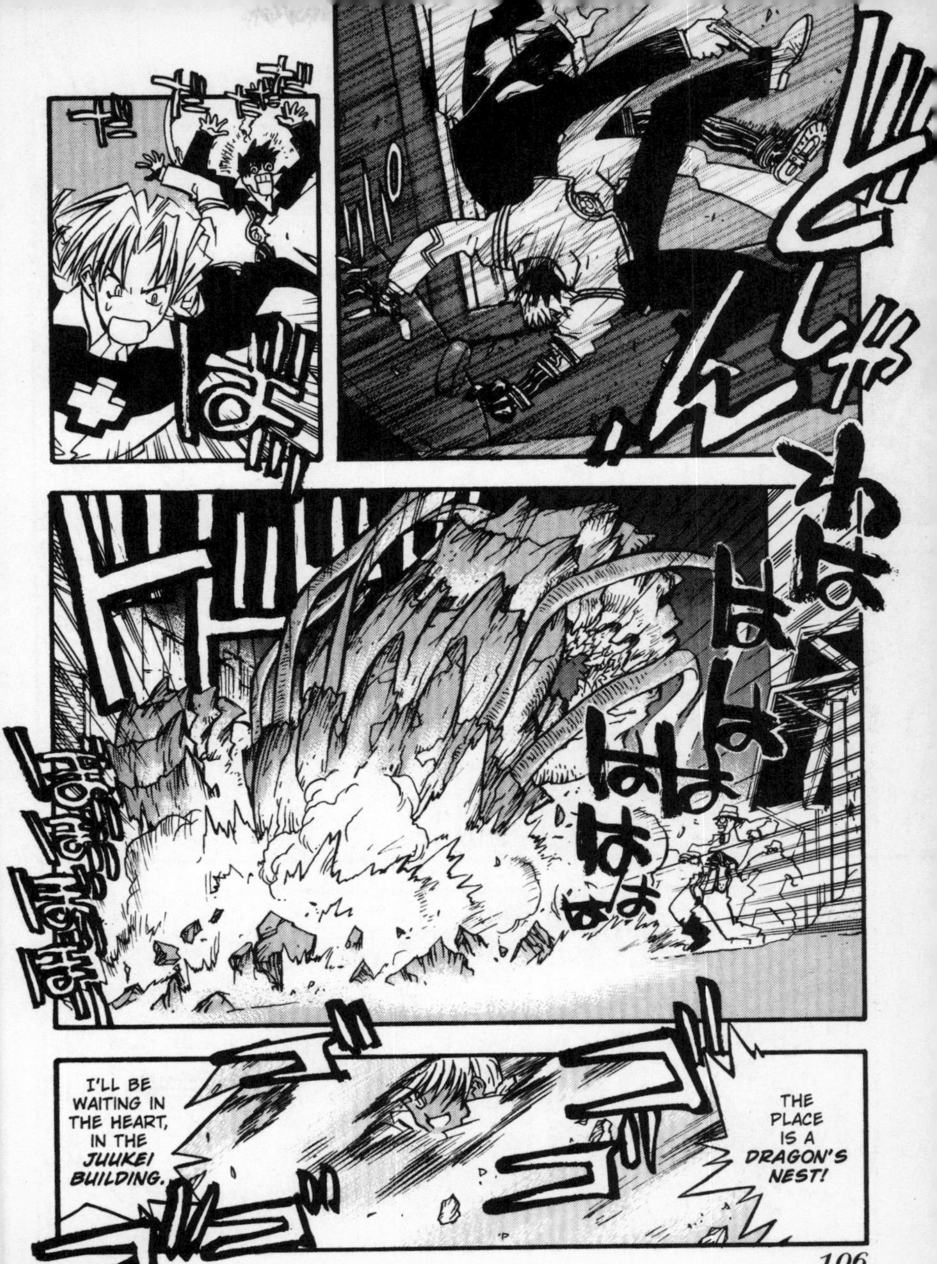
THE PLACE IS A DRAGON'S NEST!
I'LL BE WAITING IN THE HEART, IN THE JUUKEI BUILDING.

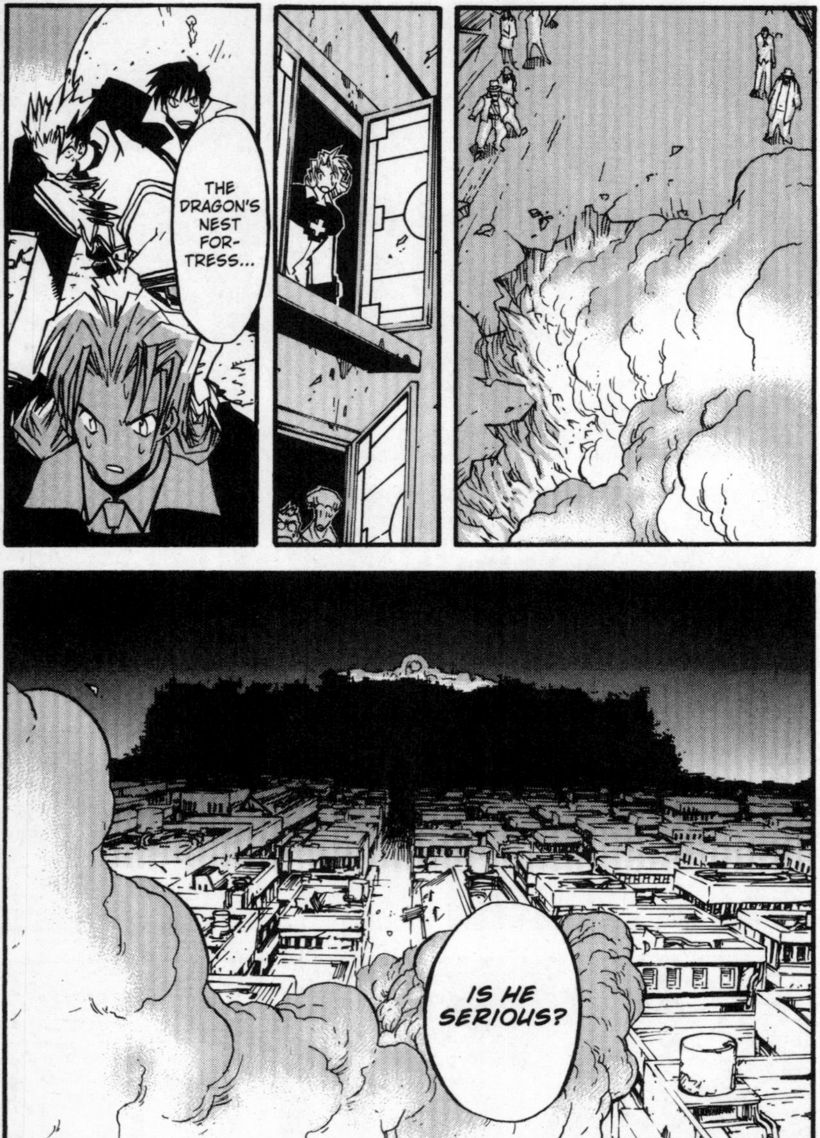
THE DRAGON'S NEST FOR-TRESS...
IS HE SERIOUS?

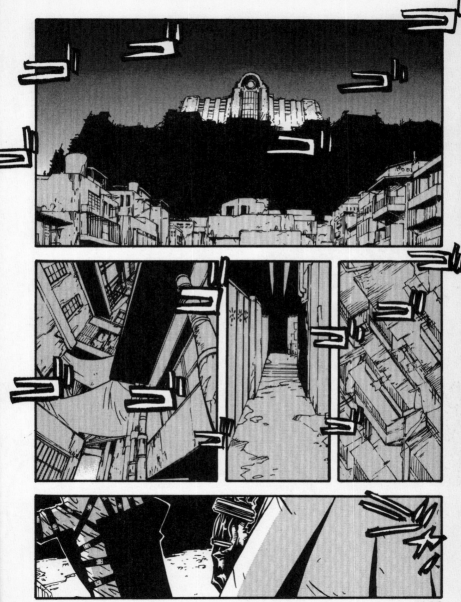

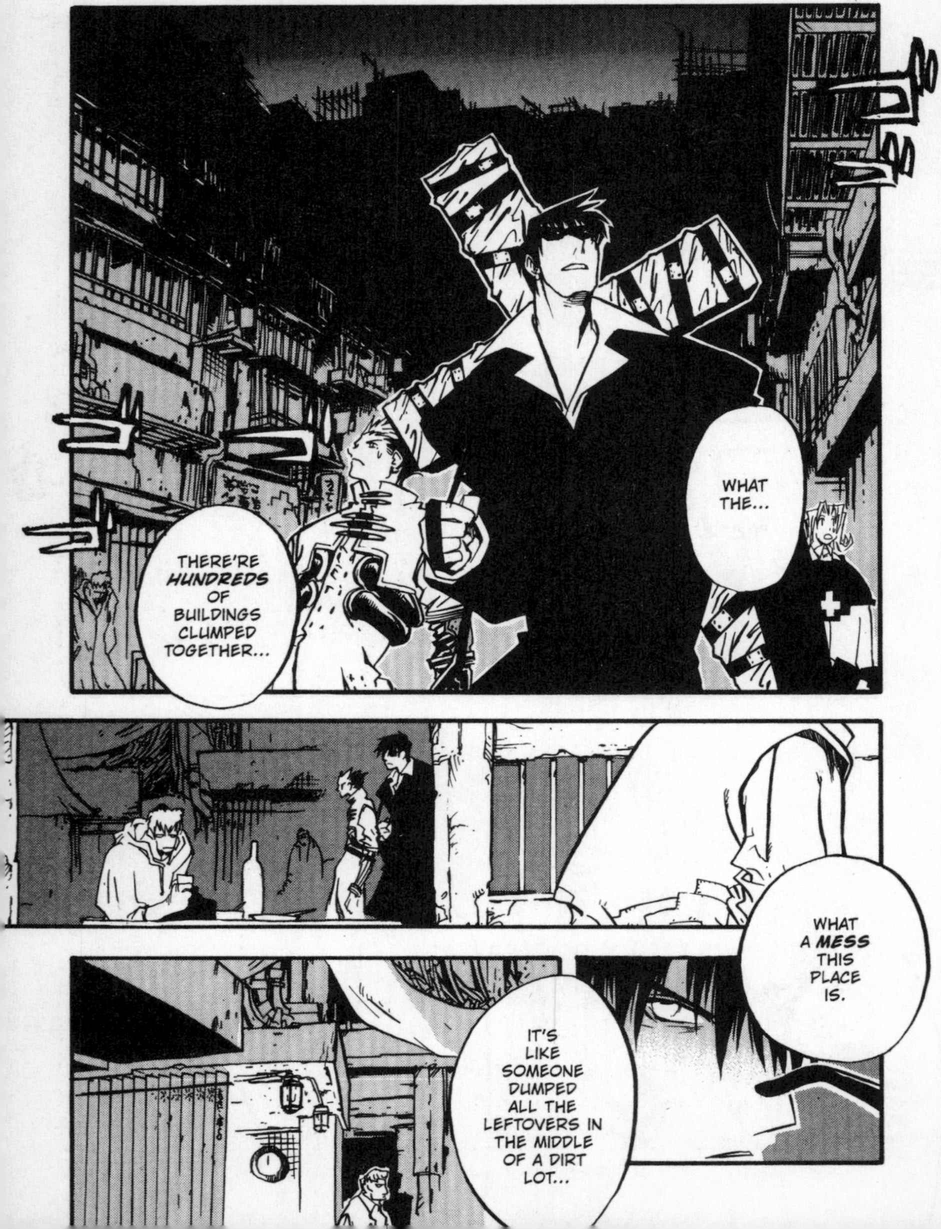
WHAT THE...
THERE'RE HUNDREDS OF BUILDINGS CLUMPED TOGETHER...
WHAT A MESS THIS PLACE IS.
IT'S LIKE SOMEONE DUMPED ALL THE LEFTOVERS IN THE MIDDLE OF A DIRT LOT...

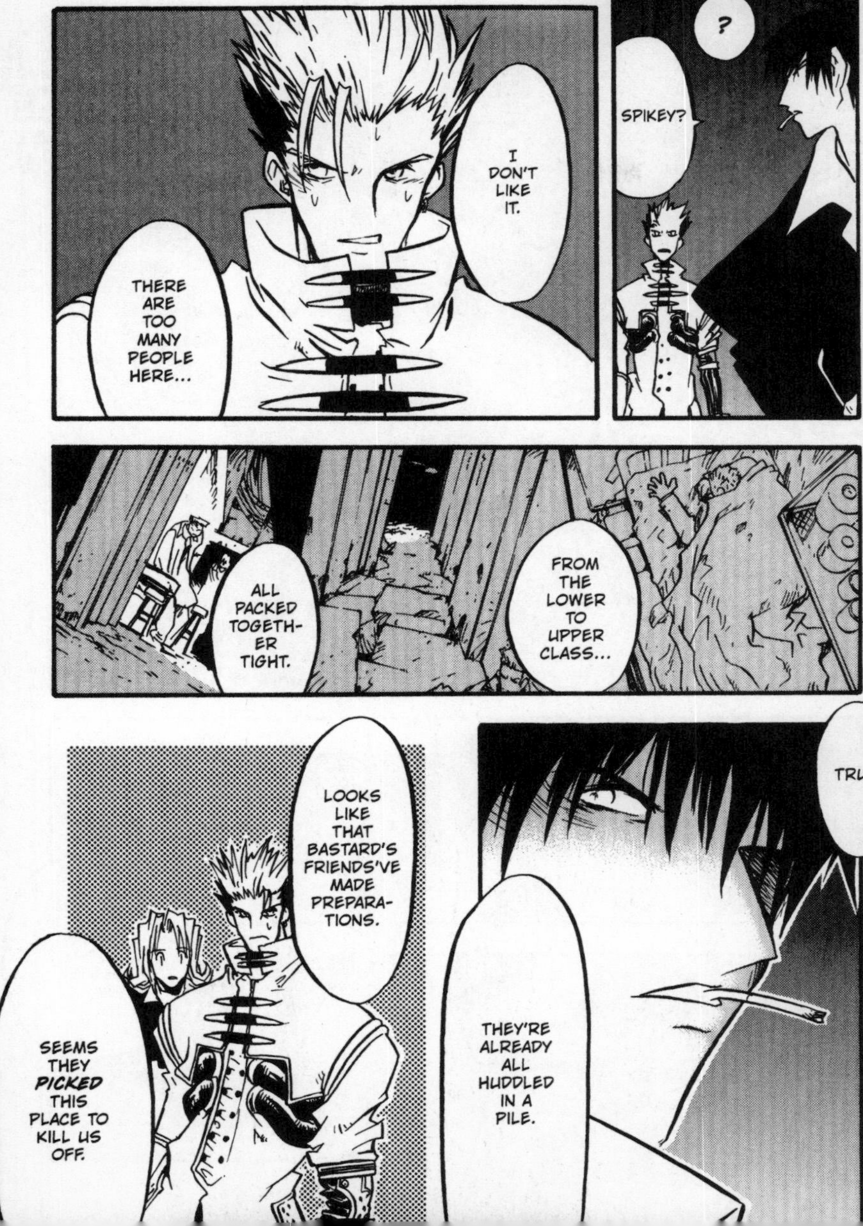
?
SPIKEY?
I DON'T LIKE IT.
THERE ARE TOO MANY PEOPLE HERE...
FROM THE LOWER TO UPPER CLASS...
ALL PACKED TOGETHER TIGHT.
TRUE.
THEY'RE ALREADY ALL HUDDLED IN A PILE.
LOOKS LIKE THAT BASTARD'S FRIENDS'VE MADE PREPARATIONS.
SEEMS THEY *PICKED* THIS PLACE TO KILL US OFF.

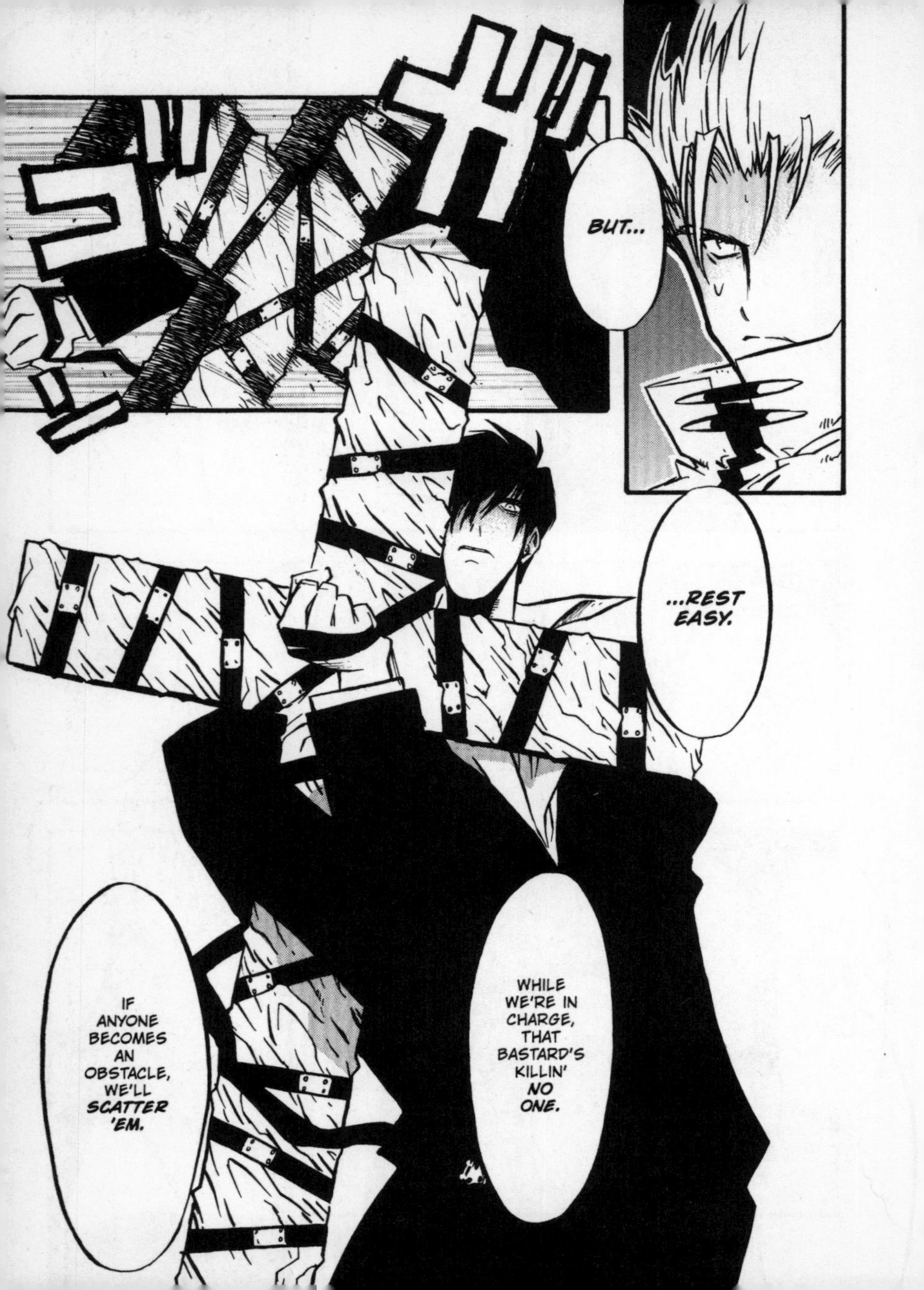
BUT...
...REST EASY.
WHILE WE'RE IN CHARGE, THAT BASTARD'S KILLIN' NO ONE.
IF ANYONE BECOMES AN OBSTACLE, WE'LL SCATTER 'EM.

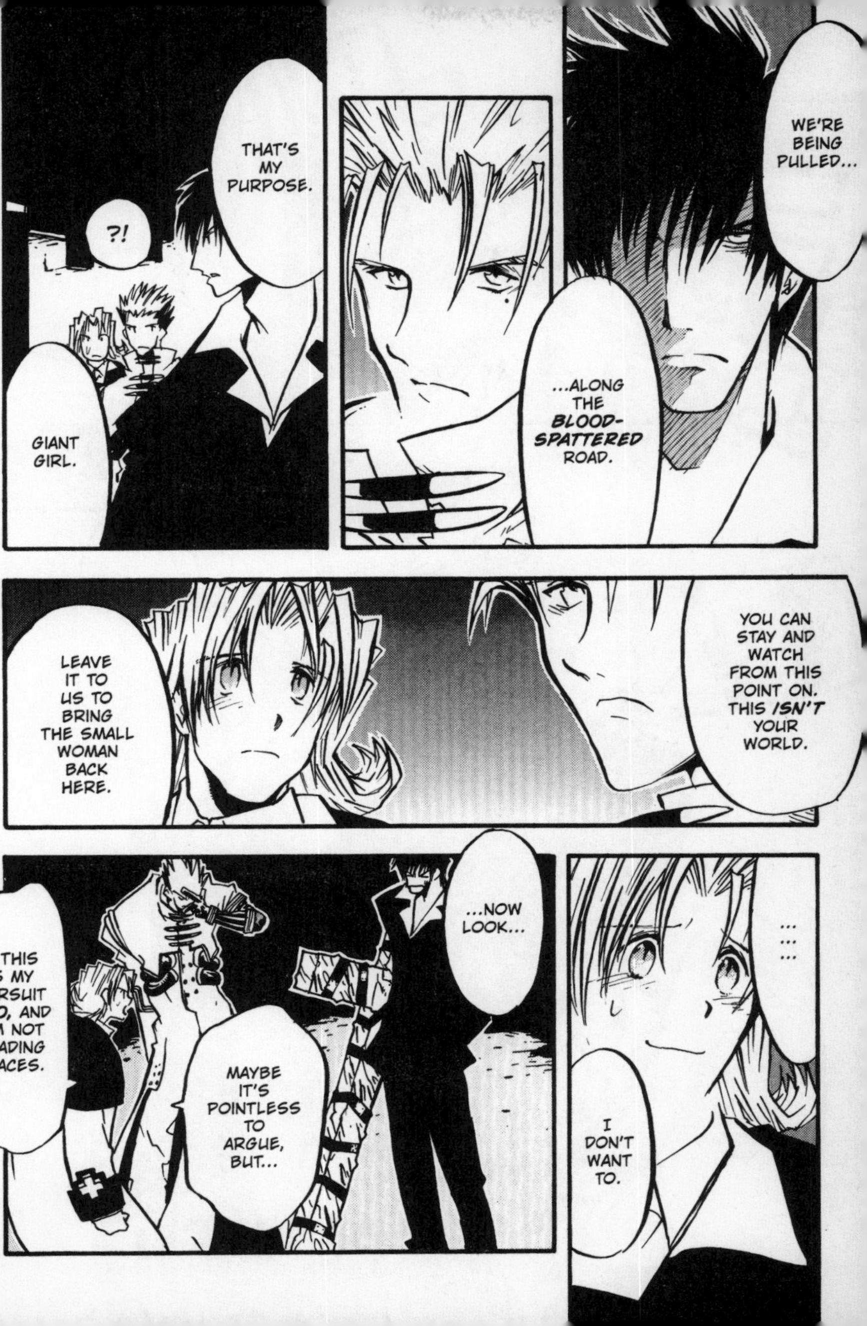
WE'RE BEING PULLED...
...ALONG THE *BLOOD-SPATTERED* ROAD.
THAT'S MY PURPOSE.
?!
GIANT GIRL.
YOU CAN STAY AND WATCH FROM THIS POINT ON. THIS *ISN'T* YOUR WORLD.
LEAVE IT TO US TO BRING THE SMALL WOMAN BACK HERE.
....
I DON'T WANT TO.
...NOW LOOK...
MAYBE IT'S POINTLESS TO ARGUE, BUT...
...THIS IS MY PURSUIT *TOO*, AND I'M NOT TRADING PLACES.

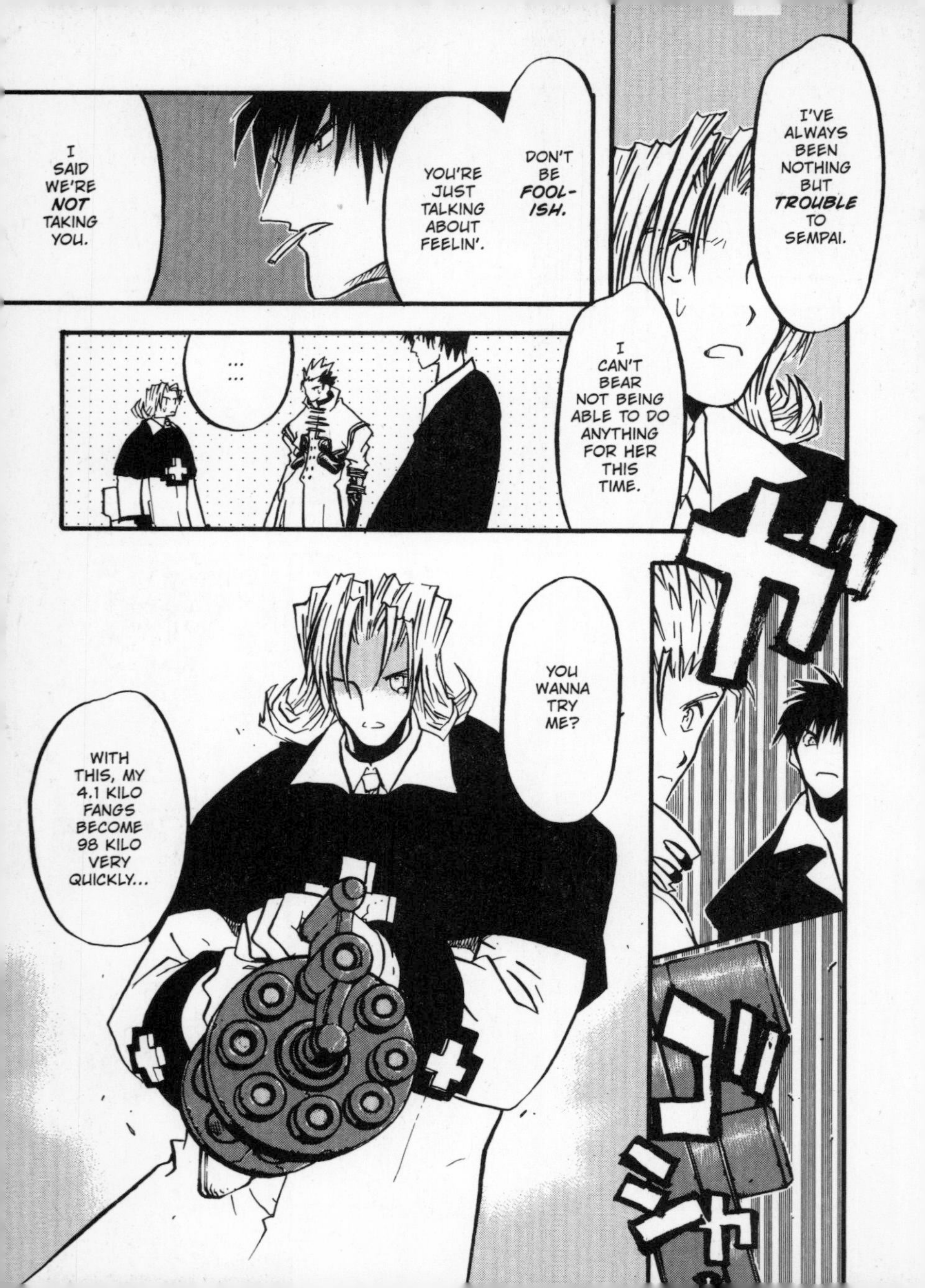
I'VE ALWAYS BEEN NOTHING BUT TROUBLE TO SEMPAI.
I CAN'T BEAR NOT BEING ABLE TO DO ANYTHING FOR HER THIS TIME.
DON'T BE FOOL-ISH.
YOU'RE JUST TALKING ABOUT FEELIN'.
I SAID WE'RE NOT TAKING YOU.
......
YOU WANNA TRY ME?
WITH THIS, MY 4.1 KILO FANGS BECOME 98 KILO VERY QUICKLY...

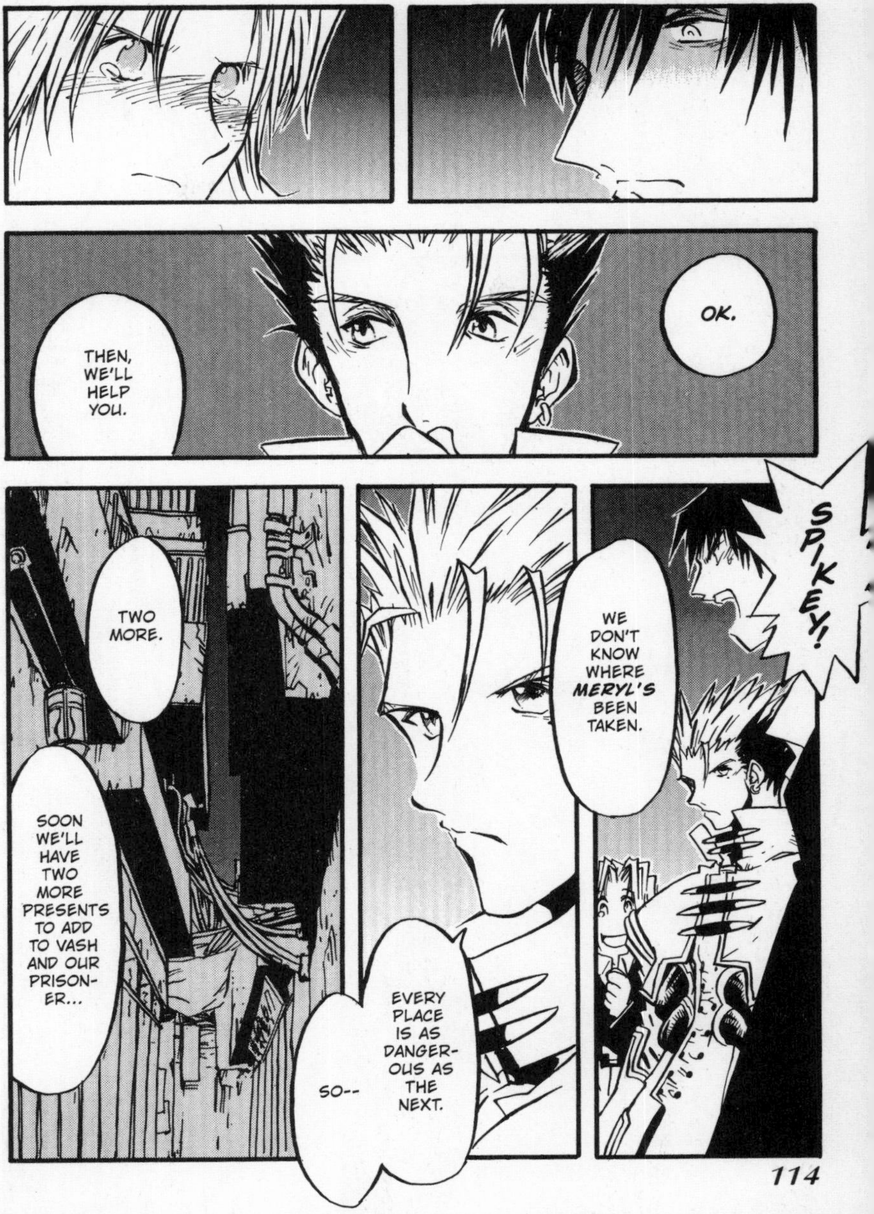
OK.
THEN, WE'LL HELP YOU.
SPIKEY!
WE DON'T KNOW WHERE ***MERYL'S*** BEEN TAKEN.
EVERY PLACE IS AS DANGER-OUS AS THE NEXT.
SO--
TWO MORE.
SOON WE'LL HAVE TWO MORE PRESENTS TO ADD TO VASH AND OUR PRISON-ER...

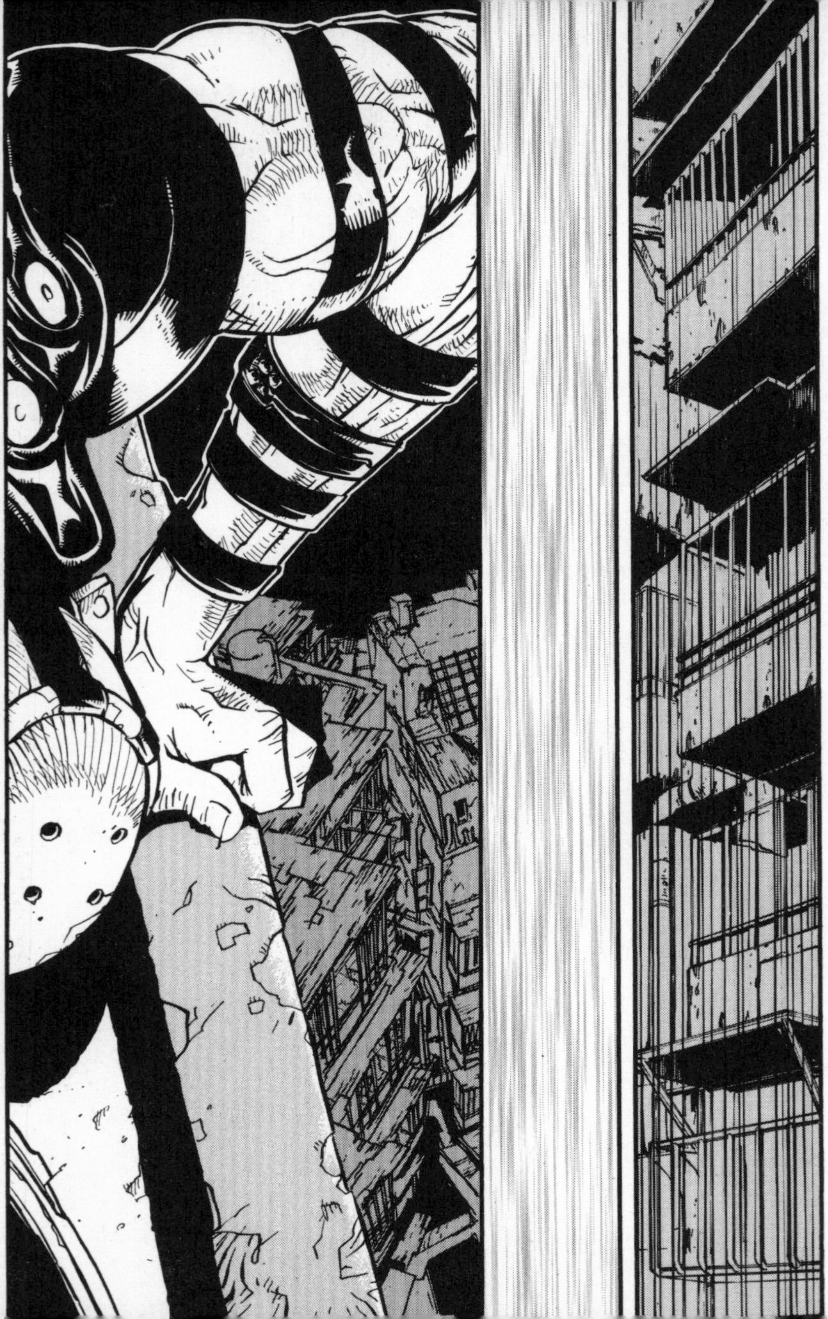

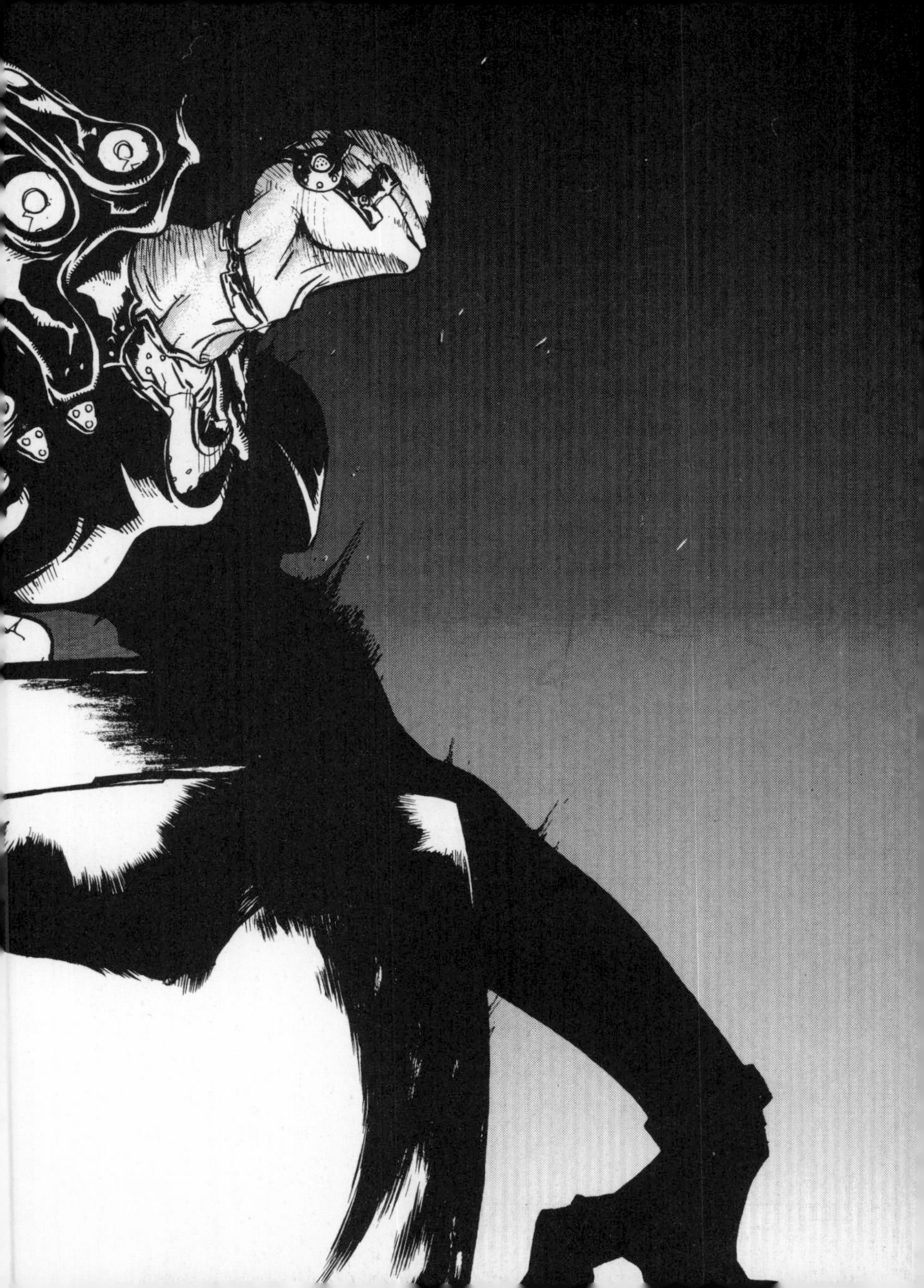

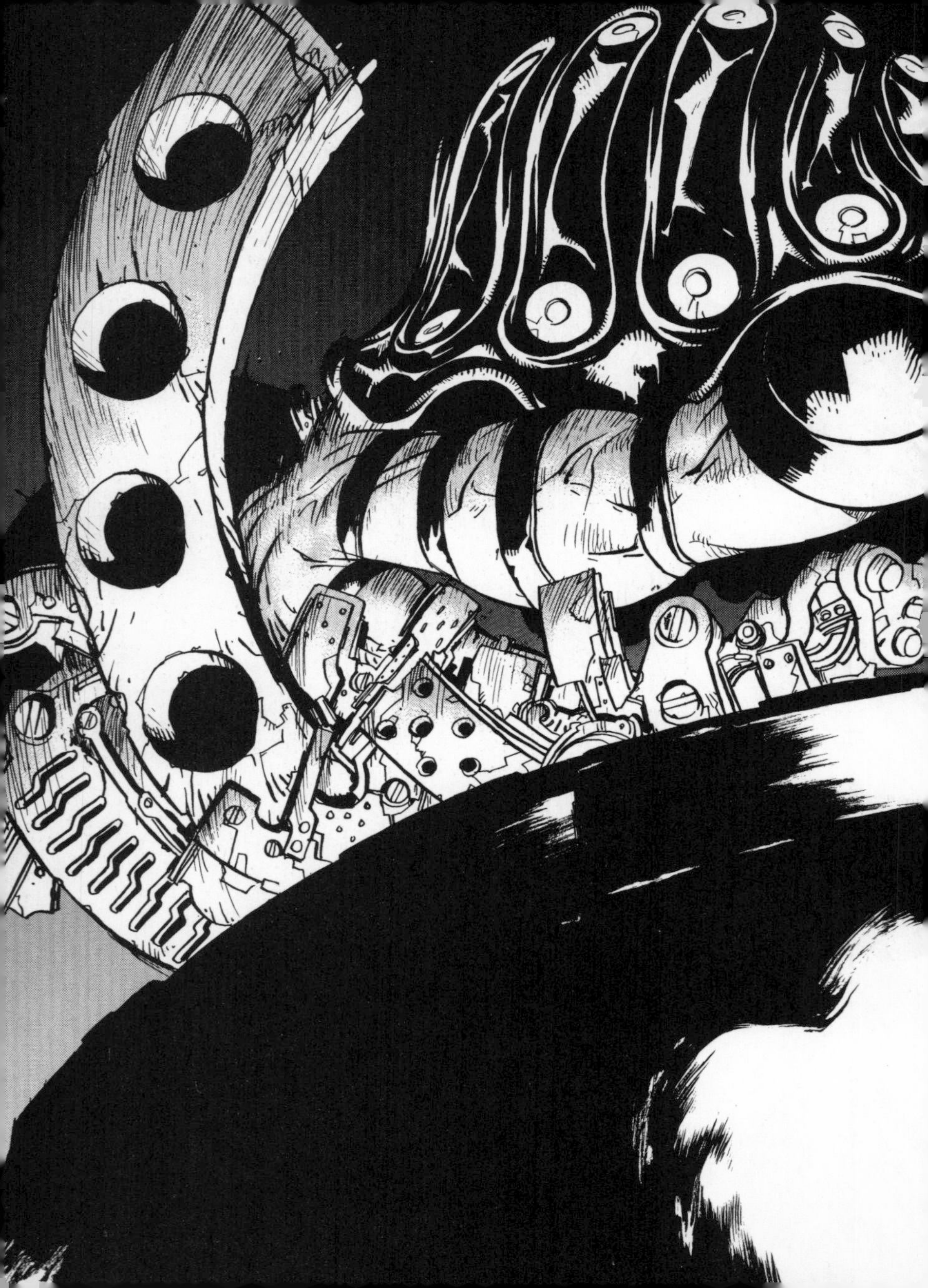

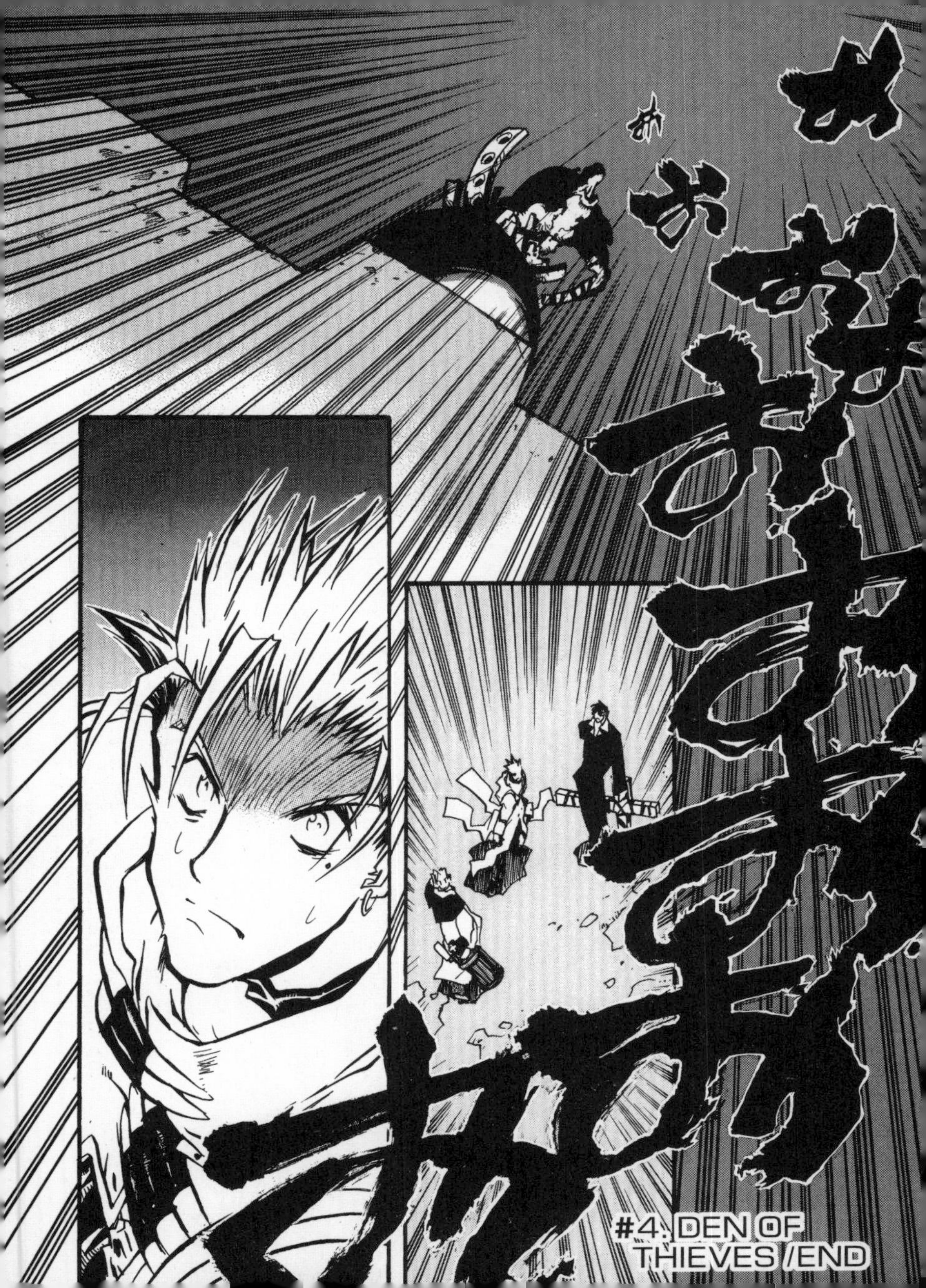
#4. DEN OF THIEVES /END

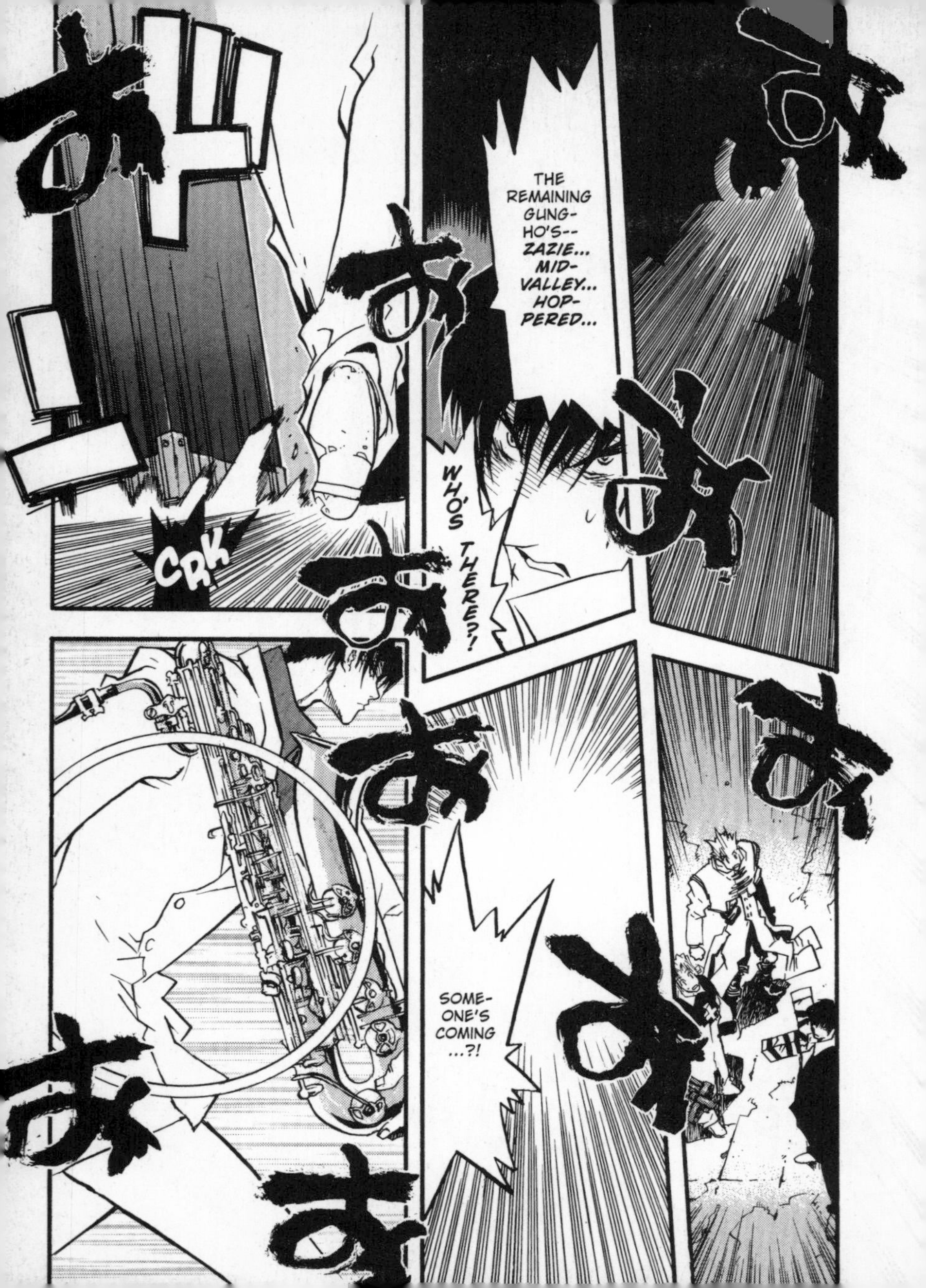
THE REMAINING GUNG-HO'S-- ZAZIE... MID-VALLEY... HOP-PERED...
WHO'S THERE?!
CRK
SOME-ONE'S COMING ...?!

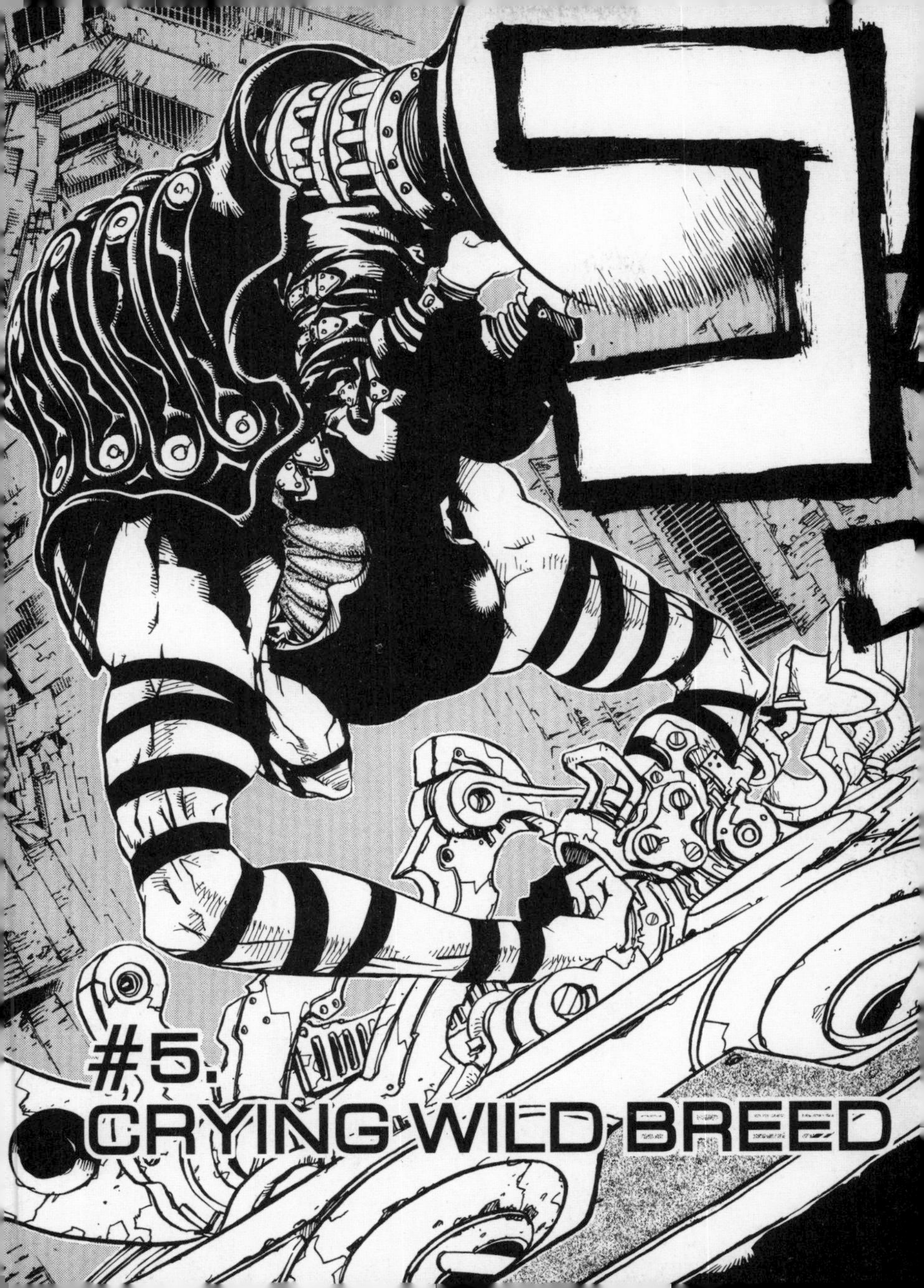
#5.
CRYING WILD BREED

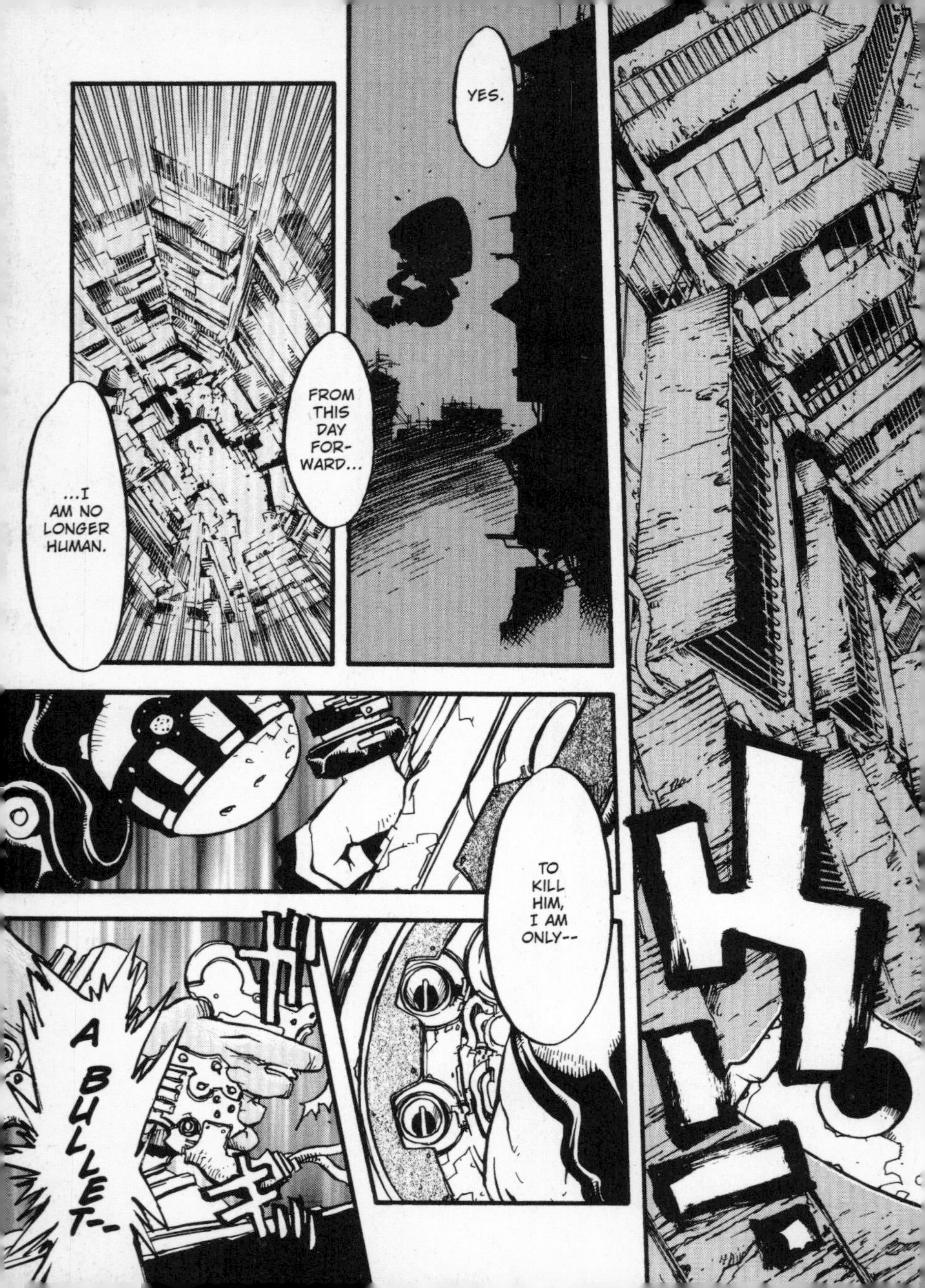
YES.
FROM THIS DAY FORWARD...
...I AM NO LONGER HUMAN.
TO KILL HIM, I AM ONLY--
A BULLET--

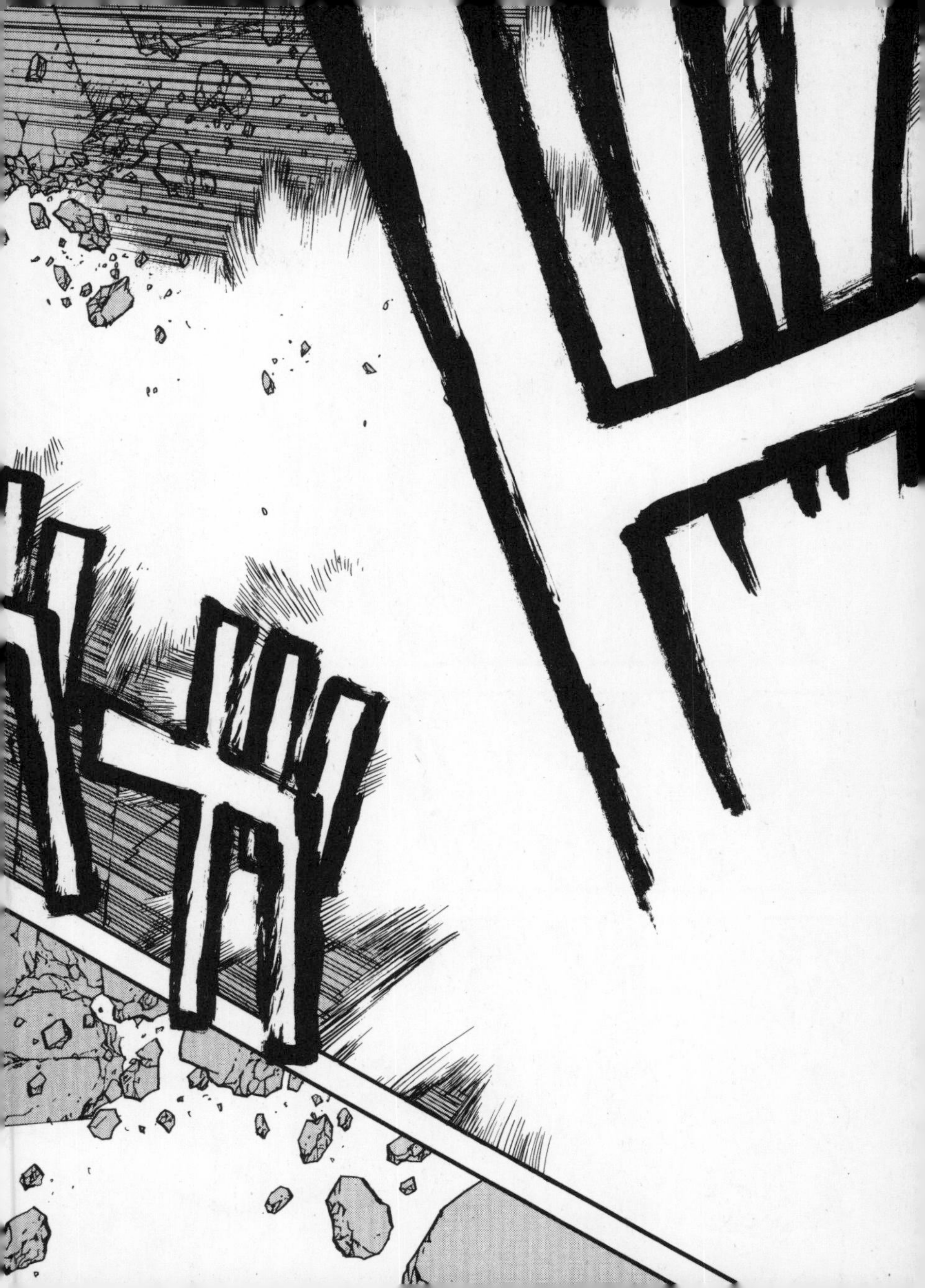

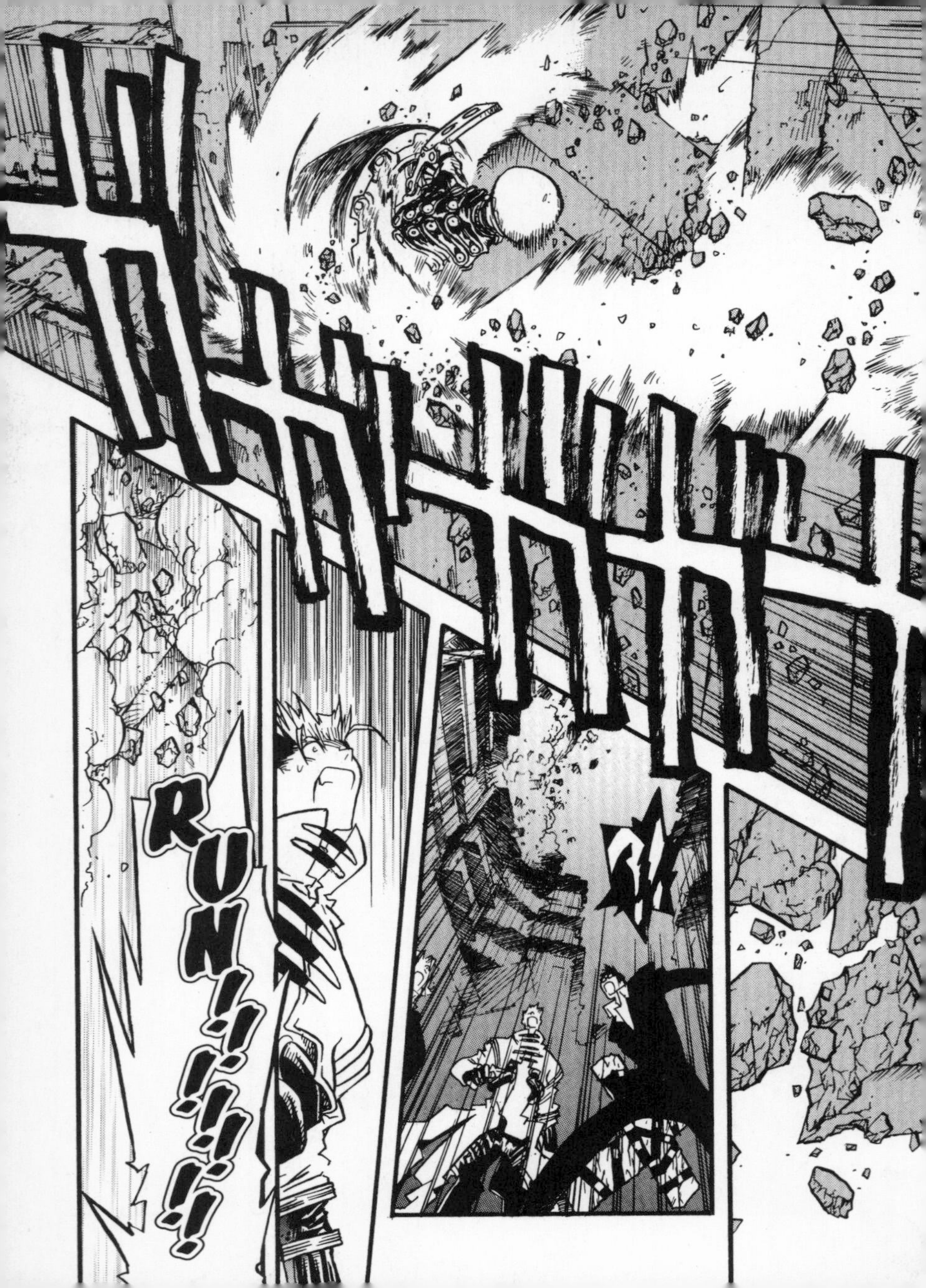
RUN!!!!!!!

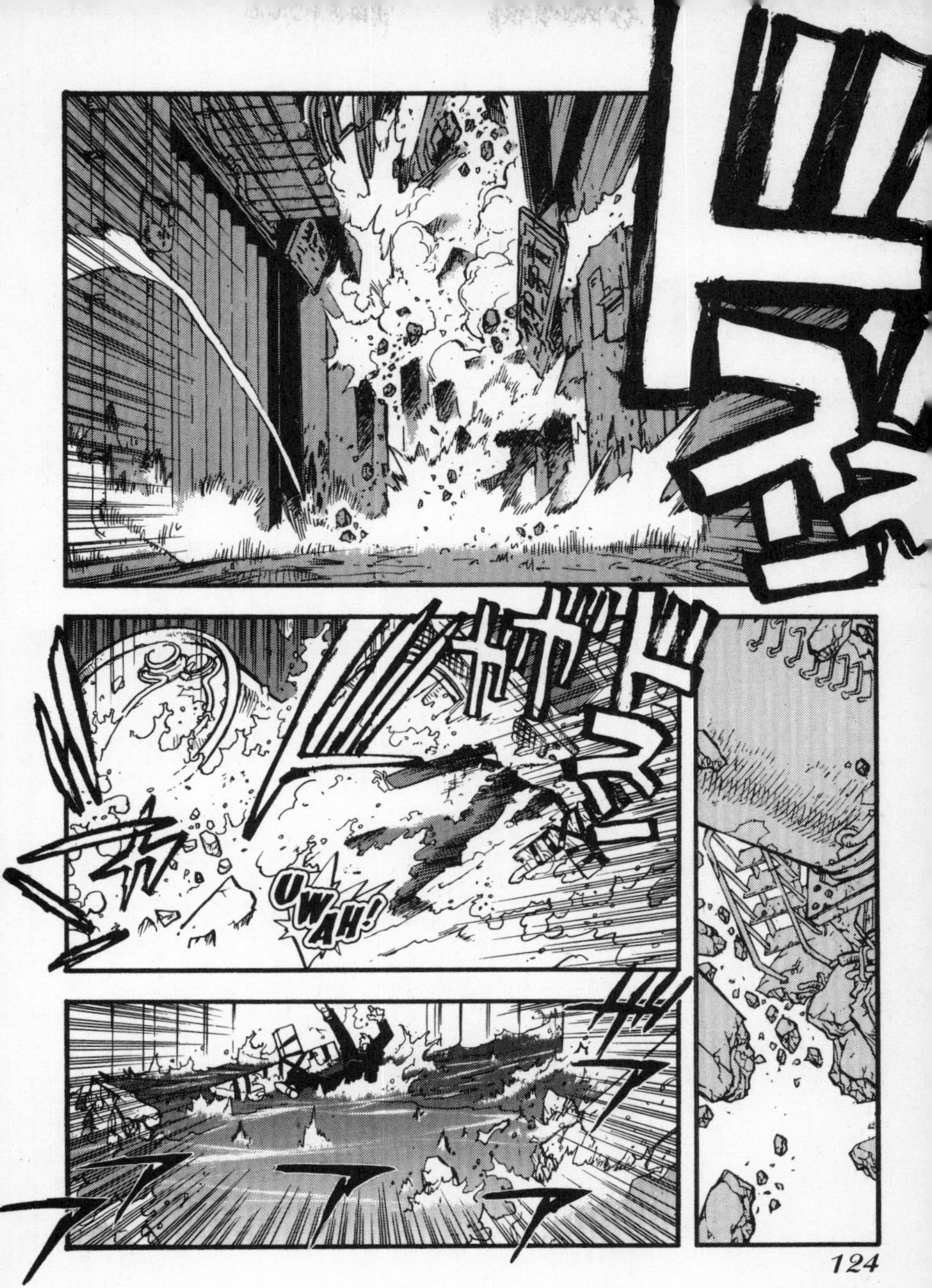
UWAH!

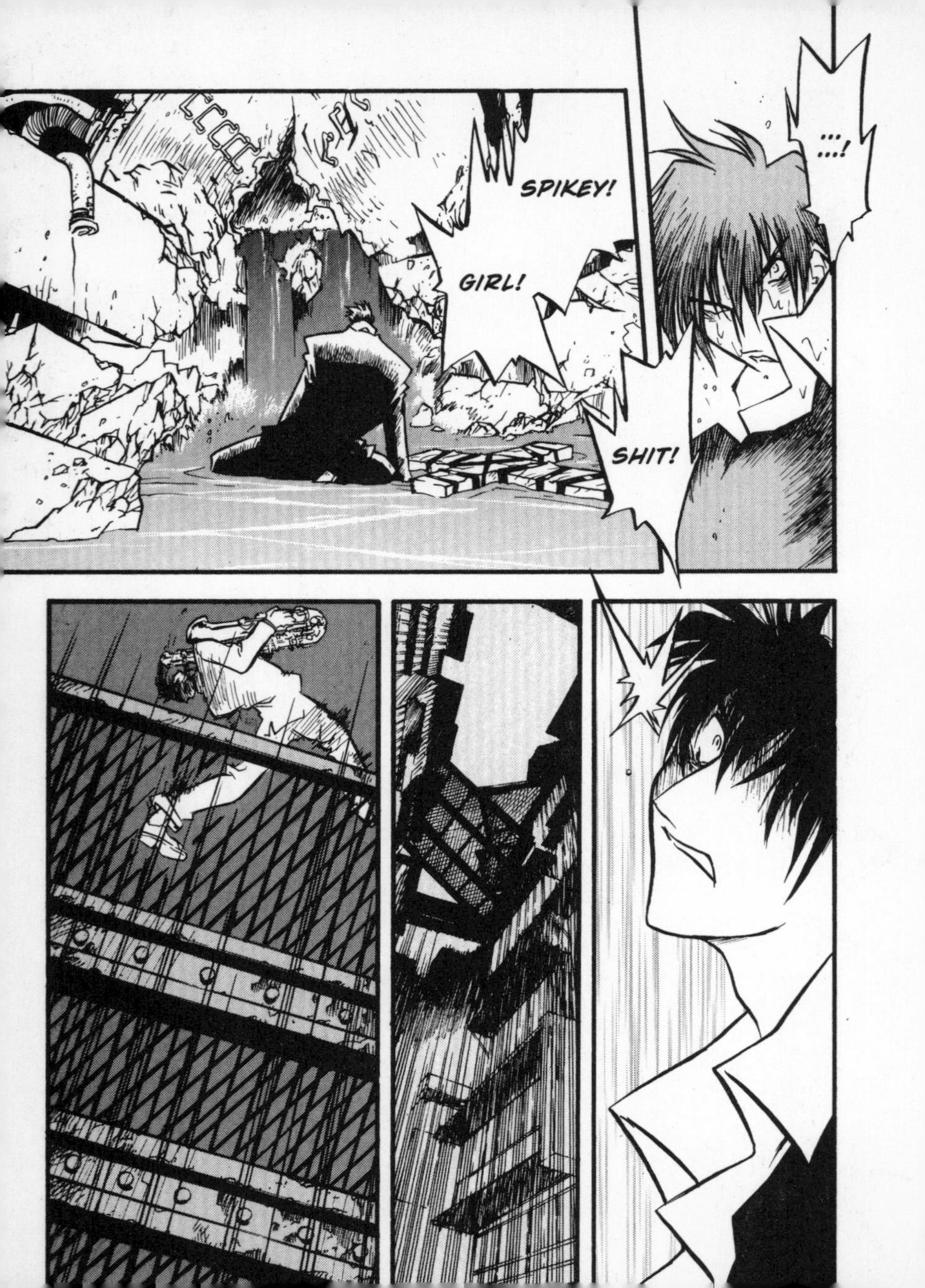
...
...!
SPIKEY!
GIRL!
SHIT!

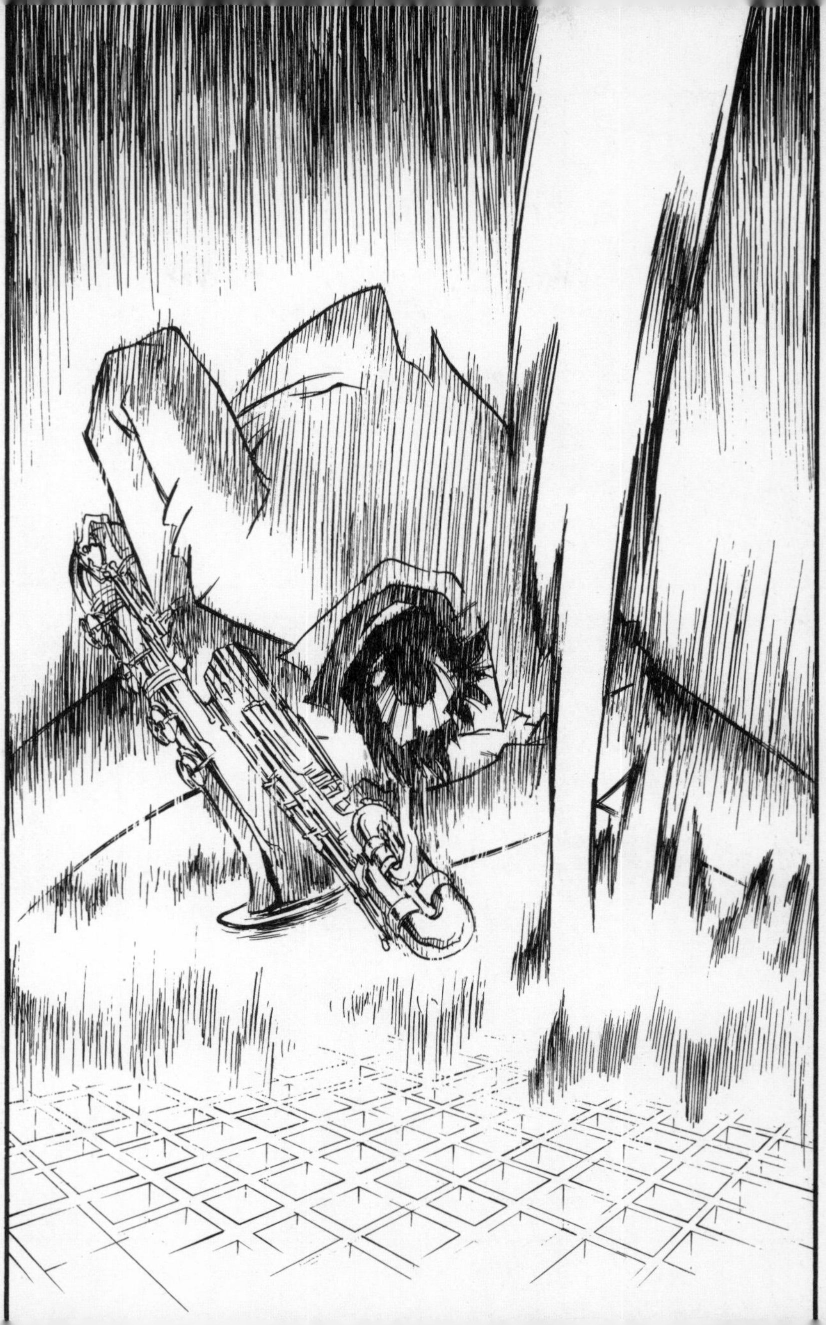

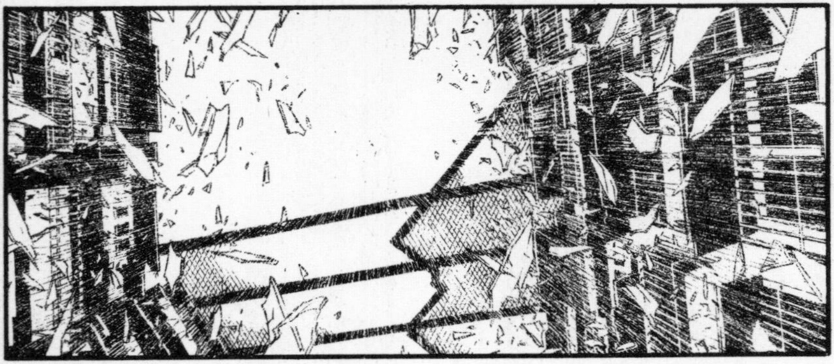
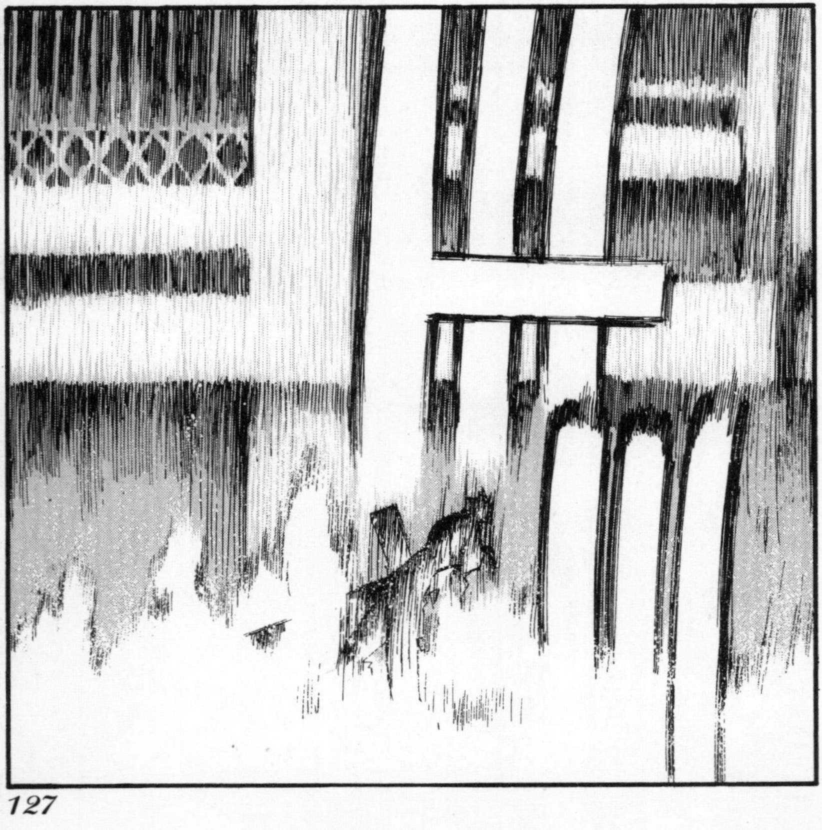

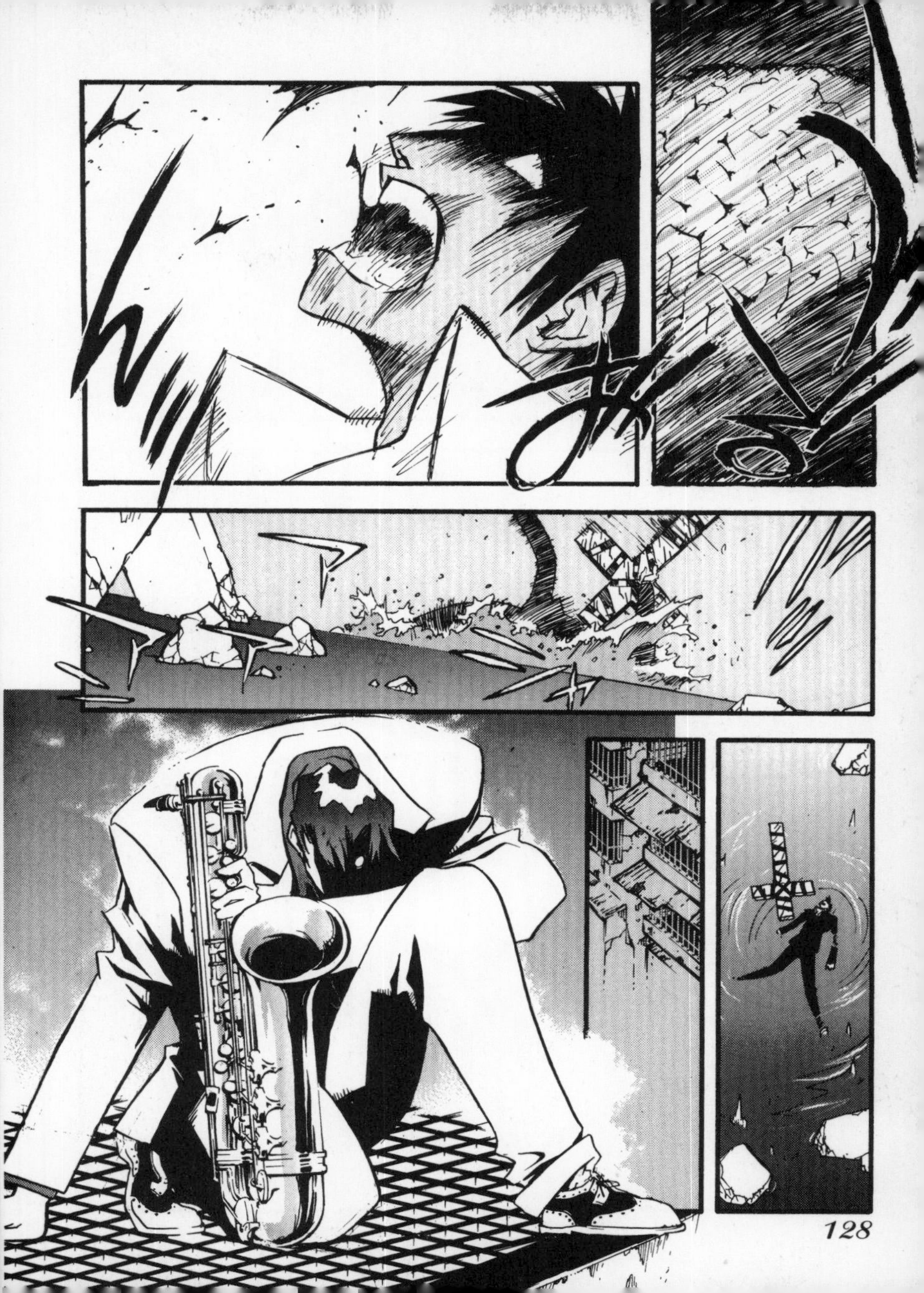

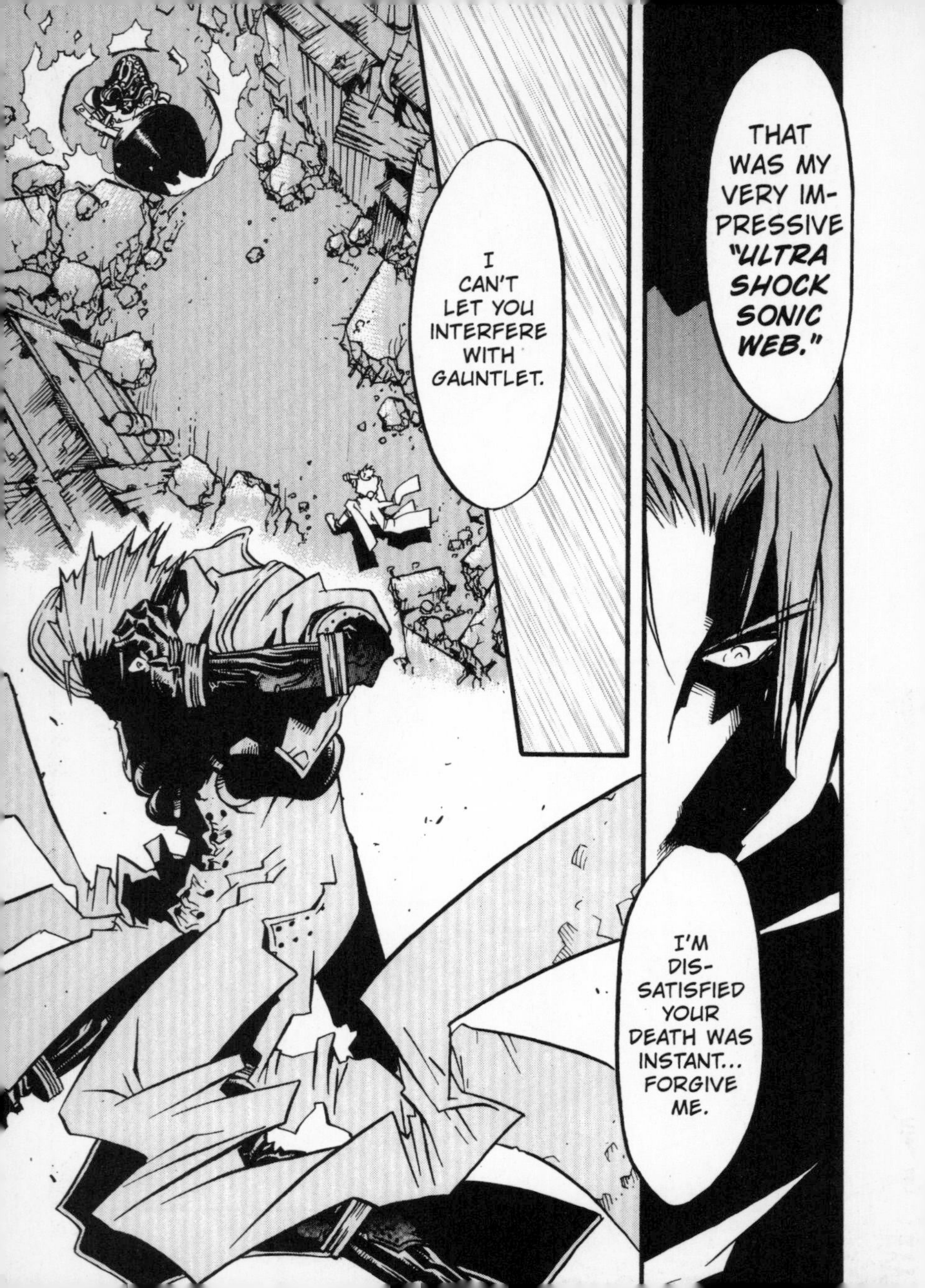
THAT WAS MY VERY IM-PRESSIVE "ULTRA SHOCK SONIC WEB."
I'M DIS-SATISFIED YOUR DEATH WAS INSTANT... FORGIVE ME.
I CAN'T LET YOU INTERFERE WITH GAUNTLET.

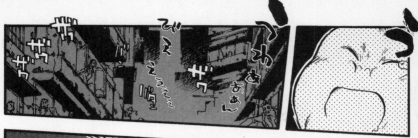

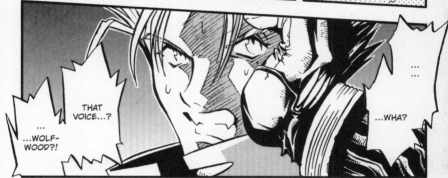

THAT VOICE...?

...

...WOLF-WOOD?!

...
...

...WHA?

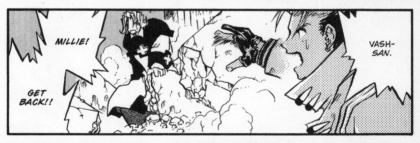

MILLIE!

GET BACK!!

VASH-SAN.

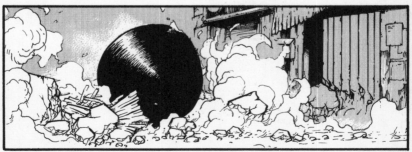

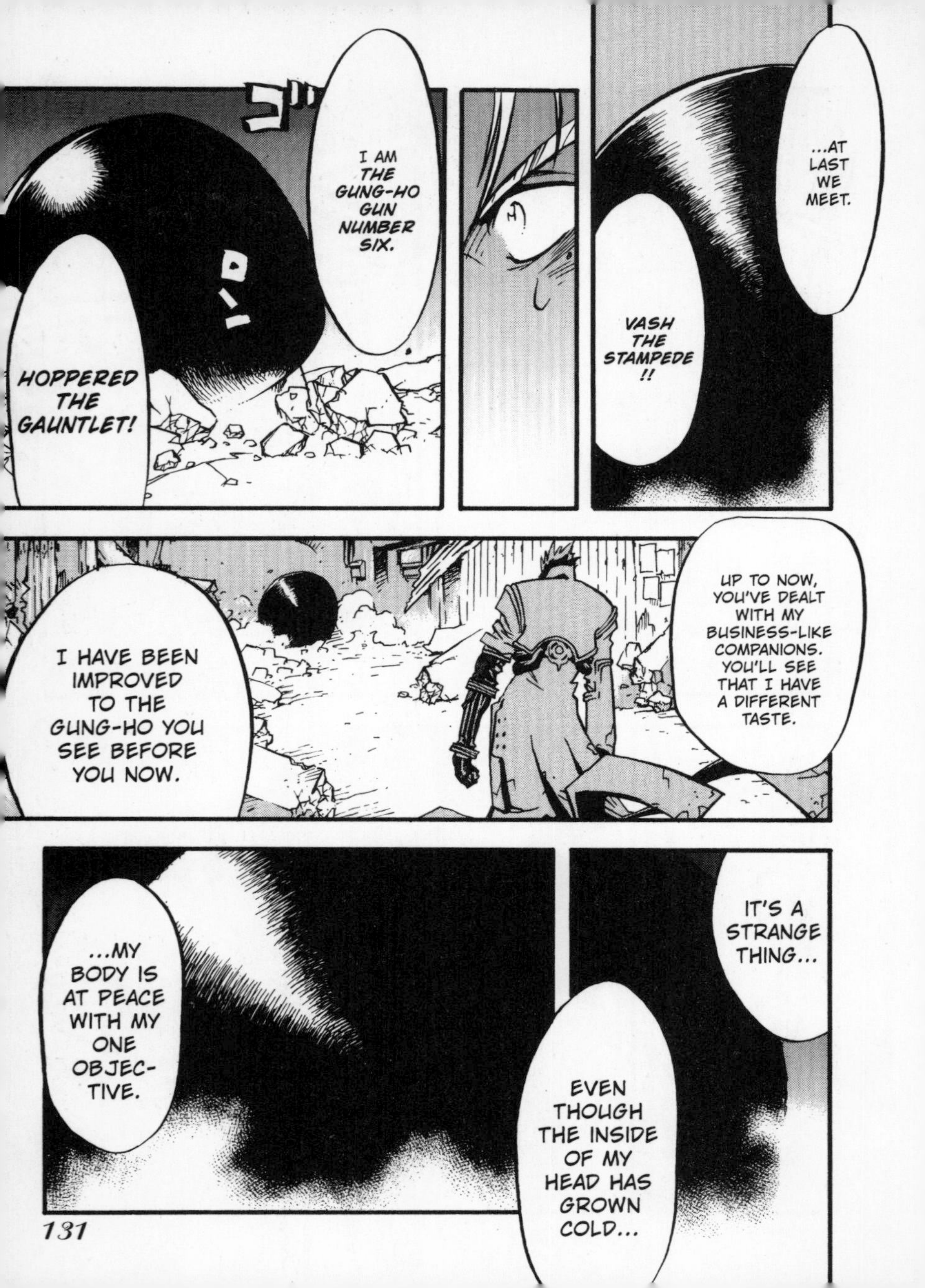
...AT LAST WE MEET.
VASH THE STAMPEDE !!
I AM THE GUNG-HO GUN NUMBER SIX.
HOPPERED THE GAUNTLET!
UP TO NOW, YOU'VE DEALT WITH MY BUSINESS-LIKE COMPANIONS. YOU'LL SEE THAT I HAVE A DIFFERENT TASTE.
I HAVE BEEN IMPROVED TO THE GUNG-HO YOU SEE BEFORE YOU NOW.
IT'S A STRANGE THING...
EVEN THOUGH THE INSIDE OF MY HEAD HAS GROWN COLD...
...MY BODY IS AT PEACE WITH MY ONE OBJEC-TIVE.

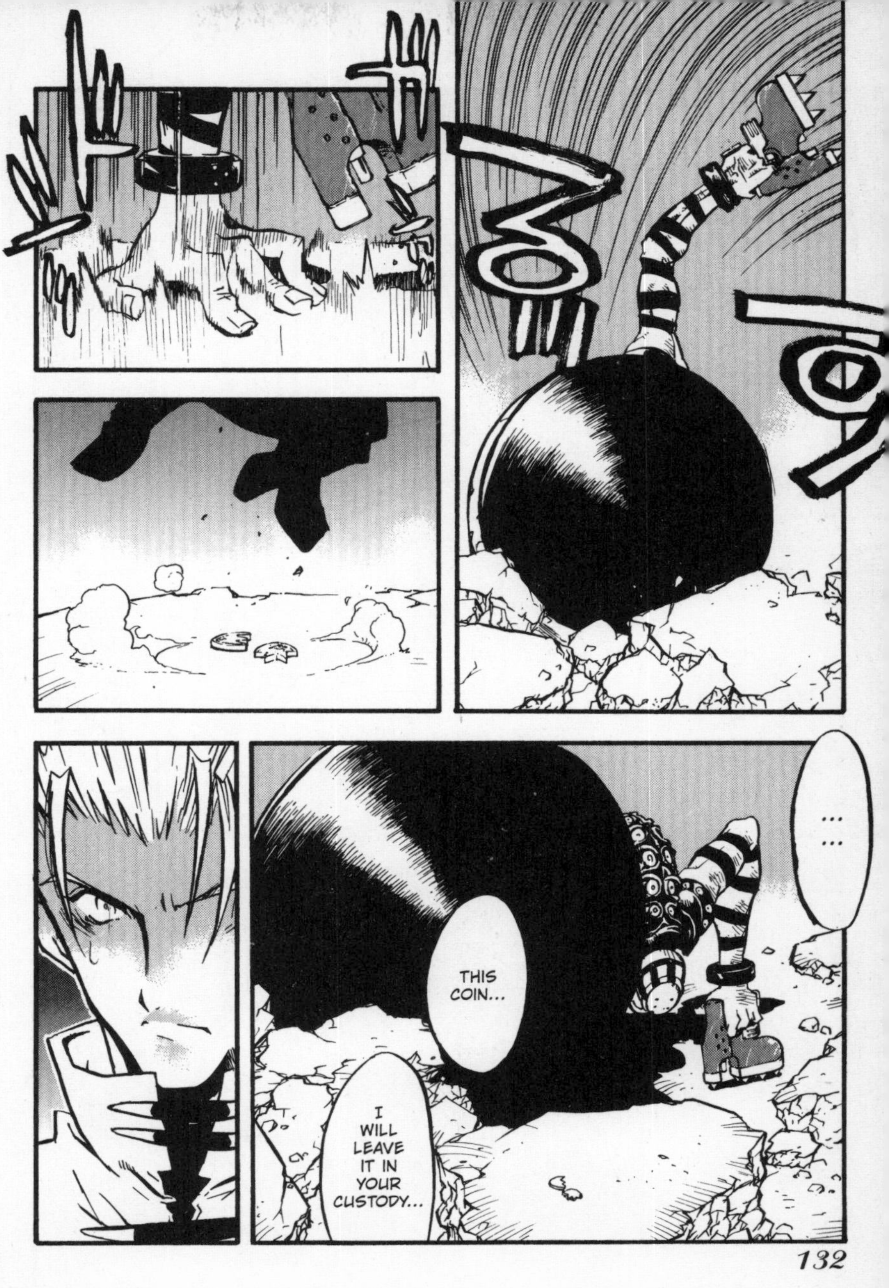
……
THIS COIN…
I WILL LEAVE IT IN YOUR CUSTODY…

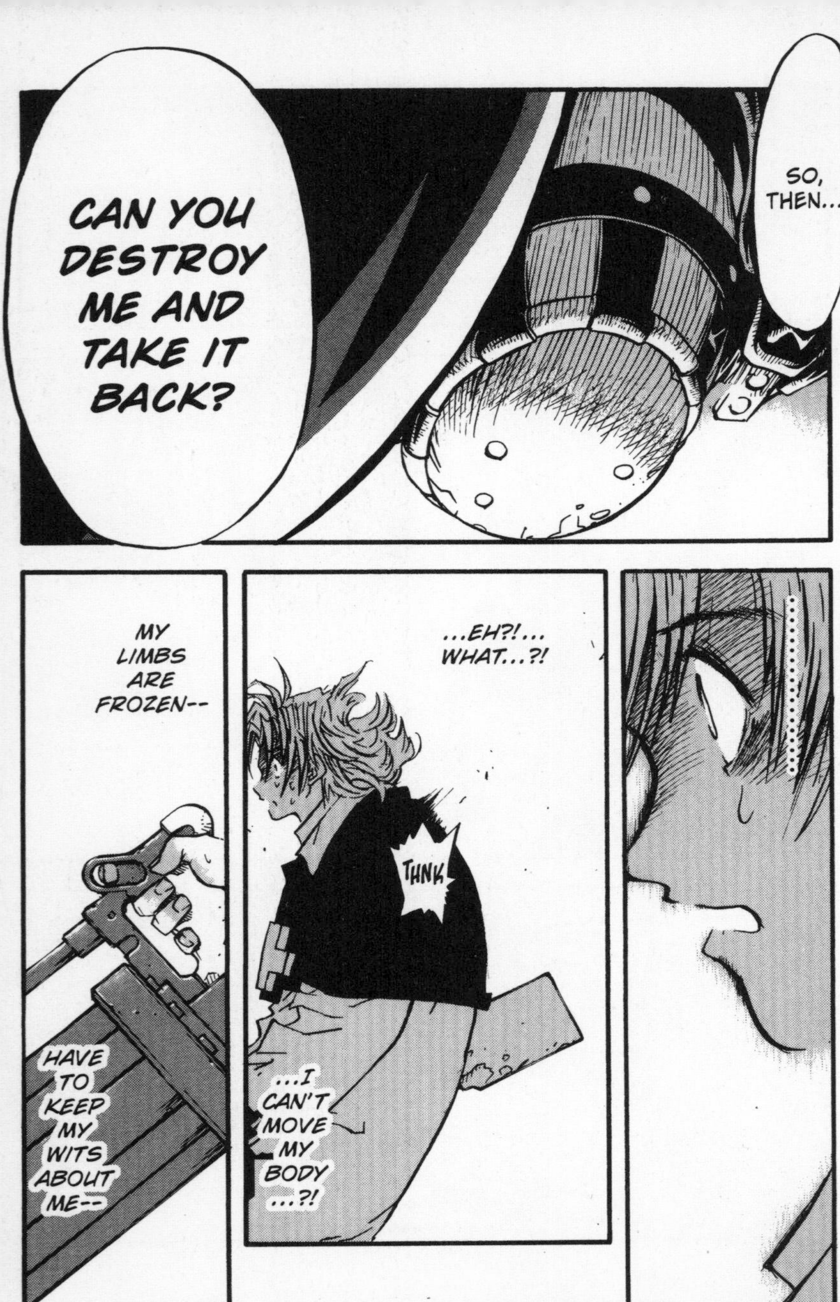
SO, THEN...
CAN YOU DESTROY ME AND TAKE IT BACK?
...EH?!... WHAT...?!
THNK
...I CAN'T MOVE MY BODY ...?!
MY LIMBS ARE FROZEN--
HAVE TO KEEP MY WITS ABOUT ME--

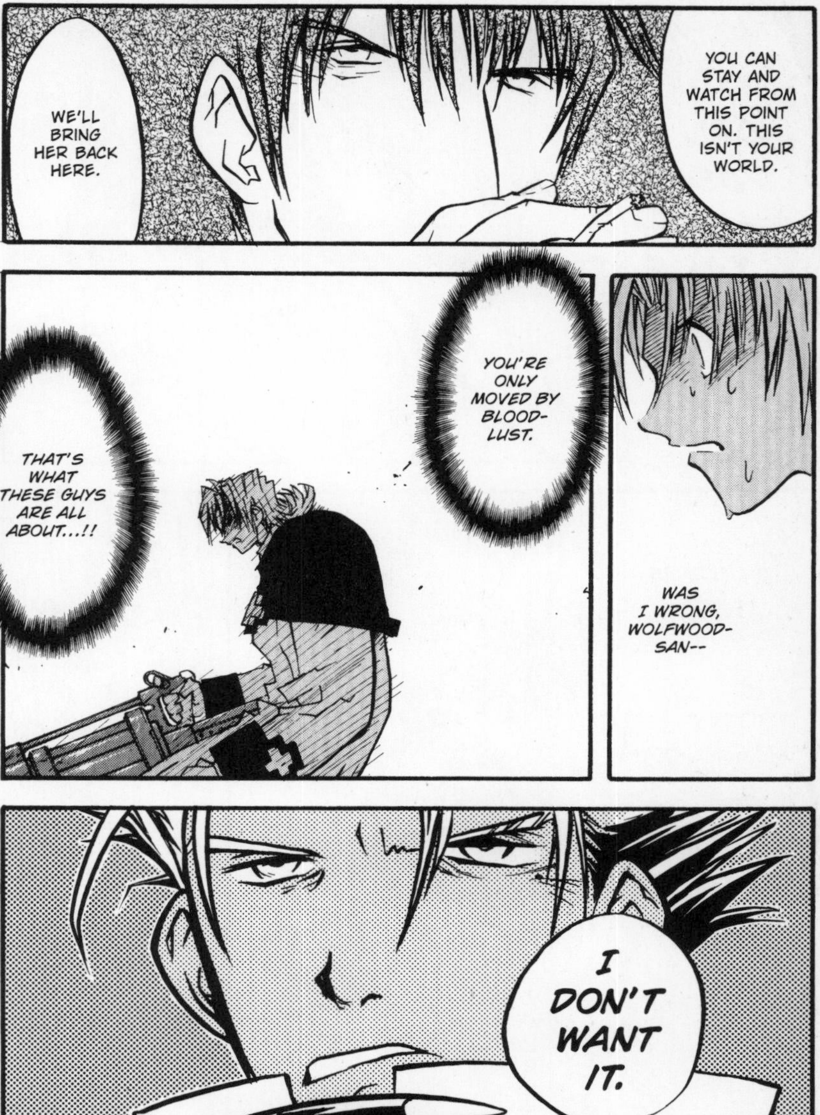
YOU CAN STAY AND WATCH FROM THIS POINT ON. THIS ISN'T YOUR WORLD.
WE'LL BRING HER BACK HERE.
WAS I WRONG, WOLFWOOD-SAN--
YOU'RE ONLY MOVED BY BLOOD-LUST.
THAT'S WHAT THESE GUYS ARE ALL ABOUT...!!
I DON'T WANT IT.

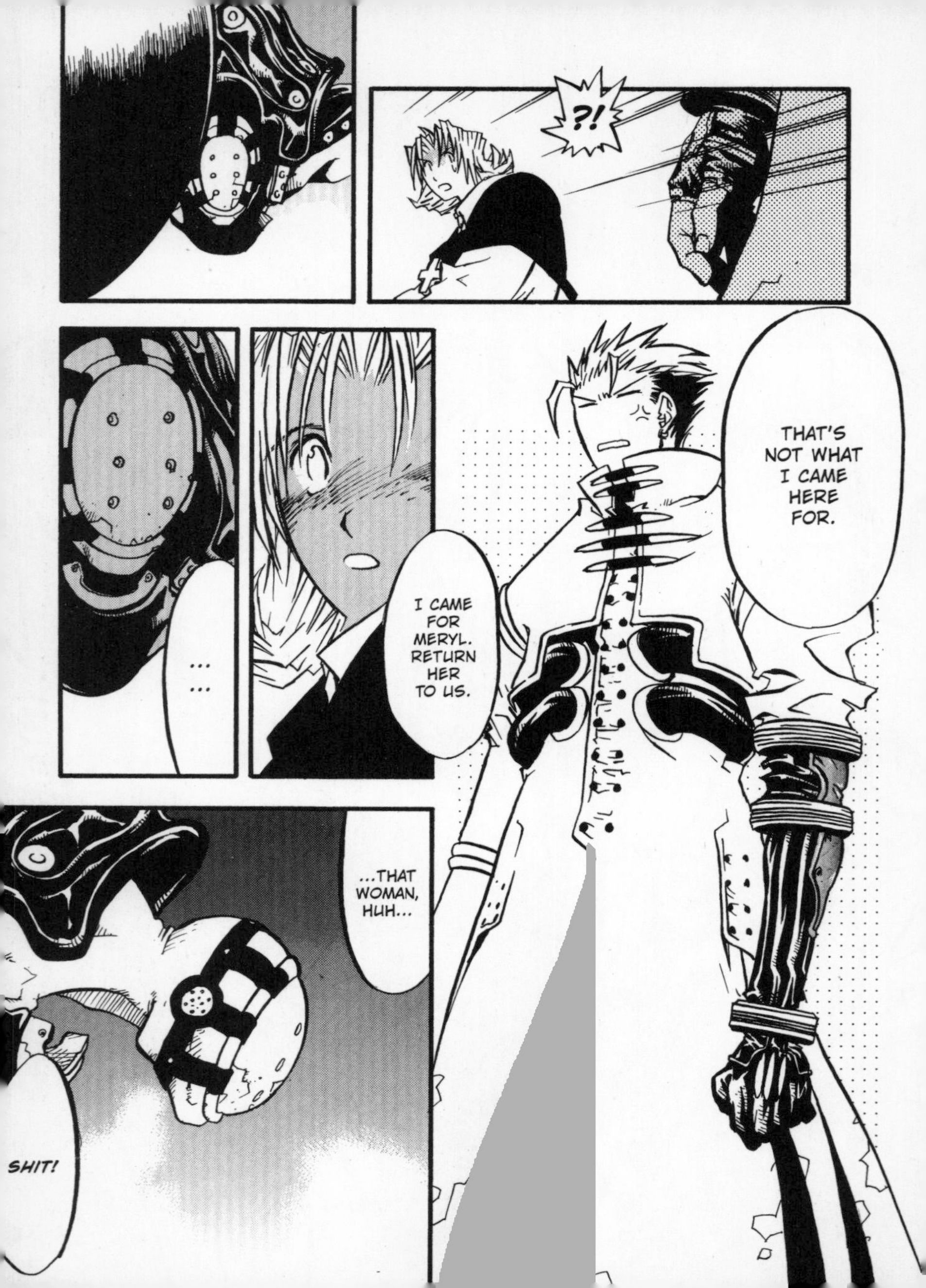
?!
THAT'S NOT WHAT I CAME HERE FOR.
I CAME FOR MERYL. RETURN HER TO US.
...
...
...THAT WOMAN, HUH...
SHIT!

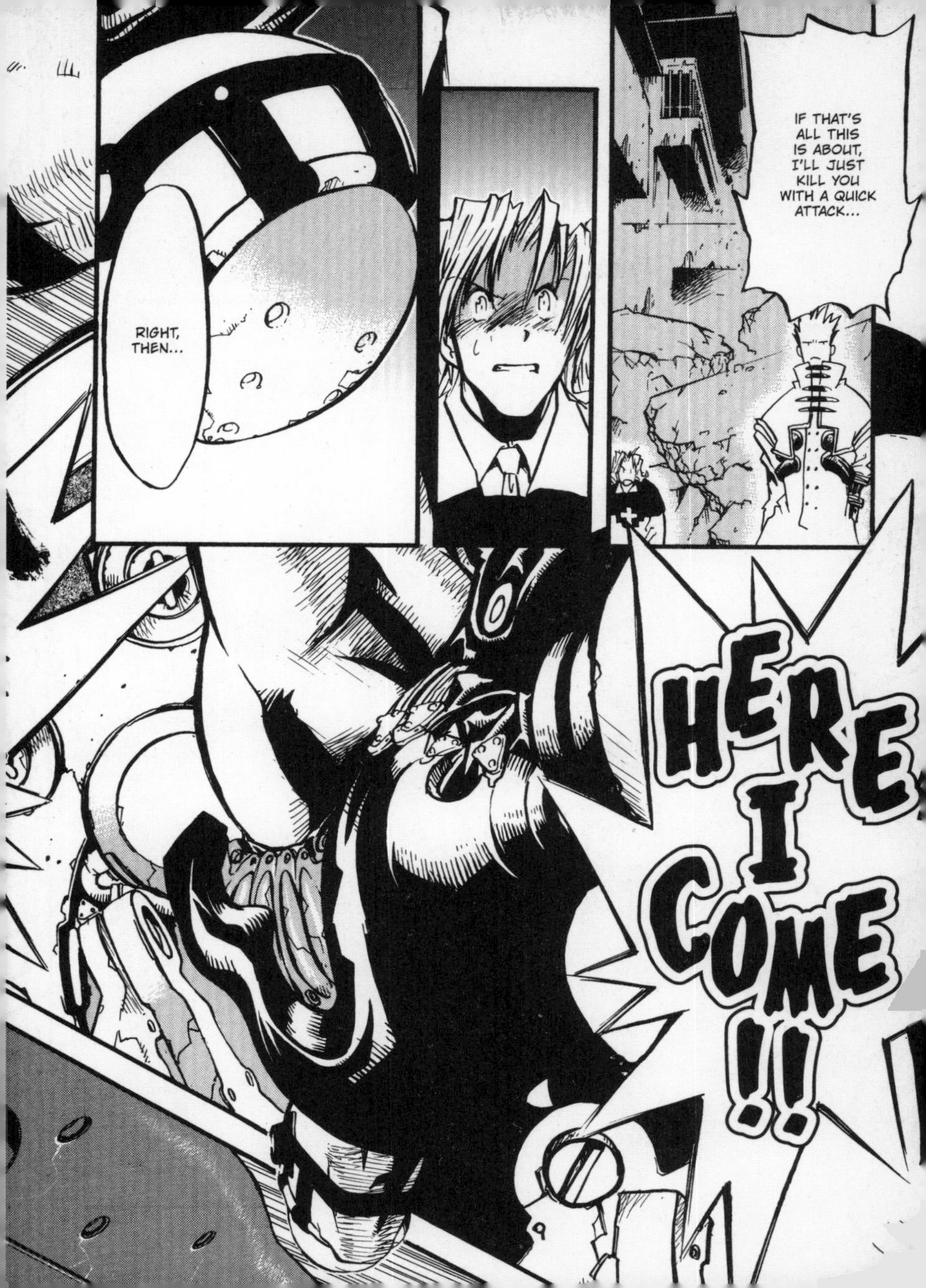
IF THAT'S ALL THIS IS ABOUT, I'LL JUST KILL YOU WITH A QUICK ATTACK...
RIGHT, THEN...
HERE I COME!!

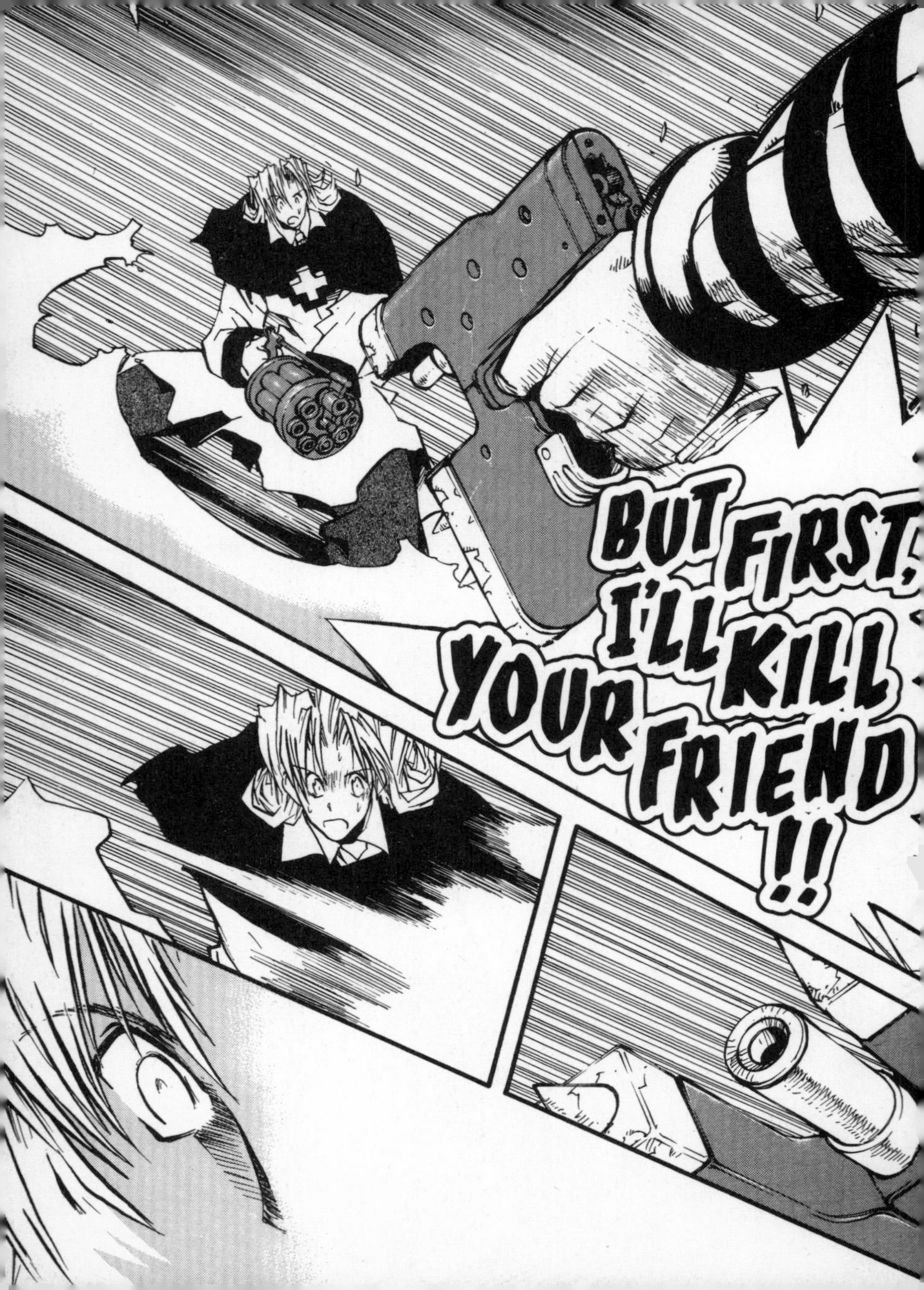
BUT FIRST, I'LL KILL YOUR FRIEND!!

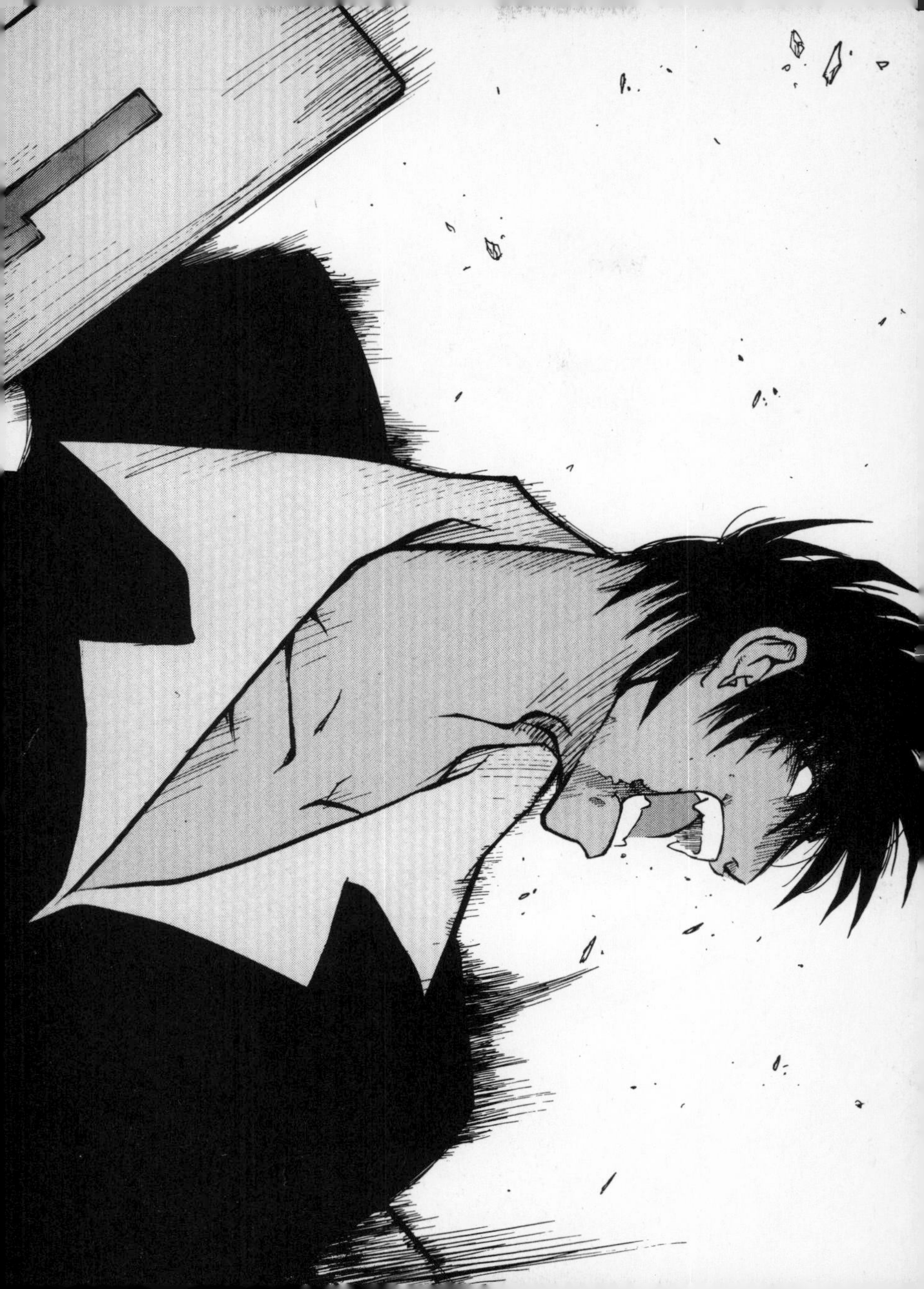

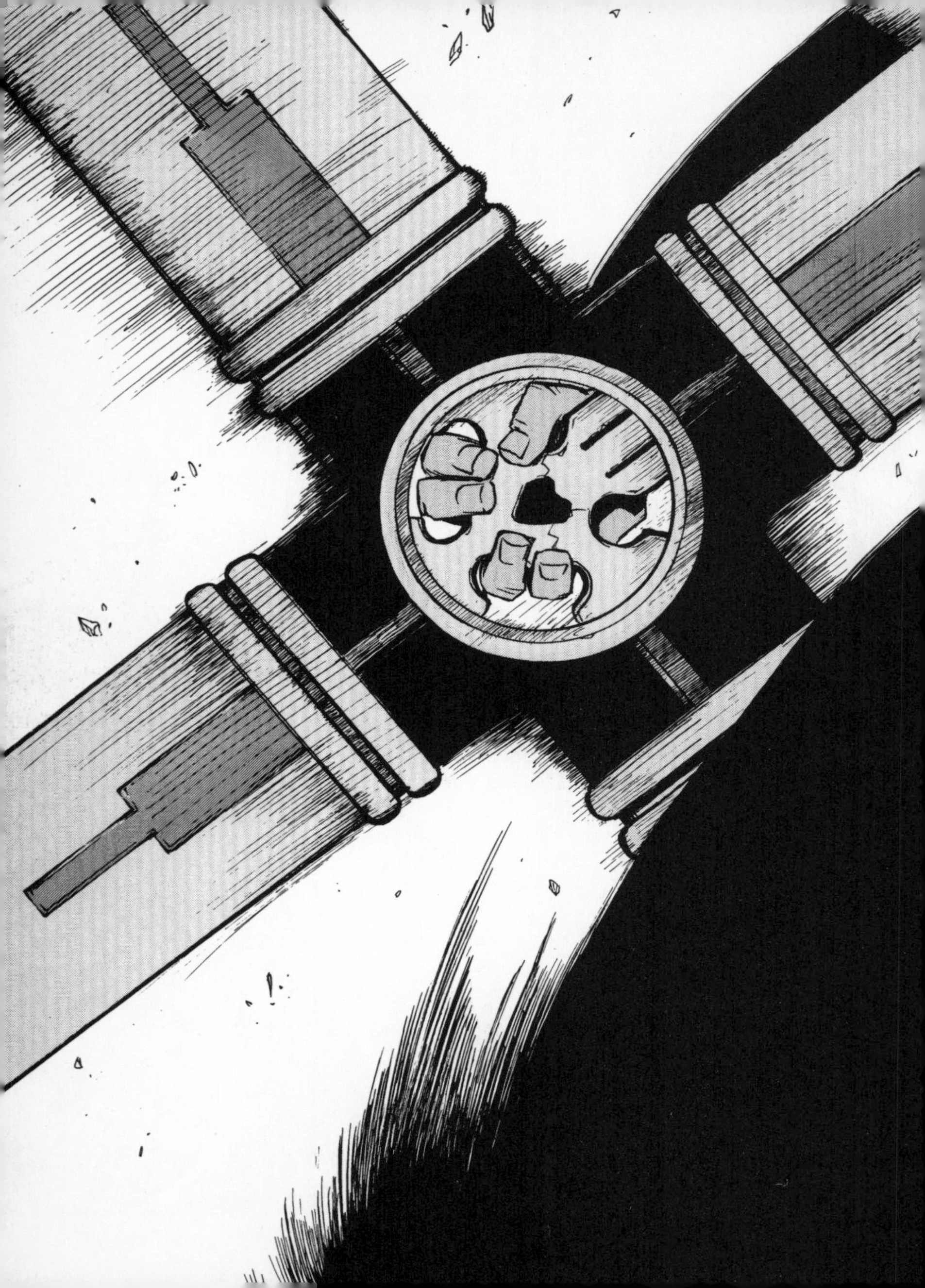

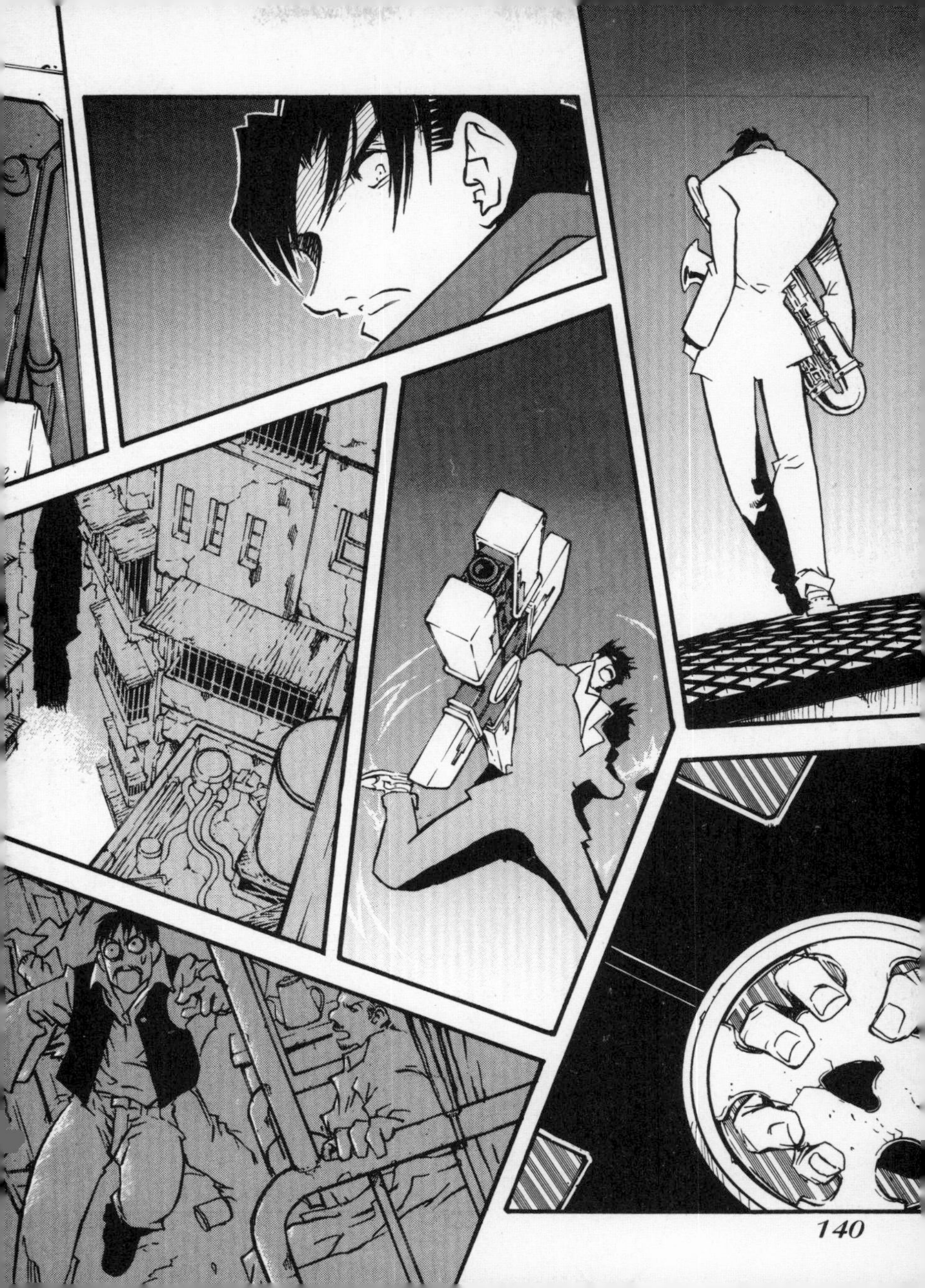

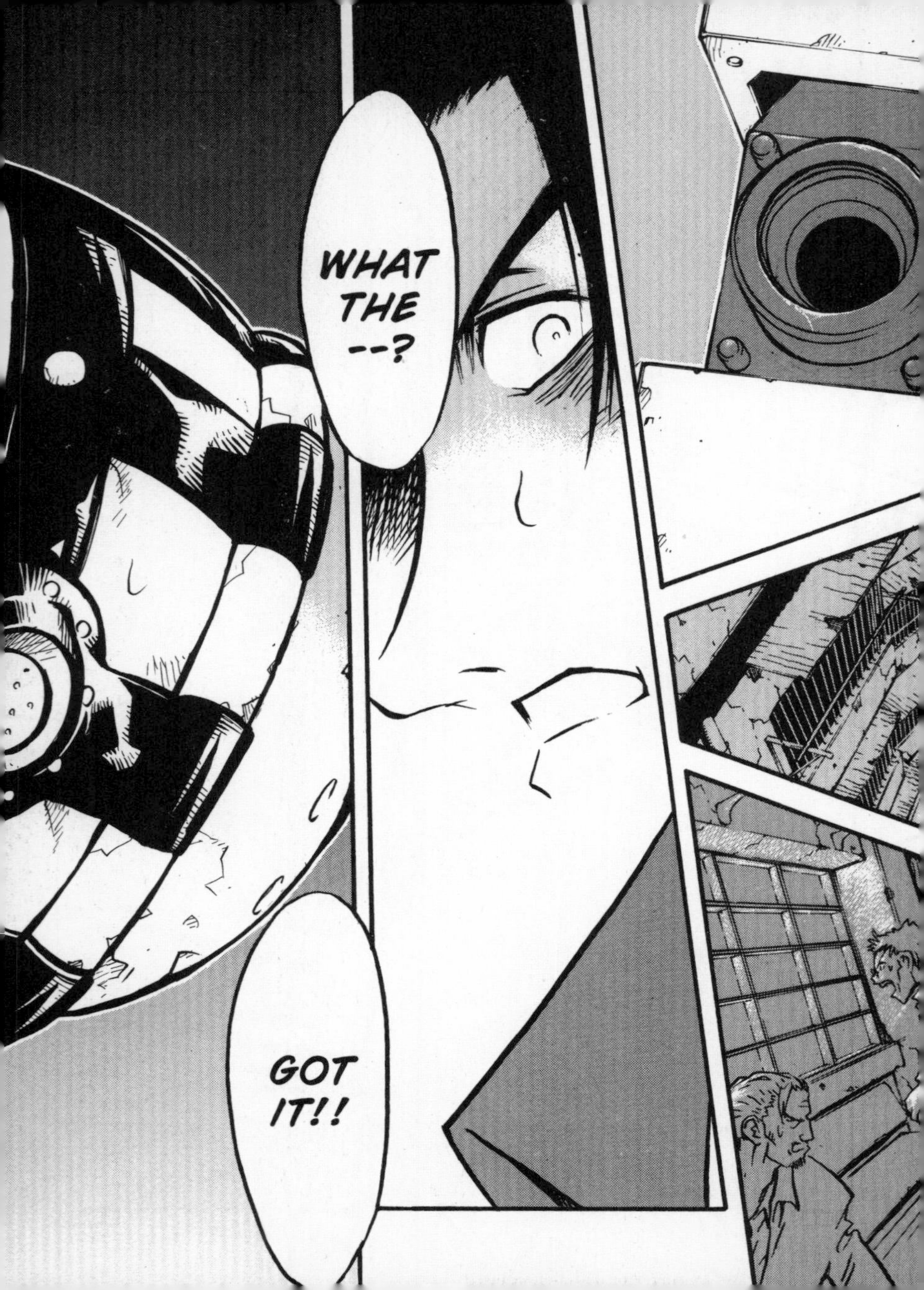
WHAT THE --?
GOT IT!!

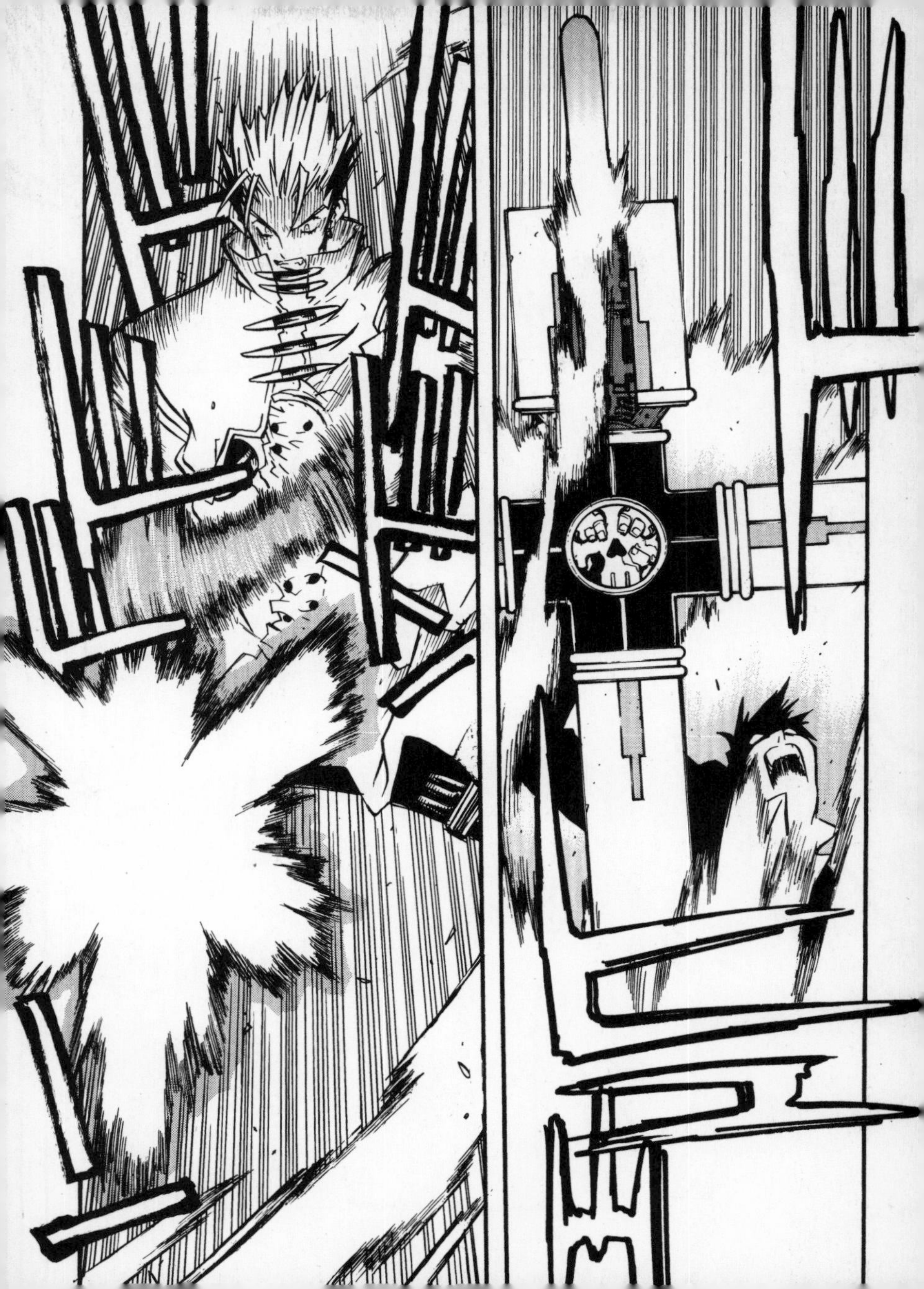

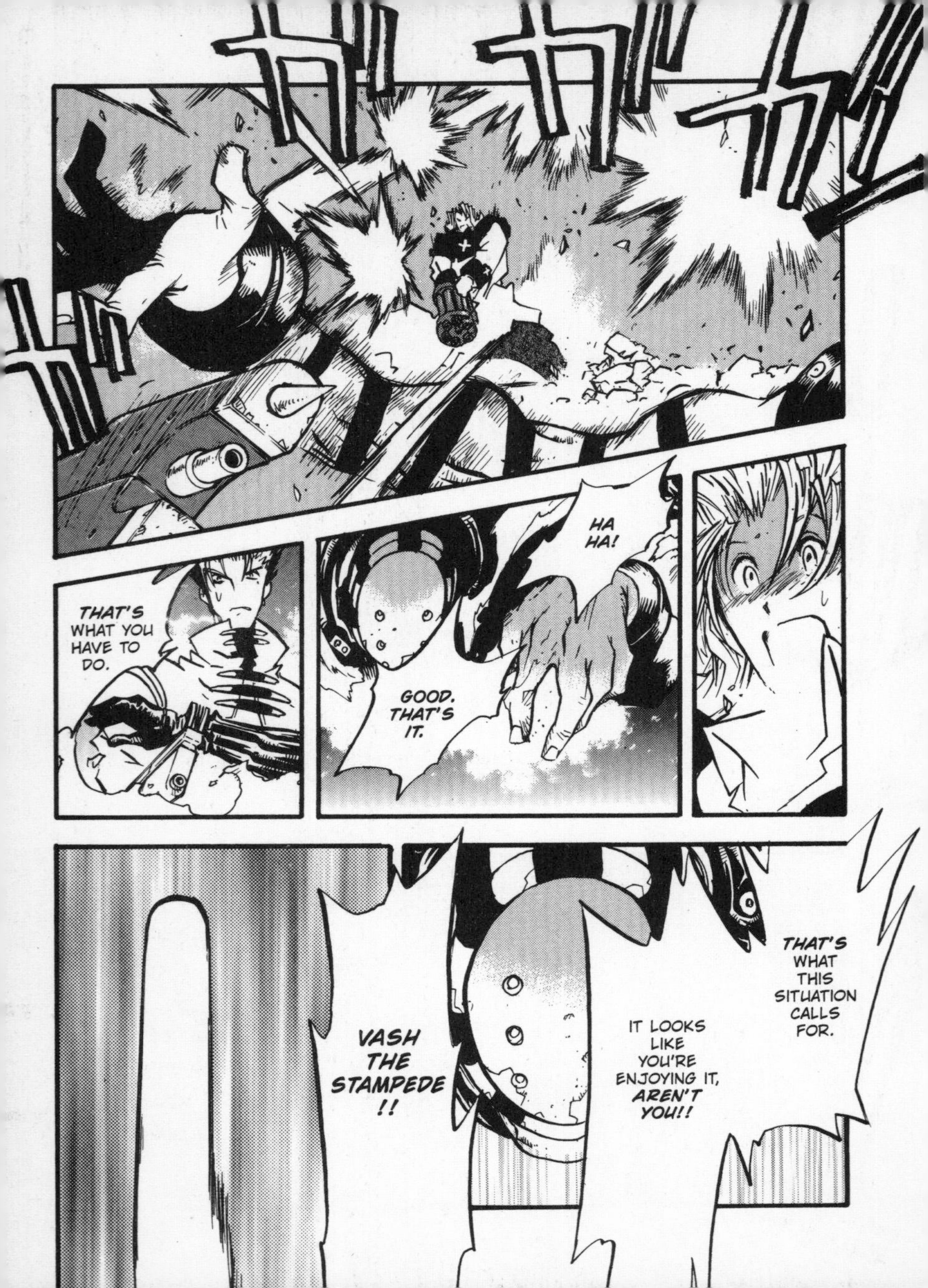
HA HA!
GOOD. THAT'S IT.
THAT'S WHAT YOU HAVE TO DO.
THAT'S WHAT THIS SITUATION CALLS FOR.
IT LOOKS LIKE YOU'RE ENJOYING IT, AREN'T YOU!!
VASH THE STAMPEDE !!

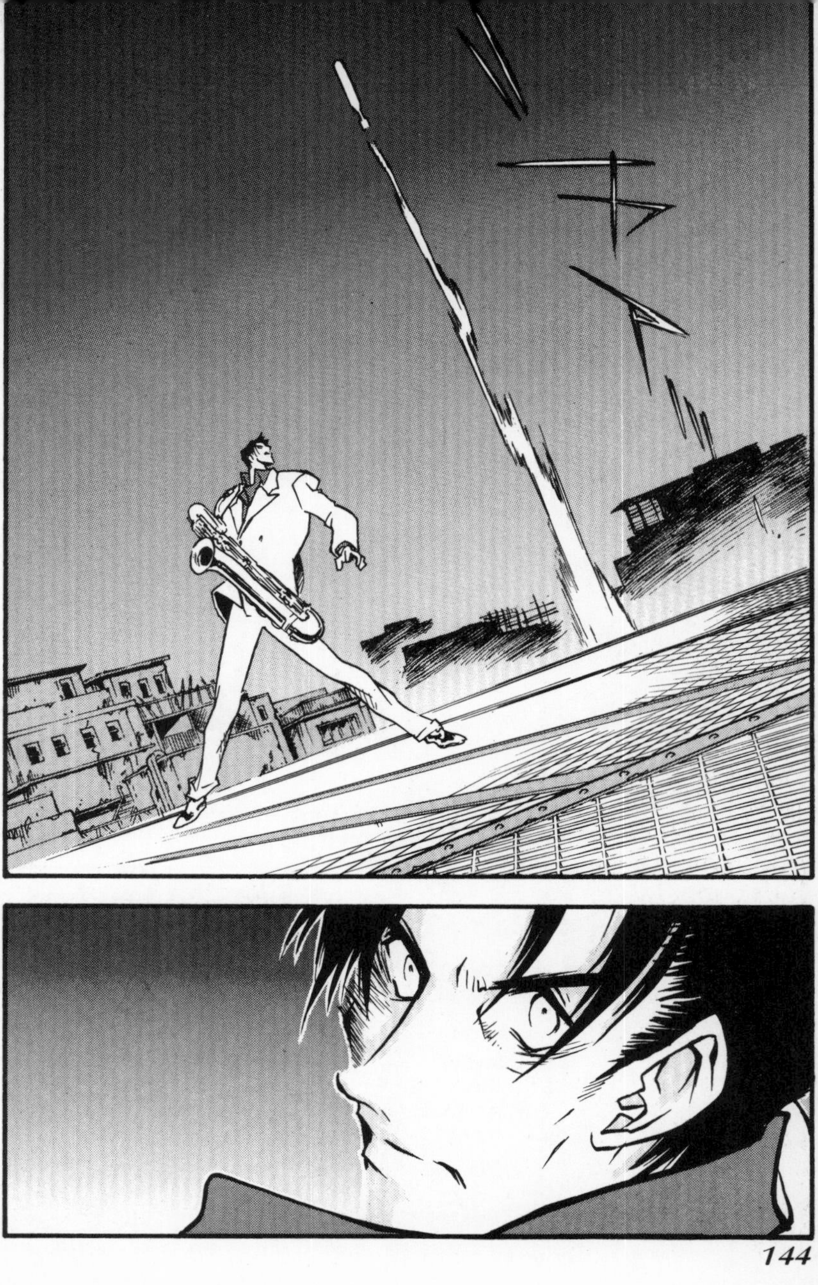

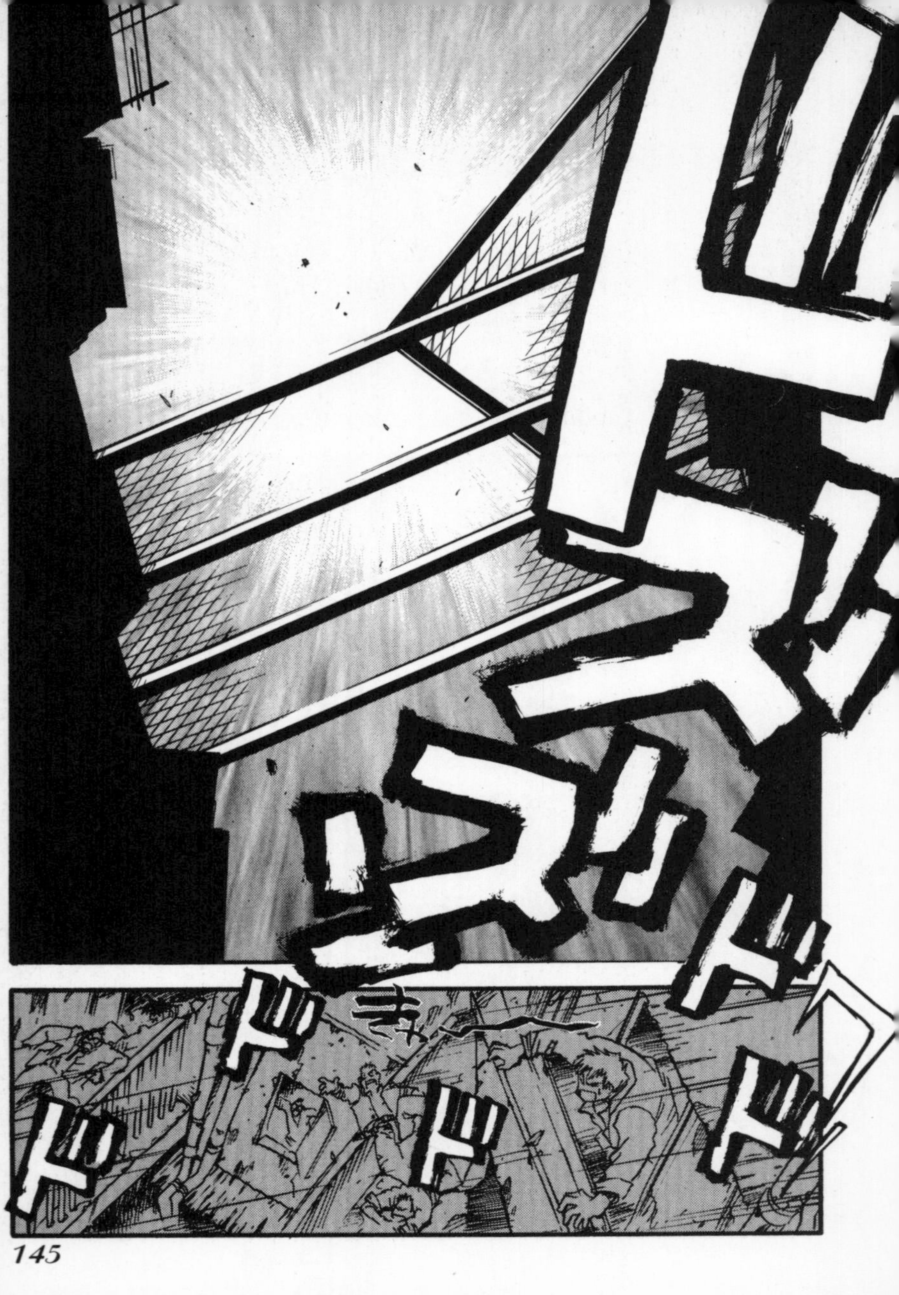
ド
ド
ド
ド

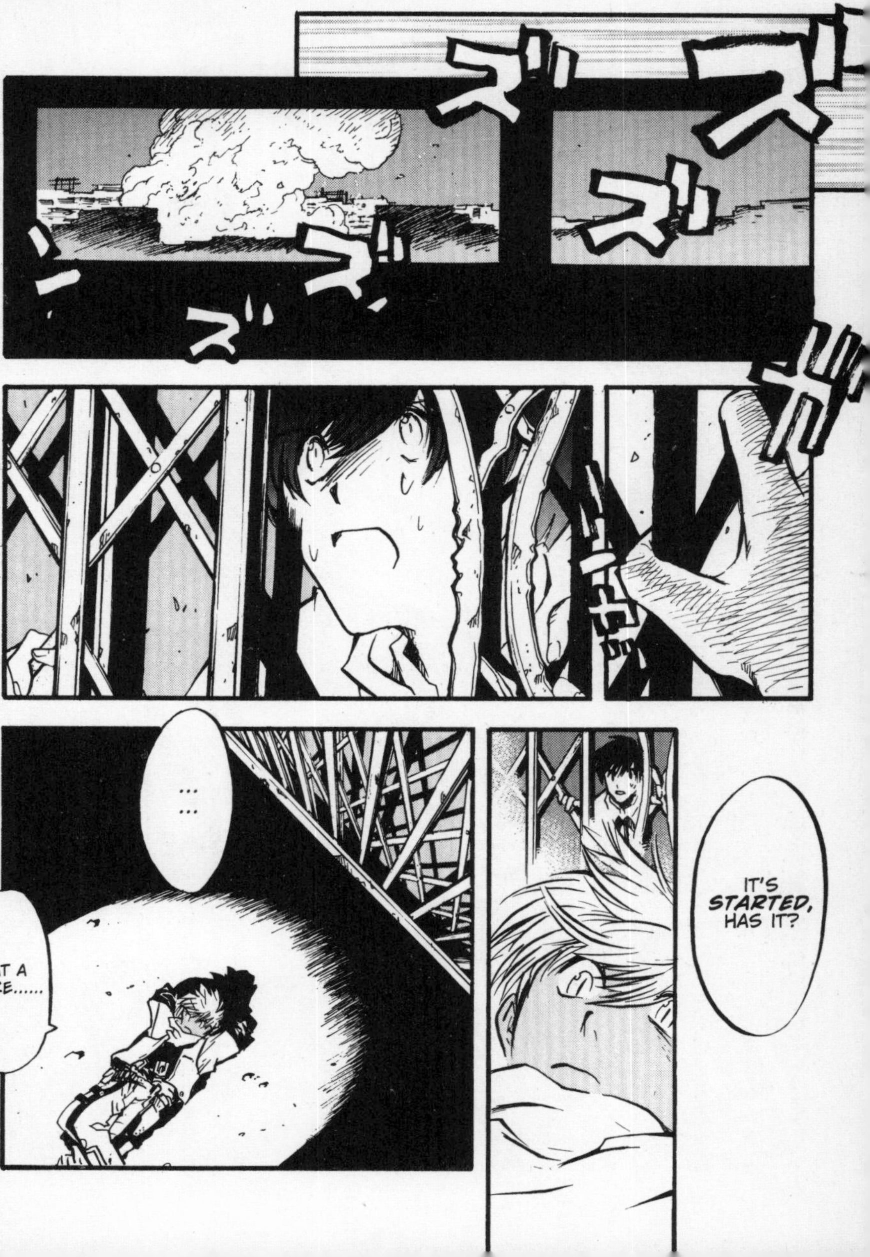
IT'S STARTED, HAS IT?
......
WHAT A BLAZE......

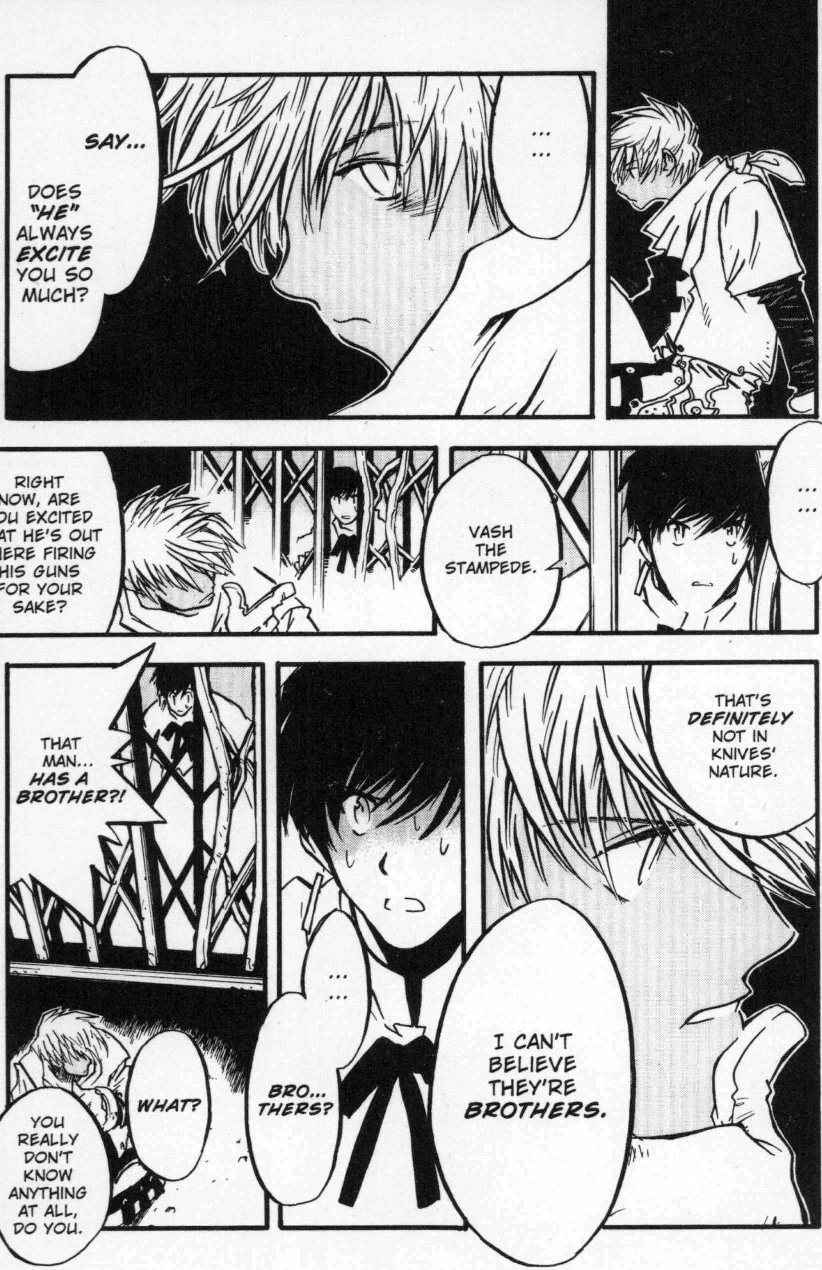
... ...
SAY...
DOES "HE" ALWAYS EXCITE YOU SO MUCH?
... ...
VASH THE STAMPEDE.
RIGHT NOW, ARE YOU EXCITED THAT HE'S OUT THERE FIRING HIS GUNS FOR YOUR SAKE?
THAT'S DEFINITELY NOT IN KNIVES' NATURE.
I CAN'T BELIEVE THEY'RE BROTHERS.
... ...
BRO... THERS?
THAT MAN... HAS A BROTHER?!
WHAT?
YOU REALLY DON'T KNOW ANYTHING AT ALL, DO YOU.

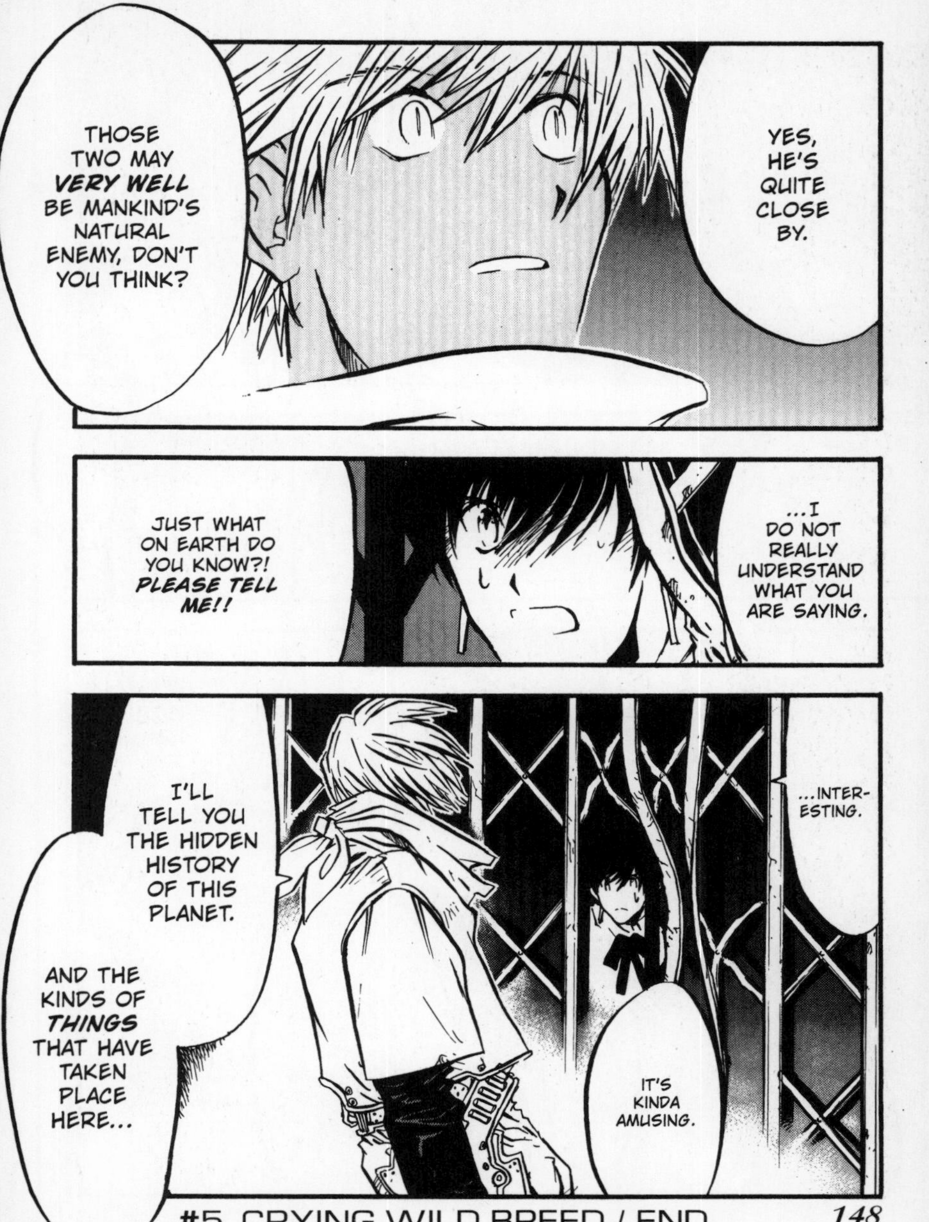
YES, HE'S QUITE CLOSE BY.
THOSE TWO MAY ***VERY WELL*** BE MANKIND'S NATURAL ENEMY, DON'T YOU THINK?
...I DO NOT REALLY UNDERSTAND WHAT YOU ARE SAYING.
JUST WHAT ON EARTH DO YOU KNOW?! ***PLEASE TELL ME!!***
...INTERESTING.
IT'S KINDA AMUSING.
I'LL TELL YOU THE HIDDEN HISTORY OF THIS PLANET.
AND THE KINDS OF ***THINGS*** THAT HAVE TAKEN PLACE HERE...

#5. CRYING WILD BREED / END

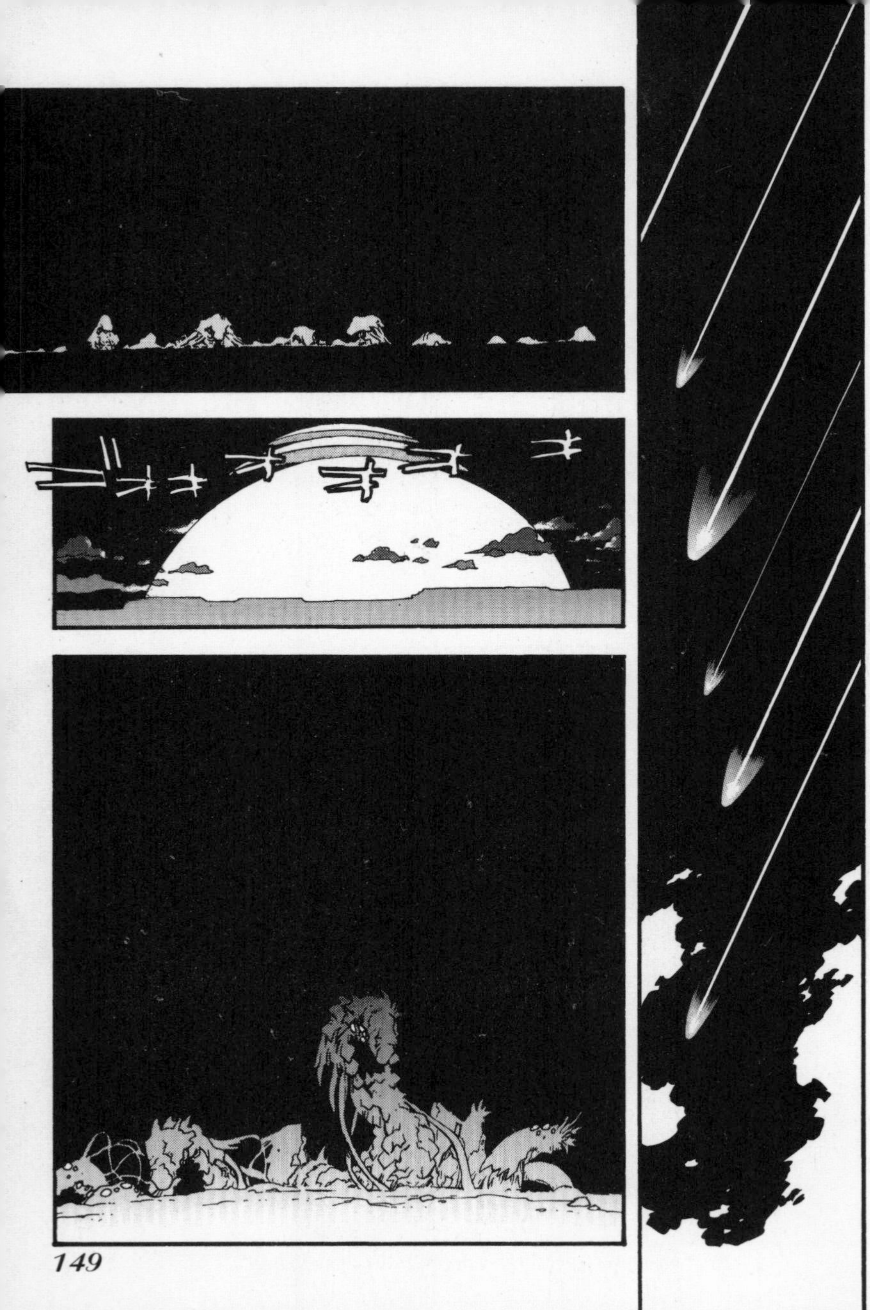
ゴォォォォォォ

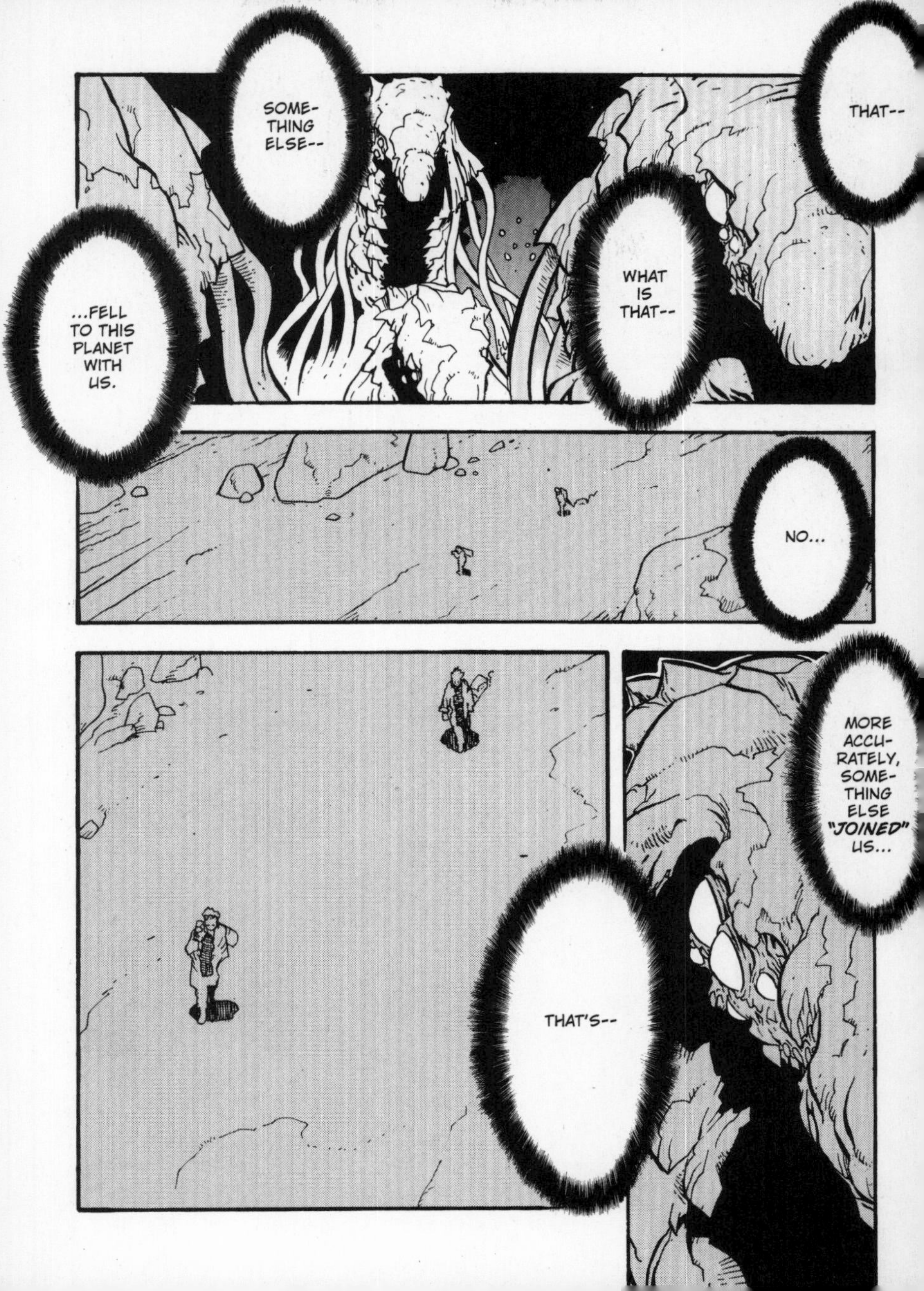
THAT--
WHAT IS THAT--
SOME-THING ELSE--
...FELL TO THIS PLANET WITH US.
NO...
MORE ACCU-RATELY, SOME-THING ELSE *"JOINED"* US...
THAT'S--

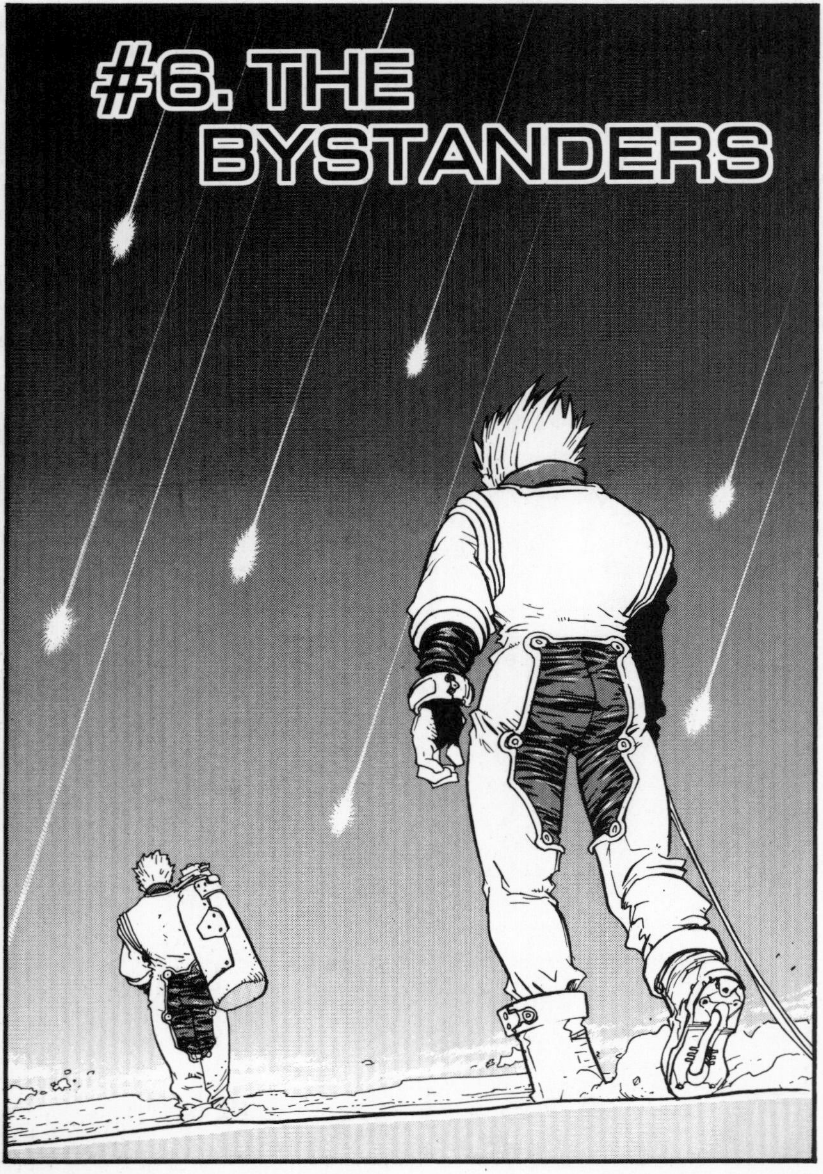
#6. THE
BYSTANDERS

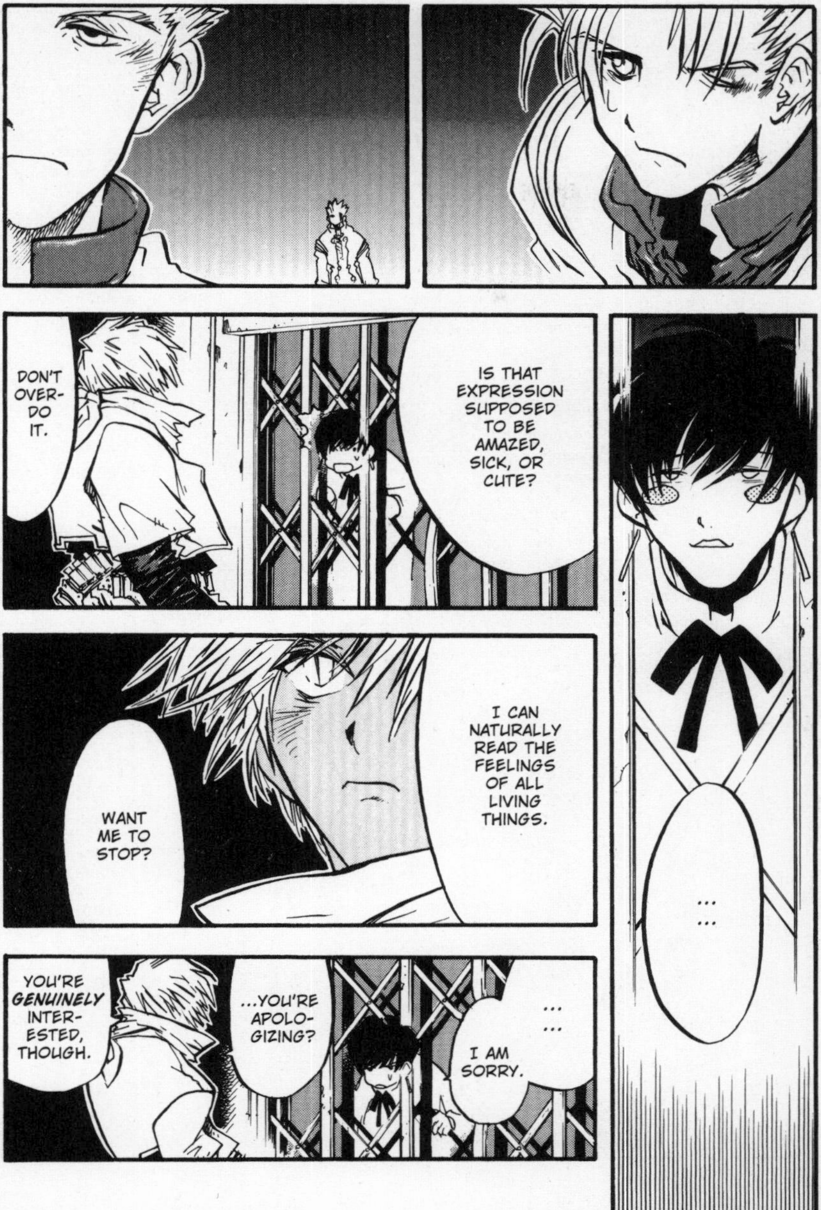
... ...
IS THAT EXPRESSION SUPPOSED TO BE AMAZED, SICK, OR CUTE?
DON'T OVER-DO IT.
I CAN NATURALLY READ THE FEELINGS OF ALL LIVING THINGS.
WANT ME TO STOP?
... ... I AM SORRY.
...YOU'RE APOLOGIZING?
YOU'RE *GENUINELY* INTERESTED, THOUGH.

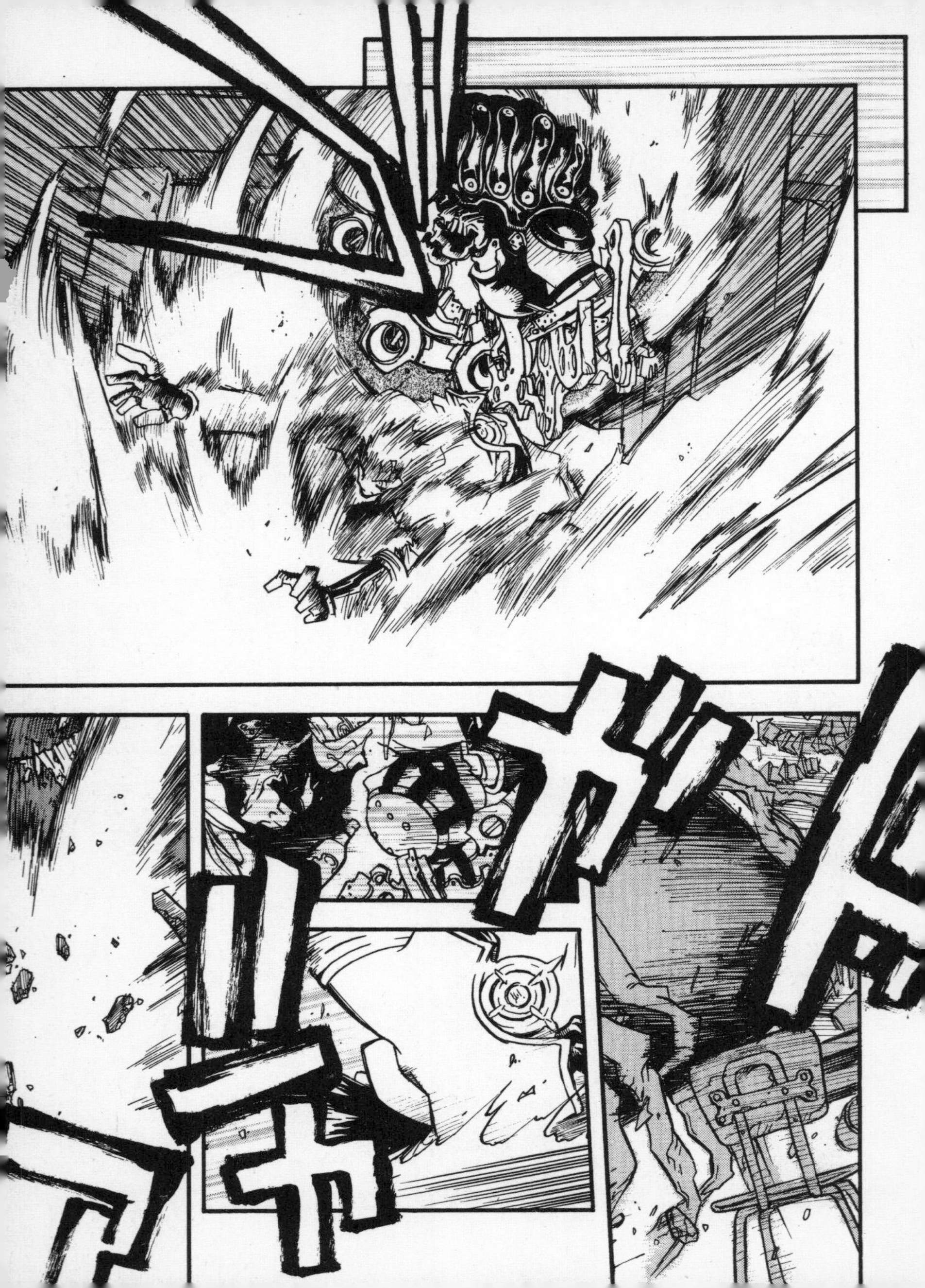

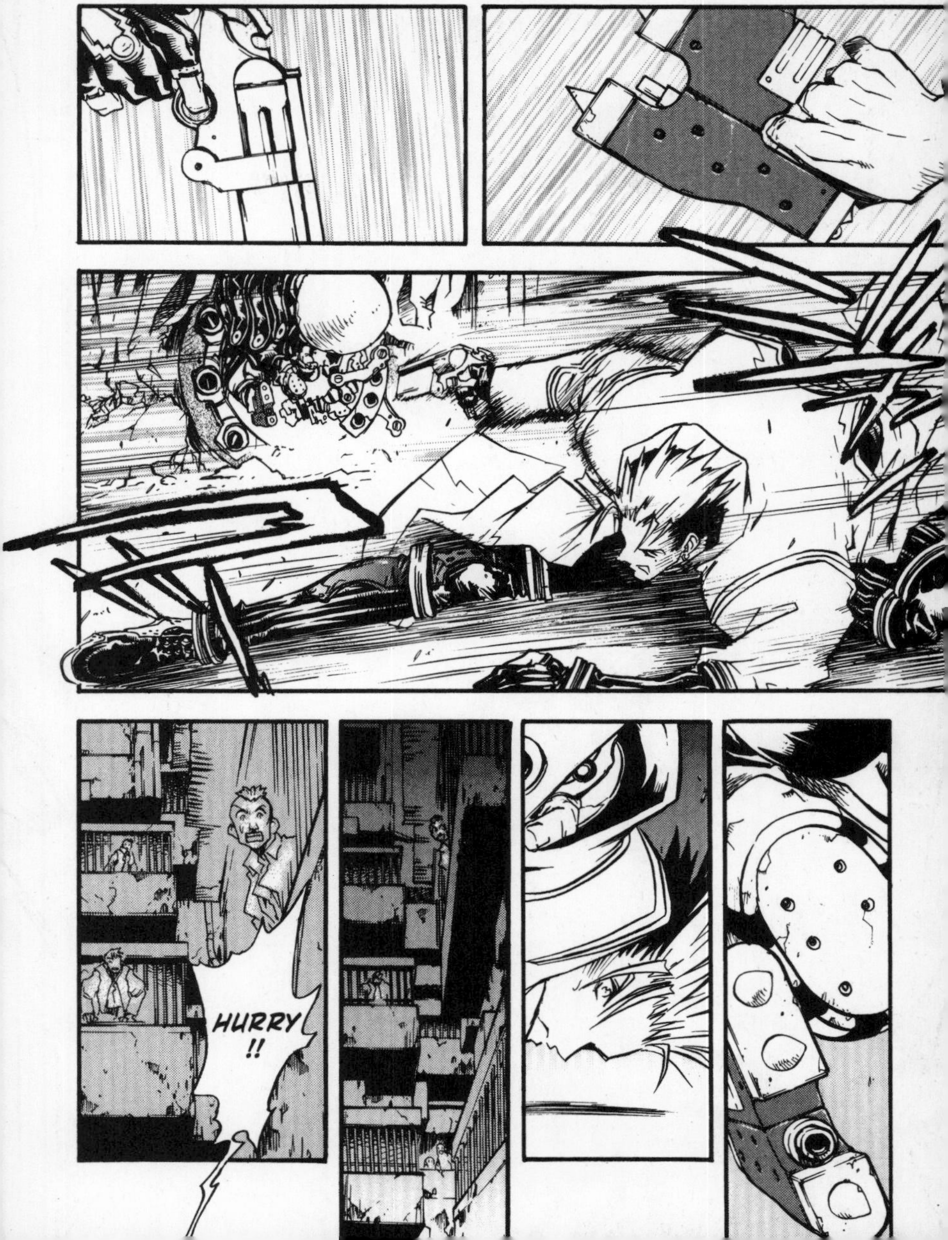
HURRY !!

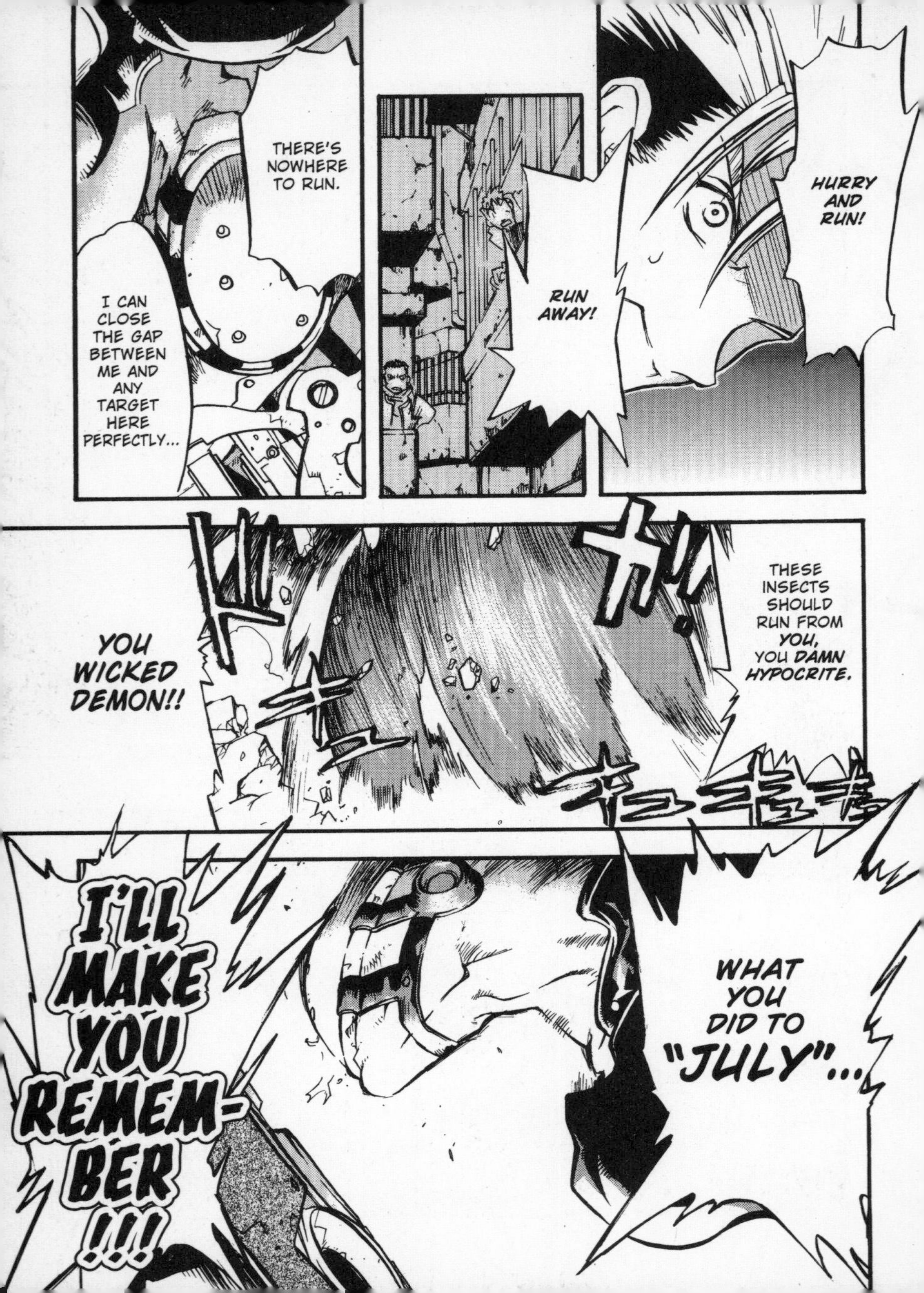
HURRY AND RUN!
RUN AWAY!
THERE'S NOWHERE TO RUN.
I CAN CLOSE THE GAP BETWEEN ME AND ANY TARGET HERE PERFECTLY...
THESE INSECTS SHOULD RUN FROM YOU, YOU DAMN HYPOCRITE.
YOU WICKED DEMON!!
WHAT YOU DID TO "JULY"...
I'LL MAKE YOU REMEMBER!!!

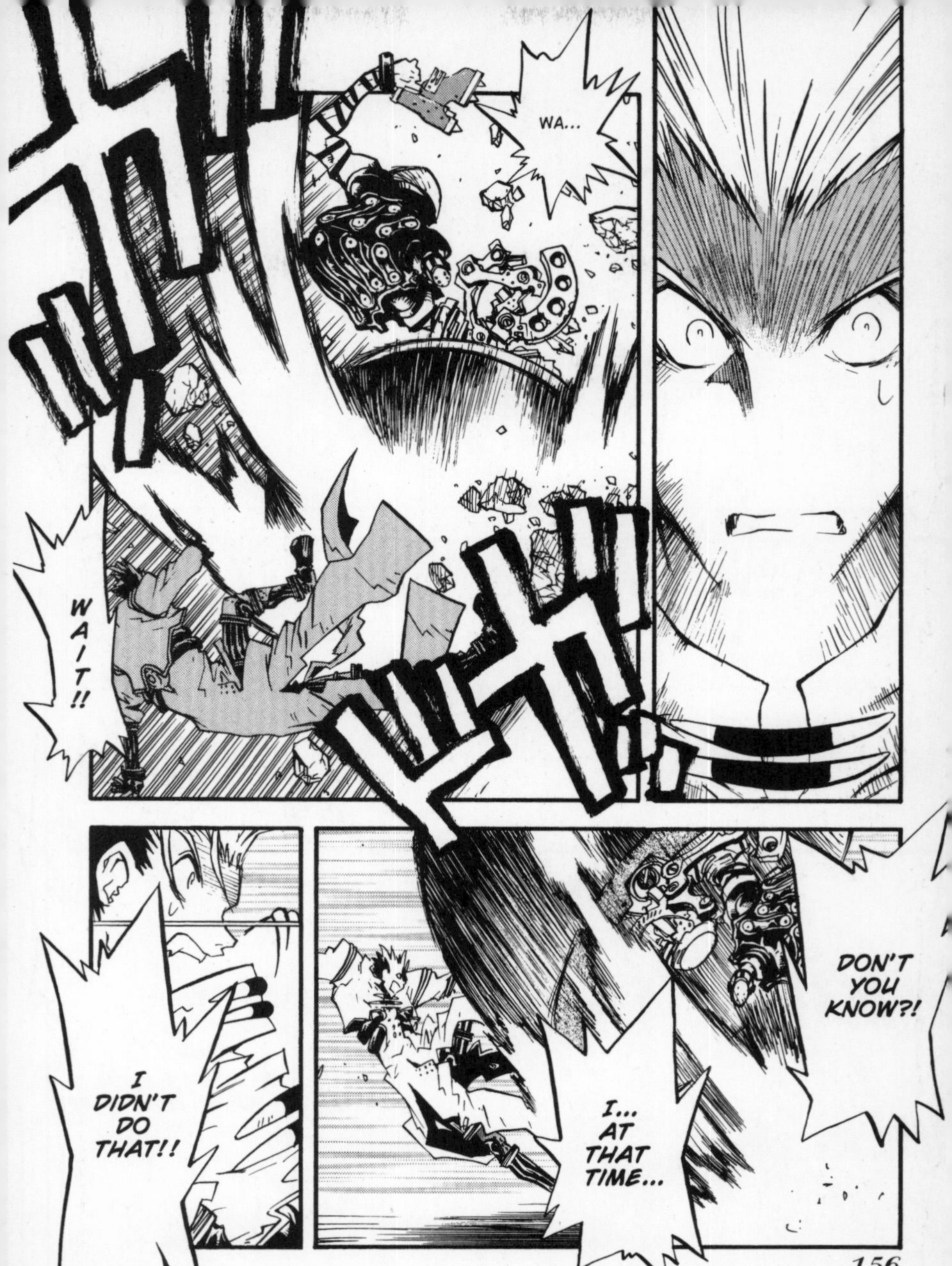
WA...
WAIT!!
DON'T YOU KNOW?!
I... AT THAT TIME...
I DIDN'T DO THAT!!

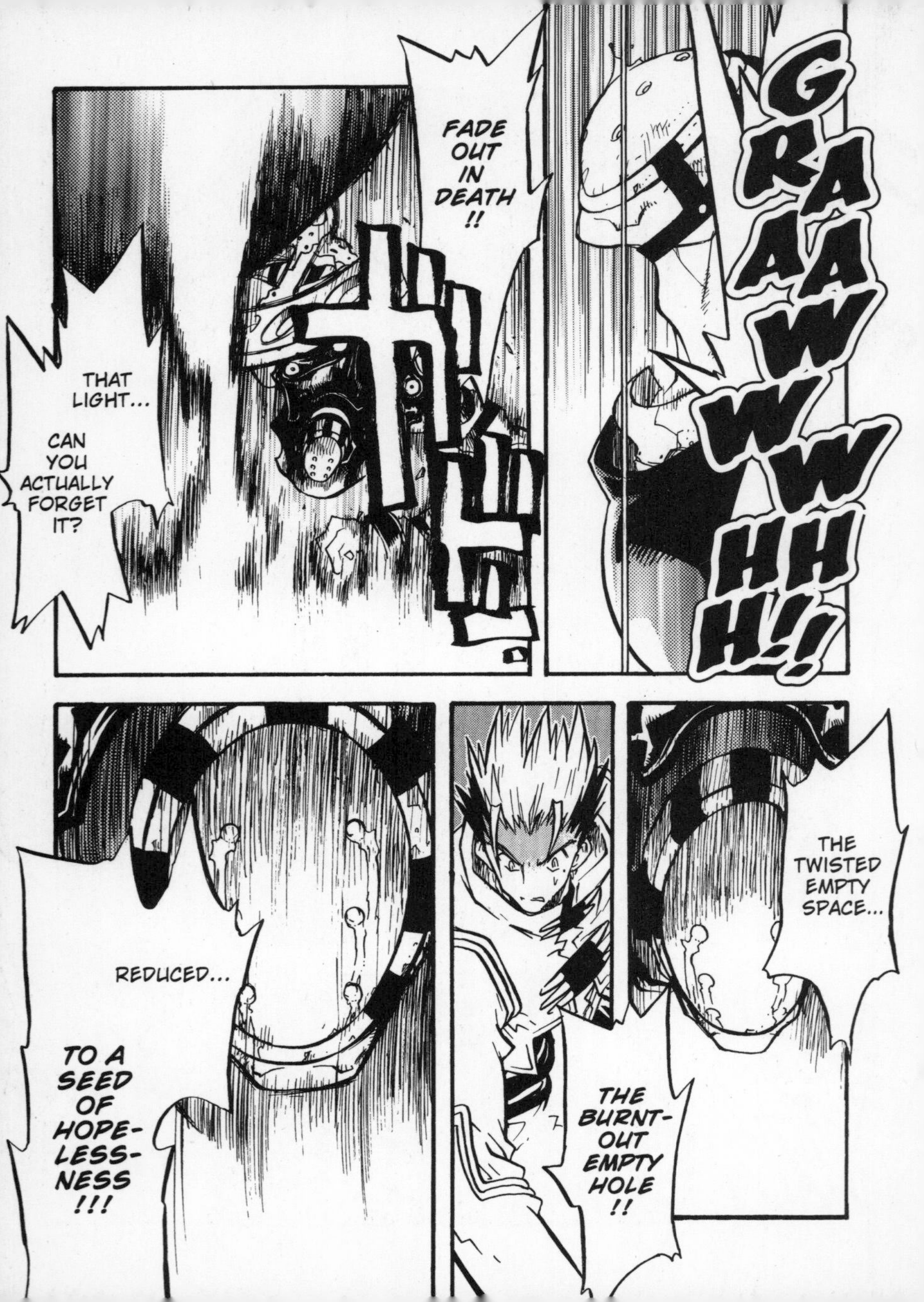
GRAAAWWWHHH!!
FADE OUT IN DEATH!!
THAT LIGHT...
CAN YOU ACTUALLY FORGET IT?
THE TWISTED EMPTY SPACE...
THE BURNT-OUT EMPTY HOLE!!
REDUCED...
TO A SEED OF HOPE-LESS-NESS!!!

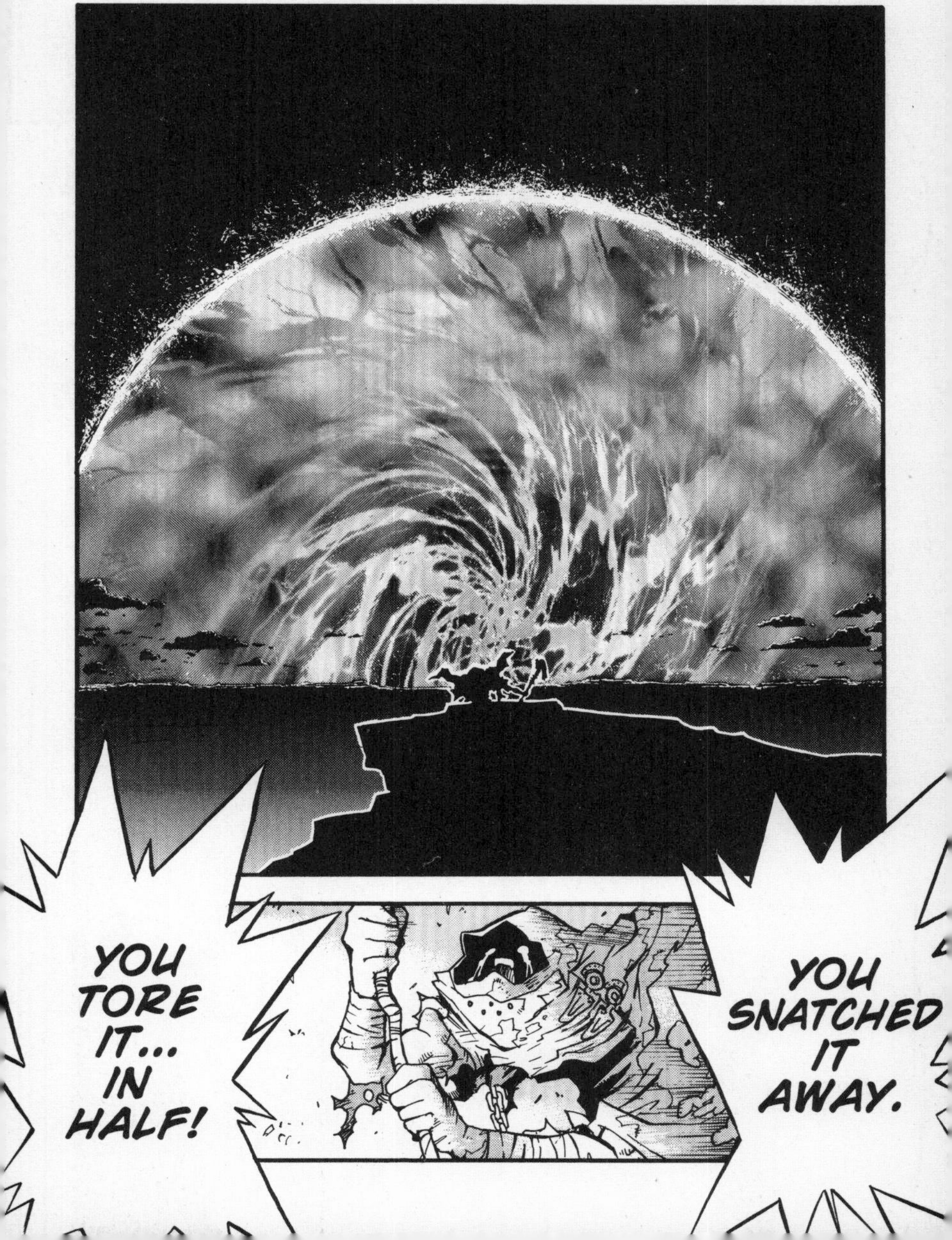
YOU SNATCHED IT AWAY.
YOU TORE IT... IN HALF!

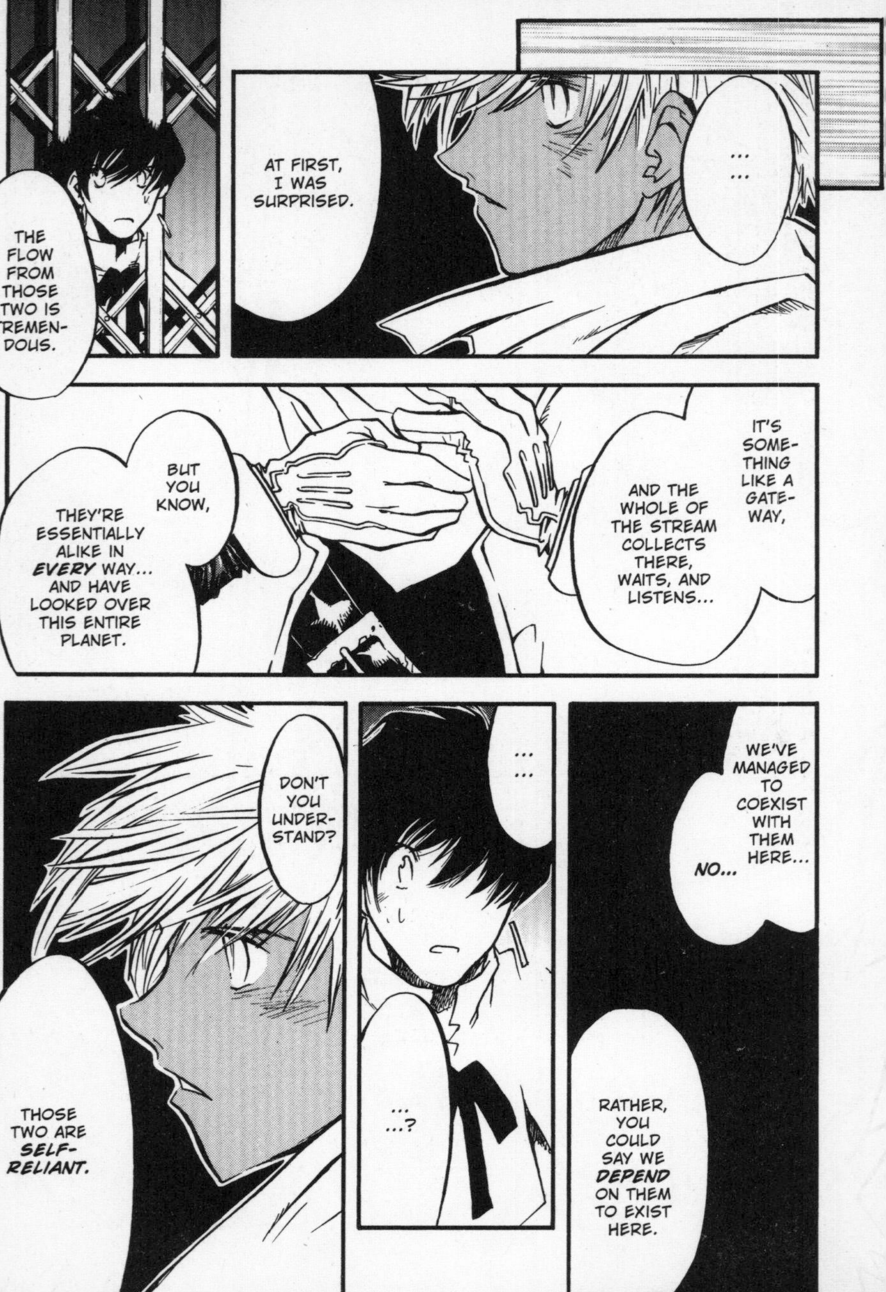

... ...
AT FIRST, I WAS SURPRISED.
THE FLOW FROM THOSE TWO IS TREMENDOUS.
IT'S SOMETHING LIKE A GATEWAY,
AND THE WHOLE OF THE STREAM COLLECTS THERE, WAITS, AND LISTENS...
BUT YOU KNOW,
THEY'RE ESSENTIALLY ALIKE IN EVERY WAY... AND HAVE LOOKED OVER THIS ENTIRE PLANET.
WE'VE MANAGED TO COEXIST WITH THEM HERE... NO...
RATHER, YOU COULD SAY WE DEPEND ON THEM TO EXIST HERE.
... ...
... ...?
DON'T YOU UNDERSTAND?
THOSE TWO ARE SELF-RELIANT.

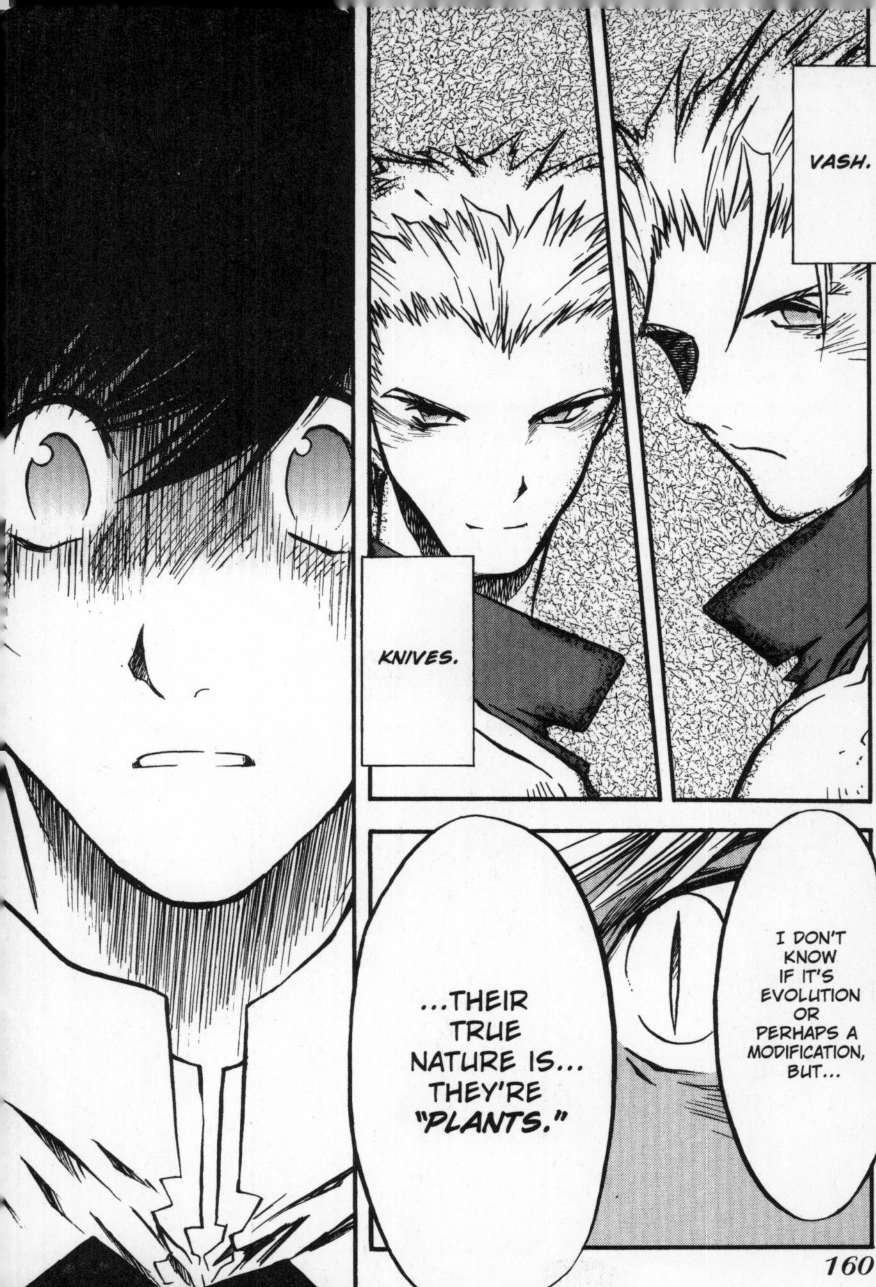
VASH.
KNIVES.
I DON'T KNOW IF IT'S EVOLUTION OR PERHAPS A MODIFICATION, BUT...
...THEIR TRUE NATURE IS... THEY'RE *"PLANTS."*

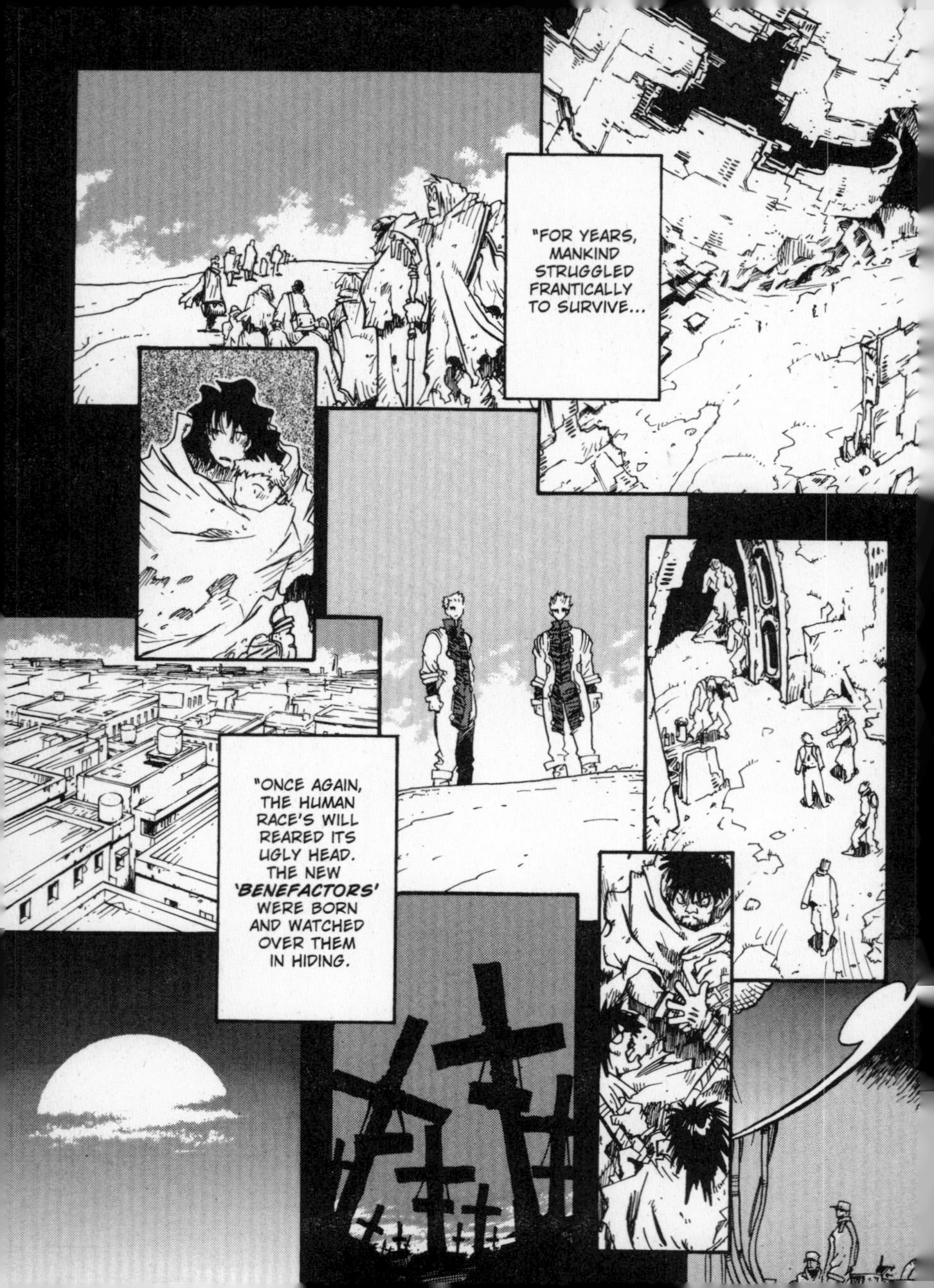
"FOR YEARS, MANKIND STRUGGLED FRANTICALLY TO SURVIVE...
"ONCE AGAIN, THE HUMAN RACE'S WILL REARED ITS UGLY HEAD. THE NEW 'BENEFACTORS' WERE BORN AND WATCHED OVER THEM IN HIDING.

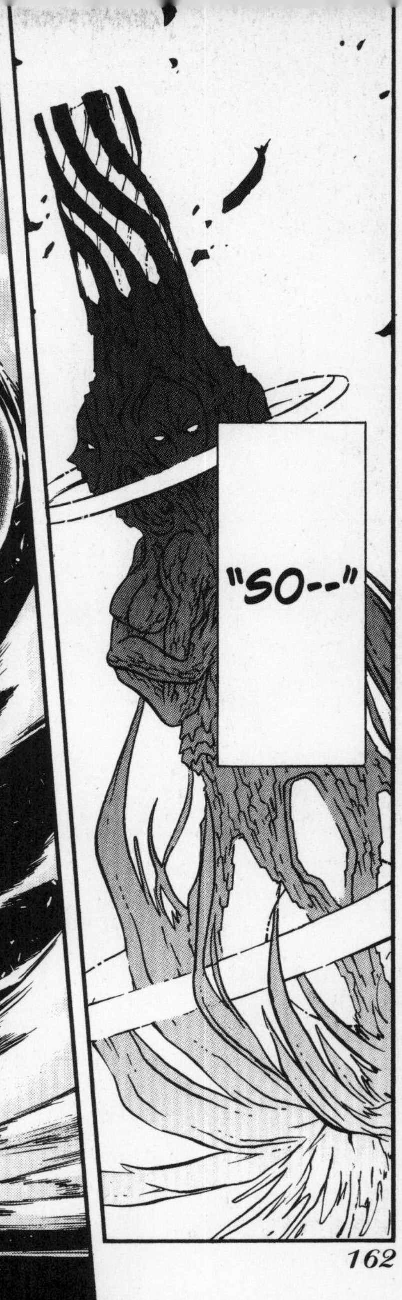
"SO--"
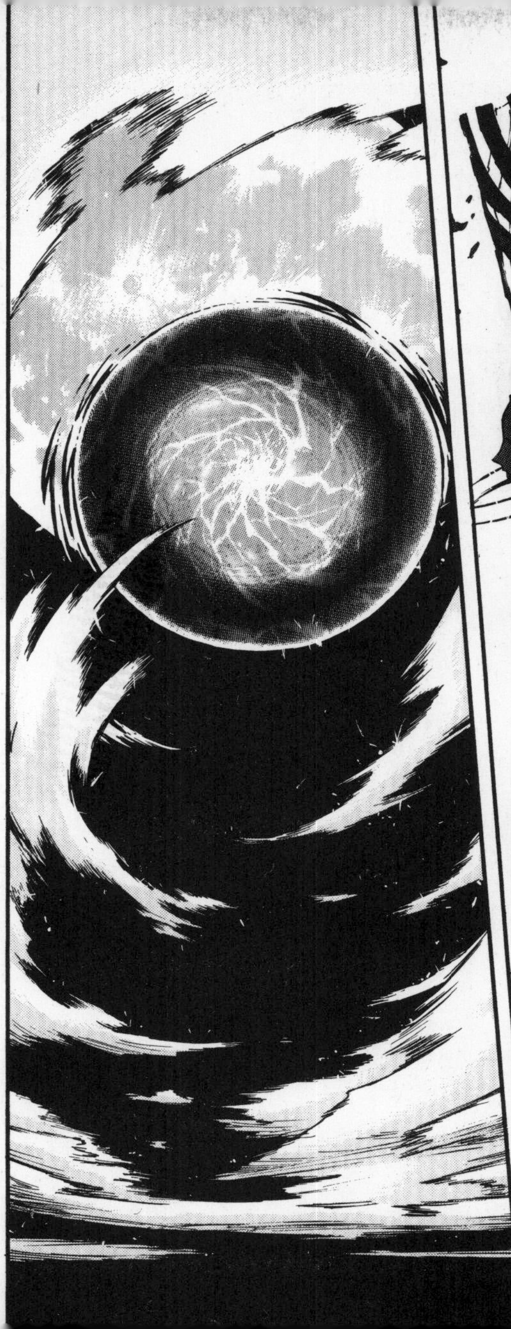

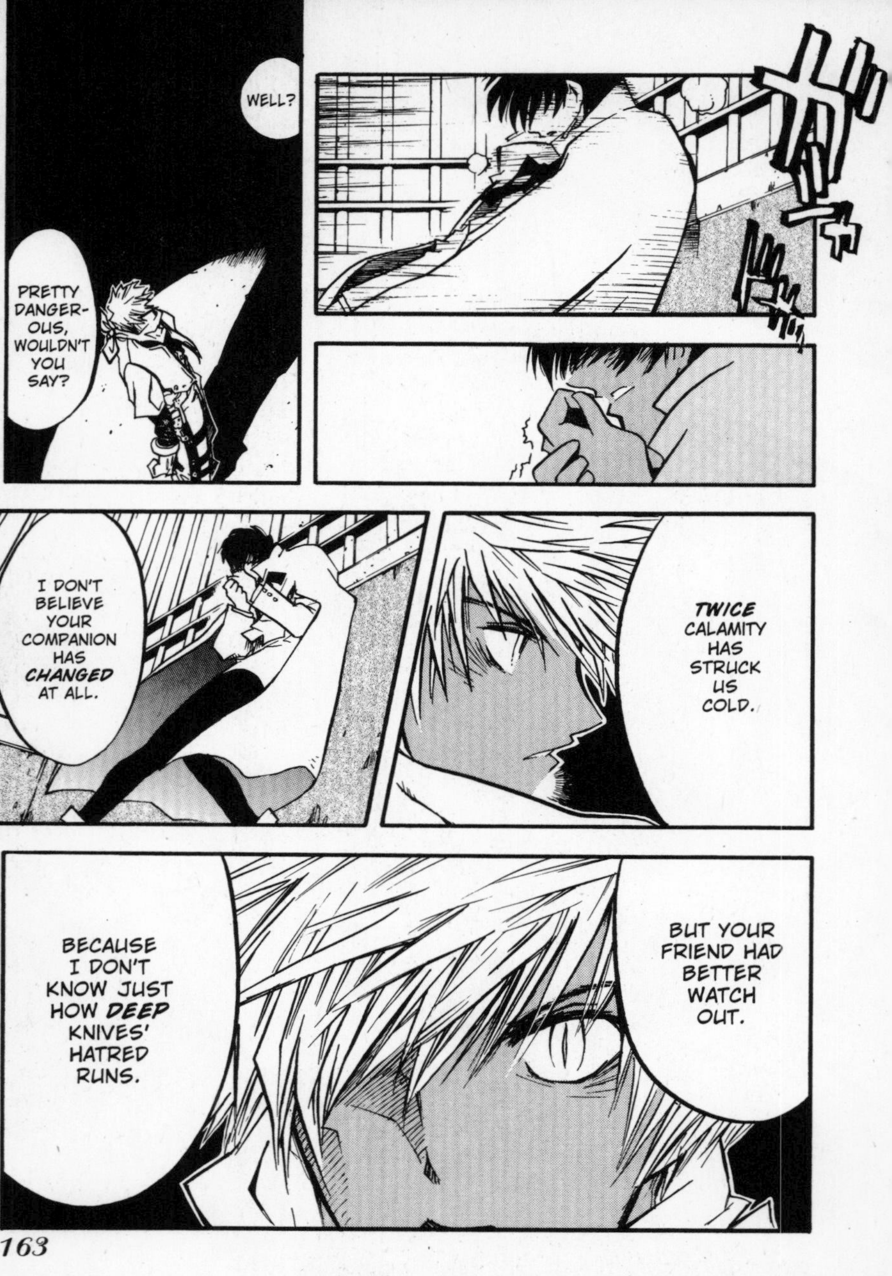
WELL?
PRETTY DANGER-OUS, WOULDN'T YOU SAY?
TWICE CALAMITY HAS STRUCK US COLD.
I DON'T BELIEVE YOUR COMPANION HAS *CHANGED* AT ALL.
BUT YOUR FRIEND HAD BETTER WATCH OUT.
BECAUSE I DON'T KNOW JUST HOW *DEEP* KNIVES' HATRED RUNS.

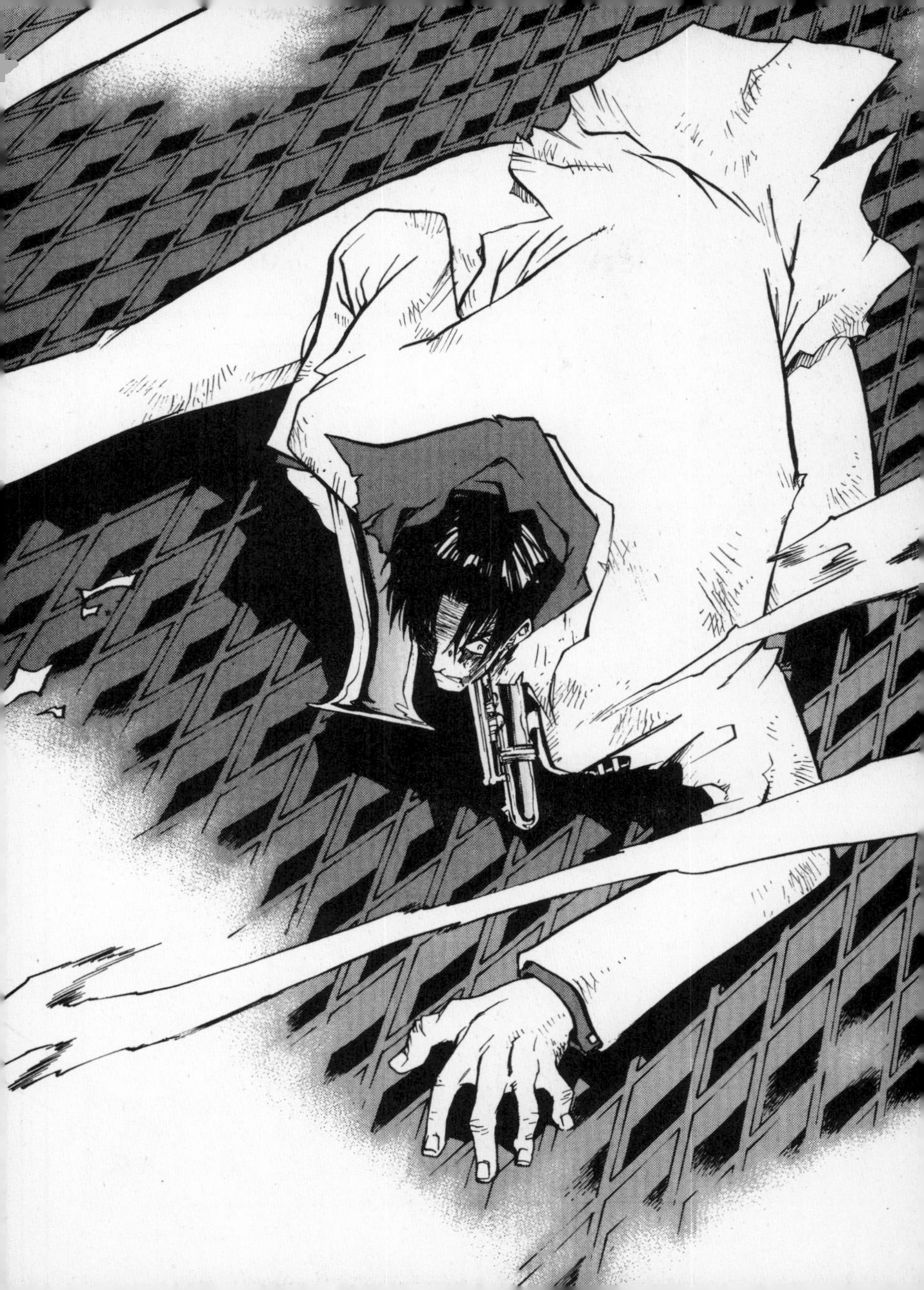

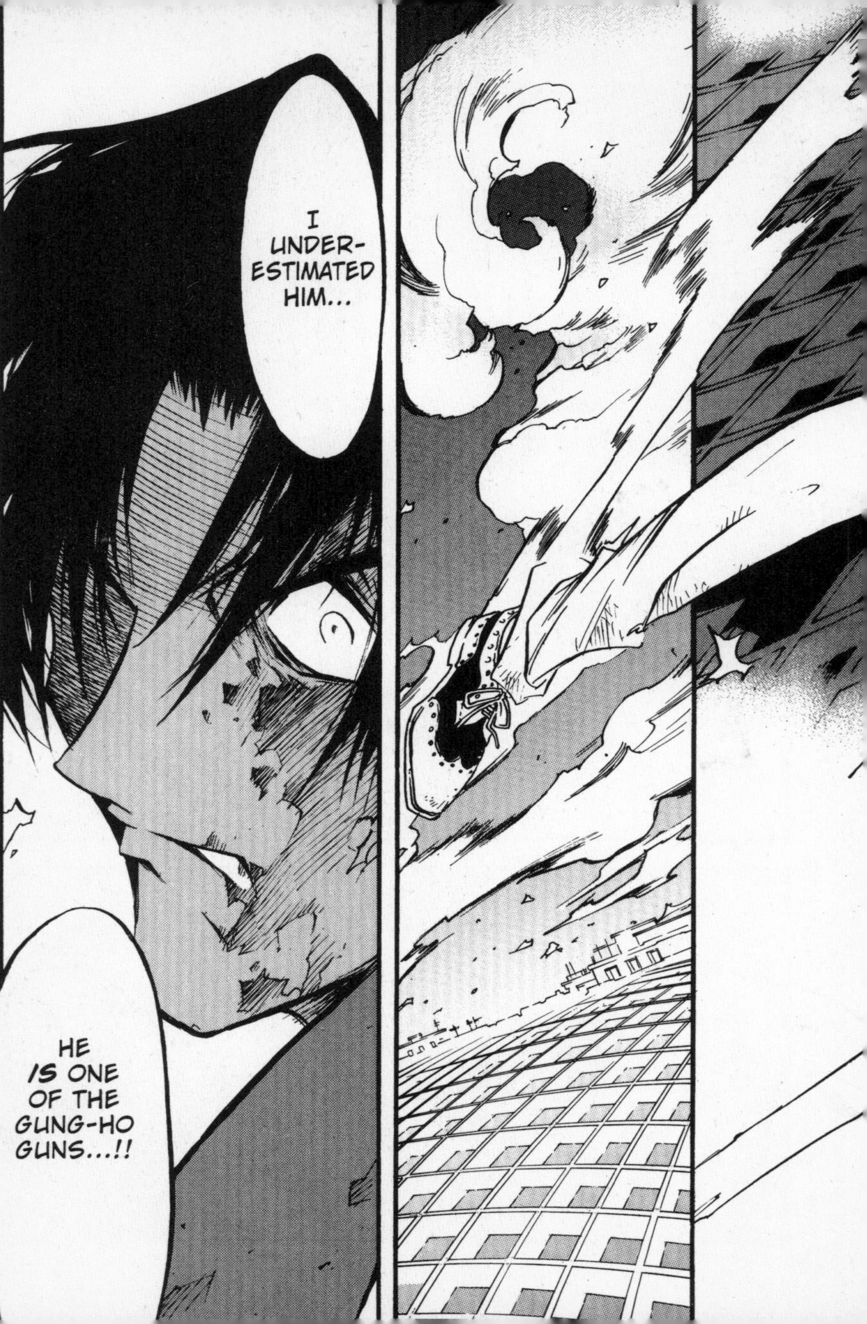
I UNDER-ESTIMATED HIM...
HE *IS* ONE OF THE GUNG-HO GUNS...!!

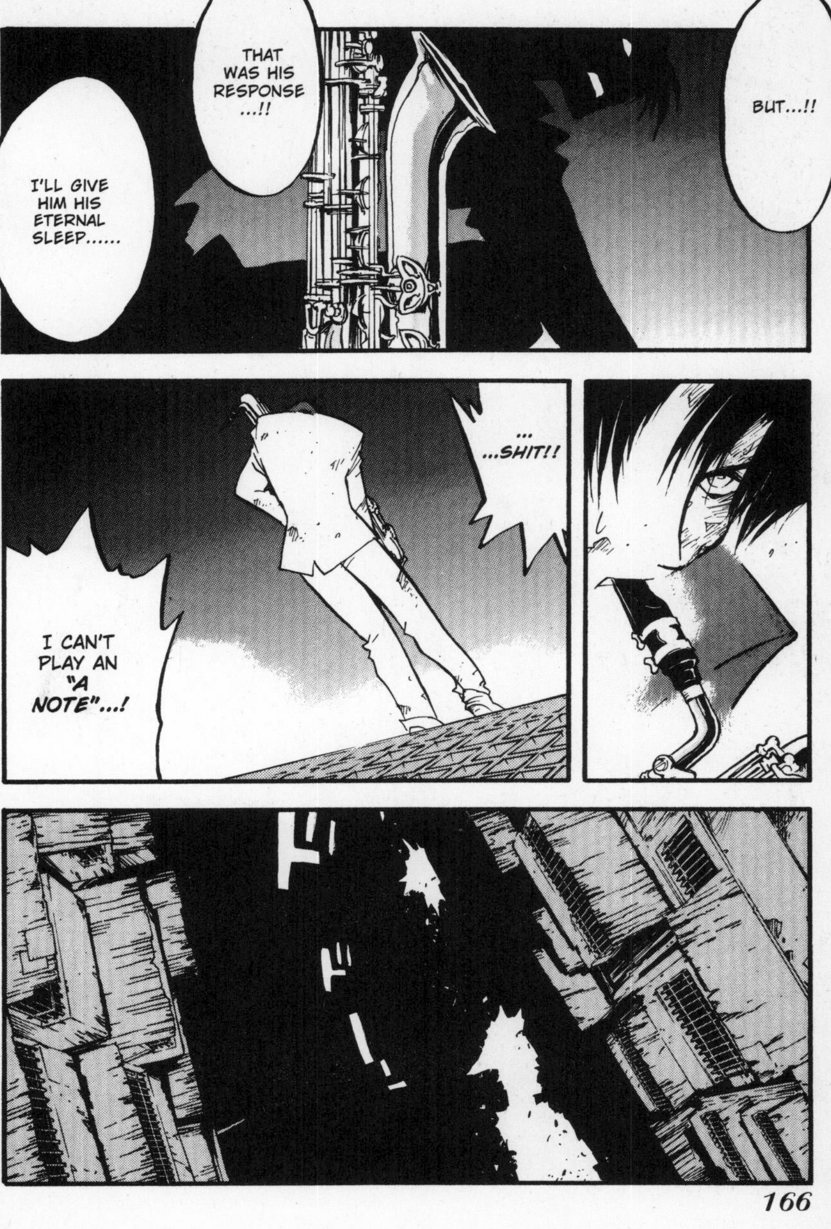
BUT...!!
THAT WAS HIS RESPONSE ...!!
I'LL GIVE HIM HIS ETERNAL SLEEP......
... ...SHIT!!
I CAN'T PLAY AN "A NOTE"...!

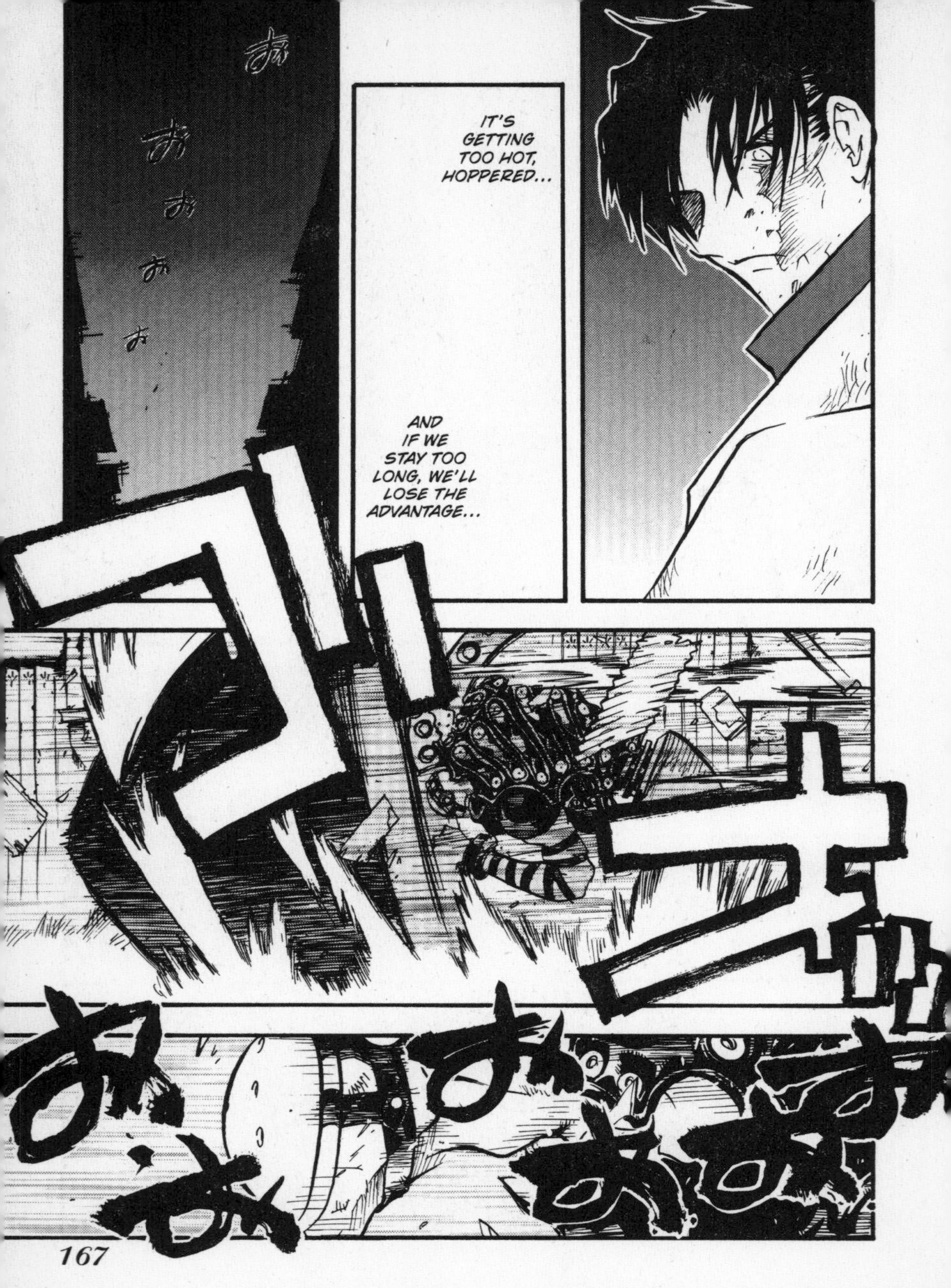
IT'S GETTING TOO HOT, HOPPERED...
AND IF WE STAY TOO LONG, WE'LL LOSE THE ADVANTAGE...

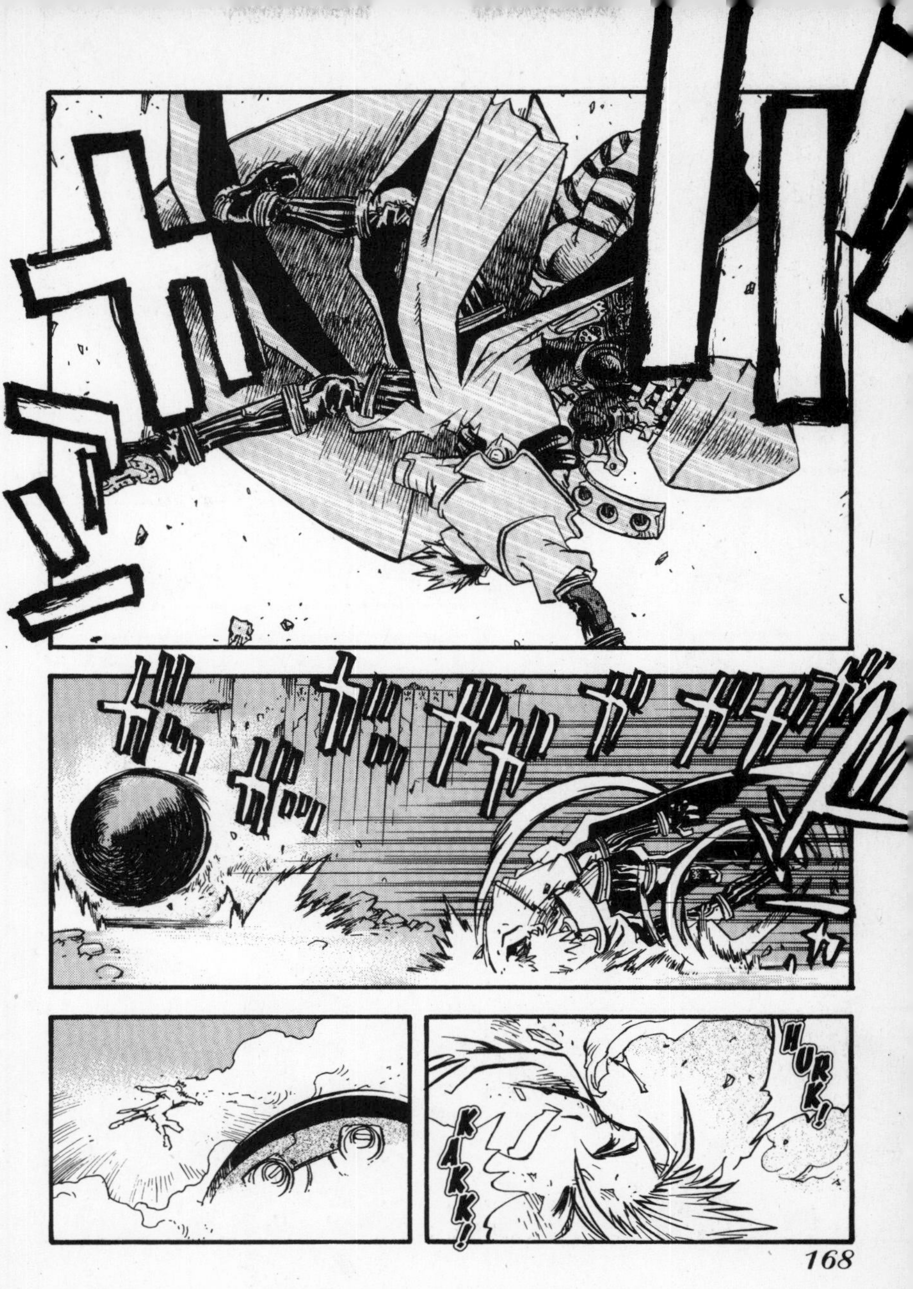
HURK!
KAKK!

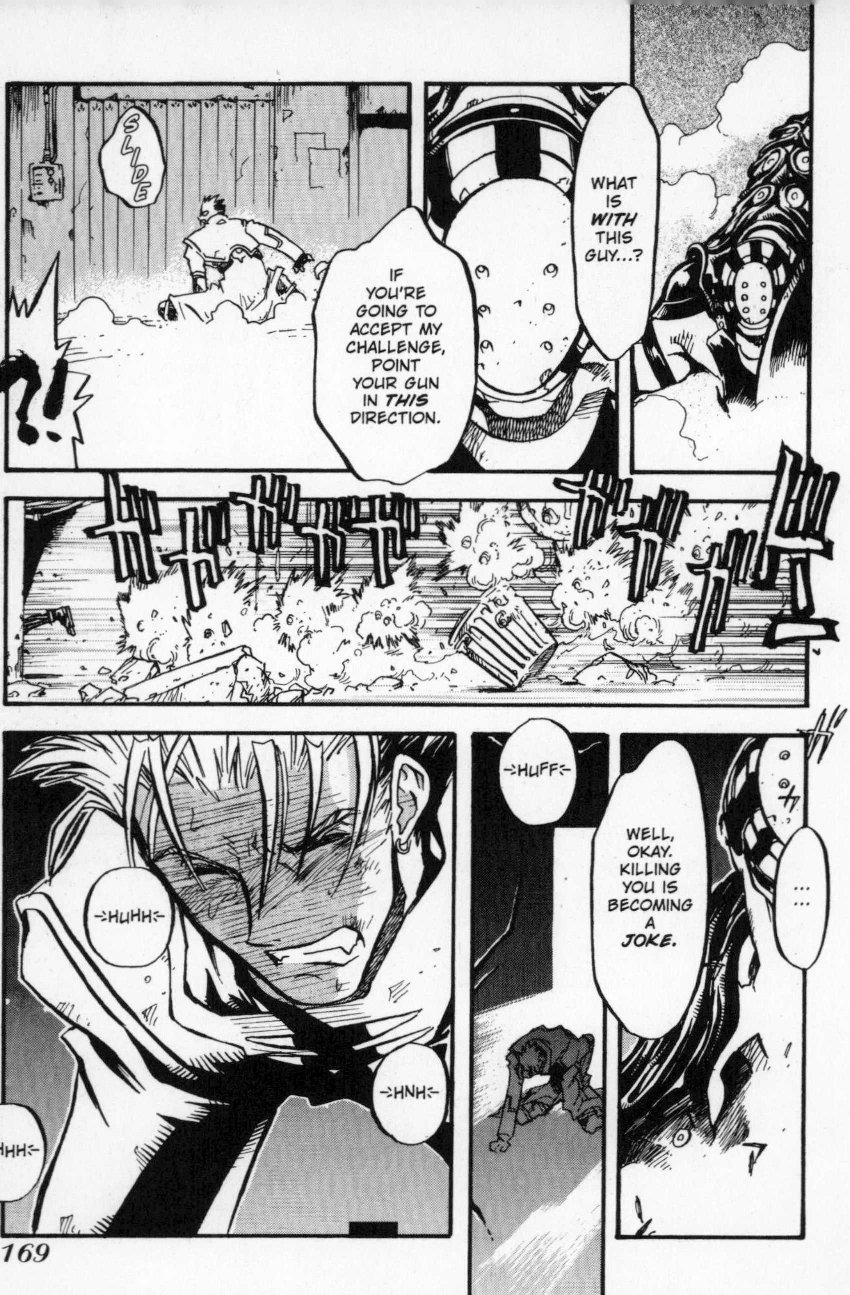

WHAT IS *WITH* THIS GUY...?
IF YOU'RE GOING TO ACCEPT MY CHALLENGE, POINT YOUR GUN IN *THIS* DIRECTION.
SLIDE
?!!
......
-HUFF-
WELL, OKAY. KILLING YOU IS BECOMING A *JOKE*.
-HUHH-
-HNH-
-HNHHH-

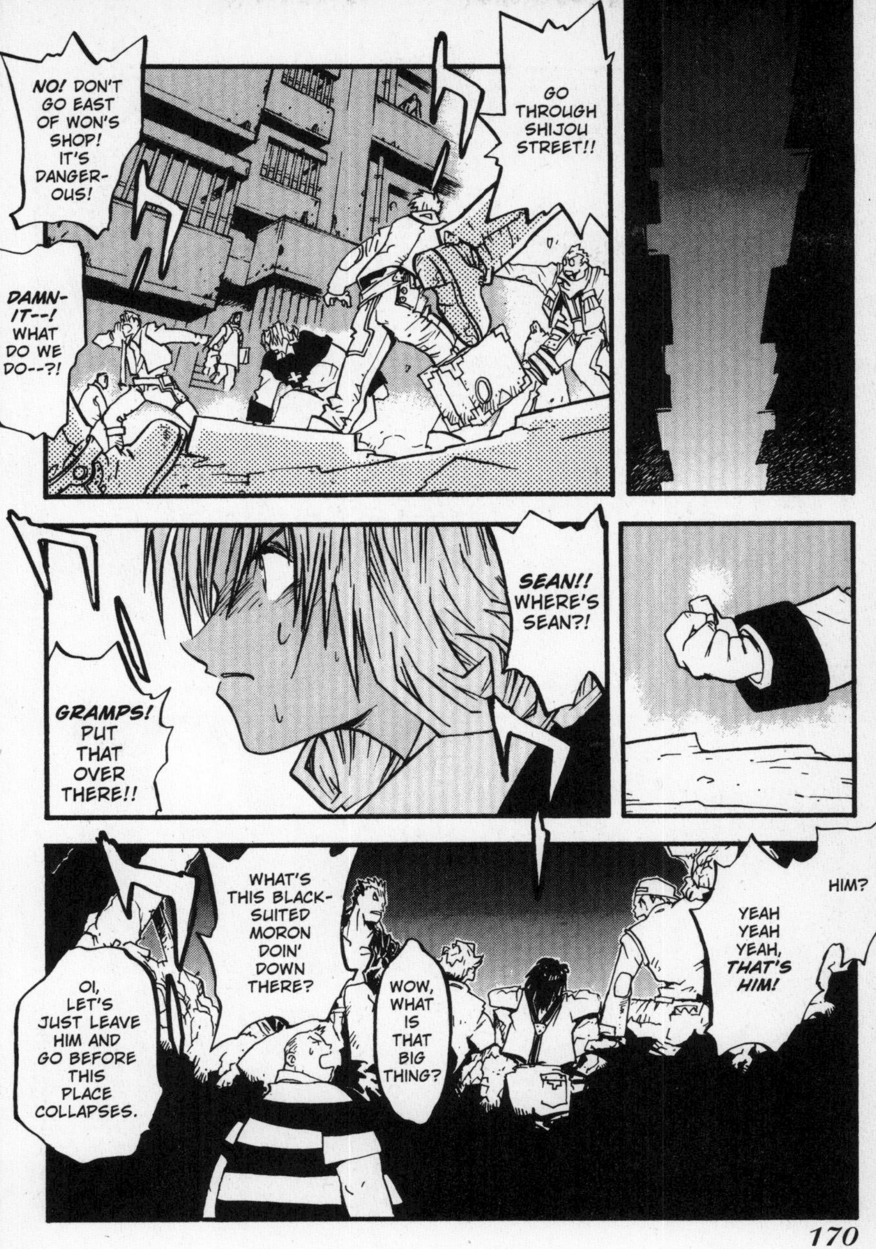
GO THROUGH SHIJOU STREET!!
NO! DON'T GO EAST OF WON'S SHOP! IT'S DANGER-OUS!
DAMN-IT--! WHAT DO WE DO--?!
SEAN!! WHERE'S SEAN?!
GRAMPS! PUT THAT OVER THERE!!
HIM?
YEAH YEAH YEAH, **THAT'S HIM!**
WHAT'S THIS BLACK-SUITED MORON DOIN' DOWN THERE?
WOW, WHAT IS THAT BIG THING?
OI, LET'S JUST LEAVE HIM AND GO BEFORE THIS PLACE COLLAPSES.

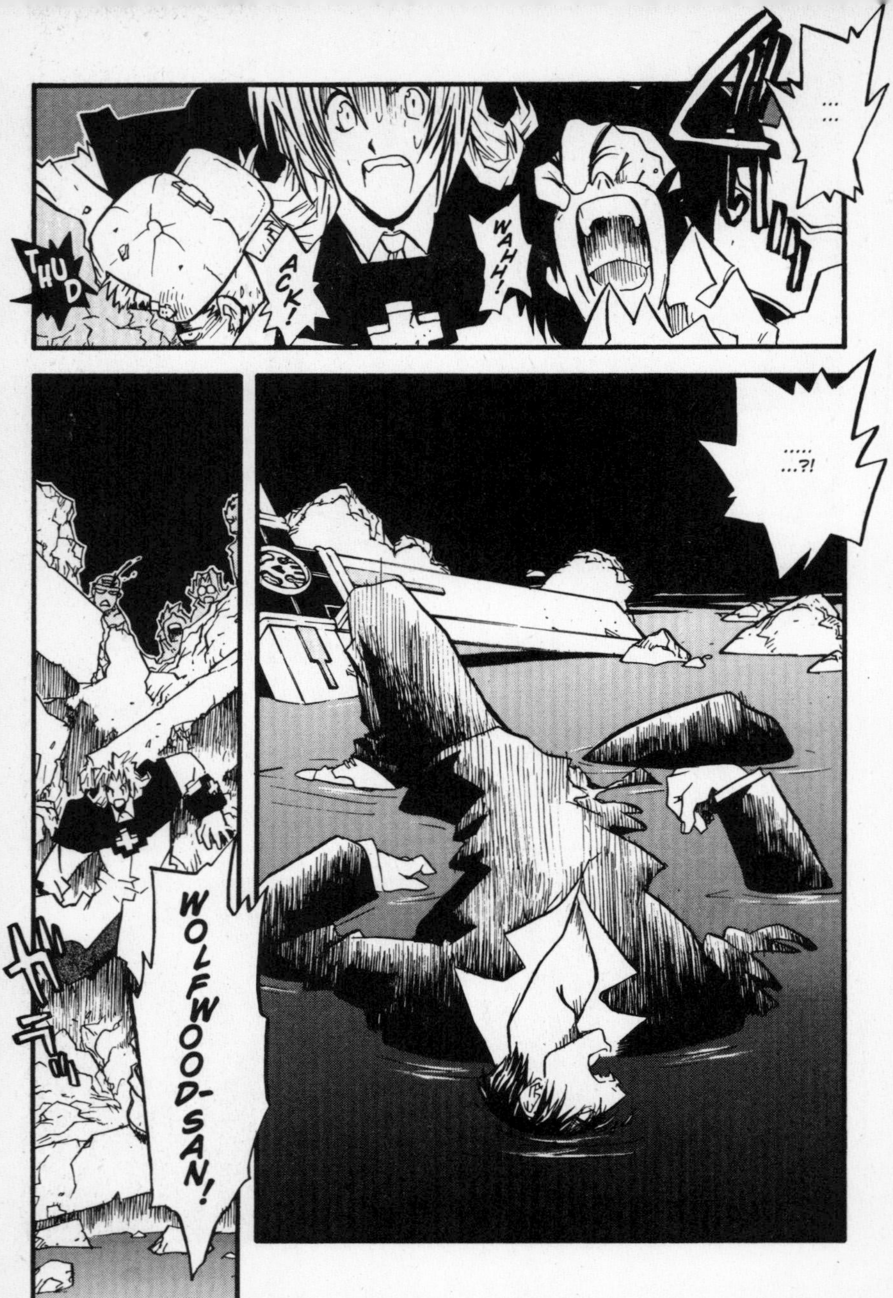
......
WAHH!
ACK!
THUD
......
...?!
WOLFWOOD-SAN!

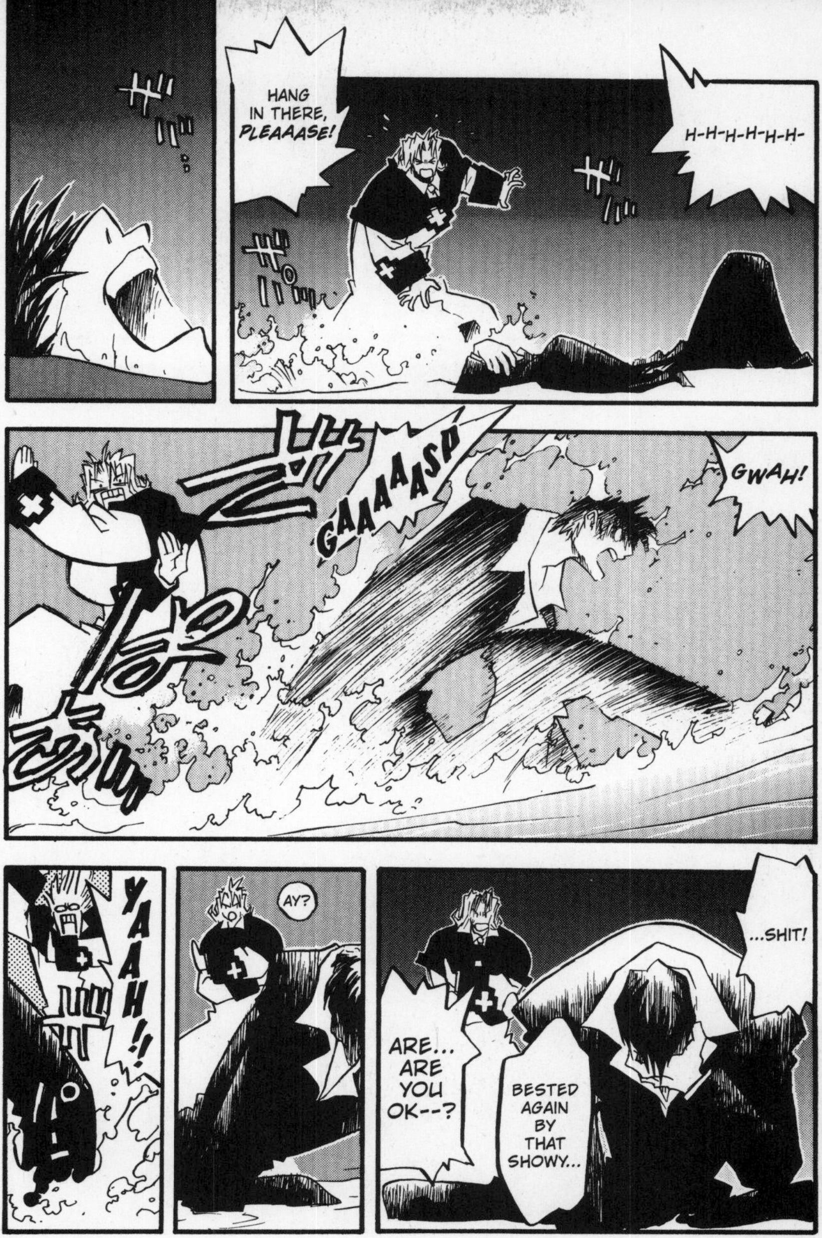
H-H-H-H-H-H-
HANG IN THERE, PLEAAASE!
GWAH!
GAAAAASP
...SHIT!
BESTED AGAIN BY THAT SHOWY...
ARE... ARE YOU OK--?
AY?
YAAAH!!

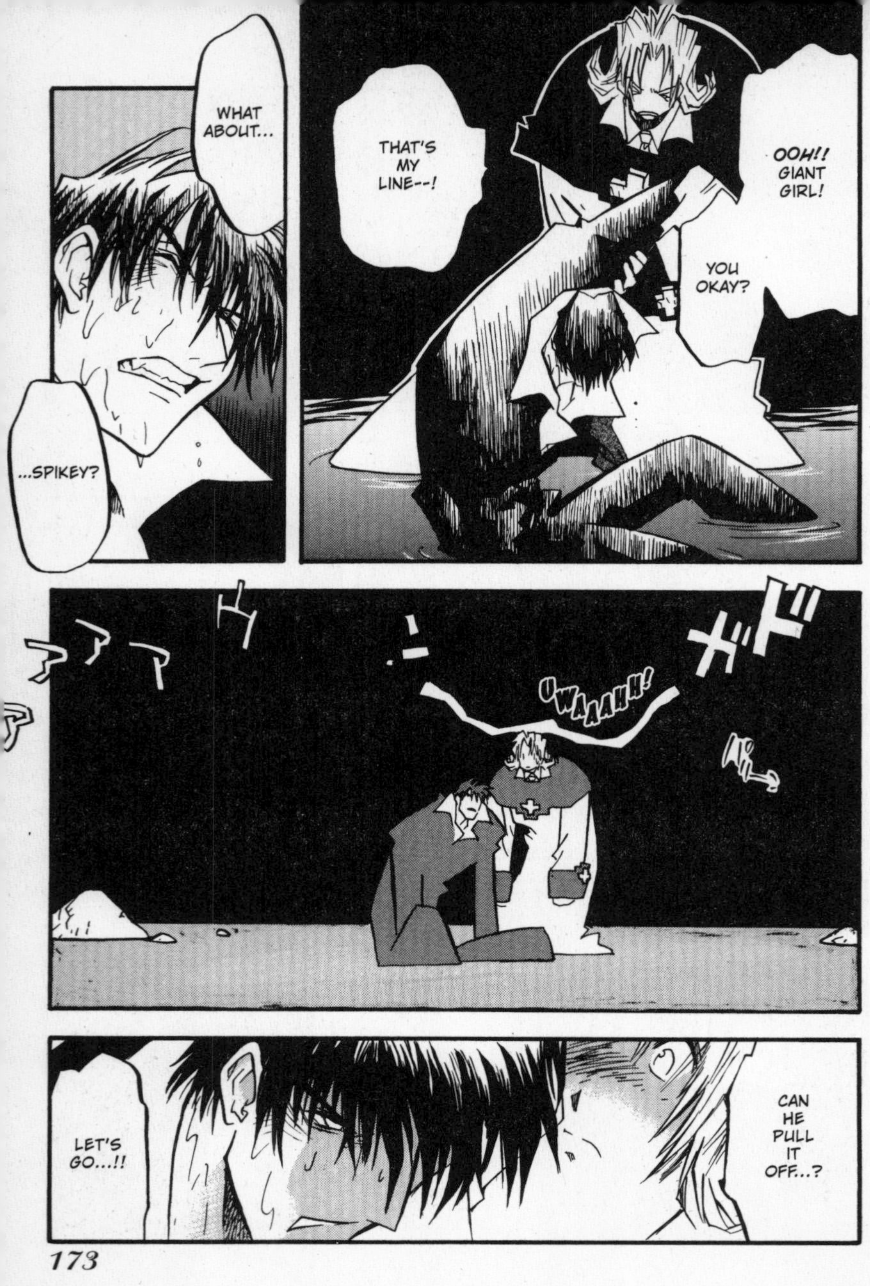
OOH!! GIANT GIRL!
YOU OKAY?
THAT'S MY LINE--!
WHAT ABOUT...
...SPIKEY?
OWAAAHH!
CAN HE PULL IT OFF...?
LET'S GO...!!

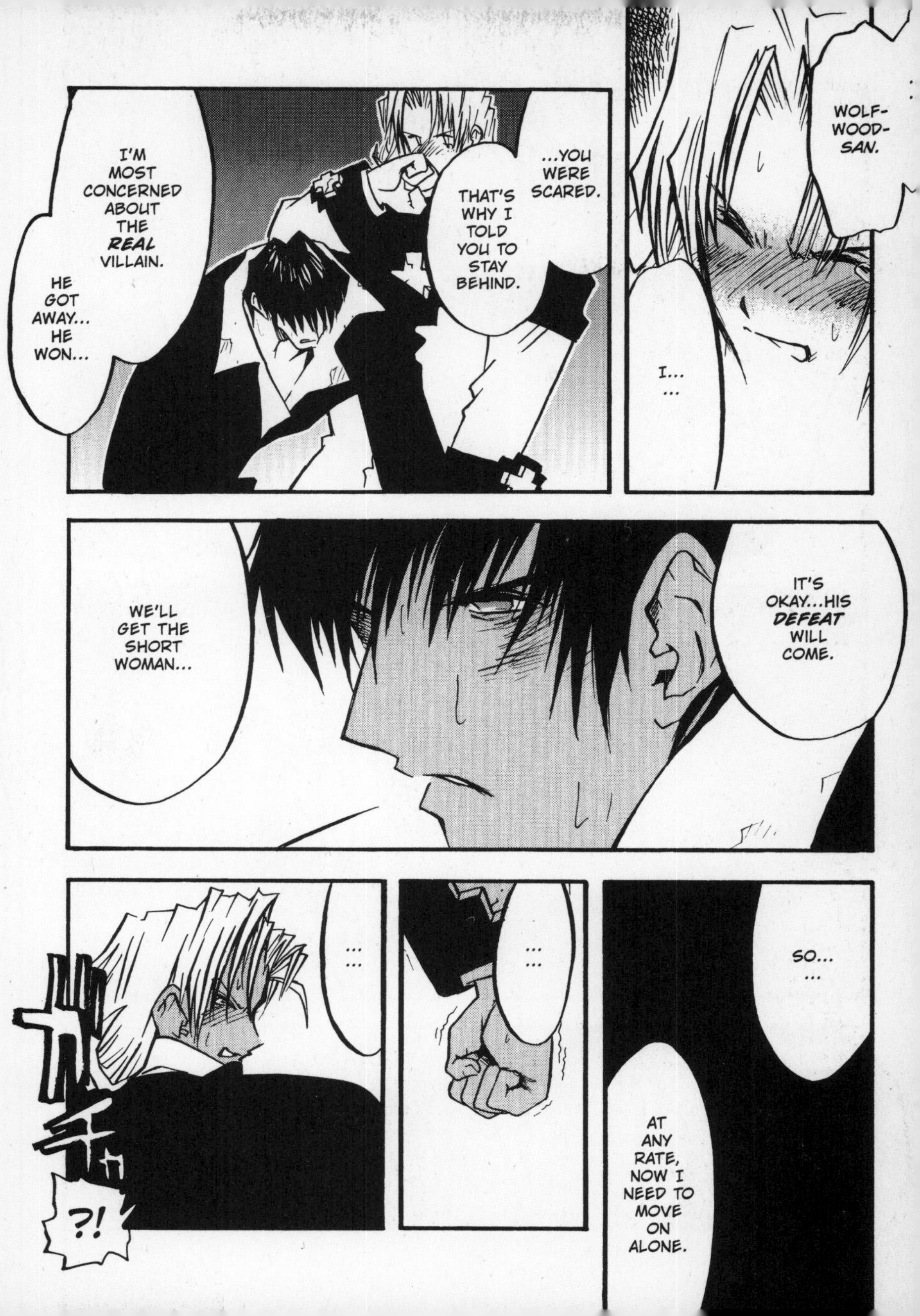
WOLF-WOOD-SAN.
I... ...
...YOU WERE SCARED.
THAT'S WHY I TOLD YOU TO STAY BEHIND.
I'M MOST CONCERNED ABOUT THE REAL VILLAIN.
HE GOT AWAY... HE WON...
IT'S OKAY...HIS DEFEAT WILL COME.
WE'LL GET THE SHORT WOMAN...
SO... ...
AT ANY RATE, NOW I NEED TO MOVE ON ALONE.
... ...
... ...
?!

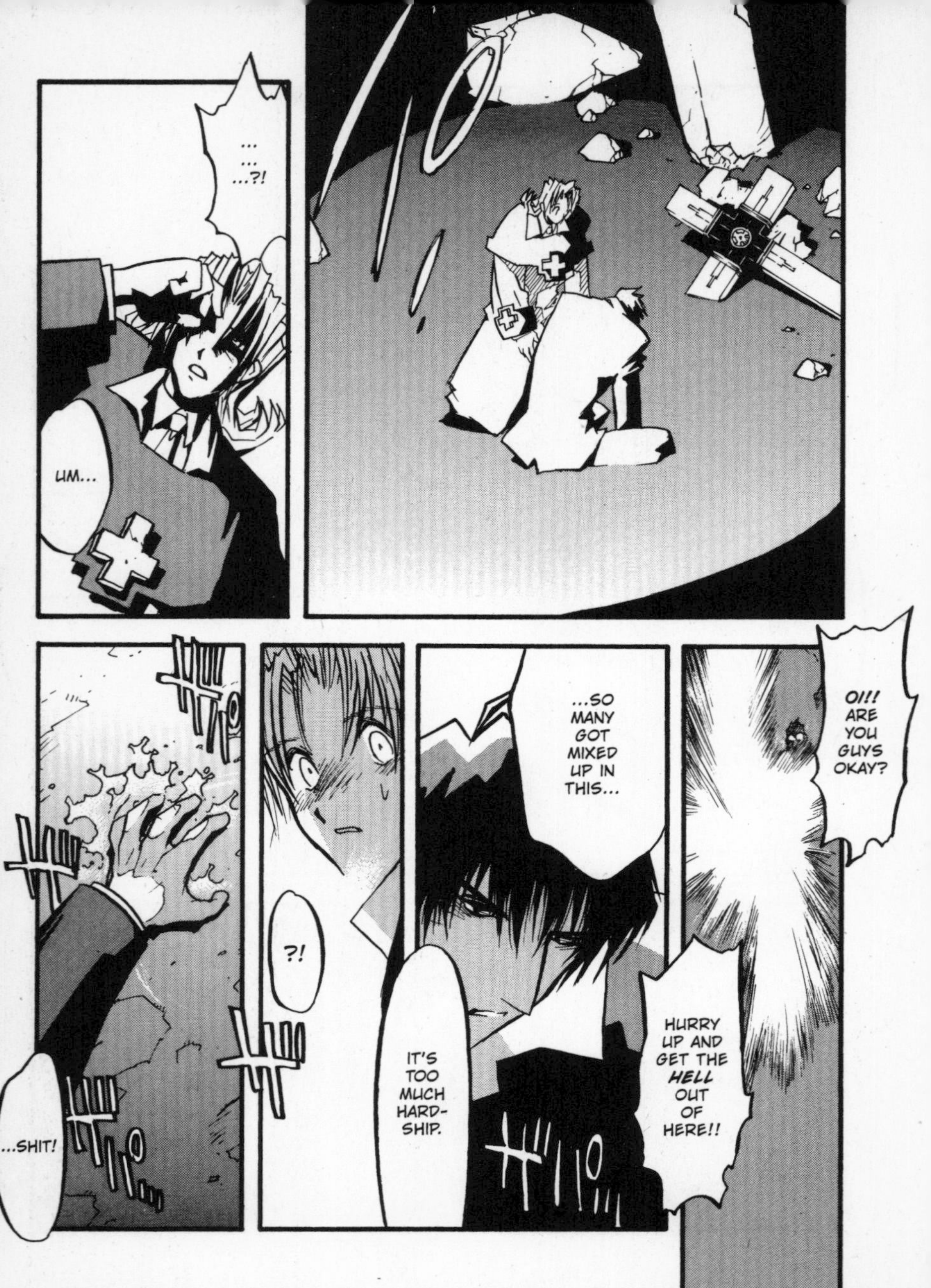
... ...?!
UM...
OI!! ARE YOU GUYS OKAY?
HURRY UP AND GET THE HELL OUT OF HERE!!
...SO MANY GOT MIXED UP IN THIS...
IT'S TOO MUCH HARD-SHIP.
?!
...SHIT!

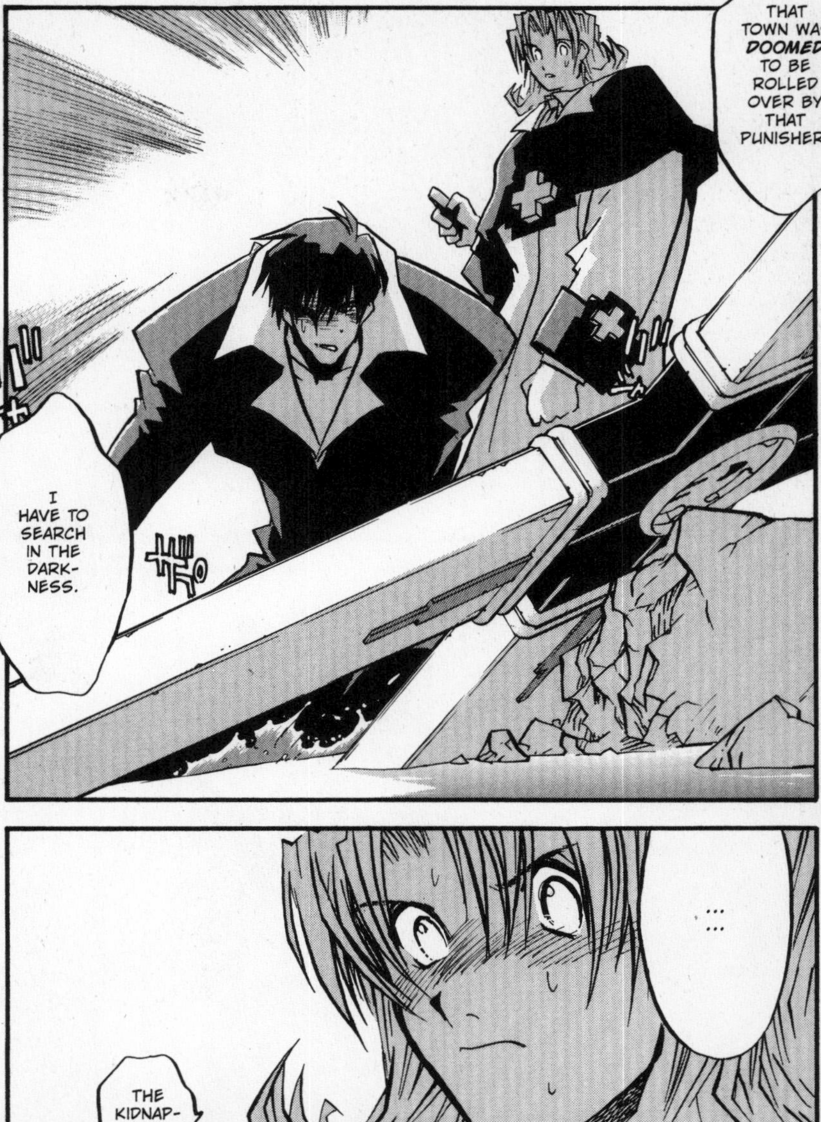
THAT TOWN WAS ***DOOMED*** TO BE ROLLED OVER BY THAT PUNISHER.
I HAVE TO SEARCH IN THE DARK-NESS.
......
THE KIDNAP-PER.

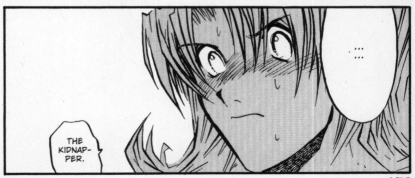

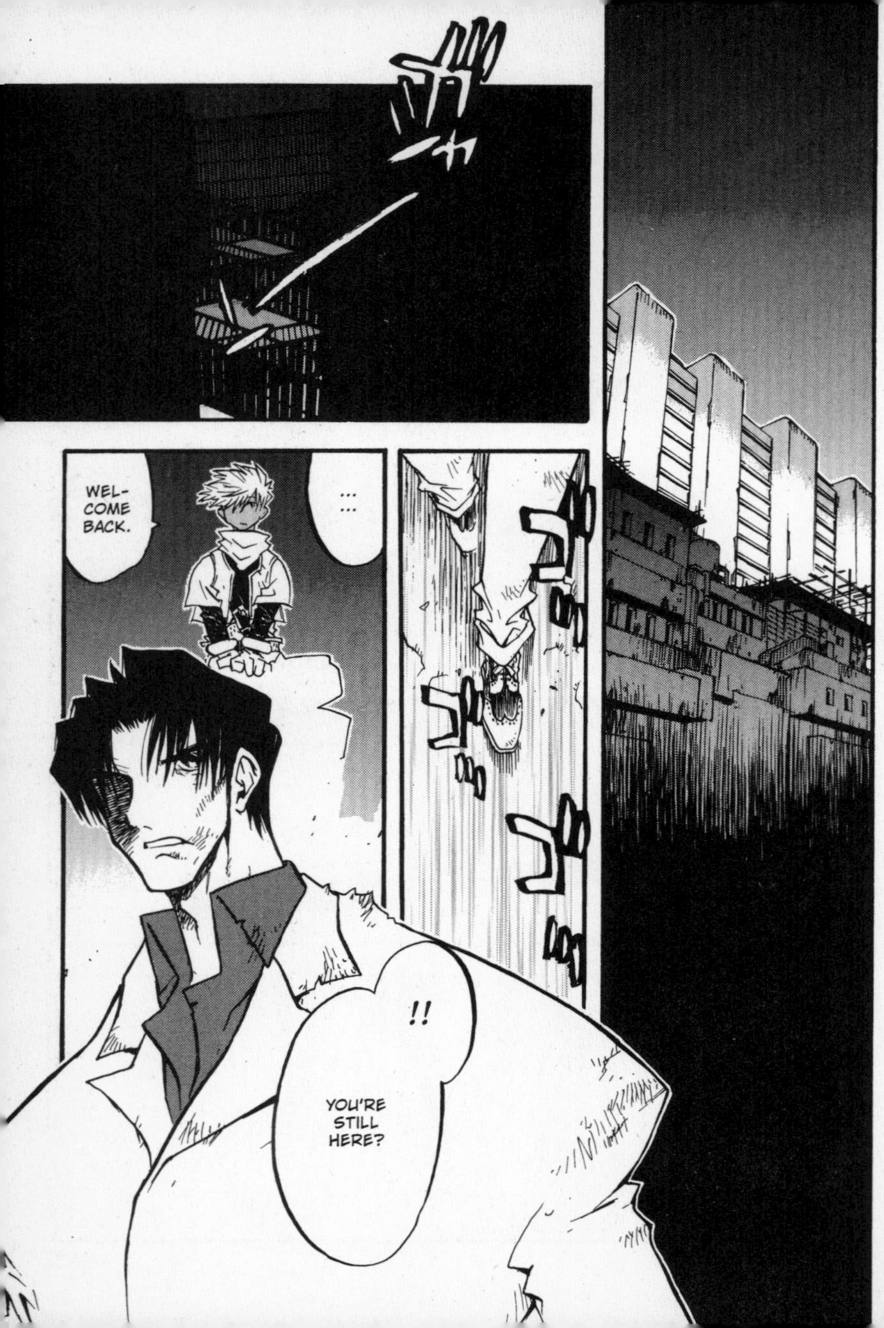
...
...
WEL-
COME
BACK.
!!
YOU'RE
STILL
HERE?

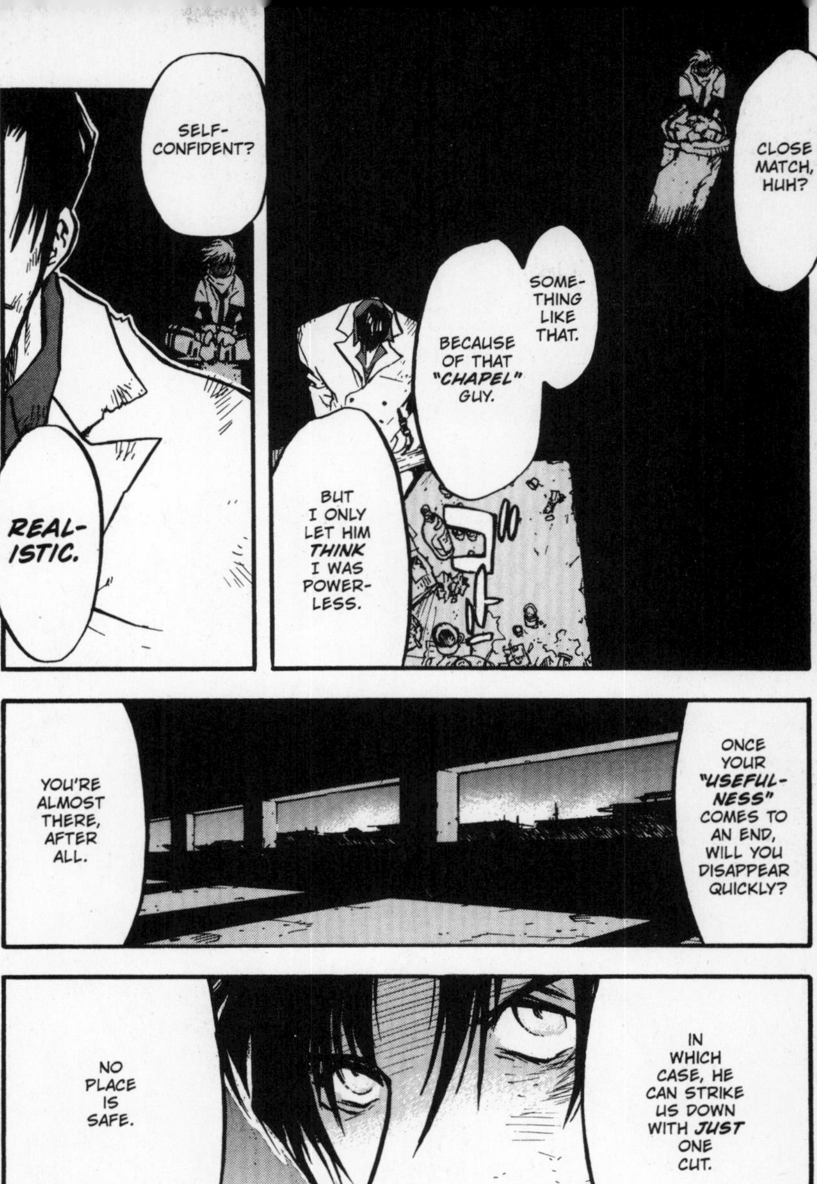
CLOSE MATCH, HUH?
SOME-THING LIKE THAT.
BECAUSE OF THAT "CHAPEL" GUY.
BUT I ONLY LET HIM THINK I WAS POWER-LESS.
SELF-CONFIDENT?
REAL-ISTIC.
ONCE YOUR "USEFUL-NESS" COMES TO AN END, WILL YOU DISAPPEAR QUICKLY?
YOU'RE ALMOST THERE, AFTER ALL.
IN WHICH CASE, HE CAN STRIKE US DOWN WITH JUST ONE CUT.
NO PLACE IS SAFE.

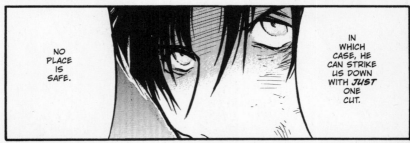

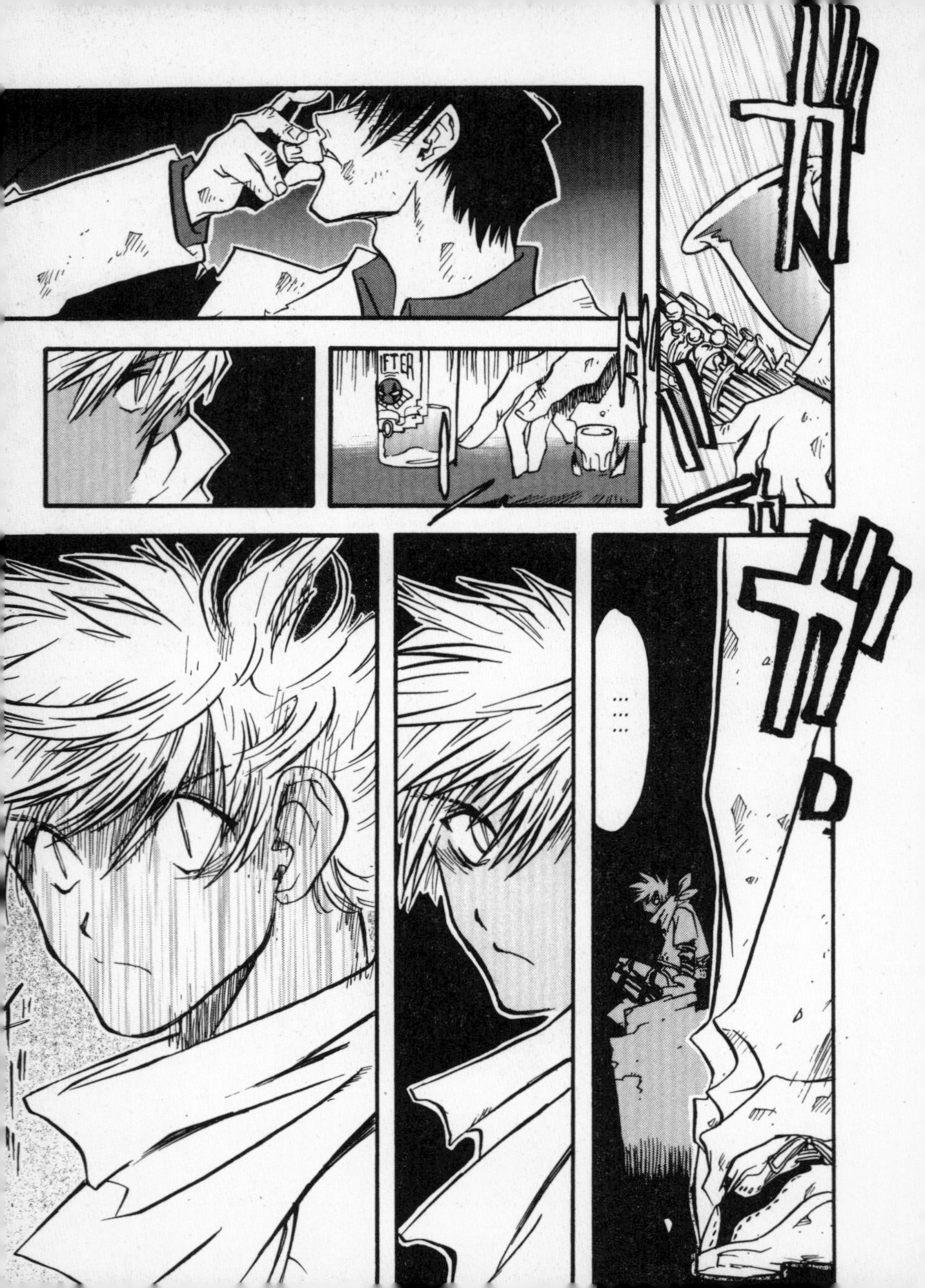

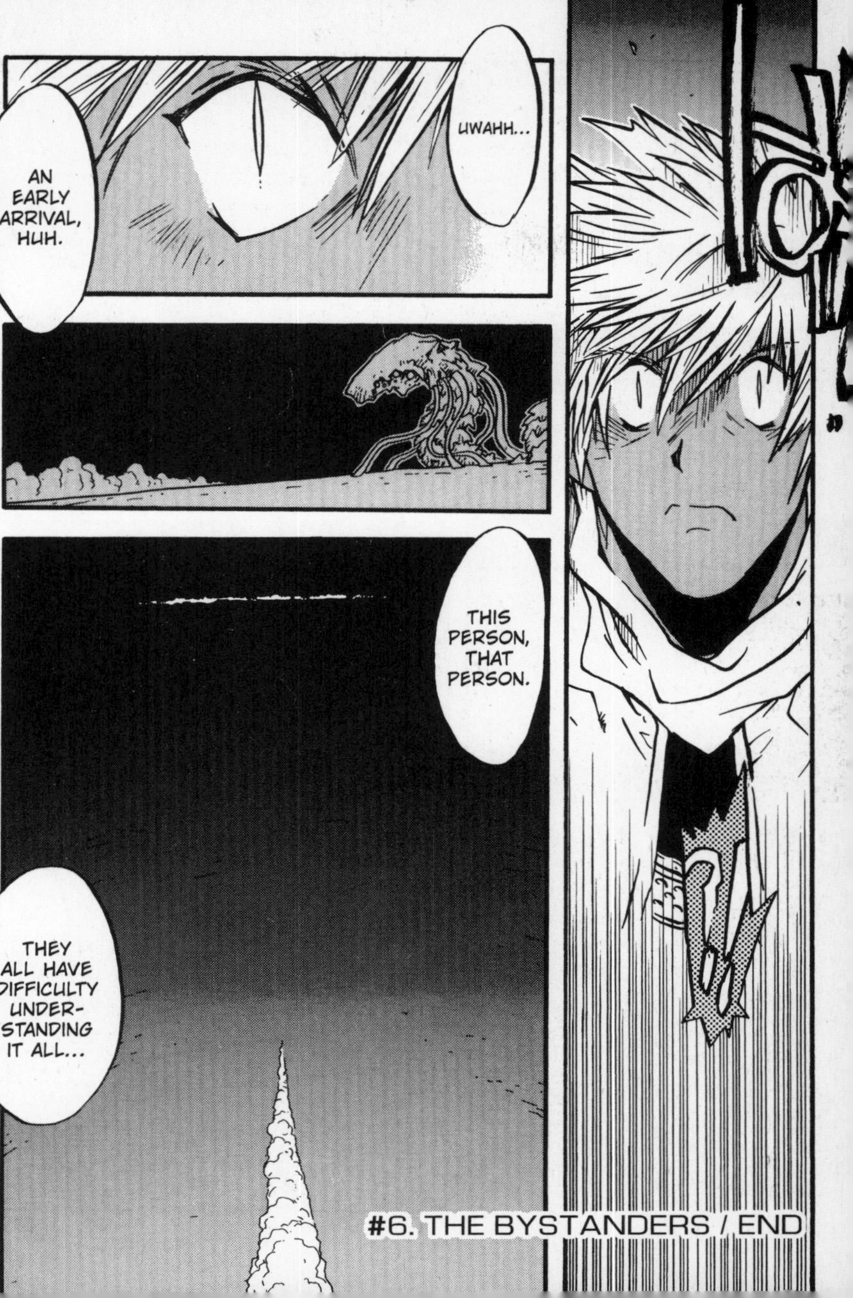
#6. THE BYSTANDERS / END
UWAHH...
AN EARLY ARRIVAL, HUH.
THIS PERSON, THAT PERSON.
THEY ALL HAVE DIFFICULTY UNDER-STANDING IT ALL...

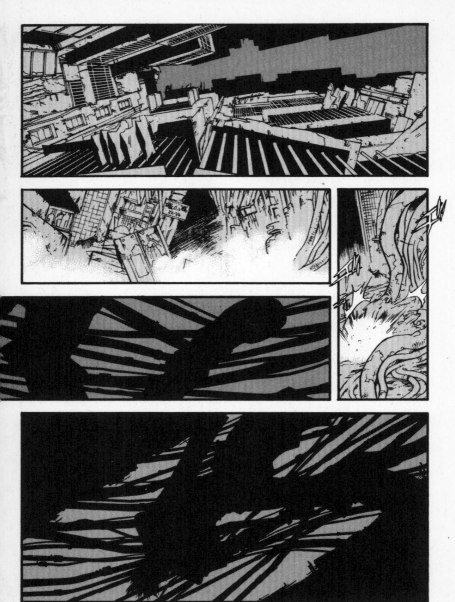

181

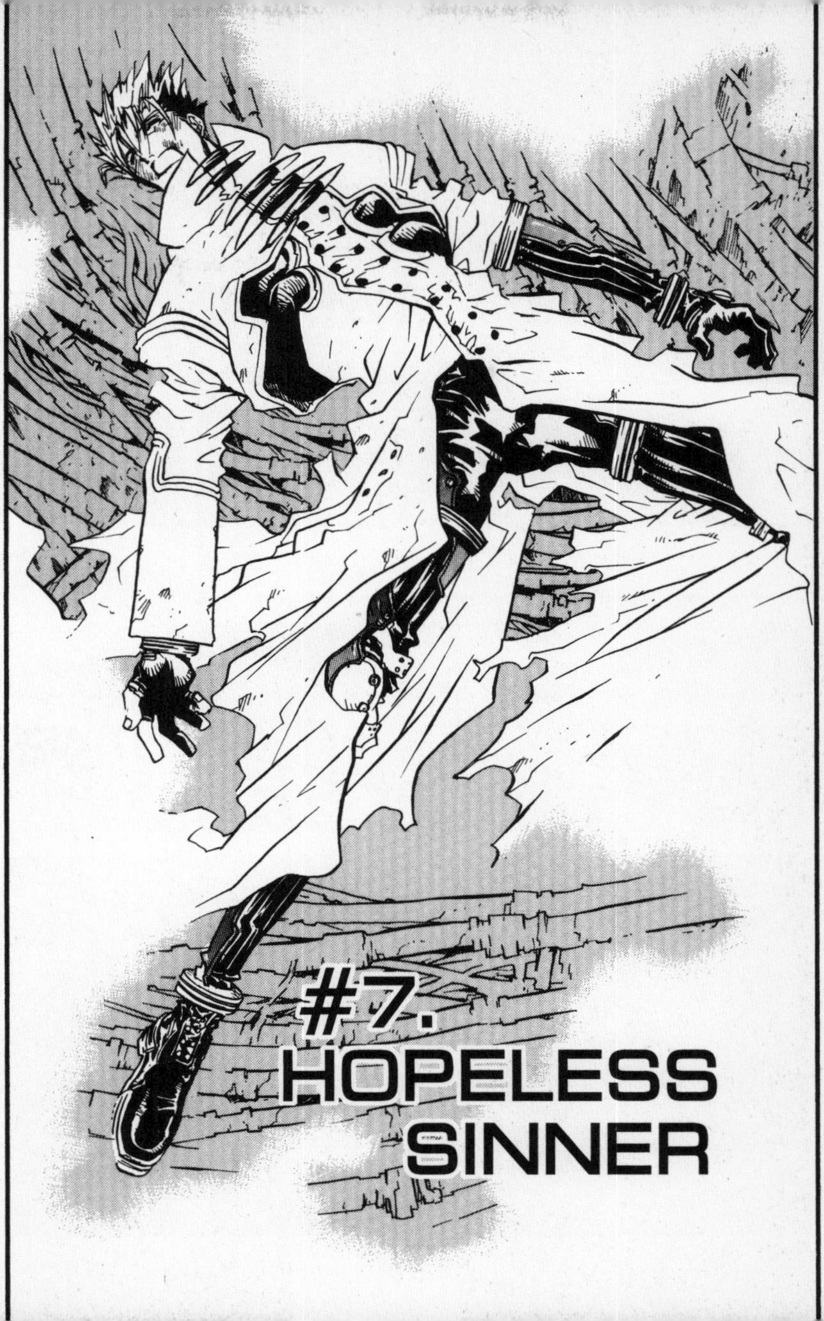
#7.
HOPELESS
SINNER

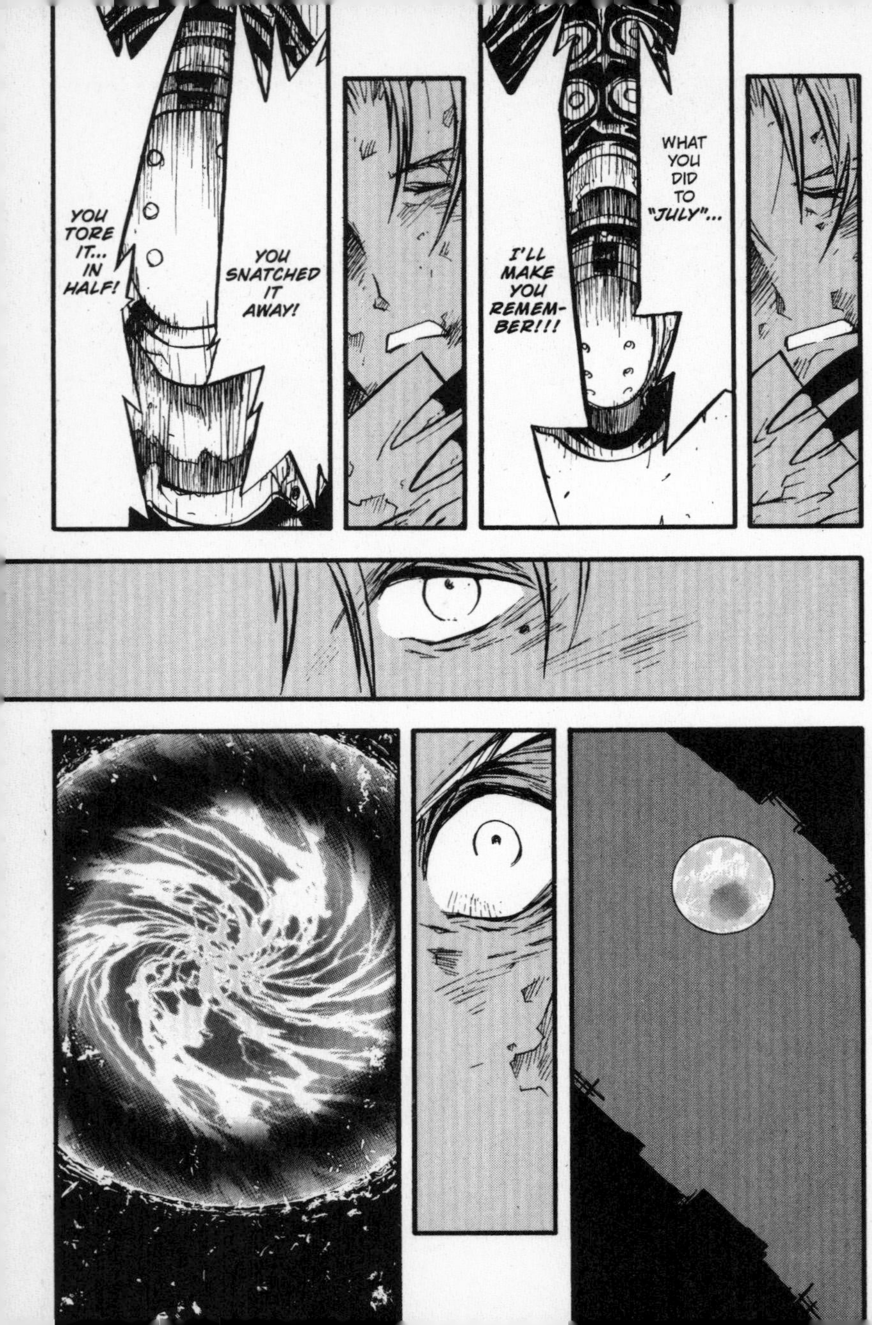
WHAT YOU DID TO "JULY"...
I'LL MAKE YOU REMEMBER!!!
YOU SNATCHED IT AWAY!
YOU TORE IT... IN HALF!

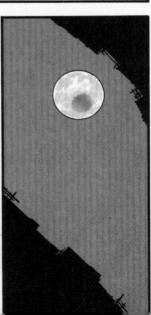

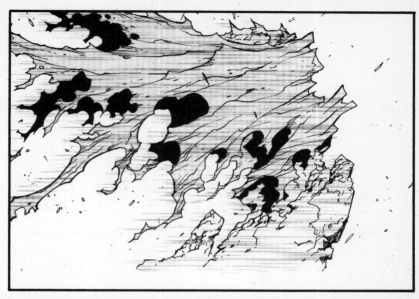

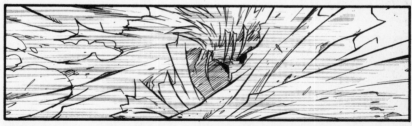

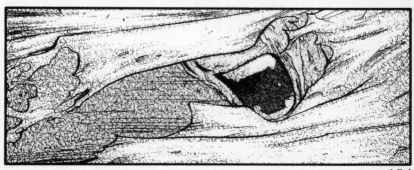

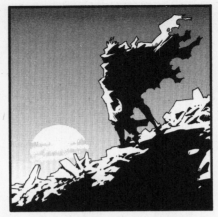

YES.

I BROUGHT THE NIGHT-MARE.

MAYBE I HAVEN'T GIVEN IT ENOUGH THOUGHT.

ONE HUNDRED THOUSAND PEOPLE WIPED AWAY...

IT WAS MY OWN SIN...

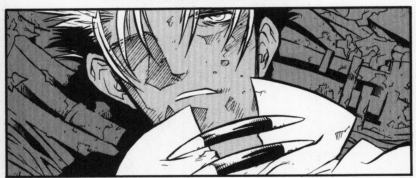

I AM A MURDERER.

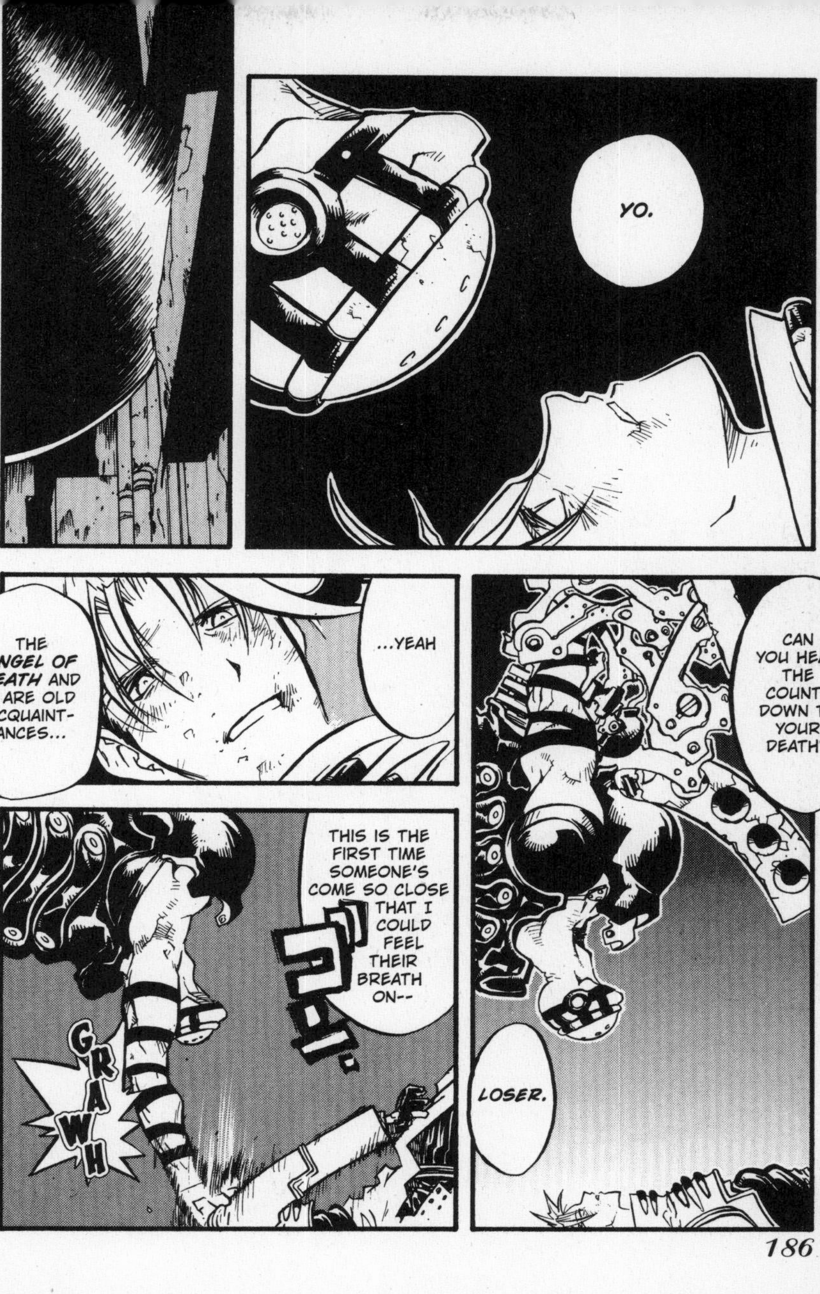
YO.
CAN YOU HEAR THE COUNT-DOWN TO YOUR DEATH?
LOSER.
...YEAH
THE *ANGEL OF DEATH* AND I ARE OLD ACQUAINT-ANCES...
THIS IS THE FIRST TIME SOMEONE'S COME SO CLOSE THAT I COULD FEEL THEIR BREATH ON--
GRAWH

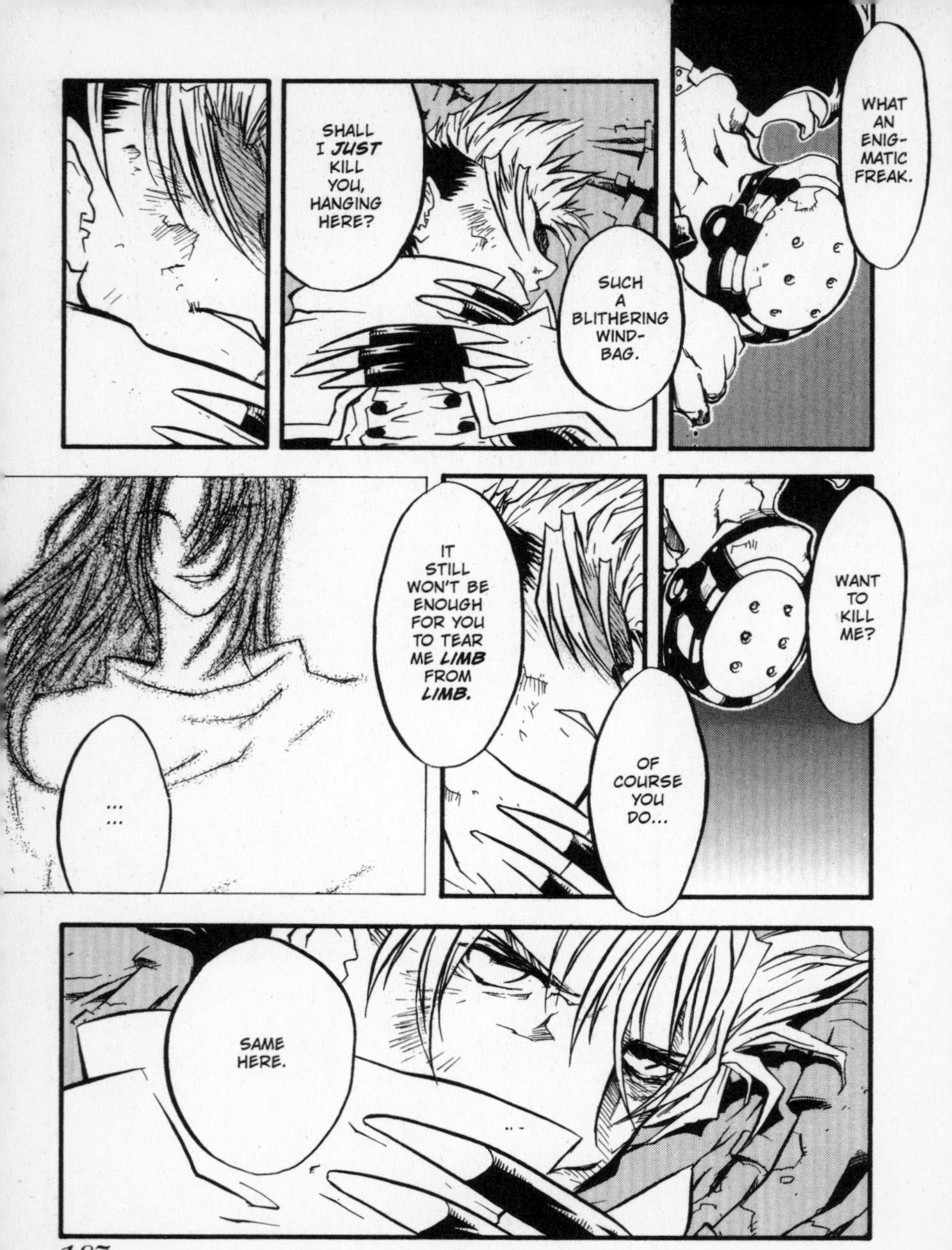
WHAT AN ENIG-MATIC FREAK.
SUCH A BLITHERING WIND-BAG.
SHALL I *JUST* KILL YOU, HANGING HERE?
WANT TO KILL ME?
OF COURSE YOU DO...
IT STILL WON'T BE ENOUGH FOR YOU TO TEAR ME *LIMB* FROM *LIMB.*
... ...
SAME HERE.

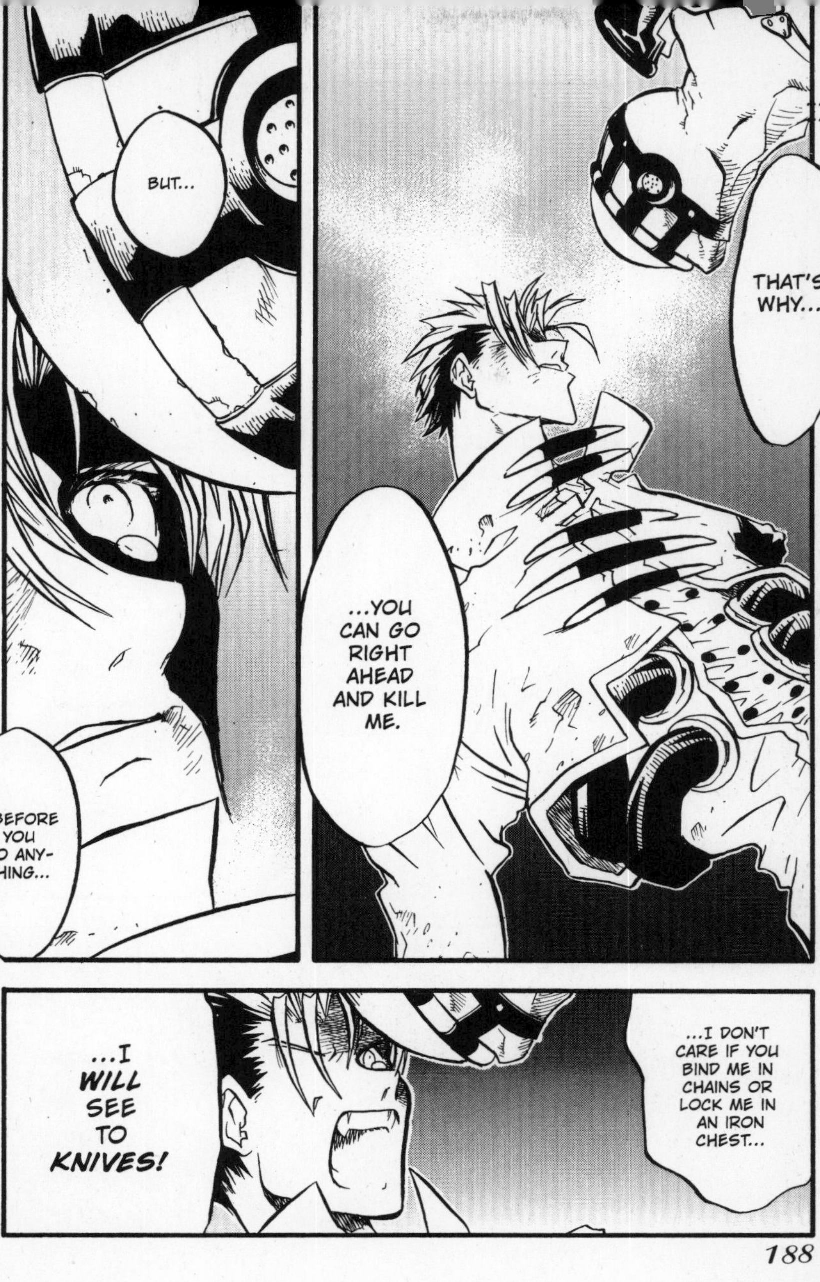
THAT'S WHY...
...YOU CAN GO RIGHT AHEAD AND KILL ME.
BUT...
...BEFORE YOU DO ANYTHING...
...I DON'T CARE IF YOU BIND ME IN CHAINS OR LOCK ME IN AN IRON CHEST...
...I *WILL* SEE TO *KNIVES!*

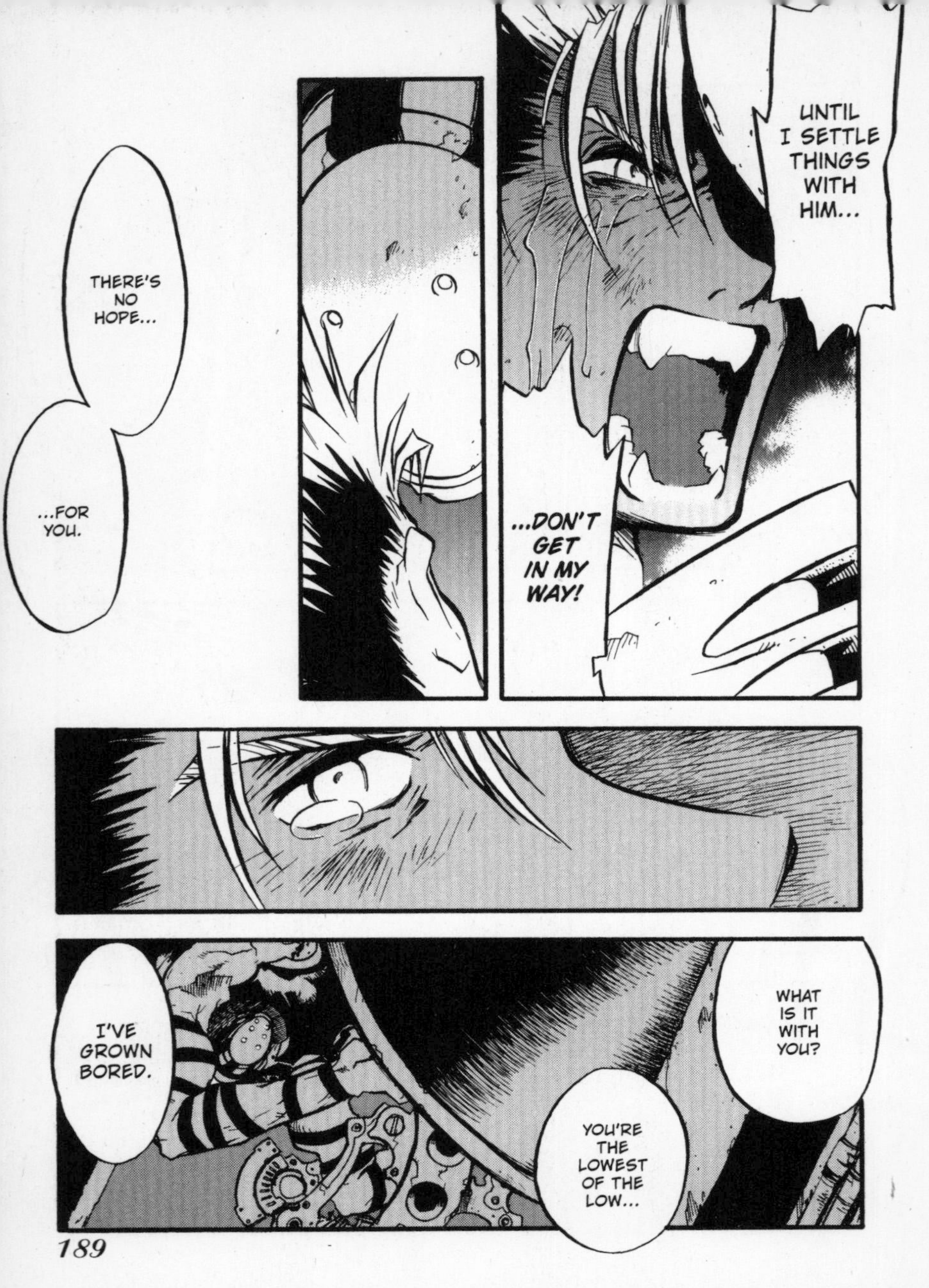
UNTIL I SETTLE THINGS WITH HIM...
...DON'T GET IN MY WAY!
THERE'S NO HOPE...
...FOR YOU.
WHAT IS IT WITH YOU?
YOU'RE THE LOWEST OF THE LOW...
I'VE GROWN BORED.

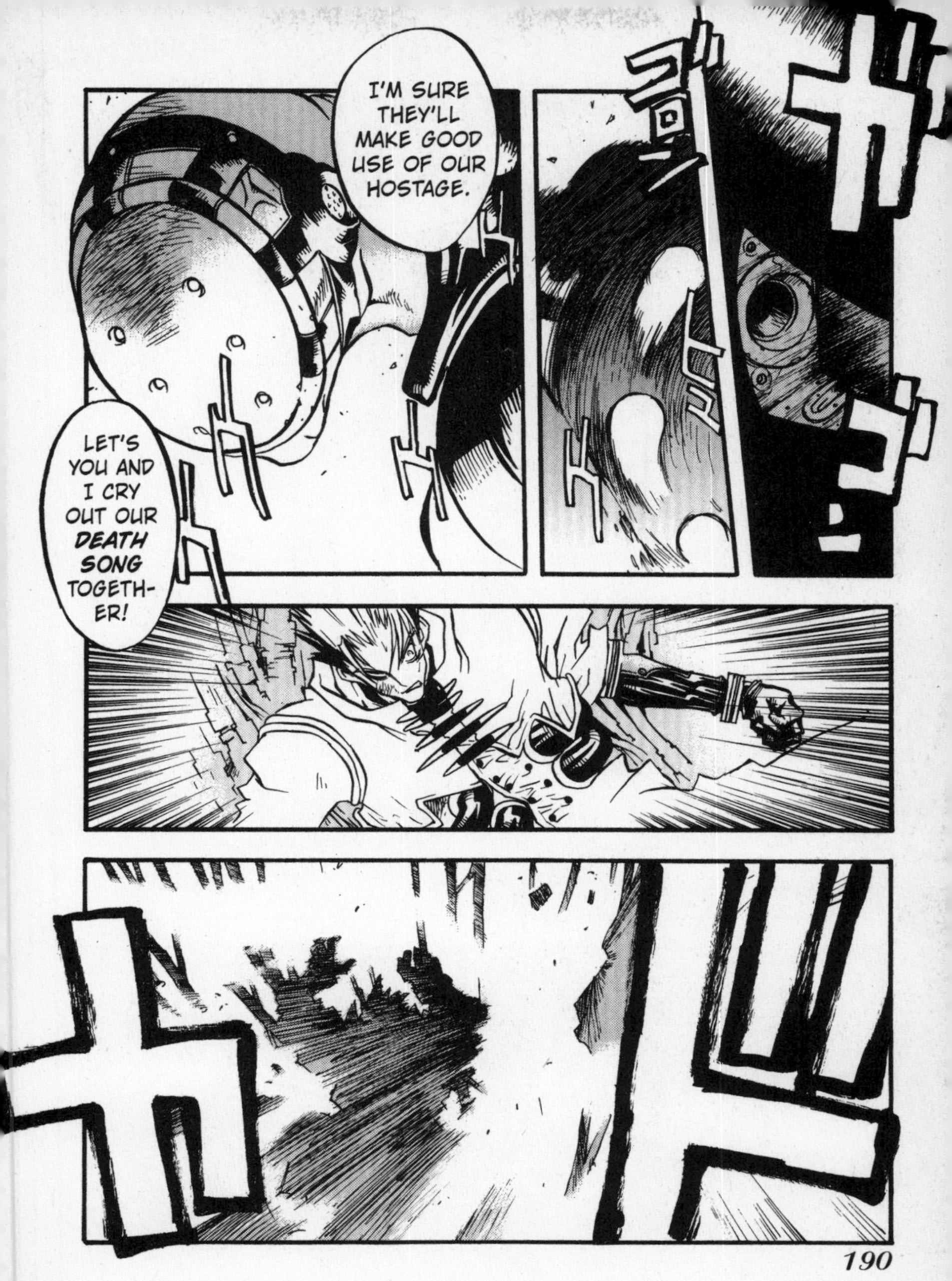
I'M SURE THEY'LL MAKE GOOD USE OF OUR HOSTAGE.
LET'S YOU AND I CRY OUT OUR *DEATH SONG* TOGETHER!

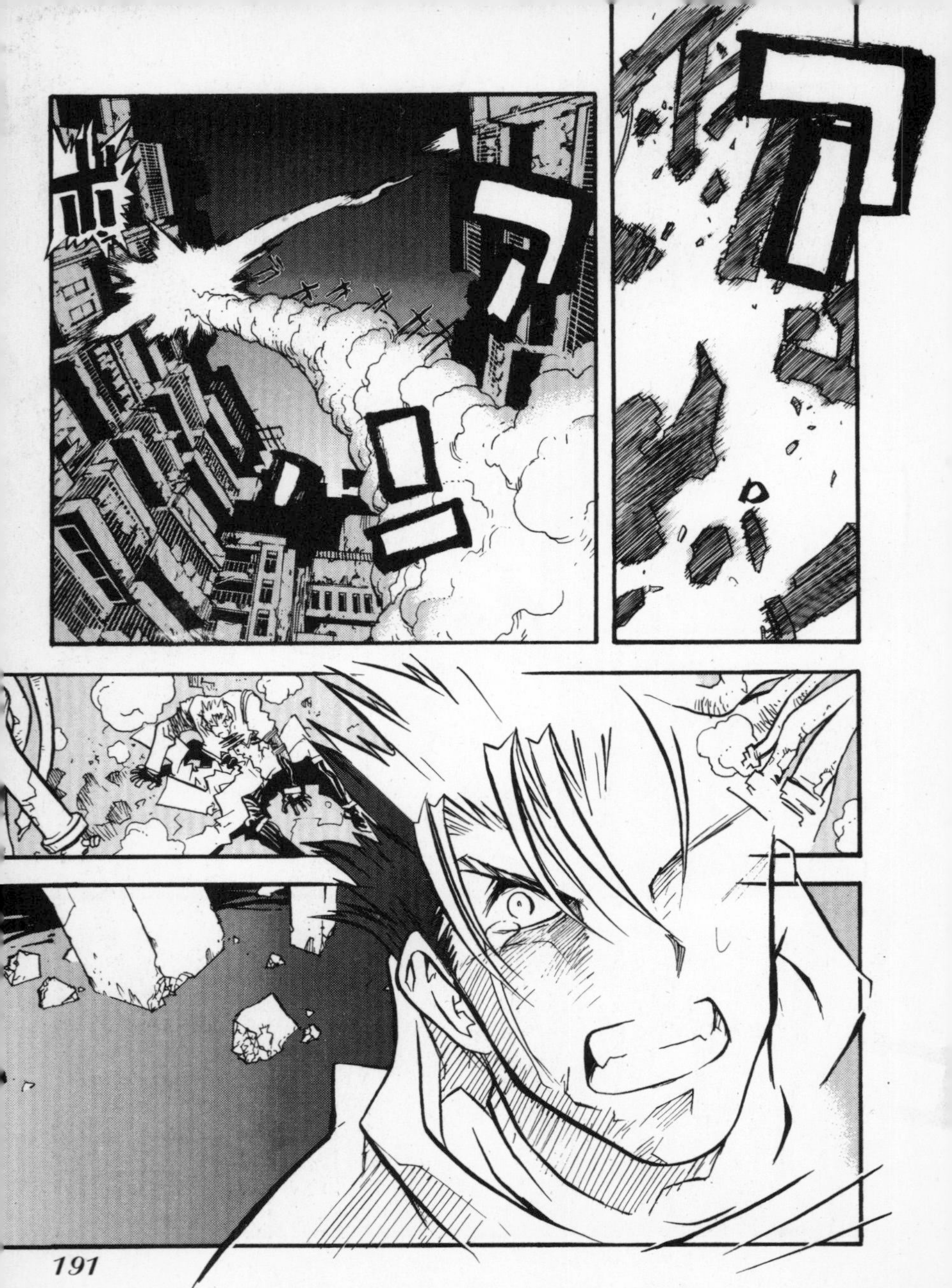

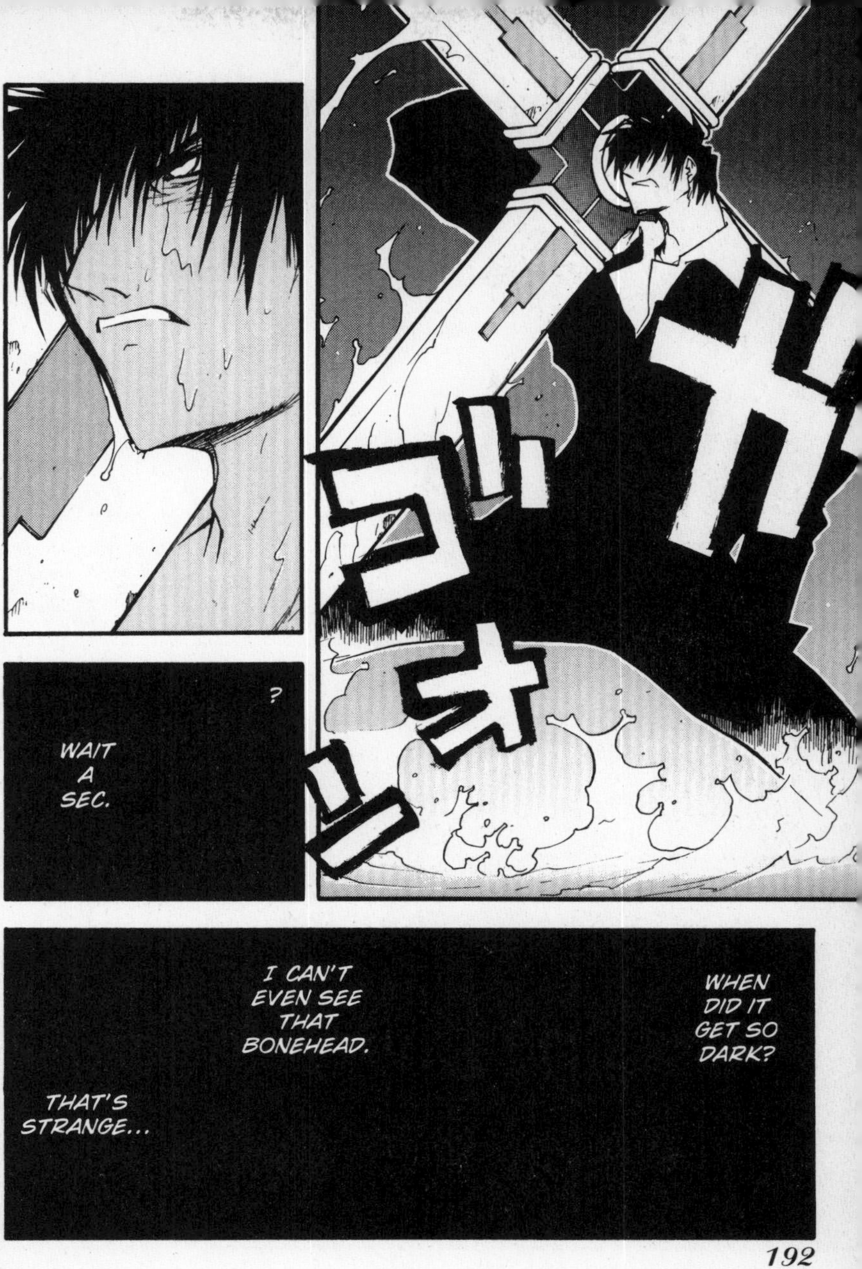
ガ
ゴォン
?
WAIT A SEC.
WHEN DID IT GET SO DARK?
I CAN'T EVEN SEE THAT BONEHEAD.
THAT'S STRANGE...

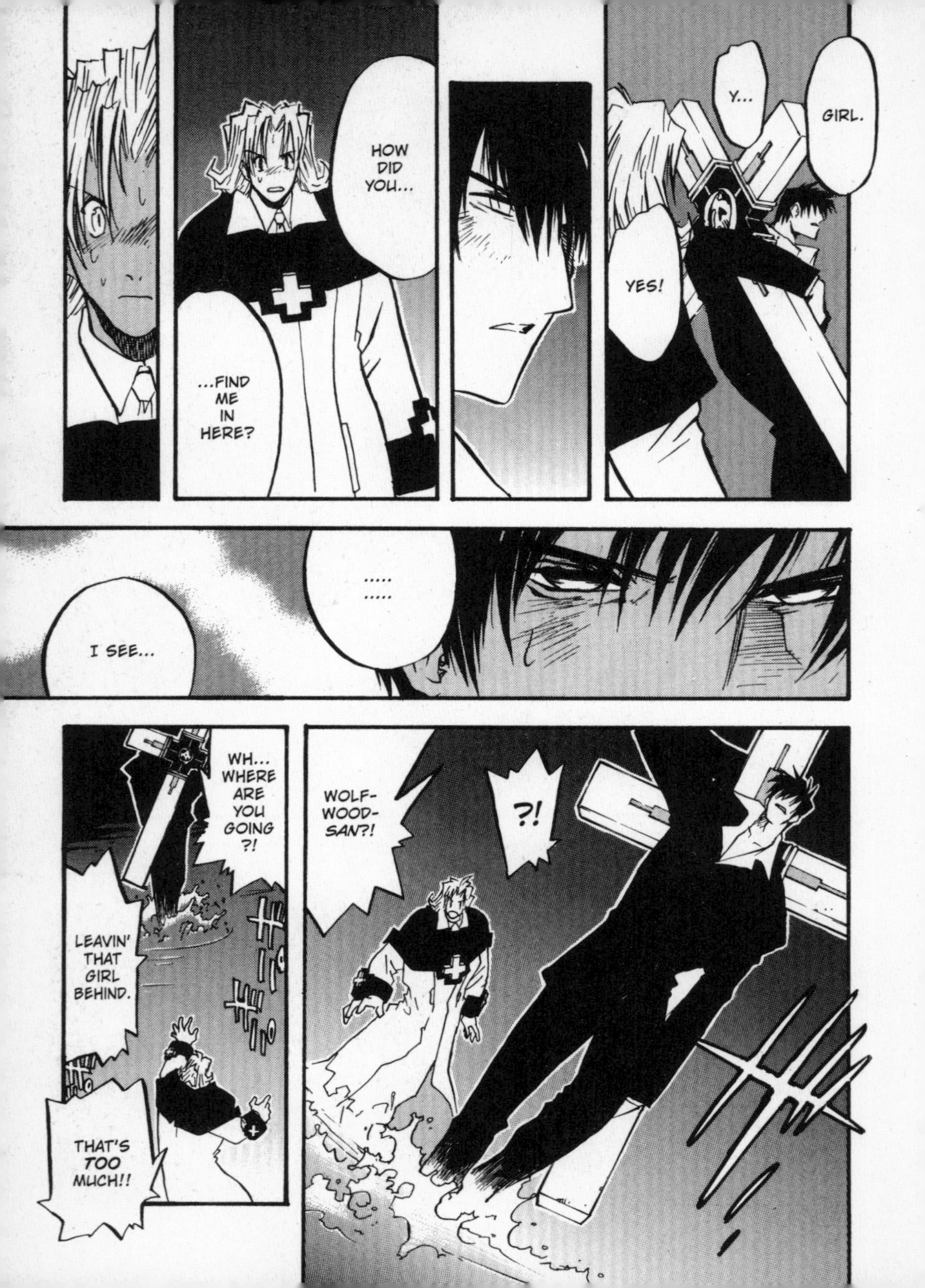
GIRL.
Y...
YES!
HOW DID YOU...
...FIND ME IN HERE?
.....
.....
I SEE...
?!
WOLF-WOOD-SAN?!
WH... WHERE ARE YOU GOING?!
LEAVIN' THAT GIRL BEHIND.
THAT'S *TOO* MUCH!!

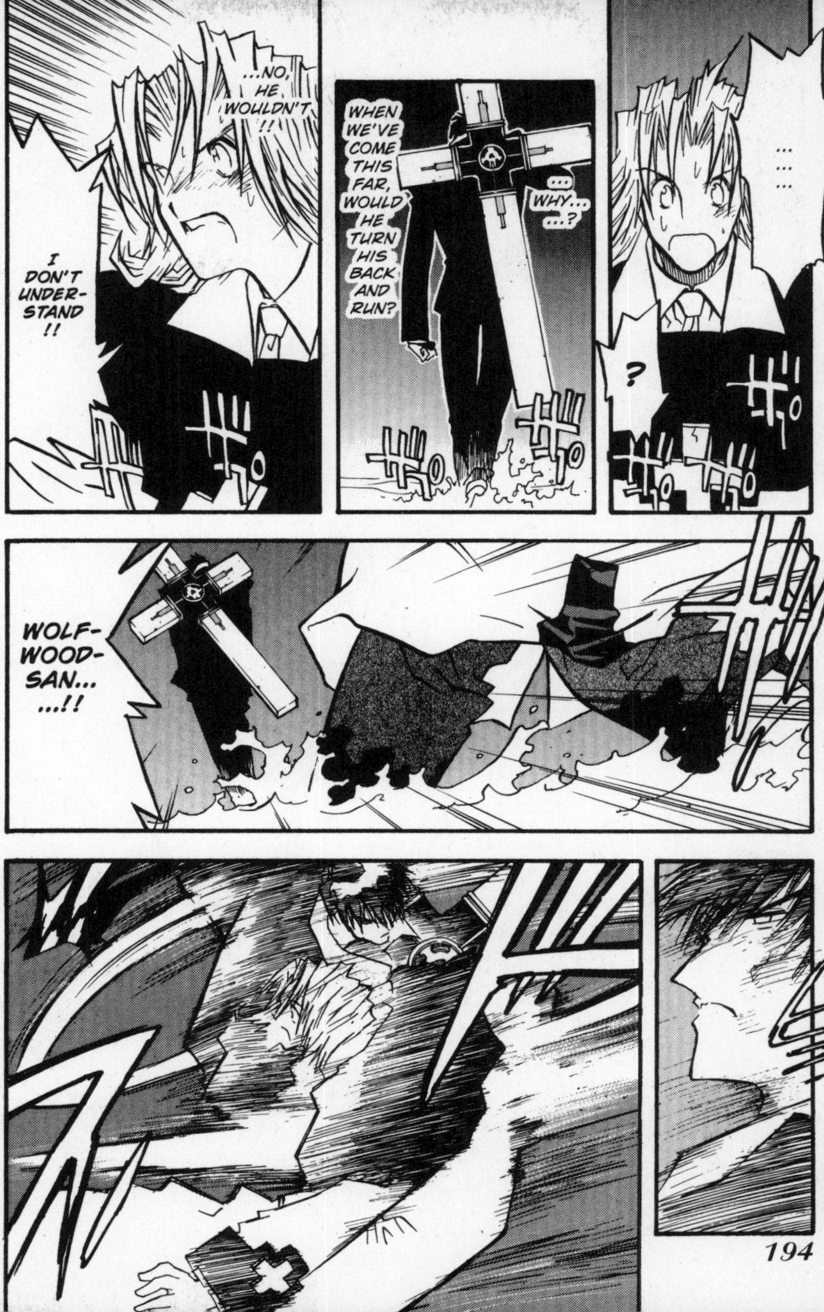
...
...
...
?
...WHY...
...?
WHEN WE'VE COME THIS FAR, WOULD HE TURN HIS BACK AND RUN?
...NO, HE WOULDN'T !!
I DON'T UNDER-STAND !!
WOLF-WOOD-SAN...
...!!

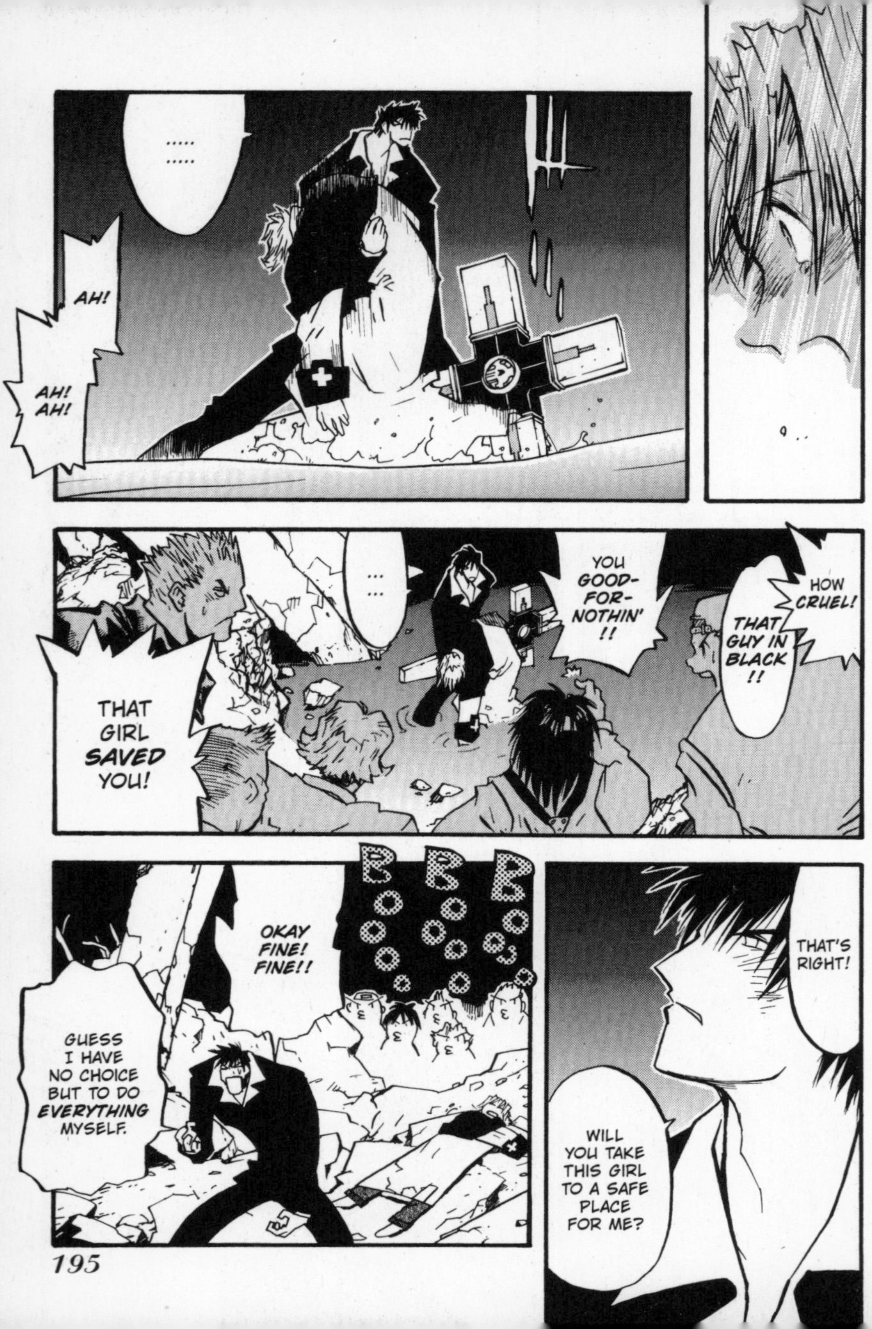

......
......
AH!
AH! AH!
HOW CRUEL! THAT GUY IN BLACK!!
YOU GOOD-FOR-NOTHIN'!!
......
THAT GIRL SAVED YOU!
THAT'S RIGHT!
WILL YOU TAKE THIS GIRL TO A SAFE PLACE FOR ME?
BOOOOO
OKAY FINE! FINE!!
GUESS I HAVE NO CHOICE BUT TO DO EVERYTHING MYSELF.

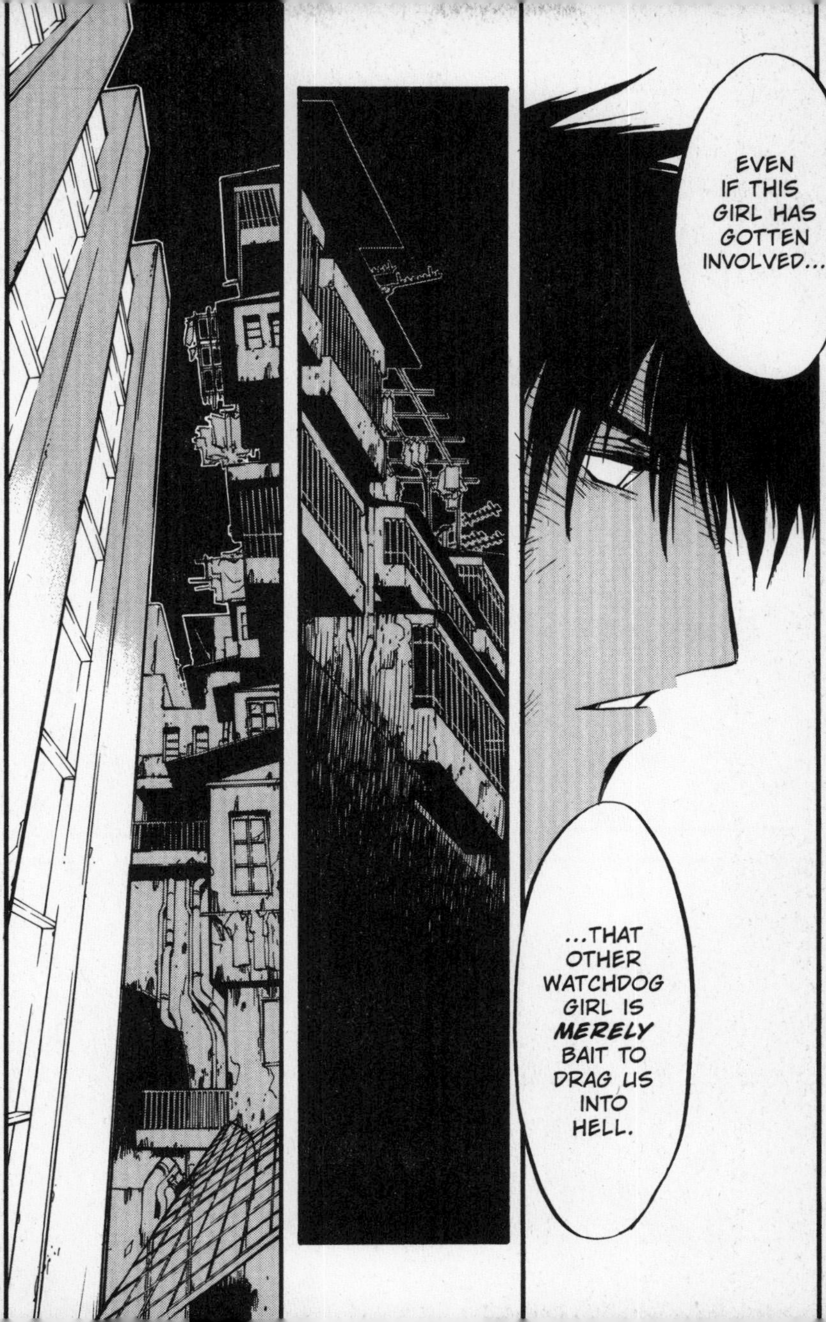
EVEN IF THIS GIRL HAS GOTTEN INVOLVED...
...THAT OTHER WATCHDOG GIRL IS *MERELY* BAIT TO DRAG US INTO HELL.

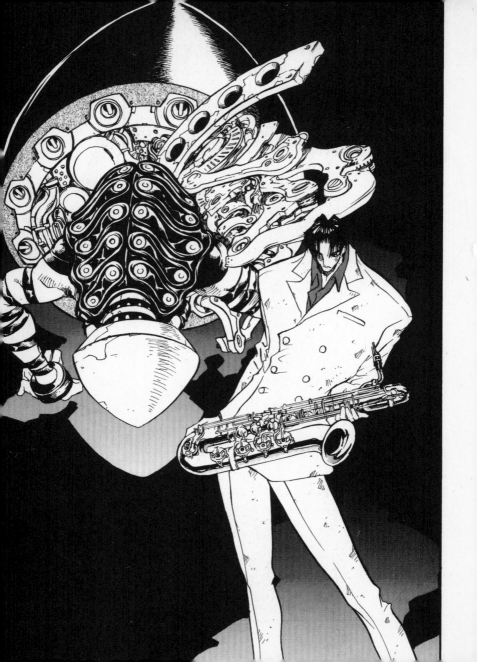

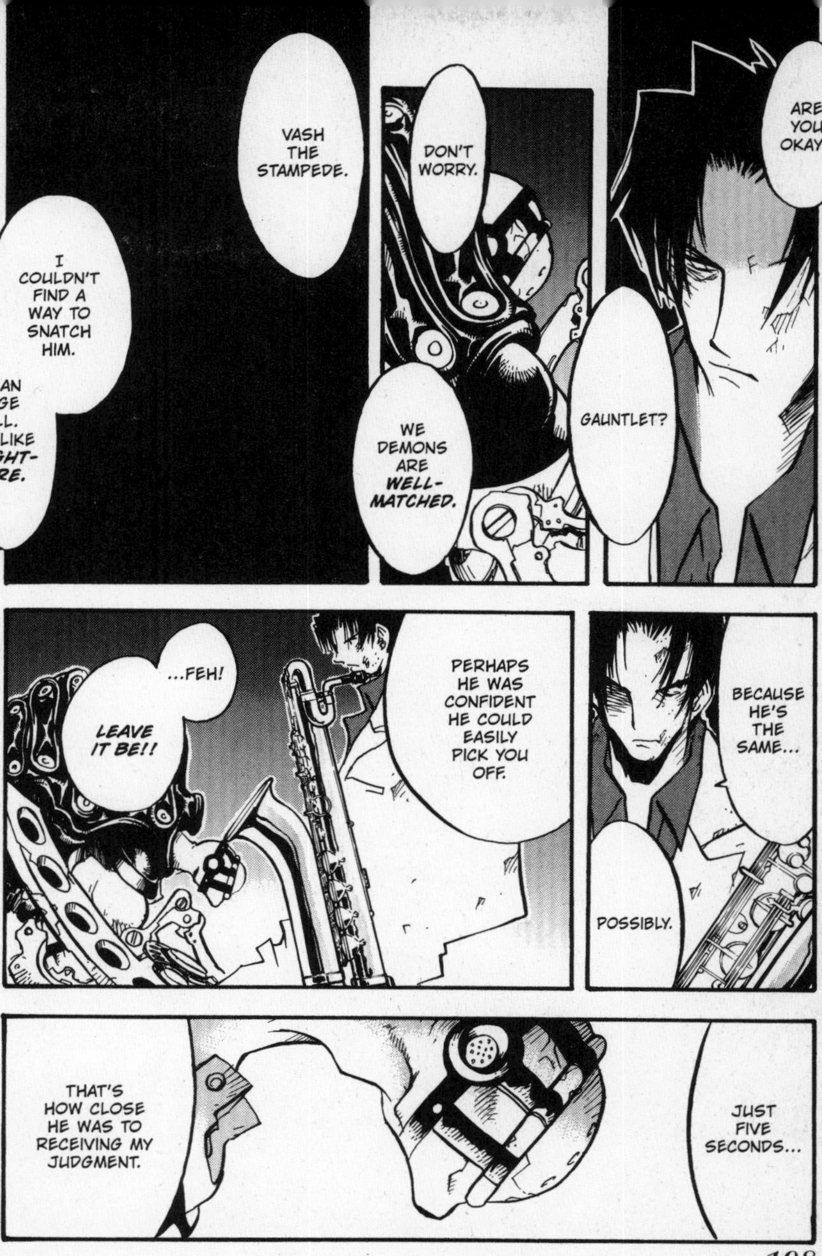
ARE YOU OKAY?
GAUNTLET?
DON'T WORRY.
WE DEMONS ARE *WELL-MATCHED.*
VASH THE STAMPEDE.
I COULDN'T FIND A WAY TO SNATCH HIM.
HE CAN DODGE IT ALL. HE'S LIKE A *NIGHT-MARE.*
BECAUSE HE'S THE SAME...
POSSIBLY.
PERHAPS HE WAS CONFIDENT HE COULD EASILY PICK YOU OFF.
...FEH!
LEAVE IT BE!!
JUST FIVE SECONDS...
THAT'S HOW CLOSE HE WAS TO RECEIVING MY JUDGMENT.

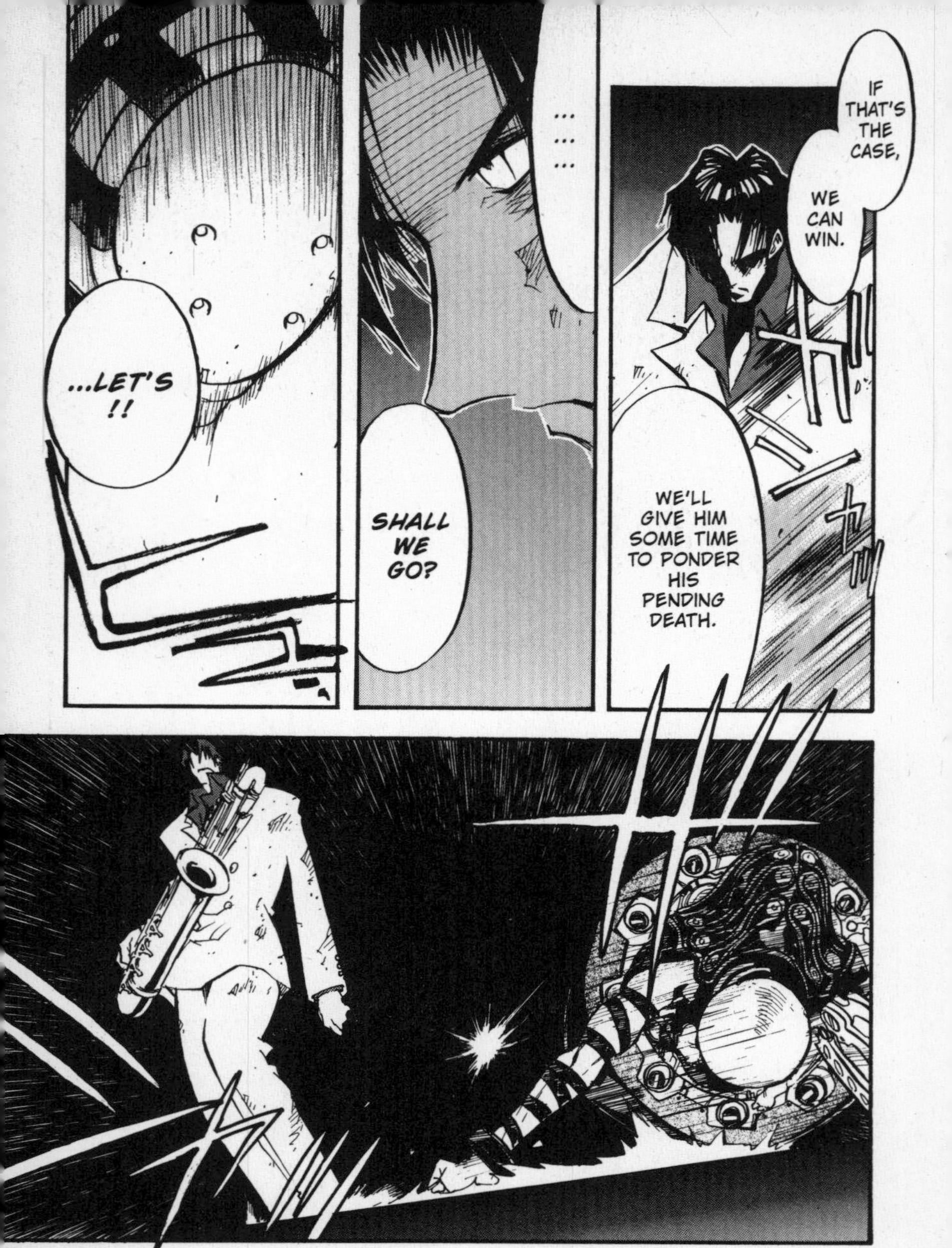
IF THAT'S THE CASE,
WE CAN WIN.
WE'LL GIVE HIM SOME TIME TO PONDER HIS PENDING DEATH.
... ...
SHALL WE GO?
...LET'S !!

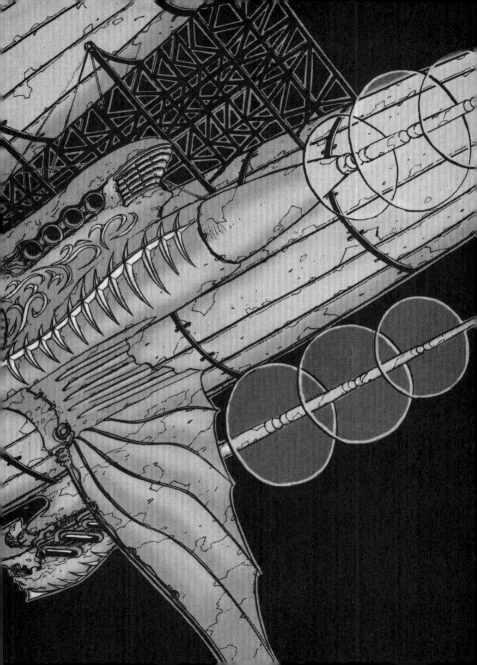

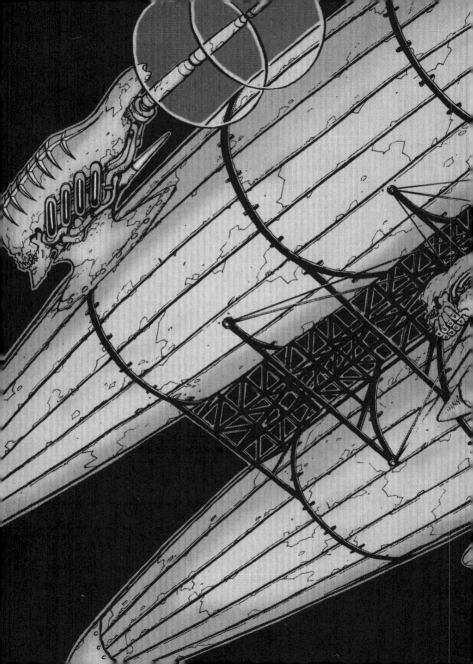

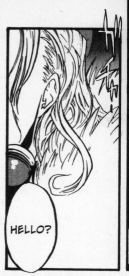
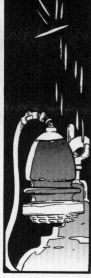
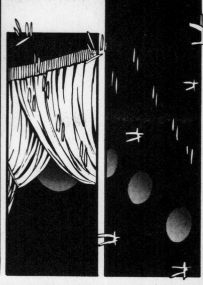

HELLO?

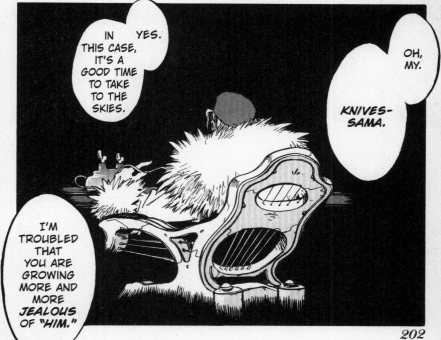

IN THIS CASE, IT'S A GOOD TIME TO TAKE TO THE SKIES.

YES.

OH, MY.

KNIVES-SAMA.

I'M TROUBLED THAT YOU ARE GROWING MORE AND MORE *JEALOUS* OF "*HIM*."

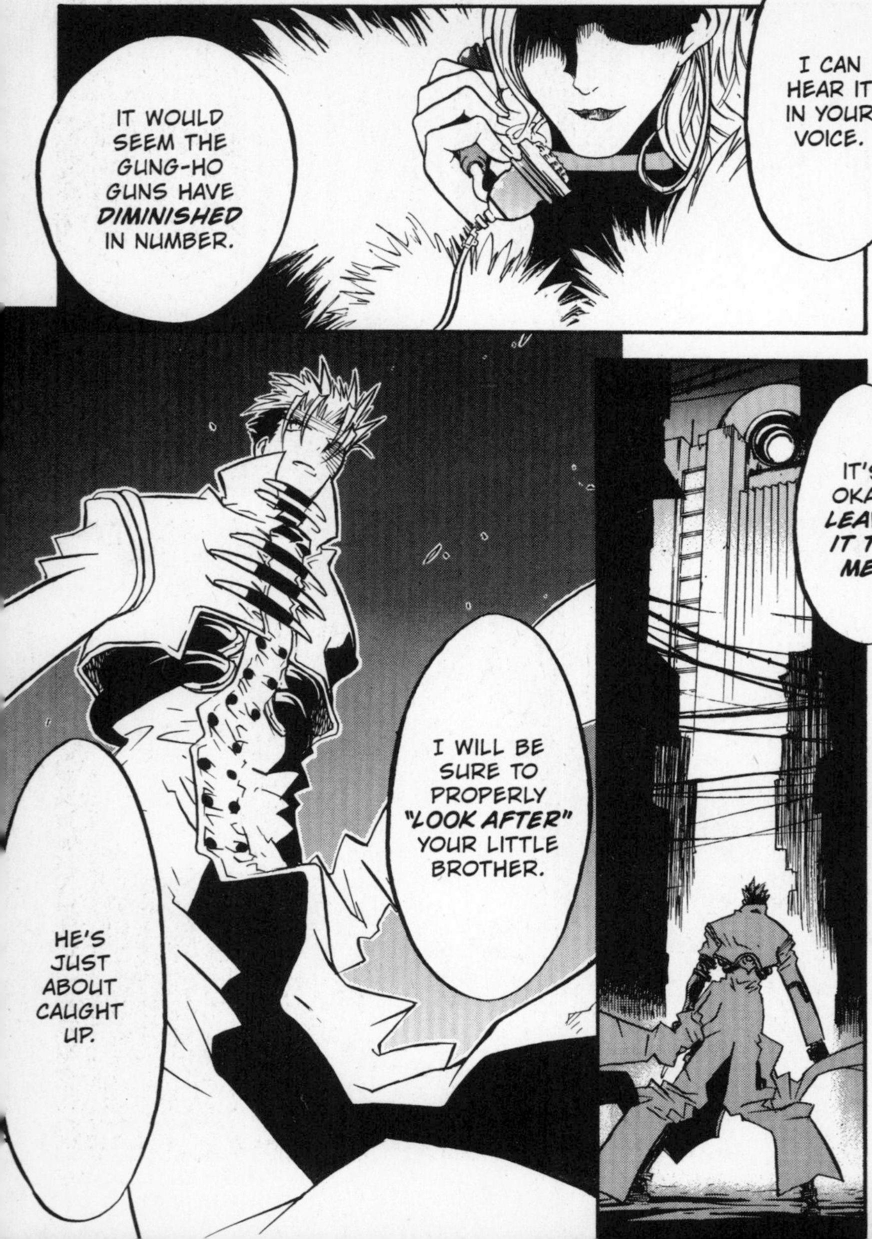
I CAN HEAR IT IN YOUR VOICE.
IT WOULD SEEM THE GUNG-HO GUNS HAVE *DIMINISHED* IN NUMBER.
IT'S OKAY. *LEAVE IT TO ME.*
I WILL BE SURE TO PROPERLY *"LOOK AFTER"* YOUR LITTLE BROTHER.
HE'S JUST ABOUT CAUGHT UP.

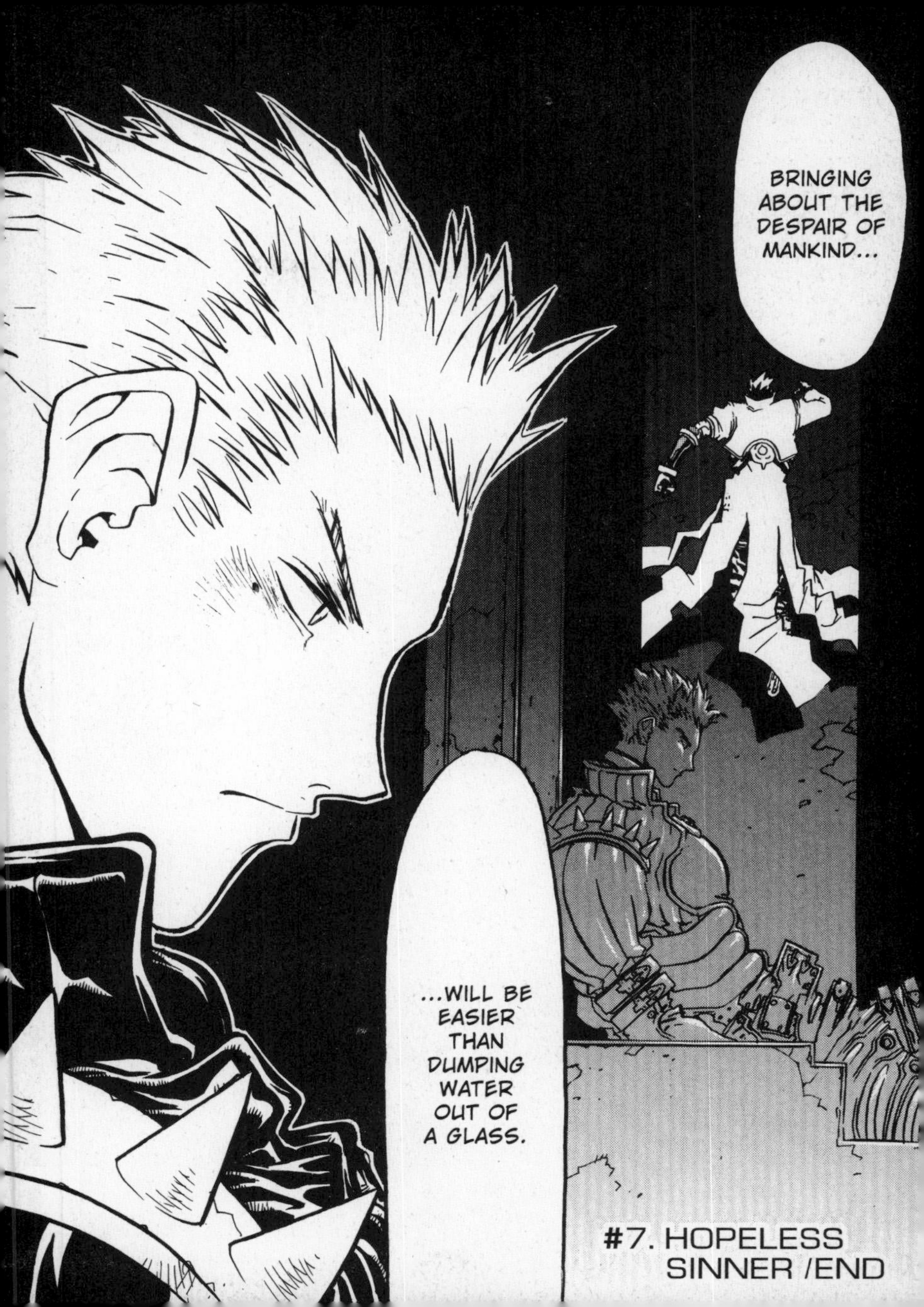
BRINGING ABOUT THE DESPAIR OF MANKIND...
...WILL BE EASIER THAN DUMPING WATER OUT OF A GLASS.
#7. HOPELESS SINNER /END

TURN TO THE NEXT

TRIGUN MAXIMUM

YASUHIRO NIGHTOW

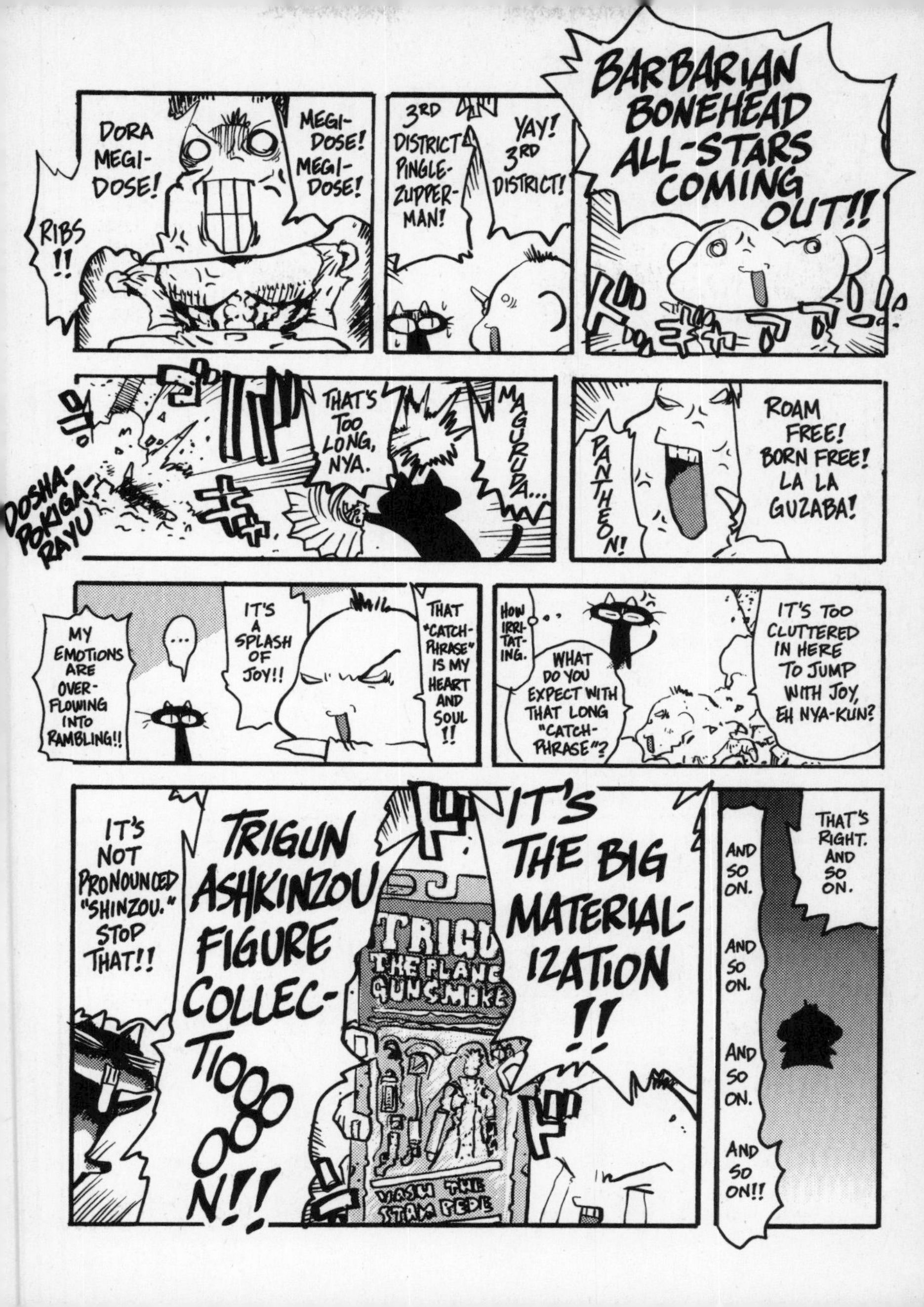
BARBARIAN BONEHEAD ALL-STARS COMING OUT!!
YAY! 3RD DISTRICT!
3RD DISTRICT PINGLE-ZUPPERMAN!
MEGI-DOSE! MEGI-DOSE!
DORA MEGI-DOSE!
RIBS!!
ROAM FREE! BORN FREE! LA LA GUZABA!
PANTHEON!
MAGURUDA...
THAT'S TOO LONG, NYA.
DOSHA-POKIGA-RAYU
IT'S TOO CLUTTERED IN HERE TO JUMP WITH JOY, EH NYA-KUN?
WHAT DO YOU EXPECT WITH THAT LONG "CATCH-PHRASE"?
HOW IRRITATING.
THAT "CATCH-PHRASE" IS MY HEART AND SOUL!!
IT'S A SPLASH OF JOY!!
...
MY EMOTIONS ARE OVERFLOWING INTO RAMBLING!!
THAT'S RIGHT. AND SO ON.
AND SO ON. AND SO ON. AND SO ON. AND SO ON. AND SO ON!!
IT'S THE BIG MATERIALIZATION!!
TRIGUN ASHKINZOU FIGURE COLLEC-TIOOOOOOON!!
IT'S NOT PRONOUNCED "SHINZOU." STOP THAT!!

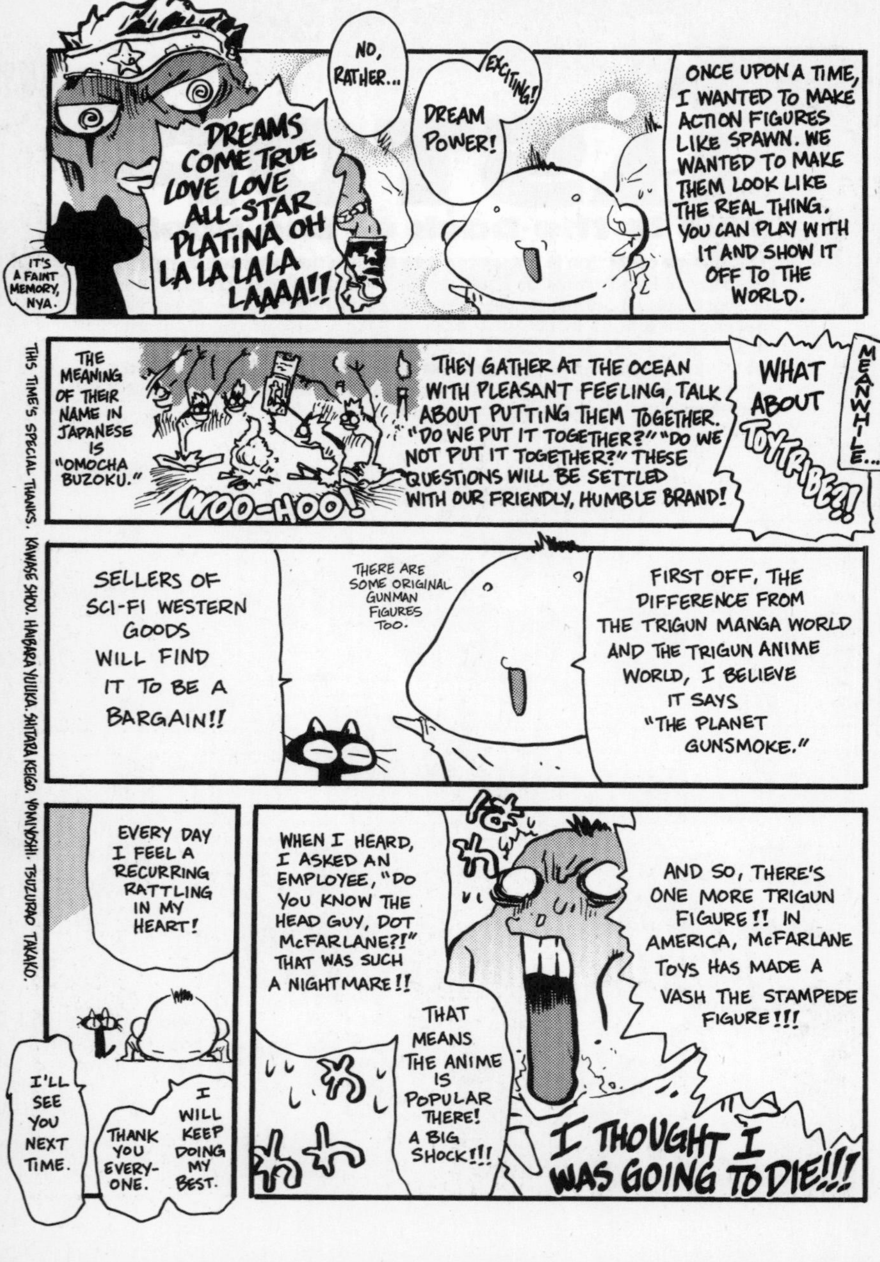
ONCE UPON A TIME, I WANTED TO MAKE ACTION FIGURES LIKE SPAWN. WE WANTED TO MAKE THEM LOOK LIKE THE REAL THING. YOU CAN PLAY WITH IT AND SHOW IT OFF TO THE WORLD.
EXCITING!
DREAM POWER!
NO, RATHER...
DREAMS COME TRUE LOVE LOVE ALL-STAR PLATINA OH LA LA LA LA LAAAA!!
IT'S A FAINT MEMORY, NYA.
MEANWHILE...
WHAT ABOUT TOYTRIBE?!
THEY GATHER AT THE OCEAN WITH PLEASANT FEELING, TALK ABOUT PUTTING THEM TOGETHER. "DO WE PUT IT TOGETHER?" "DO WE NOT PUT IT TOGETHER?" THESE QUESTIONS WILL BE SETTLED WITH OUR FRIENDLY, HUMBLE BRAND!
THE MEANING OF THEIR NAME IN JAPANESE IS "OMOCHA BUZOKU."
WOO-HOO!
FIRST OFF, THE DIFFERENCE FROM THE TRIGUN MANGA WORLD AND THE TRIGUN ANIME WORLD, I BELIEVE IT SAYS "THE PLANET GUNSMOKE."
THERE ARE SOME ORIGINAL GUNMAN FIGURES TOO.
SELLERS OF SCI-FI WESTERN GOODS WILL FIND IT TO BE A BARGAIN!!
AND SO, THERE'S ONE MORE TRIGUN FIGURE!! IN AMERICA, McFARLANE TOYS HAS MADE A VASH THE STAMPEDE FIGURE!!!
WHEN I HEARD, I ASKED AN EMPLOYEE, "DO YOU KNOW THE HEAD GUY, DOT McFARLANE?!" THAT WAS SUCH A NIGHTMARE!!
I THOUGHT I WAS GOING TO DIE!!!
THAT MEANS THE ANIME IS POPULAR THERE! A BIG SHOCK!!!
EVERY DAY I FEEL A RECURRING RATTLING IN MY HEART!
I WILL KEEP DOING MY BEST.
THANK YOU EVERYONE.
I'LL SEE YOU NEXT TIME.
THIS TIME'S SPECIAL THANKS. KAWASE SHOU. HAIBARA YUUKA. SHITARA KEIGO. YOMIYOSHI. TSUZURAO TAKAKO.

This !

This ma t-to-left reading format at the creator's request, maintaining the artwork's visual orientation as originally published in Japan. If you've never read manga in this way before, take a look at the diagram below to give yourself an idea of how to go about it. Basically, you'll be starting in the upper right corner and will read each balloon and panel moving right to left. It may take some getting used to, but you should get the hang of it very quickly. Have fun!

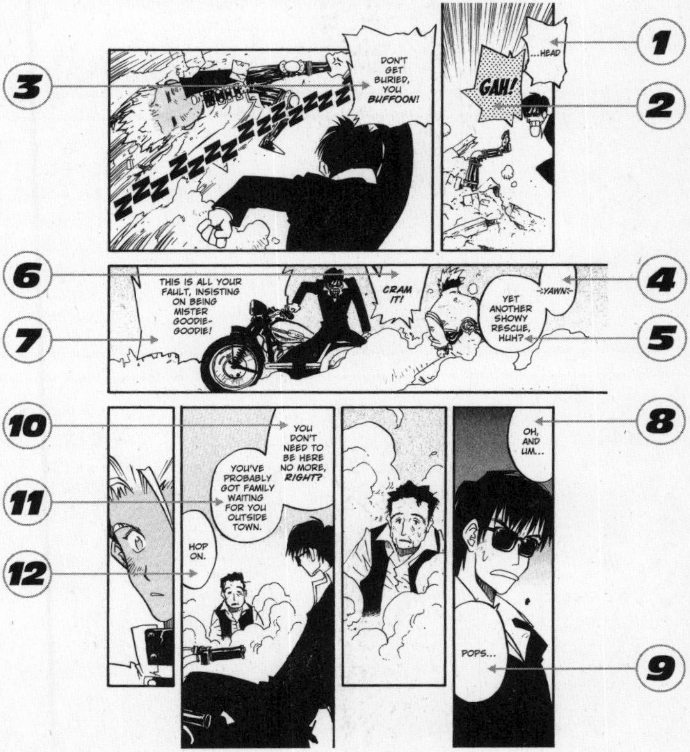
1
...HEAD
2
GAH!
3
DON'T GET BURIED, YOU BUFFOON!
4
~YAWN~
5
YET ANOTHER SHOWY RESCUE, HUH?
6
CRAM IT!
7
THIS IS ALL YOUR FAULT, INSISTING ON BEING MISTER GOODIE-GOODIE!
8
OH, AND UM...
9
POPS...
10
YOU DON'T NEED TO BE HERE NO MORE, RIGHT?
11
YOU'VE PROBABLY GOT FAMILY WAITING FOR YOU OUTSIDE TOWN.
12
HOP ON.